The Quest for Core Values in the Application of Legal Norms

Prof. Mordechai (Mota) Kremnitzer

Khalid Ghanayim • Yuval Shany
Editors

The Quest for Core Values in the Application of Legal Norms

Essays in Honor of Mordechai Kremnitzer

Springer

Editors
Khalid Ghanayim
Faculty of Law
University of Haifa
Haifa, Israel

Yuval Shany
Faculty of Law
Hebrew University of Jerusalem
Jerusalem, Israel

ISBN 978-3-030-78952-7 ISBN 978-3-030-78953-4 (eBook)
https://doi.org/10.1007/978-3-030-78953-4

This Springer imprint is published by the registered company Springer Nature Switzerland AG.
The registered company address is: Gewerbestrasse 11, 6330 Cham, Switzerland

Preface

This collection of essays celebrates the life and career of Prof. Mordechai (Mota) Kremnitzer, one of the most prominent jurists in Israel's legal history, who has had an exceptional impact on criminal and public law theory and practice in Israel and beyond and who has been and still is a strong advocate for upholding fundamental human rights and values in law and society. Prof. Kremnitzer's work has received wide acclaim throughout the international academic world, and he is broadly admired for his analytical precision, moral aptitude, and personal courage. In Israel, he is viewed by many as capturing the notion of speaking law to power.

Prof. Kremnitzer was born in Germany in 1948 to Holocaust survivors and immigrated to Israel at the age of one year. He studied law at the Hebrew University of Jerusalem—an academic institution to whose faculty he joined in 1981 and which he led as Dean between 1990 and 1993. Prof. Kremnitzer's initial specialization was in the field of criminal law. He served as a prosecutor and Judge in military court, drafted together with Prof. S. Z. Feller a major revision of Israeli criminal law (which went into effect in 1994), and led public committees dealing with issues such as police violence and the reform of homicide offences (which was enacted in 2019). Gradually, however, his professional work expanded to encompass broader public law and human rights themes. Among many of his activities in these fields, he served as Vice-President for Research of the Israel Democracy Institute, headed the Minerva Center for human rights, served as chair of the Israeli Press Council, and led notable public committees on reforming civic education in Israel and civil service discipline. He also served on several notable international bodies, including the board of governors of the UN International Anti-Corruption Academy, the International Association of Penal Law, and advised for the Constitutional Assembly of Thailand. During his rich career, he taught as guest lecturer and served as visiting researcher in numerous leading universities around the world, including the Central European University, Budapest, Hungary; University of Zurich, Switzerland; McGill University, Montreal, Canada; University of Tulane, New Orleans, Louisiana, USA; the Wissenschaftskolleg zu Berlin, Germany; Max Planck Institute for the Study of Crime, Security and Law, Freiburg, Germany and the Free University of Berlin. His many achievements have been acknowledged by many local and international prizes, awards, and grants, including the 2009 Humboldt Research Award, an honorary doctorate from the University of Lucerne (2009), and a major European Research Council grant (2012).

A central theme in Prof. Kremnitzer's scholarship and in his contributions as a public intellectual to public discourse has been an understanding of law as a vehicle for upholding the core values of society and advancing the cause of justice. The rule of law itself is among those core values, as are respect for human dignity, protecting liberty and equality, and adhering to the truth. All of these values serve as building blocks for a just society. The unique ability of Prof. Kremnitzer to credibly and effectively bridge the gap between *lex lata* and *lex ferenda* by way of creative interpretations of existing law, the development of new public law doctrines, and advocacy of legal reform aimed at better implementing core values makes his contribution to the legal world so powerful.

Both of us—the two book editors—are former students and current colleagues of Prof. Kremnitzer. We are pleased to have been able to assemble some of the world's leading criminal law and public law theory scholars—many of whom are friends and admirers of Prof. Kremnitzer—to write chapters in his honour. The chapters they contributed offer a variety of legal perspectives—public law, criminal law, international law, and legal theory—on the quest for core values in the application of legal norms, which characterizes Prof. Kremnitzer's professional path. The chapters in this book also address the complex relationship between important societal values and legal doctrine, discuss the manner in which law advances or fails to advance core values such as human rights, dignity, freedom, truth, or accountability, and analyse legal frameworks for balancing competing interests, such as proportionality, legal defences, and modes of responsibility.

The first cluster of chapters (Part I) deals with the quest for core values in public law. *Prof. Dieter Grimm's* contribution reviews the manner in which the public law principle of proportionality has been addressed and criticized in the writings of famous German philosopher Jürgen Habermas. Grimm discusses how a legal interpretation of the principle of proportionality can be kept within the boundaries of the rule of law and separation of powers, with a view to refraining from encroaching upon the competencies of the legislature. The second chapter in the same cluster, authored by *Prof. Matthias Mahlmann*, reviews the foundations of a democratic culture of freedom in law and in art. Mahlmann's chapter deals with the paradox of democratic freedom to give up freedom and proposes that art has a role to play in sustaining the culture of democratic freedom as an ideal which can be utilized by supporters of democracy in struggles over attempts to limit democratic freedoms.

The third chapter in Part I was written by *Prof. Christoph Burchard*. It considers the dialectic of rights in the context of what he considers as 'the new liberal desire for criminal law'. At the heart of his chapter is the claim that the constitutional right discourse is increasingly placing demands on the state to actively use criminal law to uphold individual rights as part of a liberal desire for a more coercive criminal law and justice system. The fourth and final chapter in this cluster is *Prof. Mohammed S. Wattad's* 'Crime, Guilt, and Punishment: Dignifying Criminal Law'. This chapter discusses the effects of constitutional law discourse (including right balancing) and justifications on the application of substantive criminal law.

The second cluster of chapters (Part II) focuses on criminal law theory and doctrine and the quest for core values in this legal context. The first chapter in this part—*Prof. Tatjana Hörnle's* 'Criminal Law in Multicultural Societies'—addresses the manner in which legislatures and courts should respond to the challenges of cultural diversity in loaded fields of criminal law such as defamation of religions and the so-called honour killings and killings in the context of blood feuds. The next chapter contains a discussion by *Prof. Thomas Weigend* of new development in the direction of introducing corporate responsibility in Germany. Prof. Weigend explains the terms of the German debate of this doctrinal question—which has increasingly become an outlier in Europe—and how developing a notion of corporate accountability can be reconciled with principles of due process and fair trial. The third chapter in this part, authored by *Prof. Vincenzo Militello* looks comparatively at questions of accountability of legal entities under European and South American laws governing corporate responsibility.

The fourth chapter in Part II is *Prof. Liat Franco* and *Prof. Khalid Ghanayim's* 'Proposal for Criminalization of Cyberbullying among Children'. It proposes to adjust the criminal law framework to three aggravating features of harm to social values inflicted by cyberbullying. The fifth chapter, authored by *Prof. Eric Hilgendorf,* discusses the German Network Enforcement Act and its implications for provider accountability, with a view to effectively curbing hate speech and disinformation. The following chapter by *Prof. Kurt Graulich* deals with anti-terrorism power of surveillance and on the manner in which the German Constitutional Court has balanced fundamental rights against the positive duty of protection of citizen's rights incurred by the State.

The seventh chapter, written by *Prof. Francisco Muñoz Conde*, addresses the specific problem of 'putative self-defence' which juxtaposes objective necessity in using force with normative considerations about self-defence as justified when addressing a wrong. The eighth chapter in this cluster, by *Prof. Raimo Lahti* deal with reforms in Finnish criminal law and penal policy relating to life imprisonment and other long-term sentences, revealing changes in the weight given to different societal goals associated with criminal punishment. The ninth and final chapter in Part II comprises excerpts from a dialogue conducted face to face and by correspondence during 2019 between *Prof. George P. Fletcher* and *Prof. Shachar Eldar* about the evolution of Israeli criminal law, with emphasis on its distinctive history, idiosyncratic terminology, and the core values it represents.

Part III includes three chapters demonstrating the quest for core values in the field of international law. The first, written by *Prof. Albin Eser*, reflects on recent German court judgments on co-responsibility for collateral damage caused by foreign drone attacks supported by activities originating from German territory. These cases ultimately delineate the scope of the obligation to protect the right to life and accountability for violation of such obligations. The following chapter, by *Prof. Kai Ambos* and *Ms. Susann Aboueldahab,* reviews another difficult problem of accountability—the application of the doctrine of command responsibility in connection with the Colombian Peace Process and the differences between domestic and international notions of accountability in this regard. The third and last chapter in this part, co-authored by *Prof. Florian Jeßberger* and *Dr. Julia Geneuss*, reflects on peace and punishment from the perspective of international criminal law. In particular, it delves on the ways in which the value of advancing peace is integrated into criminal law at both the domestic and international law and affects the development of these legal branches.

Part IV contains one entry on core values in legal research: an essay by *Prof. Otto Lagodny* and *Mr. Julius Lagodny*, on "Law as 'Argumentative Science': Functional Transfer of Basics of Scientific Theory", which explores what is the functional equivalent in legal research to finding 'the truth' in other types of academic research. This chapter can be seen as addressing the grounds on which the research for all chapters included in the book has been built. Finally, an annex to this book provides a CV and list of academic publications of Prof. Kremnitzer for the readers' perusal.

We would like to thank all authors for their contribution to this project. We are also grateful to the editorial team at Springer Nature for effectively managing the publication process. Special thanks are due to our research assistant, Ms. Tal Gross, for her hard work in helping us prepare the chapters for publications. Finally, we are immensely indebted to Prof. Kremnitzer for his support, guidance, and friendship throughout the years and for being such an impressive academic role model for us and for his many students, colleagues, and admirers throughout the world.

Haifa, Israel
Reut, Israel
2021

Khalid Ghanayim
Yuval Shany

Contents

List of Contributors

Susann Aboueldahab Georg-August-Universität, Göttingen, Germany

Kai Ambos Georg-August-Universität, Göttingen, Germany

Christoph Burchard Goethe-Universität, Frankfurt am Main, Germany

Francisco Muñoz Conde Universidad Pablo de Olavide, Sevilla, Spain

Shachar Eldar Ono Academic College, Kiryat Ono, Israel

Albin Eser Max Planck Institute for the Study of Crime, Security and Law, Freiburg, Germany

George P. Fletcher Columbia University, New York, NY, USA

Liat Franco Zefat Academic College, Safed, Israel

Julia Geneuss Universität Hamburg, Hamburg, Germany

Khalid Ghanayim Faculty of Law, University of Haifa, Haifa, Israel

Kurt Graulich Humboldt-Universität zu Berlin, Berlin, Germany

Dieter Grimm Wissenschaftskolleg zu Berlin, Berlin, Germany

Eric Hilgendorf Julius Maximilians Universität, Würzburg, Germany

Tatjana Hörnle Max Planck Institute for the Study of Crime, Security and Law, Freiburg, Germany

Florian Jeßberger Humboldt-Universität zu Berlin, Berlin, Germany

Julius Lagodny Cornell University, Ithaca, NY, USA

Otto Lagodny Paris London Universität, Salzburg, Austria

Raimo Lahti University of Helsinki, Helsinki, Finland

Matthias Mahlmann University of Zurich, Zürich, Switzerland

Vincenzo Militello University of Palermo, Palermo, Italy

Mohammed S. Wattad Zefat Academic College, Safed, Israel

Thomas Weigend Universität zu Köln, Cologne, Germany

Part I
Core Values in Public Law

Habermas on Proportionality

Dieter Grimm

It does not happen frequently that philosophers take a position on questions of legal doctrine. Jürgen Habermas, however, did it in the case of proportionality.[1] Proportionality is Germany's most successful contribution to contemporary constitutional law. In Germany, it carries the main burden of fundamental rights protection. The rules in the Basic Law which govern the limitation of fundamental rights range far behind the proportionality principle in importance. The provision in article 19 section 2, that no limitation may affect the very essence of a right, has become virtually meaningless because the proportionality principle intervenes before the question as to whether the core of a right has been touched comes up. Offences against the specific limitation clauses that are attached to most fundamental rights occur rarely. If laws are found to be unconstitutional, they mostly fail on the proportionality stage.

Outside Germany, many jurisdictions have adopted proportionality.[2] This happened partly by way of interpretation. Canada is one such example. The Canadian Charter of Fundamental Rights and Freedoms of 1982 contains in article 1 a general limitation clause applicable to all charter rights. It permits "such reasonable limits prescribed by law as can be demonstrably justified in a free and democratic society." In the first case in which the Canadian Supreme Court had to determine the meaning of article 1, Chief Justice Dixon declared that it means proportionality.[3] Other countries included proportionality into their constitutional documents such as

[1] Habermas (1992). English edition: Habermas (1996). References in this article are from the original German text. I partly draw on my article "Justiz und Gesetzgebung" in: Koller and Hiebaum (eds) (2016), p. 99.

[2] See Barak (2012), especially the map on p. 182 that shows the world-wide spread of the concept.

[3] R. v. Oakes (1986) 1 SCR 103.

D. Grimm (✉)
Humboldt-Universität zu Berlin, Berlin, Germany
e-mail: weva@wiko-berlin.de

K. Ghanayim, Y. Shany (eds.), *The Quest for Core Values in the Application of Legal Norms*, https://doi.org/10.1007/978-3-030-78953-4_1

South Africa and Israel. In the booming field of comparative constitutional law, proportionality has become a preferred subject.

Unlike countries where proportionality has a basis in the text of the constitution, nothing in the German Basic Law hints to proportionality. The Basic Law, drafted in 1948–1949 with the atrocities of the Nazi regime in mind, took great pains to strengthen fundamental rights protection. There are elaborate rules for the limitation of rights, limits on limitation, so to say. A few general provisions applicable to all rights are contained in article 19 and specific limitation clauses are attached to most fundamental rights. That, in addition, every law which limits a fundamental right has to be proportionate is an innovation of the Federal Constitutional Court.

The consequences are far reaching. This becomes visible if one asks how the scrutiny of a law that limits a fundamental right would proceed without the proportionality test. Imagine a law that permits to administer a medicine on criminal offenders in mental hospitals without their consent.[4] Such a law affects the physical integrity of a person guaranteed in article 2 section 2 of the Basic Law, to be sure a right of some importance. Nevertheless, this right has but a simple limitation clause: Infringements need a basis in law. If we assume that the law was adopted correctly and article 19 section 1 has been observed, the only remaining question is whether the law touches upon the very essence of the right (article 19 section 2), which we would probably have to negate. Nothing else is required by the text of the constitution. Consequently, the law would be upheld. By contrast, the proportionality principle strengthens the negatory effect of fundamental rights beyond the limits drawn explicitly in the constitution itself.

But this is only one side of the consequences, the rights side. The other side concerns the democratic legislature. If the principle of proportionality applies, the legislature is more restrained than the constitutional text indicates. This is why proportionality, if not entrenched in the constitution, presents a democracy problem. Everything that has been regulated on the constitutional level is thereby withdrawn from the democratic process. It is no longer an object of, but a premise for political decision-making. This is what we have constitutions for. They exist to limit government power, yet no farther than the constitution requires.

The problem appears even more clearly if one realizes that the power which the legislature loses, does not disappear. It accrues somewhere else, namely with the constitutional court. The German Court developed the proportionality principle in order to improve fundamental rights protection, but by the same token, it enhanced its own power. The Court decides what the legislature may and may not do. The introduction of the proportionality principle results in a power shift from the democratically legitimated and accountable organs to the unelected and not accountable judiciary. With proportionality the scope for the democratic process is narrower than without.

Consequently, if proportionality is not explicitly guaranteed in the constitutional text, it must at least be possible to derive it from the text. Otherwise, there would be a

---

[4]A similar case was decided by the Federal Constitutional Court in 2013, see BVerfGE 133, 112.

usurpation of power by the Court. Hence, the question is how the German Constitutional Court arrived at the assumption that the legislature is constrained by the principle of proportionality. Yet, the proportionality principle appeared on the scene without a justification, like a maxim that could be taken for granted.

And in a certain way, it was taken for granted since the late nineteenth century when the Prussian Superior Administrative Court started to limit police discretion by proportionality considerations.[5] In this form, every German lawyer was familiar with it. But it had its field of application in administrative law. Administrative acts that affected the liberty or property of citizens were regarded as legal only if they were suitable and necessary to reach their purpose. The Constitutional Court, to the contrary, transferred the proportionality principle from administrative law into constitutional law. Here the addressee was not only the executive, but also the legislature. In addition, the Court emphasized a third element next to suitability and necessity, which had had little impact in administrative law: proportionality in the narrower sense, the appropriateness of the measure—i.e., the balancing stage.

How can the missing justification be explained? It seems that, in the beginning, the Court was not aware of the impact proportionality would have in the future. In the judgment that first mentions proportionality, a case from 1954,[6] it just mentions this word, not yet a developed notion, let alone a doctrinal concept. In the pharmacy judgement of 1958,[7] the principle takes shape, but related to the peculiar formulation of article 12 (freedom of occupation). In 1961, all elements of the test are present, but their order is still unstable.[8] As late as 1963, it is disconnected from article 12 and recognized as applicable to all fundamental rights.[9] Finally, in 1965 after much admonition from academia, the Court furnishes a justification.[10] According to this judgement, the principle flows from the rule of law or from the very essence of the fundamental rights themselves, which, as expressions of the citizen's general claim to liberty vis-à-vis the state, can be limited by public authority only in so far as indispensable for the protection of the public interest. In 1969 the test is fully developed,[11] and from now on routinely applied, altogether a process of 15 years in the making.

The democratic problem that goes along with proportionality was not considered when the Court tried to justify the proportionality principle. Before it will be discussed, a reminder of how the principle works might be useful because it helps to identify the problematic zones of the principle. It operates in four consecutive steps. A law that limits a fundamental right needs (1) a legitimate purpose. Furthermore, the limitation has to be (2) suitable and (3) necessary to reach the purpose of

[5]See Remmert (1995), pp. 99–166; Hirschberg (1981).

[6]BVerfGE 3, 383.

[7]BVerfGE 7, 377.

[8]BVerfGE 13, 97.

[9]BVerfGE 16, 194.

[10]BVerfGE 19, 342.

[11]BVerfGE 27, 211, and described in greater detail in BVerfGE 30, 292.

the law. Finally, the legislature must (4) strike a reasonable balance between the harm to the fundamental right that is limited and the gain for the legal interest in whose name the right is limited.

How can this be justified constitutionally? Laws are valid only if compatible with fundamental rights. The Basic Law states this in article 1 section 3, thus distancing itself from previous German constitutions under which fundamental rights were not regarded as binding for the legislature. It is evident that limitations of fundamental rights, which do not serve a legitimate purpose, are unconstitutional, provided that legitimate means a purpose that is not prohibited by the Basic Law. This is indeed the understanding of the German Constitutional Court. The broad definition may explain why cases where a law fails already on stage 1 of the test are extremely rare.

But there are also narrower definitions. According to the Canadian Supreme Court, only an important purpose can justify a limitation of fundamental rights.[12] An explanation for this qualification may be Chief Justice Dixon's statement that limitations of fundamental rights should be rare exceptions. The rule for him is unlimited freedom. However, this assumption seems questionable. Freedoms can be misused. The use of a liberty may produce unwanted effects. Various conflicting rights must be reconciled. All this creates a need for the limitation of fundamental rights. Different from Dixon's expectation, limited freedom is the rule, not the exception.

Yet, the Canadian view is problematic still for another reason. The importance of a legislative purpose cannot be determined in absolute terms. Importance is a relational notion. The purpose must be important enough to justify the limitation of the fundamental right at stake. Accordingly, importance of the law's purpose is one element in the weighing or balancing process. If one follows the Canadian way, the question of importance is asked before all the elements necessary to answer it are gathered. It does not take cases into account in which the purpose of the limitation is not very important, but the limitation itself is minimal. The Canadian jurisprudence runs the risk that it declares a law unconstitutional on step 1, which would easily meet the requirements of the following steps.[13] At this point, the German Constitutional Court is more democracy-conscious than the Canadian Court. It allows legislature to pursue every purpose that is not explicitly prohibited by the constitution.

Furthermore, the second step does not seem problematic. Here again, it is evident that a limitation of a fundamental right which cannot even attain its purpose, is unconstitutional. Consequently, cases where a law fails on step 2 are rare.[14] This is, however, different with step 3, the necessity of the limitation. In general, this requirement is plausible as well. A law that could reach its purpose by employing

[12] R. v. Oakes (1986) 1 SCR 103.

[13] It seems that the Canadian Supreme Court in more recent decision no longer emphasizes the importance of the purpose on step 1 of the proportionality test.

[14] A nice case is Falconry BVerfGE 55, 195.

a less intrusive means than the one chosen by the legislature goes too far and is therefore unconstitutional.

The difficulties appear on the factual level. It will often be doubtful whether an alternative means is less intrusive, but still attains the purpose as effectively. Experience may be lacking; expert knowledge may be controversial. Especially with regard to laws that regulate the economy or technology, the legislature must often rely on prognosis. In such cases, the judiciary does not have superior insight. Therefore, the democratic principle requires that the legislature has its way. However, the court may oblige the legislature to observe the development and amend the law if the prognosis turns out to be wrong.

The most problematic step is the last one, the comparison of the gains that the impugned law provides for the purpose sought and the harm that the fundamental right will suffer, the true balancing stage. The criticism of the last step of proportionality is partly logical, partly doctrinal and partly democratic. The logical objection is often presented in form of the well-known saying that one cannot compare apples with pears. However, this argument, should it be valid at all, is based on the misunderstanding that the proportionality principle requires the balancing of two fundamental rights: Does freedom of assembly weigh heavier than freedom of property? Or the other way round? It is likewise a misunderstanding that proportionality analysis means a weighing of the values that have found legal expression in fundamental rights: Is freedom or security the higher value? However, this is not how the question arises. Rather, what has to be balanced are the loss that a right suffers from the law by which it is limited on the one hand, and the gain for the good (often itself a fundamental right) in whose interest the fundamental right is limited, on the other hand. This is by no means impossible.

The doctrinal objection claims that balancing is not sufficiently determined by law and can therefore not be regarded as a legal operation. The democratic objection starts from the assumption that balancing implies a policy choice that must be left to politics. These two objections are apparently connected to each other. If the result of balancing cannot be based on legal reasoning, it is a matter for the political and not the legal process. This is the second democracy problem that goes along with proportionality.

Many debates have been conducted about this question, which I do not want to reiterate here. Instead, I will turn to the particularly sharp criticism of proportionality which was launched by Jürgen Habermas. Habermas develops his criticism in chapter VI of his book "Faktizität und Geltung", where he treats the relationship between the legislature and the judiciary and especially the legitimacy of constitutional adjudication as questions of separation of powers. The central question of this chapter is how a legal interpretation can be kept within the boundaries of the rule of law and separation of powers and be prevented from encroaching upon the competencies of the legislature.[15]

[15]Habermas (1992), p. 292.

Democracy is not mentioned in this context. However, it plays a crucial role when Habermas develops his concept of separation of powers in chapter IV. For him, separation of powers does not exist, as usually presumed, to prevent the abuse of power, but to uphold the different conditions of rationality which govern the making and the application of the law. Its sole purpose is upholding the primacy of democratic law-making.[16] A law which is produced in the discursive process of democratically accountable representatives of the people and derives its legitimacy just from this process must not be tampered in the stage of application. However, precisely this threat emanates for him from the process of balancing.

For Habermas, the fundamental evil is the understanding of fundamental rights as values,[17] which manifested itself already in the early jurisprudence of the German Constitutional Court and saw its final breakthrough in the Lüth Case of 1958.[18] Habermas sees values in contrast to norms.[19] Norms have passed a generality test and apply universally. Values apply only selectively. They are shared preferences that a certain collective deems desirable. Norms are binding, values are recommendable. Complying with norms is morally required, following values is but ethically demanded. Values may contradict each other; norms form a system in which contradiction is excluded. Norms are absolute, values are relative. If a norm is applied to a case, only one correct solution exists. Values allow divergent solutions. Habermas concludes that a court that understands fundamental rights not as norms but as values misconceives the legal character of the constitution and takes political decisions.[20]

As a matter of fact, the Federal Constitutional Court's interpretation of the Basic Law is based on a conception of fundamental rights as values or, more precisely, legal expressions of values. If one wants to reduce the Court's practice of interpretation to a simple formula, one might say: Give utmost effect to the value that has found legal expression in the constitution under changing conditions. In case of a collision of fundamental rights, try to establish "practical concordance"[21] among them instead of prioritizing one over the other. The question then is whether the value jurisprudence that Habermas criticizes is identical to the value-oriented approach of the Court's interpretation of fundamental rights. This can be ascertained only by an analysis of the judgments, which Habermas avoids. It would also exceed the limits of this article. But it seems possible to gain more clarity about the Court's approach if one asks against what it was directed.

Everything hints to the assumption that, with its methodological premise, the Court wanted to distance itself from the type of positivism that had been

[16]Ibid, p. 230.

[17]Ibid, p. 309, 314 ss.

[18]BVerfGE 7, 198.

[19]Habermas (1992), p. 139, 197 ss., 310 ss.

[20]Ibid, p. 312.

[21]A term introduced by Konrad Hesse, following Richard Bäumlin, and now established case law of the Federal Constitutional Court. See Hesse (1995), 142 s.

predominant in German constitutional law thinking since the foundation of the Empire in 1871. Positivism as a method of constitutional interpretation was aimed at purifying the understanding of legal norms from all subjective, especially all political elements. Constitutional interpretation could only claim scientific quality if it was completely legal. The only admissible tools were grammar and logic.[22] Every reference to extra-legal elements would have contaminated the interpretation. Even the purpose of a constitutional provision was regarded as political and therefore outside the scope of the law. Still, one should not misunderstand this form of positivism as crude textualism. It rather allowed to discover notions behind the various provisions and to combine them to form a system from which it was then possible to determine the meaning of a provision or to fill gaps in the law.

In this form, positivism proved to be a very productive method. However, in the way it was practiced it transformed itself to a large extent to formalism. The constitution was regarded as a statute like every other one with the sole difference that amendments to it required a super majority. Democracy was identified with the majority principle. The rule of law meant just the submission of the administration to statutes. The function of fundamental rights was limited to the requirement of a legal basis for infringements. They had no impact on the content of the law and were thus reduced to the principle of legality of state action. The anti-formalist opposition against positivism, which began in the Weimar Republic, was interrupted by the NS dictatorship.

After realization that the formalist understanding of the constitution had contributed to Hitler's rise to power, positivism as legal method was discredited. The immediate post-war period saw a revival of natural law thinking. This did not last very long, but what remained was a strong conviction that a substantive concept of constitutionalism, especially of fundamental rights, was needed. The Basic Law nourished this understanding by building the whole constitutional edifice on the idea of human dignity which found expression in article 1. The Federal Constitutional Court adopted this idea and promoted it by interpreting the Bill of Rights as a system of values and the individual rights as legal expressions of these values. The reference to the Nazi past is clearly visible in the early judgments like the prohibition of the SRP, a Neo-Nazi party, and Elfes where the Court interpreted the right of free development of one's personality in article 2 section 1 as general freedom right.[23] Lüth draws the consequence from the value approach and thus revolutionizes the theory and practice of fundamental rights.[24]

This shows that the foremost goal of the Court was to overcome the formalist notion of constitutionalism, which missed its essential characteristics. For this purpose, it used in line with the feelings and needs of the time the word "value", yet without adopting all the implications with which Habermas burdens the notion of value. When the critical discussion of the Court's methodology in the 60's and 70's

[22]See the uncontested head of the positivistic school in constitutional law Laband (1888), preface.

[23]BVerfGE 2, 1; BVerfGE 6, 32.

[24]BVerfGE 7, 198. For an overview see Grimm (2015).

of the twentieth century disclosed some problems related with the notion of value, the Court did not hesitate to give up the word and replaced it by "principles" or "functions", however, without any change in substance.

What, then, is Habermas' methodological proposal to avoid the danger of a judicial encroachment upon the realm of the legislature? The question is crucial because Habermas, too, cannot escape the basic condition of the application of law, namely the gap between the general and abstract norm and the individual and concrete case, which has to be bridged by interpretation. This condition can in no way be eliminated by an understanding of fundamental rights as norms instead of values. Regardless of whether conceived as norms or values, the constitutional provisions have to be concretized to a more precise rule before they are applicable to a case, and the faithfulness of this process to the text of the constitution has to be secured by the method of interpretation.

Concretization will sometimes be easy, at other times difficult; in some cases it will need a long chain of argumentation, in others the way may be short, depending on the degree of vagueness and age of the norm and the complexity and novelty of the case. When the interpretation of fundamental rights is at stake, the way from the constitutional text to the solution of the case is usually long. This is not only so because fundamental rights are much more open-ended than the majority of other constitutional or even more so of statutory norms. They also have a different structure. While the usual norm follows an if-then-pattern, fundamental rights name a certain object, mostly described with just one word: speech, press, home, belief etc., and proclaim it to be free. In a second step they authorize the legislature to limit the freedom.

This means that on the side of the object as well as on the limitation side, everything is open-ended. Hence, there is no way to avoid interpretation. And interpretation is not just disclosing a meaning that has been deposited in the fundamental right from the time of its adoption onwards. Rather, it leaves options of which it is impossible to say that one is right and the others are wrong. To be sure, there are interpretations that are clearly wrong, but hardly is a legal norm so determinate that it never leaves any doubt about the right solution of a case. A specific norm may be clear with regard to one set of facts and unclear with regard to another. This is widely agreed nowadays, and the advocates of the opposite view have become few in number.

Nevertheless, Habermas sticks to the idea that there is only one correct solution to a legal problem. But he does not tell how this solution might be found, given the open-endedness of the norm. At this point, he contents himself with saying: The norm simply finds its unequivocal meaning in the process of application.[25] But how? This is the crucial question, and the answer determines the rationality or irrationality of the process of law application.

The problem becomes even more pressing if two or more fundamental rights enter into collision. This is by no means a rare exception. It occurs regularly. The

[25] Habermas (1992), p. 317.

Constitutional Court's extensive interpretation of fundamental rights—Article 2 section 1 as a residual right which covers every human activity that has not become the object of a special right; the duty of the legislature to protect individual freedom if it is menaced not from government, but from private actors who are also protected by fundamental rights—has even increased the frequency of collisions. Behind every law that limits a fundamental right there may be another right in whose interest the limitation was enacted. The Court's reaction to this problem is proportionality, in particular the last step, balancing the costs and benefits of a law that limits a fundamental right. But balancing is what Habermas condemns because, for him, by balancing the Court transgresses the border between law making and law application and becomes an "authoritarian instance."[26] Hence the question is what other solution he imagines for the above-mentioned problem.

Habermas assumes that fundamental rights collide not really but only seemingly. In his view, only one right is applicable to a specific case. This right has to be ascertained before the process of its application to the facts of the case can start. The selection of the single applicable norm out of a set of prima facie applicable norms is therefore decisive for him. He calls this selection a matter of "appropriateness,"[27] but adds in the same vein that this has nothing to do with balancing according to the principle of proportionality. The excluded norms do not lose their legal validity, but only their applicability to the case at hand. Their relationship is not one of competing values but of fitting and not fitting norms, in short, the opposite of practical concordance.

Habermas's conception causes two difficulties. Both result from his silence about how to select the applicable norm and how to apply it to the case. If we first turn to selection, it seems difficult to determine the applicable norm without some sort of balancing. Habermas explains that the applicable norm among the plurality of prima facie relevant norms is the one that, taking all relevant viewpoints into consideration, fits the situation to which it will be applied.[28] My assumption is that at this stage the same considerations that the Constitutional Court takes into account when balancing have to be made. If this is true, Habermas would need the proportionality aspects, which he wants to eliminate from norm application, for the preceding stage of ascertaining the norm that shall govern the case. Compared to the practice of the Constitutional Court, this would simply mean a shifting from one step in the process of decision-making to another.[29]

The ensuing process of application of the relevant right is described by Habermas as a determination of which claim and which act is lawful and not as balancing goods

[26]Ibid, p. 314 s.

[27]Ibid, p. 317.

[28]Ibid, p. 317.

[29]A similar shifting, although within the proportionality test, can be observed in the jurisprudence of the Canadian Supreme Court. The Court shies away from the last stage of the proportionality test, balancing, for fear that it might be political. But the Court considers the elements that are relevant for balancing on the necessity stage, where they are systematically misplaced, and settles the balancing stage with the remark that here no new viewpoints are visible, see Grimm (2007).

or comparing values.[30] Yet, the fundamental right that has been ascertained as relevant for the case is not immediately ready for application. It remains as indefinite as before. It needs concretization as Habermas admits. The case, however, is characterized by a collision of two or more fundamental rights. This means that the decision of the court will affect the fundamental rights of third persons. But these rights may no longer be taken into account in the process of concretization because they have been eliminated on the initial stage of determining the governing right. Therefore, Habermas either runs the risk of reaching unbalanced results or he must repeat the considerations that he had eliminated on the preceding level.

There is, of course, a way to solve collisions of fundamental rights without balancing. This would be possible if the various fundamental rights followed a hierarchical order. The higher ranking right would trump the lower ranking. However, Habermas rejects this way, just as the Constitutional Court does. And it would not be recommendable to adopt it, even if one were to succeed in establishing a hierarchy. It would fail to handle cases in which the higher-ranking right is minimally constrained in order to protect the lower ranking from great harm. If a hierarchy is not accepted, there remains only one further way to avoid balancing, namely that the balancing undertaken by the legislature to solve a collision of various rights is exempted from judicial scrutiny according to the last prong of the proportionality principle. The proportionality test would end at prong three (necessity). This is the suggestion that among others Bernhard Schlink has made.[31]

What would be the consequences? I reiterate here an example that I used in another context.[32] Most countries' police laws authorize a policeman to shoot a perpetrator to death who is about to kill a person, if this is the only remaining way to save the innocent victim. Imagine a law that extends this authorization from the protection of life to the protection of property. Protection of property is certainly a legitimate purpose (1). Killing the person that threatens to destroy property is suitable to reach its end (2). If the perpetrator is dead, he can no longer execute his plan. It is also necessary, as the necessity requirement is already made a condition of the police action in the text of the law (3). If the test were to end here, the law would be constitutional.

The example shows that there is an often overlooked, but fundamental difference between prongs 2 and 3 of the proportionality test on the one hand and prong 4 on the other. Prongs 2 and 3 are immanent to the law that limits the fundamental right. The question is how the purpose of the law and the means that the law employs to reach the purpose are related. The constitutional level is not yet reached. The fundamental right that is limited does not come into the play. Only when prong 4 is addressed do we enter constitutional ground again. The proportionality test without the last step only sorts out some evident violations, but severely weakens the protection of the fundamental right at stake.

[30]Habermas (1992), p. 317.

[31]See Schlink (1976).

[32]See Grimm (2007).

Even if these considerations justify the proportionality test including the balancing stage, the democratic concerns are not completely dispelled because the balancing stage is susceptible to misuse. The risk can, however, be avoided if there is clarity about the objects of balancing so that the two scales of the balance are filled with utmost care. As mentioned before, when a court balances, the question is not which fundamental right outweighs another one, freedom of speech or protection of someone's honour or reputation, freedom of religion or gender equality. Even less so does balancing require a choice between the overarching values like freedom vs. security, functioning of criminal justice vs. protection of criminals, and certainly not between competing policy goals like the export capacity of the German automobile industry vs. climate protection.[33]

Rather, the object of constitutional scrutiny is always a certain law that will never raise the big questions like liberty vs. security. Even if the law's purpose is to fight terrorism, it will affect a specific right, say the freedom of telecommunication, and it will affect this right not in its totality, but in a certain aspect and to a certain degree. It will do so in order to increase the protection of another specific right, say privacy, vis-à-vis a specific danger, say the infiltration of computer systems and databases, and in a specific aspect and to a specific degree. These detailed circumstances have to go into the scales: the concrete harm that the limited right suffers from the law that stands constitutional scrutiny and the concrete gain or expectation of advancement of an interest (mostly itself a fundamental right) in whose name the right is limited.

If this is done, the balancing itself can take place. However, even when balancing, the court does not change its role as a reviewing power. For the court, the question to be asked is not what it deems proportionate, but whether the balance that the legislature struck is proportionate. If the scales have been filled as carefully as possible, the balancing, more precisely the scrutiny of the legislature's balancing, is not an irrational act of judicial arbitrariness whose result is unforeseeable. Rather, it remains within the legal realm, so that the risk for democracy is minimized. In any case, such a risk is smaller than the threat posed to fundamental rights protection if no balancing takes place.

References

Barak, A. (2012). *Proportionality*. Cambridge: Cambridge University Press.

Grimm, D. (2007). Proportionality in Canadian and German constitutional jurisprudence. *University of Toronto Law Journal, 57*, 383.

Grimm, D. (2015). The role of fundamental rights after 65 years of constitutional jurisprudence in Germany. *I-CON, 13*, 9.

[33]Habermas refers to examples of this type when he tries to demonstrate that balancing is a political and not a legal operation, see Habermas (1996), p. 316 (quoting Ingeborg Maus). It may therefore be that his rejection of the proportionality test is influenced by a—admittedly existing—contestable practice of balancing.

Habermas, J. (1992). *Faktizität und Geltung. Beiträge zur Diskurstheorie des Rechts und des demokratischen Rechtsstaats*. Frankfurt: Suhrkamp Verlag.

Habermas, J. (1996). *Between facts and norms*. Cambridge: The MIT Press.

Hesse, K. (1995). *Grundzüge des Verfassungsrechts der Bundesrepublik Deutschland* (20th ed.). Heidelberg: C.F. Müller.

Hirschberg, L. (1981). *Der Grundsatz der Verhältnismäßigkeit*. Göttingen: Schwartz.

Koller, P., & Hiebaum, C. (Eds.). (2016). *Jürgen Habermas: Faktizität und Geltung*. Berlin: De Gruyter.

Laband, P. (1888). *Das Staatsrecht des Deutschen Reiches* (Vol. I, 2nd ed.). Tübingen und Leipzig: J.C.B. Mohr.

Remmert, B. (1995). *Verfassungs- und verwaltungsgeschichtliche Grundlagen des Übermaßverbotes*. Heidelberg: Müller.

Schlink, B. (1976). *Abwägung im Verfassungsrecht*. Berlin: Duncker & Humblot.

On the Foundations of a Democratic Culture of Freedom: Law and the Normative Resources of Art

Matthias Mahlmann

1 The Culture of Freedom

The struggle for human freedom has taken many forms in human history—political reforms; revolutions, violent and peaceful; the slow work of liberation from the fetters of traditions without justified purpose, of religious and non-religious prejudice, of self-righteousness, of resentment and of culturally entrenched powerful folly. The struggles were sometimes successful, sometimes not and, if successful, did not always secure liberty for a very long time.

There are many preconditions to a political order of liberty—institutional, legal and social. Theories of a teleology in history have never been convincing and there is, in particular, no reason to think that it is a necessary outcome of history that human beings ultimately organize themselves under the banner of liberty. Moreover, liberty is a vulnerable political achievement. Not surprisingly, then, in political history a stable political order of freedom is the exception, not the rule.

The vagaries of the fate of the search for—if not permanently—at least durably institutionalized liberty are vividly illustrated by recent events, too. When the Soviet Empire sank to its well-deserved grave, the time of constitutionally entrenched liberty seemed to have finally dawned around the globe. Thirty years later the situation has changed radically. The time of constitutionally camouflaged, freely elected authoritarianism seems to have come—at least in an increasing number of countries. In these systems, democracy is no longer meaningful autonomous self-determination in the public sphere, but has turned into a hollow exercise to legitimize authoritarian and often visibly kleptocratic rule. Arguably, the most astonishing thing is that people freely vote for the forces that subvert their freedom by undermining the separation of powers, in particular the power of independent courts,

M. Mahlmann (✉)
University of Zurich, Zürich, Switzerland
e-mail: lst.mahlmann@rwi.uzh.ch

K. Ghanayim, Y. Shany (eds.), *The Quest for Core Values in the Application of Legal Norms*, https://doi.org/10.1007/978-3-030-78953-4_2

the rule of law and the normative force of fundamental rights. In relation to the international community, a new contempt for international law has become widely practiced, yet another self-destructive policy option that people choose at the ballot box. These developments stand alongside the thriving authoritarian systems who can observe with glee how democracy destroys itself.

These developments show that it is of persistent interest and immediate political relevance to reflect substantially about the foundations of human rights and democracy as the institutional embodiment of human freedom. This includes, as a central issue, the reasons for the success of the enemies of democracy and how to meet their challenge. There are many problems that need further consideration in this regard. This essay will focus on one of them: the cultural preconditions for a political order of freedom that sustains itself long term because it offers an attractive way of life. This is particularly important because democracy—given its defining characteristic of being an order of liberty—necessarily implies the possibility of a use of freedom that leads to its self-destruction. There are many useful institutional safeguards to protect a democratic order against its enemies, including against those foes who use democratic means to reach their aim, e.g. the instruments of a militant democracy. Ultimately, however, a democracy that is abandoned by its citizens will cease to exist. There is no democracy without democrats who make it a living thing.

What are the roots of a democratic culture? What is its appeal that human beings overlook who become ensnared by the lure of democratically camouflaged authoritarianism? A useful, thought-provoking means to attempt to contribute to answering this major question is to look in the mirror of the poetical representation of the human world. The following remarks hope to show why this is a fruitful approach and a supplement to arguments from other theoretical angles. The piece of art chosen is one of the most profound reflections on liberty in world drama, Friedrich Schillers *Don Carlos*, first staged in 1787, as a drama of a "new kind",[1] expansive, sometimes with a labyrinthine course of action, but painting with strikingly effective, bold brush strokes a personal drama of love and brutally defeated idealism that is an aesthetic representation of great political conflicts in world history, epitomized by the ultimately successful struggle for liberation of the Spanish Dutch provinces. It is the expression of the desire of human beings for individual and political freedom, the forces that quash these hopes and the tragic choices and errors their often-desperate situation forces upon human beings seeking to overcome established structures of repression. It masters, as a new form of Schiller's dramatic art, unrhymed iambic pentameters that express naturally the cruelty of potentates as well as moments of great tenderness and bleak despair. Among the impressive achievements of its

[1]Alt P A (2009) Schiller. C.H. Beck, München, 1:433: "Drama neuen Typs". Cf. for some background Reed T (1991) Schiller. Oxford University Press, Oxford, p 36ff; Sharpe L (1991) Friedrich Schiller: Drama, Thought and Politics. Cambridge University Press, Cambridge, p 76ff; Janz R P (2005) Great Emotions – Great Criminals? Schiller's Don Carlos. In: Martinson S D (ed) A Companion to the Works of Friedrich Schiller. Camden House, New York, p 137ff; Safranski R (2004) Friedrich Schiller oder Die Erfindung des deutschen Idealismus. Carl Hanser Verlag, München.

intricately drawn characters is the humanization of the inhuman—not as an apology but as a downright indispensable means to understand its nature—and to drain springs. It contains passages of such beauty that it "cracks", as Tonio Kröger, a character in Thomas Mann's famous story observes as a school boy,[2] expressing nothing but the aesthetical experience of Mann himself,[3] and of many others who try to fathom the depth of this play.

Schiller wrote great works about the problem of freedom besides *Don Carlos*, *Wilhelm Tell* for instance, dramatizing a foundational Swiss myth (of, however, Danish origin) about the struggle against feudal rule. If an ultimate proof for the quality of a writer is that his or her work was forbidden by the Nazis, Schiller passed this test with this latter play, despite the efforts of the Nazis to exploit Schiller's works (including *Tell*) for their propaganda purposes: Wilhelm Tell's powerful appeal to human rights and resistance against illegitimate power was ultimately too dangerous a challenge for a regime based on the lethal contempt for human beings to be allowed on a Nazi stage.[4]

Moreover, Schiller also made the pursuit of freedom a central piece of his theoretical writings, which are without doubt of great philosophical substance.[5] Schiller outlined in his reflections about the aesthetical education of human beings[6] a famous aesthetical utopian vision that inspired other searches for the contours of un-estranged human life in the sphere of art's beauty.[7] It culminated in the aesthetical state, an order of universal freedom, freely granted by everyone to everyone: "The basic law of this realm is to give freedom by means of freedom. Here, the individual may not dispute the whole, nor the whole with the individual. One may not become strong through the submission of the other; there may only be victors, and no vanquished."[8] The philosophical root of this political vision is an aesthetical theory in which beauty's hidden root is freedom: The beautiful is, for him, inspired by a critical reflection of Kant's aesthetics,[9] an embodiment of freedom in a meaningful form borne by human creativity. Art is not turned into morality or

---

[2]Mann T (1990) Tonio Kröger. In: Gesammelte Werke, Bd. VIII. S. Fischer Verlag, Frankfurt, p 277.

[3]Mann T (1990) Versuch über Schiller. In: Gesammelte Werke, Bd. IX. S. Fischer Verlag, Frankfurt, p 892ff.

[4]Schiller F (1987) Wilhelm Tell. In: Sämtliche Werke II, Hanser, München, p 913ff.

[5]For some comments, Beiser F (2005) Schiller as Philosopher: A Re-examination. Oxford University Press, Oxford; Moland L L (2017) Friedrich Schiller. In: Zalta E N (ed) The Stanford Encyclopaedia of Philosophy. https://plato.stanford.edu/archives/sum2017/entries/schiller/.

[6]Schiller F (2000) Über die ästhetische Erziehung des Menschen. In: Berghahn K L (ed) einer Reihe von Briefen. Reclam, Stuttgart.

[7]Habermas J (1985) Der philosophische Diskurs der Moderne. Suhrkamp Verlag, Berlin, p 59: "erste programmatische Schrift zu einer ästhetischen Kritik der Moderne" (first programmatic treatise on a aesthetical critique of modernity).

[8]Schiller, supra note 6, p 120; Schiller F (2016) On the Aesthetic Education of Man (Trans: Tribe K). Penguin Books, London, p 110.

[9]Kant I (1913) Kritik der Urteilskraft, Akademie Ausgabe, Bd. V. De Gruyter, Berlin, New York.

politics. Its autonomy is defended. The experience of beauty is, however, a source to strengthen and re-awaken the human existential desire for freedom and respect for human worth.

The background for his thoughts on the foundation of political freedom and its relation to aesthetical experience is the torn path taken shortly after the completion of *Don Carlos* in the *French Revolution,* after the *American Revolution* had started the epoch of constitutionalism. The experience that the attempt to gain freedom in France had led to the rule of terror is of central importance for Schiller, because it dispelled hopes that freedom could be easily won if the downtrodden only shake off their chains.[10]

---

[10]Cf. Schiller's famous poem, Die Glocke (The Bell), by some admired and, since the Romantics, by some derided: Schiller F (1987) Sämtliche Werke I. Hanser, München, p 429 ff, 440:

Wo rohe Kräfte sinnlos walten,
Da kann sich kein Gebild gestalten,
Wenn sich die Völker selbst befrein,
Da kann die Wohlfahrt nicht gedeihn.

Weh, wenn sich in dem Schoß der Städte
Der Feuerzunder still gehäuft,
Das Volk, zerreissend seine Kette,
Zur Eigenhilfe schrecklich greift!
Da zerret an der Glocke Strängen
Der Aufruhr, daß sie heulend schallt,
Und nur geweiht zu Friedensklängen
Die Losung anstimmt zur Gewalt.

Freyheit und Gleichheit! hört man schallen,
Der ruhge Bürger greift zur Wehr,
Die Straßen füllen sich, die Hallen,
Und Würgerbanden ziehn umher,
Da werden Weiber zu Hyänen
Und treiben mit Entsetzen Scherz,
Noch zuckend, mit des Panthers Zähnen,
Zerreissen sie des Feindes Herz.
Nichts heiliges ist mehr, es lösen
Sich alle Bande frommer Scheu,
Der Gute räumt den Platz dem Bösen,
Und alle Laster walten frey.
Gefährlich ist's den Leu zu wecken,
Und grimmig ist des Tigers Zahn,
Jedoch der schrecklichste der Schrecken
Das ist der Mensch in seinem Wahn.
Weh denen, die dem Ewigblinden
Des Lichtes Himmelsfackel leihn!
Sie leuchtet nicht, sie kann nur zünden
Und äschert Stadt' und Länder ein.

Translation by Lytton E B (1844) The Poems and Ballads of Schiller. W. Blackwood and sons, Edinburgh, p 157 f:

These events underlined for him, as for others of his time like Immanuel Kant or Friedrich Hölderlin, that the struggle for human freedom forms a particularly difficult task with many preconditions if it is to succeed. It is not only necessary to win against the old powers who try to prevent the establishment of new orders of liberty. It is also important to ensure that the liberated people use their newly gained freedom reasonably and do not destroy what they have just achieved. Schiller is disillusioned by the experience that "the natural state" (Naturstaat) of his time, which is based only on power, had been shaken, but without the historical opportunity thus opened up being used to create a freer political order. He observes: "The fabric of the natural state is tottering, its rotting foundations give way and there seems to be the physical possibility of enthroning the law, of finally treating humans as ends in themselves, and making true liberty the foundation of political association. Vain

When rages strength that has no reason,
There breaks the mould before the season;
When numbers burst what bound before,
Woe to the State that thrives no more!
Yea, woe, when in the city's heart,
The latent spark to flame is blown;
And millions from their silence start,
To claim, without a guide, their own!

Discordant howls the warning Bell,
Proclaiming discord wide and far,
And, born but things of peace to tell,
Becomes the ghastliest voice of war:
"Freedom! Equality!"—to blood
Rush the roused people at the sound!
Through street, hall, palace, roars the flood,
And banded murder closes round!
The hyena-shapes (that women were!),
Jest with the horrors they survey;
They hound—they rend—they mangle there—
As panthers with their prey!
Naught rests to hallow—burst the ties
Of life's sublime and reverent awe;
Before the Vice the Virtue flies,
And Universal Crime is Law!
Man fears the lion's kingly tread;
Man fears the tiger's fangs of terror;
And still the dreadliest of the dread,
Is Man himself in error!
No torch, though lit from heaven, illumes
The Blind!—Why place it in his hand?
It lights not him—it but consumes
The city and the land!

hope! The moral possibility is lacking, and a moment of such possibility finds itself confronted with an unreceptive generation."[11]

It is, thus Schiller concludes, necessary to prepare human beings under the conditions of political suppression for a political use of their autonomy in such a way that the political conquest of their freedom does not already ring its death bell. Schiller consequently develops a new attempt to prepare human beings for the use of freedom that secures the continuing possibility of a free political order. The key is aesthetical education: "I hope to convince you that this matter is far less alien to the needs of the age than it is to its taste; and that if one is to resolve this political problem one must in practice take the aesthetic path, for it is by way of beauty that one approaches liberty."[12]

In the aesthetical sphere, one finds embodied what has not yet been achieved or what has already been lost in the political world: "Mankind had lost its honour, but it was rescued by art and preserved in worthy stone; truth survives in the shape of deception, and from the copy the original will be restored."[13] But not only beautiful stones have the task of keeping alive the traces of human dignity that can be the seeds of a new harvest of human autonomy. In Schiller's case, it is his poems, stories and plays. They offer on the one hand the possibility to ascertain the way in which this aesthetical program with a purpose to realize human freedom has been able to determine and guide a poetical practice. On the other hand, they may provide substantial insights that are useful if one tries to face the task outlined above to understand more about the cultural foundations of human freedom in order to strengthen them in times that endanger their political and legal survival and to restate their true appeal as powerfully as possible. After all, these works are not just pieces of high art irrelevant for the real path of history but, in addition, are part of the cultural developments that created the political will to freedom in the first place, and that led to the establishment of democratic orders in the last 200 years or so. What needs to be scrutinized, is with which ideas such works fostered the case of freedom and whether they provide us with insights about the political, philosophical and ethical foundations of a social order that takes freedom as seriously as it deserves.

---

[11]Schiller, supra note 6, p 18: "Das Gebäude des Naturstaates wankt, seine mürben Fundamente weichen, eine physische Möglichkeit scheint gegeben, das Gesetz auf den Thron zu stellen, den Menschen endlich als Selbstzweck zu ehren und wahre Freyheit zur Grundlage der politischen Verbindung zu machen. Vergebliche Hoffnung! Die moralische Möglichkeit fehlt und der freygiebige Augenblick findet ein unempfängliches Geschlecht." Translation by Tribe K, Schiller, supra note 8, p 14, adapted by the author.

[12]Schiller, supra note 6, p 11: "Ich hoffe, Sie zu überzeugen, daß diese Materie weit weniger dem Bedürfnis als dem Geschmack des Zeitalters fremd ist, ja daß man um jenes politische Problem in der Erfahrung zu lösen, durch das ästhetische den Weg nehmen muß, weil es die Schönheit ist, durch welche man zu der Freyheit wandert." Translation by Tribe K, Schiller, supra note 8, p 6.

[13]Ibid, p 35: "Die Menschheit hat ihre Würde verloren, aber die Kunst hat sie gerettet und aufbewahrt in bedeutenden Steinen; die Wahrheit lebt in der Täuschung fort, und aus dem Nachbilde wird das Urbild wieder hergestellt werden." Translation by Tribe K, Schiller, supra note 8, p 30.

As we have seen, the present indicates that this question is relevant not only for historic moments of profound revolutionary change, but also under the conditions of established democracies. Today, too, the question must be asked of how irresponsive the current generation is to the idea of freedom protected by fundamental rights and guaranteed equally for all in the framework of a democratic constitutional state under the rule of law. Schiller posed a question with which we are now confronted again and most probably, given the historical record, with which future generations will struggle, too. It may be helpful, therefore, to see whether one can learn something from his insights and the errors of his analysis.

Engaging with these problems, it is not assumed that reading an eighteenth century play will provide us with all the keys to counter current populist authoritarianism instrumentalizing the new communicative patterns of a digital society and playing the surprisingly effective card of xenophobic identity politics. Nor is it proposed that the current crisis and the new challenges of the future will be solved by increased visits to theaters and museums. This was not what Schiller hoped, either. But the cultural undercurrents that are the preconditions for the functioning of democratic constitutional states that take human liberty and dignity seriously are doubtlessly of great importance. The enemies of these orders have learned this lesson very well and are therefore at the moment quite successfully at work to shift the cultural framework of the thoughts and hopes of many human beings in various political orders of this world, so as to enable a new grim reign of elected authoritarianism. It is important to learn this lesson and to try to remind a perhaps increasingly unreceptive generation of the many roots and the deep human appeal of a culture of freedom. The power of art and the force of beauty should not be underestimated in this struggle for the survival of a great idea.

Mordechai Kremnitzer has set out powerfully the task of law and literature after the experience of the Holocaust: Both should have a preventive role, helping to answer the question: "How can we prevent the next atrocity? The next atrocity need not take the same form and need not be as extreme as genocide to justify this preventive aim. Prevention refers not only to the final phase – the atrocity. The immediate stages must also be prevented, assuming that there is a gradual process of democracy's erosion, which does not necessarily – or usually – have a specific turning point, but takes rather the form of progressive abrasion, which hollows out democracy."[14]

Living up to this task needs many efforts. We will investigate below whether Schiller's attempt is a contribution to the struggles for freedom that is still worth some attention.

---

[14]Kremnitzer M (2013) Der Holocaust in Recht und Literatur. In: Kilcher A, Mahlmann M, Müller Nielaba D (eds) Fechtschulen und phantastische Gärten. Recht und Literatur, Zürich, p 57, 70 (translation M.M.).

2 The King's Heir

Don Carlos belongs to Schiller's central texts dealing with the idea and problems of political freedom. This play is of particular interest because it not only makes the case for human liberty and the existential importance of respect for the intrinsic worth of human beings. It also identifies a trap on the path of human liberation that, not only on the stage of the theater but also on the stage of world history, turns the attempt by human beings to gain their freedom into a tragedy. The play is not a shallow and boring celebration of liberty, no High Mass of idealism sounding hollow because it is disconnected from political realities, but rather a profound reflection about its normative roots and a striking anticipation of the dangers that the fight for liberation entails.

Don Carlos is the heir to the throne of Spain, a rather unhappy heir, however. He is an innocent, enthusiastic character full of high-flying ideas and benevolent wishes, but also quickly moved to rash decisions, too easily convinced and somewhat naïve, even though he has understood that intrigues and betrayal are the core of the society of the Spanish court in which he lives. Schiller has written a magnificent commentary on his own play in which he observes about Don Carlos: "He had to possess a gentle and benevolent heart, enthusiasm for greatness and moral beauty, delicacy, courage, firmness, disinterested generosity; he had to display beautiful and bright intuitions and capacities, but it was not my intention to endow him with wisdom."[15]

The reason for Don Carlos' somber mood is an unhappy love that he feels for Elisabeth of Valois who has—because of dynastical policies—married none other than his father Philip II. She is therefore painfully close and at the same time unreachably far removed for the kind of feelings which he entertains for her. In this situation, his old friend, the Marquis Posa, meets him. He is a decided cosmopolitan republican, who has developed with Carlos during their common youth spent at the court of Spain the ideal of a humane and free society. This idea shines not only in the far-off regions of utopian visions that cannot be realized, but contains a concrete republican program of freedom with human beings taking center stage as ends in themselves. The real-life expression is the fight for liberty of Flanders. In a famous dialogue with King Philip, Posa not only asks for freedom of thought, but develops his ideas of a new republican order:

[15]Schiller F (1987) Briefe über Don Carlos. In: Sämtliche Werke II. Hanser, München, p 255: "Ein weiches, wohlwollendes Herz, Enthusiasmus für das Grosse und Schöne, Delikatesse, Mut, Standhaftigkeit, uneigennütziger Grossmut sollte er besitzen, schöne und helle Blicke des Geistes sollte er zeigen, aber weise sollte er nicht sein." Translation by Hempel C J et al. (1861) Schiller's Complete Works. L. Kohler, Philadelphia, 2:342.

Your subjects must be what they were once more,
The crown's unique concern. Can there be any
Holier duty than equality?[16]

This ideal Schiller saw manifested in the sixteenth century, the time of his play, by the rebellion of the Estates in the Netherlands: "The circumstances favored my plan; the love of liberty struggling with despotism, the fetters of stupidity broken, hoary prejudices shaken, a nation reclaiming its human rights, republican virtue practiced in life, clearer notions circulating among the people, the minds in a state of fermentation, the hearts inspired with noble sympathies for the public good."[17]

Posa intends to save the freedom of Europe in Flanders. The path he has elected to reach this aim is not only to win over Carlos for this cause, but also to use him as a means to achieve this aim without his knowledge. First, however, his attempts take an unexpected turn. The King is the object of an intrigue at the court pursued with perfidious purpose. Elisabeth of Valois does not live in a happy marriage with Philip II, which is not unknown to him. The King remembers full of pain the shocked view with which his young wife regarded his gray hair when he received her as his bride. His courtiers' aim is to increase his jealousy and to let him doubt the loyalty of his wife, more concretely to ask whether his wife is betraying him with his son. This question torments him profoundly and drives him into a self-destructive circle of doubt and mistrust. The rottenness of the world of the court is a central theme of the play, which is unraveled in magnificent scenes. One element full of bitter sarcasm is that Philip's jealousy is accompanied by an affair that he demanded and finally is able to enjoy with a young lady of his court, who is a companion of his wife. The pain of the King, despite this patriarchal hypocrisy, is, however, genuine. He has humane sides and is intelligent enough to understand that he is the victim of intrigues and to desire something else. In his despair, he formulates an extraordinary wish for the environment in which he lives:

---

[16]Ibid, III/10, p 127:

Der Bürger
Sei wieder was er zuvor gewesen
Der Krone Zweck – ihn binde keine Pflicht
Als seiner Brüder gleich ehrwürdge Rechte.

Translation by Collier SyQuia H (1996) Don Carlos and Mary Stuart. Oxford University Press, Oxford, p 117. The translation lacks the emphasis on equal rights.

[17]Schiller, supra note 15, p 252: "Alles fand ich mir, wie durch einen dienstbaren Geist, dabei in die Hände gearbeitet; Freiheitssinn mit Despotimus im Kampfe, die Fesseln der Dummheit zerbrochen, tausendjährige Vorurteile erschüttert, eine Nation, die Menschenrechte wiederfordert, republikanische Tugenden in Ausübung gebracht, hellere Begriffe in Umlauf, die Köpfe in Gärung, die Gemüter von einem begeisternden Interesse gehoben." Translation by Hempel C J et al., supra note 15, p 341.

Now, Providence, good Providence, send me
A man.[18] You have been generous to me,
Now bless me with a man. You are alone,
Because unaided you see everything,
I beg you for a friend because my eyes see little by themselves. (. . .)
I am in need of truth. I need a helper,
Kings may not dig for truth where it lies buried.
Find the uncommon man whose heart is open
And pure, whose soul is clear, whose eyes unblinkered,
For he will help me seek it out. I shuffle
The destinies. Among the many thousands
Who flutter to the flam of royalty,
Let that one find me.[19]

He finally remembers Posa and a surprising fact about him: he is the only one of his noblemen who has not asked any favor of him since he returned from Flanders. This strange kind of behavior among the courtiers who desire, full of greed, nothing but favors from him, leads the King to ask himself whether he has perhaps found the person who is still a human being he is looking for. In this famous dialogue between Posa and the King, Posa does not only outline to the King his idea of a free order that takes human dignity seriously. He also tries to show that it could be a project for the King himself to create such an order of freedom—a project that would bring him true honor. He realizes with surprise that the King listens to what he says, and that he even seems to be moved by his passionate vision. The hope grows in Posa that perhaps the King himself could be the instrument to create the desired order of freedom—at least in the very first beginnings. For some time, he acts accordingly and deepens the trust of the King that he has won. One means among others to do this is to disclose Carlos's feelings towards his stepmother to the King, as Posa believes that he cannot hide them anymore anyway. Finally, however, he

[18]In the German original "Mensch," human being.

[19]Schiller, supra note 15, III/5, p 111:

Jetzt gib mir einen Menschen, gute Vorsicht –
Du hast mir viel gegeben. Schenke mir
Jetzt einen Menschen. Du – du bis allein,
Denn deine Augen prüfen das Verborgne,
Ich bitte dich um eine Freund, denn ich
Bin nicht wie du allwissend. (. . .)
Ich brauche Wahrheit – Ihre stille Quelle
Im dunkeln Schutt des Irrtums aufzugraben,
Ist nicht das Los der Könige. Gib mir
Den seltnen Mann mit reinem, offnem Herzen,
Mit hellem Geist und unbefangnen Augen,
Der mir sie finden helfen kann – ich schütte
Die Lose auf; laß unter Tausenden,
Die um der Hoheit Sonnenscheibe flattern
Den einzigen mich finden.

Translation by Collier Sy-Quia, supra note 16, p 101.

understands that the idea to bring freedom to Europe by the hands of Philip II is a futile hope. His attention is therefore directed solely towards Carlos again. Carlos, however, seems to be totally absorbed by his passion for Elisabeth. To overcome this obstacle, Posa decides that the only way to proceed is to use Carlos' passion for Elisabeth to draw his attention again to the cause of freedom. To achieve this end, he has to convince the Queen to turn Carlos's feelings into a new political, not only personal, direction:

And in this hopeless love
There was a gleam of hope for something else.[20]

The Queen, suffering under the atmosphere and repressive regime of the court where an autodafé is regarded as entertainment, is sympathetic to the cause of freedom herself. She agrees to pursue this plan. The central tragic turn of the play is rooted in the decision of Posa not to disclose his intentions to Carlos. He hides his new position with the King from Carlos. He decides to guide Carlos and his actions in the desired direction by influencing his feelings and decisions. He is not imposing any aims on Carlos that Carlos does not wholeheartedly support. On the contrary, Posa understands quite rightly that those aims that he thinks are correct for Carlos are in fact those that Carlos truly desires politically; in fact, they are an expression of his innermost political hopes.

Posa asks the Queen at the moment when he is sure of his imminent death, in verses of outstanding and deeply moving beauty not fully captured in translation, to remind Carlos to stay loyal to this cause even after he, Posa, has died:

---

[20]Ibid, IV/21, p 174:

In dieser hoffnungslosen Flamme
Erkannt ich früh der Hoffnung goldnen Strahl.

Translation by Collier Sy-Quia, supra note 16, p 163.

He must respect the dreams he had when young,
And guard his sacred gentleness of heart
Against the disenchanting touch of reason.
He must not stumble when the dust of thought
Threatens to choke his passion, heaven's gift.[21]

Schiller comments, "between the two friends the project ripens of producing the happiest state which is possible for human society to attain; it is the conflict between this enthusiastic project and personal passion, which constitutes the subject of the present drama."[22] Posa's view on Carlos' political convictions is confirmed at the end when Carlos, after Posa's death, explains to the Queen his own inner reorientation that now is directing his passion towards the political freedom of Flanders.

Posa's plan fails. Carlos cannot understand Posa's actions, starts to doubt Posa and is about to act accordingly. The total trust Posa demands is too heavy a burden for Carlos, who contributes with his doubts to the acceleration of the fatal course of events. In despair, Posa tries drastic means. He arrests Carlos due to a special warrant of the King he had obtained after Carlos discloses his secrets to a lady of the court who has already betrayed him before to the King because of disappointed love and jealousy. He does so to distract from the suspicion against Carlos and to enable Carlos to flee to Flanders and help the uprising there. Posa sacrifices himself by pretending he, himself, had intended to rebel against the King and therefore captured Carlos. The courageous and clever Queen Elisabeth understands quite well the ambivalence of this deed, which is not only altruistic, but also satisfies Posa's need to perform great deeds:

---

[21]Ibid, IV/21, p 173:

Sagen sie
Ihm, daß er für die Träume seiner Jugend
Soll Achtung tragen, wenn er Mann sein wird,
Nicht öffnen soll dem tötenden Insekte
Gerühmter besserer Vernunft das Herz
Der zarten Götterblume – daß er nicht
Soll irre werden, wenn des Staubes Weisheit
Begeisterung der Himmelstochter lästert.

Translation by Collier Sy-Quia, supra note 16, p 161.

[22]Ibid, p 253: "unter beiden Freunden bildet sich also ein enthusiastischer Entwurf, den glücklichsten Zustand hervorzubringen, der der menschlichen Gemeinschaft erreichbar ist, und von diesem enthusiastischen Entwurfe, wie er nämlich in Konflikt mit der mit der Leidenschaft erscheint, handelt das gegenwärtige Drama." Translation by Hempel C J et al., supra note 15, p 341.

No, no! This horrible catastrophe,
That you so nobly praise, you wished for it!
I know you – you have waited for this moment
Year after year. To feed your depthless pride,
A thousand hearts can break, it is no matter!
Your one desire is to be wondered at![23]

But it is not only the desire for fame that drives Posa forward, nor the demands for immediate action that clearly determine his choice, as he could have saved his friend under calm reflection through other means than self-sacrifice. He is also driven by the desire to pay back a self-sacrificial act of Carlos, who, in order to win Posa's friendship, as a child accepted the punishment for a crime that Posa himself committed. In addition, he hopes to commit his friend firmly and irrevocably to the cause of the freedom of Flanders by his own death. But Posa's plan fails again. Carlos does not save himself because of his own inability to live up to his political task. Full of despair he explains the situation to the King after Posa's death, tries to escape but is arrested during his last conversation with the Queen and is handed over to the Spanish Inquisition by his own father.

In a decisive talk with the Queen, Posa gains at the very end an idea of a kind of life in which love towards other people can become a central content of a human life. For a moment, his affection for the Queen becomes vivid and clear, whatever exact nature it may have, and he understands how beautiful life could be.[24] But, as Schiller comments dryly, this insight comes too late: "He wraps himself up in the greatness of his deed in order not to experience any regret on account of it."[25]

3 Posa's Mistake

The central problem of Posa's actions are not the aims for which he tries to win over Carlos, but that he uses Carlos as an instrument for his purposes without letting him remain the autonomous subject of his own action: "The enthusiasm of the Marquis leads him to act without noise, without companions, in silent greatness. Quietly as

---

[23]Ibid, IV/21, p 176:

Nein! Nein!
Sie stürzten sich in diese Tat, die Sie
Erhaben nennen. Leugnen Sie nur nicht.
Ich kenne Sie, Sie haben längst danach
Gedürstet – Mögen tausend Herzen brechen,
Was kümmert Sies, wenn sich Ihr Stolz nur weidet.

Translation by Collier Sy-Quia, supra note 16, p 164.

[24]Ibid, IV/22, p 177. Translation by Collier Sy-Quia, supra note 16, p 165.

[25]Ibid, p 267: "Er hüllt sich in die Größe seiner Tat, um keine Reue darüber zu empfinden." Translation by Hempel C J et al., supra note 15, p 346.

Providence takes care of a sleeping person, he desires to untie the knot of his friend's fate, he wants to save him after the fashion of a God; and by this means he ruins him. In looking up to high at his ideal of virtue, and not stooping sufficiently to watch his friend, he ruins both him and himself. Carlos perishes because his friend is not content with saving him in an ordinary manner."[26]

Posa is in every way Carlos' true friend and he feels an equally sincere and noble love for humanity. This perspective, reaching far beyond the individual person of his friend, lets Posa commit a decisive mistake that drives his friend into misfortune, that destroys his political project and that betrays the very idea at the root of his political ideals: He decides, and this is the tragic turn, to use the individual Carlos as a means to reach his political aims. This underlines dramatically the danger of missing high and well justified aims by using means that make the achievement of these aims impossible. The path pursued rings the death knell of the purpose of action: "On this account I selected a man of benevolent character soaring far above every selfish desire, I endowed him with the greatest respect for the rights of others. I made it his object to realize the enjoyment of universal liberty, and I do not believe that I have gone contrary to universal experience, in allowing him to assume the manners of despotism at the very moment when he was engaged in securing his great ideal. It was part of my plan to allow him to fall into the snares which beset every one who is engaged in similar pursuits."[27]

This political enthusiasm that breeds despotic tendencies even leads Posa to suggest to the King in their great dialogue that it is the King's duty to conquer the world if his is a happy kingdom of liberty.[28] Liberty seizes a sword that is the instrument of its death.

---

[26]Ibid, p 260: "Geräuschlos, ohne Gehülfen, in stiller Grösse zu wirken ist des Marquis Schwärmerei. Still, wie die Vorsicht für einen Schlafenden sorgt, will er seines Freundes Schicksal auflösen, er will ihn retten wie ein Gott – und eben dadurch richtet er ihn zugrunde. Daß er zu sehr nach seinem Ideal von Tugend in die Höhe und zu wenig auf seinen Freund herunterblickte, wurde beider Verderben. Carlos verunglückte, weil sein Freund sich nicht begnügte, ihn auf eine gemeine Art zu erlösen." Translation by Hempel C J et al., supra note 15, p 343f.

[27]Ibid, p 261f: "Ich wählte deswegen einen ganz wohlwollenden, ganz über jede selbstsüchtige Begierde erhabenen Charakter, ich gab ihm die höchste Achtung für anderer Rechte, ich gab ihm die Hervorbringung eines allgemeinen Freiheitsgenusses sogar zum Zwecke, und ich glaube mich auf keinem Widerspruch mit der allgemeinen Erfahrung zu befinden, wenn ich ihn, selbst auf dem Wege dahin, in Despotismus verirren ließ. Es lag in meinem Plan, daß er sich in dieser Schlinge verstricken sollte, die allen gelegt ist, die sich auf einerlei Wege mit ihm befinden." Translation by Hempel C J et al., supra note 15, p 344; Adorno T W (1998) Minima Moralia. In: Gesammelte Schriften. Suhrkamp, Frankfurt, 4:100; transl. E.F.N. Jephcott. London: Verso, 1978, p. 89, observes about Schiller that "in the innermost recesses of humanism, as its very soul, there rages a frantic prisoner who, as a Fascist, turns the world into a prison." ("Im innersten Gehäuse des Humanismus, als dessen eigene Seele, tobt gefangen der Wüterich, der als Faschist die Welt zum Gefängnis macht"). Given Schiller's treatment of Posa's tragedy which is about the very danger of abstract moral notions being turned into immoral deeds, this critique is untenable.

[28]Ibid, III/10, p 127. Translation by Collier Sy-Quia, supra note 16, p 117.

The Queen asks Posa a decisive question:

Can your good cause
Transform the evil of its means to honour?[29]

To think so, is Posa's fundamental error. It is not the error of an evil man, but of somebody driven to use fateful means by the power of the adversaries and helplessness of his position. The critique of this political choice must therefore be accompanied by the consciousness of the responsibility of those who maintain the repressive order. Political history up to the present, from the *terreur* of the French Revolution to the defense of postcolonial dictatorships to liberate human beings, has illustrated the consequences of this political error with much human suffering—and the persistent force of the motives that lead political agents to commit it.

4 The Law of Autonomous Reflection

The political ideal of Carlos and Posa is a mirror image of Schiller's own political ideas as developed in his theoretical and other writings, not least in the letters on the aesthetical education of human beings. The central normative root is the hope to create not only a political order in which human beings are the ultimate purpose of state action, but also a human life-world in which human dignity counts. This echoes Schiller's Kantianism, the leading maxim of which is respect for the worth of human beings. The idea that to treat human beings as ends in themselves is a limiting condition of any action of the state and individuals and their action-guiding intentions is expressed in the second material version of Kant's categorical imperative (though by no means invented by Kant) that demands, as a foundational ethical and legal principle, that human beings are always to be regarded as ends and never merely as means.[30]

The power of this idea is spelled out by the action of the play.

The "snake bite of suspicion"[31] determines the atmosphere of the court, as Carlos observes. It offers no true happiness, because human beings do not act because of some intrinsic motivation, but only to satisfy the demands of the ruler.[32] The King is

[29]Ibid, IV/3, p 134:

Und kann
Die gute Sache schlimme Mittel adeln?

Translation by Collier Sy-Quia, supra note 16, p 124.

[30]Kant I (1911) Grundlegung zur Metaphysik der Sitten. Akademie Ausgabe IV:429.

[31]Schiller, supra note 15, I/2, p 13; Translation by MM, cf. also Collier Sy-Quia, supra note 16, p 6.

[32]Ibid, III/10, p 120. Translation by Collier Sy-Quia, supra note 16, p 110.

part of the world of his court and its inherent contempt for human beings. His sexual overtures towards and abuse of the young court lady displays this attitude with brutal clarity. At this point, he does not know that the real reason for her acquiescence is the court lady's desire to take revenge on Carlos, who rejected her love. He knows very well, however, that she does not consent to his wishes because of affection for him, but because of the benefits she wants to reap as the price for granting a repulsive night. Notwithstanding this, he himself experiences painfully what it means to become the object of intrigues driven by the selfish interests of his courtiers. He is desperately looking for the experience of being regarded himself as an end in himself—that is the core of his search for a true human being which has become nothing less than an existential need. That he is capable of forming this desire as far as he himself is concerned but does not understand the meaning of his other behavior, epitomized by the affair with the court lady, saves the play throughout from any kind of humanistic kitsch: The King is certainly not an idealized noble sovereign. It shows, too, the importance of universalization, the need to apply the moral standards one wants to be applied to oneself to others as well, and the great psychological difficulty of doing exactly this.

This desire for a true human relation is also the source of the King's despair when he understands that Posa in the end despised him. First, he wishes to correct this image of himself:

He despised me when he died.
Summon him back, he must think differently. (...)
Who cares about the living, they can change,
One man stood up in this whole century,
One man was free – he scorned me and he died.[33]

But this pain is soon turned into merciless hatred:

But there is something he did not consider.
I am still here. Still here. Thanks be to nature
I feel the strength of youth in all my sinews.
And I will make a mockery of him,
Transforming all his dreams to fantasies,

[33]Ibid, V/9, p 205f:

Er dachte klein von mir und starb. Ich muß
Ihn wiederhaben. Er muß anders von
Mir denken. (...)
Was gehen die Lebenden mich an? Ein Geist,
Ein freier Mann stand auf in diesem ganzen
Jahrhundert – Einer – er verachtet mich
Und stirbt.

Translation by Collier Sy-Quia, supra note 16, p 191f:

His death into a fool's demise. His fall
Will shame his friend and darken the whole age.
How do men think they could survive without me?
I have the evening still and I will use it
To blight the earth for twenty generations!
He sacrificed me to humanity,
His god – I will avenge that sacrifice![34]

The intensity of the hatred that drives him to this decision to scorch the earth is yet another testimony to the force of his wish to be more than just the instrument of the petty, corrupted machinations of his court. It cannot be explained but by the depth of the wish that Posa ultimately left unfulfilled.

The Inquisition, the brutal cynical cold religious politics of power, is embodied by the Cardinal Inquisitor. The depiction of the nature of the institution he serves culminates in the magnificent scene in which the Cardinal Inquisitor informs Philip that the Inquisition had surveilled Posa and wanted him alive to teach the rebels a lesson by his punishment. That the Cardinal Inquisitor convinces Philip that he has to hand over his son to his myrmidons shows what orders look like in which individual human beings are only pawns in a religiously legitimated game of power and influence:

Why did you need a man? Mankind is numbers,
Nothing but numbers. Must my grey-haired pupil
Learn once again the law of single rule?

---

[34]Ibid, V/9, p 207:

Er könnte sich verrechnet haben. Noch,
Noch bin ich. Habe Dank, Natur. Ich fühle
In meinen Sehnen Jünglingskraft. Ich will
Ihn zum Gelächter machen. Seine Tugend
Sei eines Träumers Hirngespinst gewesen.
Er sei gestorben als ein Tor. Sein Sturz
Erdrücke seinen Freund und sein Jahrhundert!
Laß sehen, wie man mich entbehrt. Die Welt
Ist noch auf einen Abend mein. Ich will
Ihn nützen, diesen Abend, daß nach mir
Kein Pflanzer mehr in zehen Menschenaltern
Auf dieser Brandstatt ernten soll. Er brachte
Der Menschheit, seinem Götzen, mich zum Opfer;
Die Menschheit büße mir für ihn!

Translation by Collier Sy-Quia, supra note 16, p 193.

The Cardinal Inquisitor asks this with impatience when confronted with Philip's desire to find a human being in his court.[35] Institutions such as the Inquisition prostituted humanity—a humanity he intended to avenge and to pillory its enemies' shameful deeds with his play, as Schiller wrote in a letter.[36]

The violation of human dignity is thus illustrated in all its baseness and ugliness by the life-world of the court and the institutions that support it, but also, and that is the greatness of the play, by the means of Posa's fateful intrigues to topple this despised order. His means to pursue a justified and noble aim subvert the possibility of achieving his purpose. This does not delegitimize Posa's aspirations, but invites the audience to think profoundly about the means to pursue these noble aims. After all, history vindicated the power of his ideas and the possibility of successful political action. Philip and the Inquisition enjoy a grim triumph on stage, but as the reality of the fight in Flanders and its outcome underlined for any spectator—the forces they represent are not necessarily victorious in all times to come. Schiller's vision of history, as outlined on grand dramatic scale in *Wallenstein*, is not particularly rosy, but pure fatalistic pessimism is not the ultimate conclusion that he draws.

The alternative to this life-world is not only spelled out in the political terms that Posa and Carlos regard as the form of life that truly suits human beings. Posa also ultimately gains a sense of another kind of existence because of the experience that humans can become ends in themselves *for others* as one of the greatest gifts in life. Love weeds out heteronomous purposes set for others and shows that one can become as important for them oneself. Some of the dignity that is so far only promised to human beings is conserved in fleeting, but profound moments of human intimacy.

In Schiller's theoretical writings, the principle of freedom following from the intrinsic value of human persons is understood as foundational. Furthermore, the way human beings come to an understanding of this principle underlines their normative status, because ethical insight cannot be gained by anything else but the autonomous thinking of free individuals. The process of cognition manifests itself in human beings' status as reasonable subjects. The process of understanding is radically inclusive, as the cognitive aim is to think about ethics and the legitimate ethical order in a cosmopolitan perspective which at least attempts to exclude nobody from the realm of ethical consideration: "The gaze of both philosopher and man of the world is now fixed expectantly on the political domain, where the very fate of humanity is argued out (…) However important the substance and

[35]Ibid, V/10, p 213:

Wozu Menschen? Menschen sind
Für Sie nur Zahlen, weiter nichts. Muß ich
Die Elemente der Monarchenkunst
Mit meinem grauen Schüler überhören?

Translation by Collier Sy-Quia, supra note 16, p 198.

[36]Schiller F (1783) Letter to Reinwald, 14. April 1783. https://www.friedrich-schiller-archiv.de/briefe-schillers/an-wilhelm-reinwald/schiller-an-wilhelm-reinwald-14-april-1783/.

consequence of this great legal dispute might be to anyone calling himself a man, the way in which it is conducted should be of especial interest to anyone who can think for himself. A question that would otherwise be settled by the blind right of might now seems to have been brought before the tribunal of pure reason; and whoever remains capable of putting himself at the centre of things, advancing from a mere individual to a representative of the human race, might equally consider himself a member of this tribunal, as he is, a human being and citizen of the world, party at the same time and more or less caught up in its outcome. It is hence not just his own interest that will be decided by this legal process; judgement will also be made according to laws which his rational mind is competent and entitled to dictate."[37]

These foundational ideas of the critical Enlightenment are at the same time at the core of the ethical project of a democratic constitutional state embedded in a cosmopolitan legal order. It builds on the capacity of its citizens for autonomous thought guided by reasons. It attempts to overcome nationalistic antagonisms in some kind of stable, value oriented international order of cooperation under equitable international legal rules based on respect for a modest version of human rights. This presupposes that human beings can transcend their narrower group interests and can at least in some particularly important, qualified cases consider seriously the interests of the human species as part of their normative deliberation. In the eighteenth century, the issues in this respect were universalized freedom and equality, and perhaps most importantly—as Kant formulated it—perpetual peace.[38] These normative ideas are expressed today by constitutions and the supplementary, still mostly aspirational international regime of human rights in the language of law, making human dignity the guiding principle of these legal orders, however insufficiently the practice of states and the international community may live up to this task.

---

[37]Schiller, supra note 6, p 10: "Erwartungsvoll sind die Blicke des Philosophen wie des Weltmanns auf den politischen Schauplatz geheftet, wo jetzt, wie man glaubt, das grosse Schicksal der Menschheit verhandelt wird (...) So nahe dieser grosse Rechtshandel, seines Inhalts und seiner Folgen wegen, jeden der sich Mensch nennt, angeht, so sehr muss er, seiner Verhandlungsart wegen, jeden Selbstdenker ins besondere interessiren. Eine Frage, welche sonst nur durch das blinde Recht des Stärkeren beantwortet wurde, ist nun, wie es scheint, vor dem Richterstuhle reiner Vernunft abhängig gemacht, und wer nun immer fähig ist, sich in das Centrum des Ganzen zu versetzen, und sein Individuum zur Gattung zu steigern, darf sich als einen Beysitzer jenes Vernunftgerichts betrachten, so wie er als Mensch und Weltbürger zugleich Parthey ist, und näher oder entfernter in den Erfolg sich verwickelt sieht. Es ist also nicht bloss seine eigene Sache, die in diesem großen Rechtshandel zur Entscheidung kommt, es soll auch nach Gesetzen gesprochen werden, die er als vernünftiger Geist selbst zu diktiren fähig und berechtiget ist.". Translation by Tribe K, Schiller, supra note 8, p 6.

[38]Immanuel Kant (1995) Zum Ewigen Frieden. Akademie Ausgabe XX, Berlin, p 341ff.

5 A Mirror Image of the Life-Worlds to Come?

The "beautiful stones" of Schiller's play are thus an invitation to reflect not only on human dignity's content, but also on the seasoned instruments to violate its demands and, equally important, the many ways not to live up to its human promises, ruining ultimately the agent's own life, even if he is a king. The tragedy of *Don Carlos* is not just of philological interest as an odd specimen of eighteenth century German literature. It is not some moralizing sob story. It is a powerful image of a kind of life-world in which mutual instrumentalization has been universalized: Everybody is using everybody else as a tool to pursue an egoistic aim. The form of this life-world, a court, intrigues, the inquisition, the struggles in Flanders, have faded away, but that renders the ethical and political core of the matter only more visible. Of course, everybody feels that the court is rotten, that the King is ultimately a merciless potentate, the Inquisition is of appalling cruelty and its religion of supreme hypocrisy. Of course, Posa was wrong to use his friend as a tool in his plans. It is not particularly difficult to discern all of this. But to realize this is already just one step away from a critical analysis of current political phenomena with newly sharpened normative tools.

Are there, after all, no features of the world Schiller describes that can be found in our political present (and will most probably not ever disappear entirely from the surface of the earth)? What about, for instance, the attitude of populist authoritarians towards the citizens of the states they rule? What does political propaganda, a new culture of political lies, the stirring up of resentment and hatred, tell us about their mindset? What does the political attack on truth entail in this respect?

A lie is a classic example for the use of person as a means to heteronomous aims. Its purpose is manipulation. A political force that takes systematic recourse to lies is thus one that quite obviously is characterized by disrespect for human beings. The politics of hate and resentment, which have been and still are such effective tools for the machinery of power, are of a related kind. They exploit the weaknesses of human beings, their fears, their ability for fanciful self-delusion and self-righteousness, the longing to be able to feel superior to others, the malicious emotions stirred by power over others that political history has shown to be of such destructive strength. The turn to authoritarianism itself, with a democratic fig leaf or not, is another element of political orders that shows that they do not respect the worth of human beings. Freedom, the protection of humans' rights to self-fulfillment, offers them a place to be themselves and to shape their individual pursuit of happiness. An order like authoritarianism, in whatever form, that makes the enjoyment of liberty and other rights ultimately dependent on its serving the regime or that, at least, ensures that the liberty of the citizens does not create obstacles to the attainment of the regime's aims, is based on contempt for the individuals that it suppresses.

The normative ideas *Don Carlos* deals with can be spelled out in economic terms too. The critique of the instrumentalization of human beings for economic purposes is a source of the ideas that had a major impact on the formation of the movements for the emancipation of labor. Many issues arise in the context of the economic exploitation of human beings. In industrialized countries and beyond, a new threat has raised its head in recent years, the exploitation of human beings by amassing data that are commercialized and put to economic use, in particular in the advertising industry—"surveillance capitalism" as it has been called.[39] Based on these technologies, authoritarian (and not-so-authoritarian) states create a new dimension of surveillance most probably dreamed of by old-fashioned instruments of subjugation like the Stasi or the KGB.

Schiller thus wrote nothing less than a powerful parable of how a world in which human beings encounter each other predominantly as means to their narrow, egoistic aims looks like. It shows the price in freedom and happiness that human beings pay for living in this life form, even if they apparently profit from the power structure of the respective society. The characters are not Beckettian tramps but are drawn from the world of a sixteenth century court. That does not mean they are antiquated puppets on long torn theatrical strings. On the contrary, the world of courts and the Inquisition is by now so far removed from contemporary experience that this imagery powerfully focusses attention on the core of the artwork. Like Shakespeare's kings, queens and princes they visibly enact a persistently recurring human drama that, in our times, like in other times, is of paramount human importance. It explores the ethical fundamentals of a meaningful human life. It has recently gained truly existential political significance, because during the second half of the Twentieth century humanity has created a situation that puts the further existence of the species into question. That the new authoritarianism, based on a faked reality, resentment, hatred and disrespect for the worth of human beings will be able to face this challenge is impossible to conceive. Rather, it will conjure up further menaces it will ultimately not be able to contain.

By understanding the fate of Carlos, Posa, Philip and Elisabeth, the greatness of these characters and the tragedy of their actions brought into a beautiful form, those who accompany them in the realm of aesthetical intuition on the way to the abyss have already taken a decisive step into the sphere where the cultural foundations of an order of freedom have their source. The memory of how those who look for freedom with dignity can drown in the course of history, as victims, perpetrators and a troubling mixture of both, and what the alternative could promise, enlivens the consciousness of the value of human relations and such orders that, like the democratic constitutional state, do not create a political paradise, but are firmly founded on the respect for human freedom, equality and the worth of each human being. It is therefore important to remember Carlos, Posa, Elisabeth and Philip, their many siblings in other great pieces of art in different languages and aesthetical forms, and for which historical processes they stand if one asks oneself why democratic constitutional states and the wider life-world they embody deserve so much passion in their unwavering defense.

[39] Cf. Shoshana Zuboff (2019) The Age of Surveillance Capitalism. Profile Books, London.

Of Forging into Swords on the Dialectic of Rights and the New Liberal Desire for Criminal Law

Christoph Burchard

1 Introduction

Mordechai Kremnitzer's official webpage reads—and rightly so!—that he is an 'admired and leading researcher in the fields of criminal and constitutional law'. This makes praising him none the easier. After all, if one were to emphasize that he is an exquisite legal scholar and a distinguished comparativist, or to point out his fascinating intellectual curiosity and his sincere personal openness—all of this sounds somewhat unoriginal. This would also be true if one were to highlight that he is a preeminent "bridge builder": who connects different legal disciplines (most notably criminal and constitutional law);[1] who links divergent jurisdictions and legal heritages (as a German, his vast knowledge of German law and its societal backgrounds indeed makes me blush);[2] who joins diverse methodologies (think about his knowledge about theory and doctrine,[3] as well as his recent empirical work);[4] and who indeed brings together people (including, like myself when I got to know him,

The manuscript of this essay was finalized in January 2020. I will not analyze the most recent jurisprudence of the German Federal Constitutional Court, most notably its decision on 26 February 2020—2 BvR 2347/15 et al.—Thank you to an anonymous reviewer, who helped me clarify my line of argumentation; and to the participants of the Virtual Workshop on the Political Turn(s) in Criminal Law Thinking (www.viritual-workshop.info), especially to *Matt Matravers* for his extensive comments and editorial suggestions. As usual, all faults etc. are my mine alone.

[1]Only see Kremnitzer (1993), p. 84 et seq.; Kremnitzer (1999), p. 720 et seq.

[2]Only see the analysis in Kremnitzer (2014), p. 111 et seq.

[3]Only see Kremnitzer (2008), p. 78 et seq.; Ghanayim and Kremnitzer (2014), p. 329 et seq.

[4]See Sulitzeanu-Kenan et al. (2016), p. 348 et seq.

C. Burchard (✉)
Goethe-Universität, Frankfurt am Main, Germany
e-mail: burchard@jur.uni-frankfurt.de

K. Ghanayim, Y. Shany (eds.), *The Quest for Core Values in the Application of Legal Norms*, https://doi.org/10.1007/978-3-030-78953-4_3

people to whom *Mordechai Kremnitzer* is the far more senior and accomplished). So instead of repeating such praises, I rather dare to illustrate my utmost respect and deep admiration for *Mordechai Kremnitzer* by dedicating to him some tentative thoughts on matters that I still find puzzling, and that he has seen and mastered long since: namely thoughts on what I call the dialectic of rights in constitutional criminal law, and how it bespeaks a foundational transformation of the image of public penal power.

The dialectic of rights[5] is a means to analyze the new liberal desire for (the expansion and intensification of) criminal law and criminal justice[6] (at least in Germany and Europe). More concretely, the dialectic of rights is a means to appreciate legal developments in the discourse on (especially human and fundamental) rights that point to underlying social and political transformations of the image of public penal powers. In drawing on the dialectic of rights in this analytical sense, then, I wish to bring to the fore foundational questions that often only lurk in the shadow of the affirmations of an increasingly coercive criminal law, and which those desiring a more coercive criminal law rarely address. Among said questions is whether it is sociologically warranted and normatively justified that many liberal minds are no longer suspicious of the "dark side"[7] of the state and its public penal power. As a matter of fact, I only wish to raise the significance of these questions, while this paper cannot seek to reply to them. The dialectic of rights is hence a means to raise, not to answer foundational social and political questions, and to initiate a political turn in criminal law theory.

Conceptually, the dialectic of rights is that rights allow for antithetical, prima facie even paradoxical practices of justification in the legislation, administration and adjudication of criminal law and criminal justice: Rights safeguard individual freedoms and liberties, *and* encroach upon these very freedoms and liberties. Rights result in a limitation of the intrusive powers of the state,[8] *and* in the expansion of

---

[5]The term "dialectic of rights" has inter alia been used in a related, but purely theoretical manner by Menke (2009).

[6]"New" I do not use in a legal historical, but in a conceptual sense. It is to distinguish the liberal "desire for more criminal law" from the traditional liberal "skepticism about criminal law". I will not explore how new in a temporal sense this desire for criminal law really is. What is more, "liberal" I use in the Continental European way to designate a political theory based on and related to freedoms and liberties. Further, I will not reflect upon whether these freedoms and liberties are primordially given (as the concept of freedom suggests) or externally constructed (as the concept of liberties suggests).—I acknowledge that my approach is rooted in German constitutional theory. Hence, even the criminalization of murder I see as an intervention into the freedom of the offender; mind, an intervention that can be (and in effect: is!) justified. In framing this as an intervention ("Eingriff"), the burden of justification rests on the state.

[7]As aptly put by Kölbel (2019), p. 257, where one can also find references aplenty for such affirmations of a more coercive criminal law and justice in German criminal law academia.

[8]This extends to non-state polities that wield criminal power over individuals, as becomes apparent in international criminal law and justice. Here, too, (human) rights are a significant means to justify the expansion of criminal powers. After all, the fight against the impunity of human rights violations is a recurring argument for the criminalization of so-called core crimes (especially of genocide and

these very powers.[9] Rights imply freedoms and liberties against the coercive powers of a polity, and the empowerment of that very polity to coercively intervene into these very individual freedoms and liberties (be it by means of legitimate authority, or illegitimate domination).[10] Rights (the justificatory practices thereof) thus carry the potential to protect *and* infringe upon these very rights (the freedoms that they express and the liberties to which they entitle). This leads to the potential for rights (the possibility to assert one's rights in rights-based discourses against others) to expand and intensify criminal law and justice, and thus to foster coercive overreach. This must not be overlooked,[11] although it is hard to acknowledge that rights can turn into a violating enablement, as they appear as something that one cannot *not* want.[12]

The dialectic of rights becomes manifest in the field of what I call constitutional criminal law,[13] and characterizes many developments of human and fundamental rights jurisprudence in Germany and Europe. In this context, one can perceive an ever-stronger move from the (classical, at least supposedly so) defensive[14] to the offensive function of human and fundamental rights.[15] These rights increasingly formulate (or rather: are interpreted as formulating) '*coercive duties* on the state to criminalize, prevent, police, and prosecute harmful acts.'[16] Or to say it more metaphorically, German and European constitutional criminal law is progressively re-forging rights as shields into rights as swords.[17]

To no small degree, this is caused by a transforming image of public penal power in Europe. Many proponents of this turn (from rights as shields to rights as swords) no longer consider the state as the primary threat to individual freedoms and liberties, but as their central guarantor. The dialectic of rights in constitutional criminal law and justice thus prompts no less than an inquiry into our current societal and political transformations and whether they are justified. This is what I will argue in this paper

---

crimes against humanity), *and* for their prosecution beyond the state. On this offensive function of rights in international criminal law see Geneuss (2017), p. 45 et seq.

[9]Also cf Lazarus (2012a), pp. 135–155.—On the negative and positive dimension of rights also see Currie (1986), p. 864 et seq.

[10]Also cf Menke (2009), para 11.

[11]This was first stipulated by Lazarus (2012a), p. 155, and I fully agree.

[12]This draws on the post-colonial critique against liberalism by Chakravorty Spivak (1993), p. 44 et seq., but casts—consciously so—rights-based violations not as an inevitability, but as a mere possibility, which one can counter.

[13]On this term from a German perspective Burchard (2016), p. 28 et seq.; Jahn (2016), p. 63 et seq.

[14]As to this classical dimension of rights only see Hassemer (2004), pp. 312–315; Bascuñán Rodríguez (2007), p. 47 et seq. as a reply to Viganò (2014), p. 428 et seq.

[15]See inter alia: at the German level, Alexy (1996), p. 420 ff; Heinrich Rupp (1976), p. 161 et seq.; at the European level, Fredman (2008); Tulkens (2011b), p. 583 et seq.; Tulkens (2011a), p. 156 et seq.

[16]As vividly summarized by Lazarus (2012a), p. 136.

[17]Christine Van den Wyngaert is credited with the reference to the shield and sword function of human rights in the application of (international) criminal law.

by first delineating the notion of constitutional criminal law (infra Sect. 2), then conceptualizing the idea of the dialectic of rights (infra Sect. 3), before finally offering some reflections on the transforming image of public penal power and how it caters to the new liberal desire for a more coercive criminal law and justice (infra Sect. 4).

2 The Analytical Notion of Constitutional Criminal Law

The dialectic of rights is prominent in what I call constitutional criminal law. The latter comprises the constitutional legal contexts and conditions (positive requirements, negative limits, organizational constraints, and options, etc.) of an "ordinary" criminal law and its administration in a given jurisdiction. In the analytical sense advanced here, constitutional criminal law cannot be universal, but can only be particular to a given constitutional order, and it can neither be about generalizations of constitutional traditions (which may overlook what is "really" happening "on the ground") nor about prescriptions of legitimate constitutional orders and how they ought to organize their criminal laws.[18] Rather, since *a* constitutional criminal law is (part of) *a* constitutional law, it refers to the realities of a constitutional order in action, which is (normally) intrinsically interlinked with the formation of the social and the political in a given polity at a given moment in time. As constitutional law is the "supreme law of the land", it is the first and final arbiter of the legality of "its" ordinary criminal law and justice. External points of reference (like those advanced by pre-constitutional criminal law theories) hence have—analytically speaking, i.e. for good or bad—no legal sway over the internal validity of ordinary criminal law. And due to its relation to societal social and political contexts, constitutional criminal law brings particular social and political rationalities to "its" criminal law (for example about the separation of powers, which many traditional criminal law theories disregard). This constitutionalization of criminal law discards essentialist conceptions of criminal law (at least essentialization that did not make it constitutional law, its doctrines, principles, and jurisprudence), and (internally, that is constitutionally) limits the (external, for example philosophical) limits of criminal law.

As an example, consider the notion of "in dubio pro libertate", which many German criminal law theorists cherish. It means in its strong sense that a legislator must choose non- or even de-criminalization if there are doubts about whether some conduct deserves punishment ("Strafwürdigkeit" in German).[19] As a weaker rule regarding the distribution of burdens of argumentation, '*in dubio pro liberate* demands [or so it is argued, C.B.] that no criminal prohibition be made [. . .] when all prior considerations did not result in a definite judgment that criminal prohibition

[18]A normative take of constitutional criminal law is advanced by Thorburn (2010), p. 21 et seq.

[19]See Vormbaum (1995), pp. 734–760.

would be either clearly proportionate or clearly disproportionate.'[20] Although in terms of liberal criminal law theory much can and should be said to this effect, this theory ("in dubio pro libertate") does not necessarily bind a constitutional criminal law in a given jurisdiction. After all, does it not rest with a democratic legislator to make the necessary calls about the correct (and timely) balance between freedom or security? Put differently, as long as "in dubio pro libertate" is not recognized as a general constitutional doctrine that restricts legislative powers, it is but an argument that can (and possibly should) be heeded in policy making; but it is no constitutional imperative that must be complied with. Or to pick up what has been said before: Constitutional criminal law internally limits external limitations of criminalization.

Because of this setup of constitutional criminal law, I consider it a particularly rewarding "dig-site" to analytically identify, in a first step, legal developments (in my case: the way rights, due to their dialectic, are re-forged from shields into swords), which point to social and political transformations that go beyond the mere realm of criminal law and justice. These social and political transformations then require, in a second step, careful critical social and political reflections, which go beyond the focal points of many of the dominant criminal law theories, be they a-political and essentialist (as in the prevailing German tradition)[21] or moralistic in nature (as in the prevailing Anglo-American tradition).[22] The turn to (the critical analysis of legal developments in) constitutional criminal law is, therefore, part of the political turn in criminal law theory, which is now underway in many parts of the (Western) world.

Although (to my knowledge, and according to all databases that I checked) *Mordechai Kremnitzer* has technically not spoken about "constitutional criminal law" so far, he is substantively speaking one of the first and foremost constitutional criminal lawyers, and a realistic and critical one at that. Indeed, being the "bridge builder" that he is, he went into depths about the connection between constitutional and criminal law *avant la lettre*. In his highly instructive 1999 piece on the 'Constitutionalization of Substantive Criminal Law', he made the very convincing case for taking a 'Realistic View' on the subject matter at hand.[23] Interestingly enough, he expressed deep skepticism that constitutional law in general and (constitutionally induced) judicial review in particular could help in closing the gap between criminal law in theory and criminal law in practice. Inter alia the gap that '[c]riminal law in theory is an instrument of last resort, but the reality of criminal law is that it is often an instrument of first resort', and that the 'real interpretation in criminal law has very little to do with prior warning', while its most basic principle should actually be 'the principle of legality, of prior warning.' I fully agree with these diagnoses and suggest analyzing them on the level of constitutional criminal law itself. I do so by asking how and why constitutional criminal law in action

[20]Hörnle (2014), p. 678.

[21]As to a critical review of this tradition, see Vogel (2014), p. 635.

[22]As to a critical review of this tradition, see Chiao (2018), p. 144 et seq.

[23]See Kremnitzer (1999), p. 720 ff.

sanctions and caters to the practical demise of many theoretical principles of criminal law (think about the German constitutional principle of proportionality, which does not "really" treat criminal legislation as *ultima ratio*, inter alia because the German Constitutional Court delegates to parliament margins, indeed prerogatives of appreciation, in crucial areas of its application). In this respect, I very much share the sentiment of the "recent" *Mordechai Kremnitzer* that one has to take due account of the subjectivity in practices of constitutional law, which for example 'compromises the idea of proportionality analysis as an objective and neutral method of constitutional adjudicating.'[24]

3 The Analytical Notion of the Dialectic of Rights

3.1 Brief Conceptualizations

Indeed, *Mordechai Kremnitzer's* 2014 lucid critique of the realities of the proportionality principle[25] was among my inspirations for the very idea of the dialectic of rights. The justifications necessary under this principle, or so he wrote, may actually be no more than a 'nice and misleading mask concealing an ugly face', actually no more than 'an instrument that can be used to justify any kind of human rights violation.' From this, he drew the general conclusion that '[t]he discourse of human rights created initially for the purpose of the protection of rights is becoming in this way a discourse for all purposes', including—or so I would understand him—for the violations of rights. This, then, is the seeming paradox that the dialectic of rights addresses: rights allow for the protection *and* the violation of rights, at least for coercive penal action. Or to put it differently and in a less condensed way: Rights give rise to a discourse, which practically permits justifications for the protection of, *and* the invasion into, the very freedoms and liberties that these rights express. This, however, is neither an irresolvable self-contradiction, that is to say, it is not a paradox per se, nor an ambiguity[26] of rights. It is rather, or so I suggest, a dialectical feature of rights (or rather the discourses they set into motion), the consequences of which need to be reflected on carefully and critically, as the sword function puts into serious question the shield function of rights.[27]

The dialectics of rights has two emanations, a basic and a complex one. The *basic emanation* has been brought to the fore in *Mordechai Kremnitzer's* seminal 1993 piece on 'Constitutional Principles and Criminal Law'. Here, he underlined that '[b] asic to constitutional law and criminal law is a shared image of human beings. It is a conception of human beings as "morally" autonomous.' On the one hand, or so he

---

[24]Sulitzeanu-Kenan et al. (2016), p. 348 et seq.

[25]See Kremnitzer (2014), pp. 111 and 120 et seq.

[26]As suggested by Lazarus (2012a), p. 137.

[27]See also Rusterberg (2014), p. 87.

argued, this 'conception dictates the boundaries of the penal law and influences the principles of criminal responsibility, both qualitatively and quantitatively'. But on the other hand, 'the criminal law is uncompromising' in assuming—sanctioned by corresponding constitutional principles, I would add—that the individual has internalized 'the system's fundamental values and a basic commitment to those values by every competent person. Alienation, unreceptiveness, rejection, or non-internalization are neither recognized nor considered.' The general lesson I take from this insight is that rights come with preconceptions, including those that encumber the individual. Indeed, the very notion of individual autonomy, which is axiomatic to human and fundamental rights, dialectally empowers and frees as well as binds and disciplines the individual,[28] in our case most notably by requiring *and* by allowing for the individualization of criminal responsibility. On the one hand, this resists (for example very short-sighted utilitarian) mere ascriptions of criminal responsibility (and, for example, militates against the arbitrary designation of criminal scape-goats for the sake of social utility). But on the other hand, the individualization of criminal responsibility also systemically obfuscates possible collective accountabilities, and the need to address, justify and criticize them.[29]

The *complex emanation of the dialectics of rights* becomes evident in two insightful papers that *Mordechai Kremnitzer* co-authored together with *Tatjana Hörnle* on the principle of human dignity and the principle of culpability (the "Schuldprinzip" in German, a more literal translation of which is 'principle of individual guilt') in Israel and Germany in 2011. The first paper explores these

[28] See generally Menke (2009), para 11.

[29] By way of a brief example, think about a railway crossing attendant, who negligently fails his duties, thus causing the death of a cyclist who runs into a train because the gates were not duly closed. Most of us will not doubt that this "perpetrator" has indeed incurred criminal responsibility (e.g. for reckless homicide). But then consider that this could have been easily prevented by automatizing the gates, which the railway company did not do to save costs in order not to raise ticket prices (or to increase shareholder returns etc.). Under the autonomy principle, criminal law remains in the realm of "without alternatives," and is freed—for good or bad!—from questioning whether relieving railway customers from rising costs (or boosting shareholders returns) justifies the risk of a cyclist's death, and whether it is fair (or good policy) to hold a (realistically speaking, poorly paid) railway crossing attendant to personal account without duly considering prior collective failings. This case is by no way a fiction. On its (sad) real-life background see the report of the Federal German Agency for Railway Accidents on the accident in Bad Aibling on 9 February 2016: Bundesstelle für Eisenbahnunfalluntersuchung, 'Untersuchungsbericht - Zugkollision, 09.02.2016, Bad Aibling–Kolbermoor' (2018). http://tinyurl.com/53wpkdxw (last visited 22 February 2021).— The objection that one can bring tort or administrative action against the railway company, or that the shared responsibility of the latter does not affect the moral (and legal) responsibility of the railway crossing attendant, who was negligent in carrying out the duties assigned to him, only supports my argument: The possibility to hold the latter criminally accountable neatly shifts the responsibility of the railway company to "mere" civil or administrative—at least to mere "complementary"—liability. What is more, the language that the railway crossing attendant "is" morally (and legally) responsible obfuscates that "responsibility" rests on an act of ascription. This ascribed individualization of criminal responsibility may be warranted (make no mistake: I am not arguing for abolition), but it has to draw on concepts (like moral autonomy) that dialectically free and bind at the same time.

principles as defensive rights, which limit the criminal powers of the state, for example by disallowing '[a]bsolute liability as a form of criminal liability [because it] is contradictory to the principle of culpability, since liability is imposed without the need to prove any kind of mental element.'[30] But in the second paper, we can then trace how rights as shields are re-forged into rights as swords. Here, human dignity is presented as a possible 'protected legal interest in criminal law'. *Tatjana Hörnle* and *Mordechai Kremnitzer* examine various criminal offences in German and Israeli criminal law, and 'explore how such prohibitions can be justified, and, more specifically, what role human dignity plays in such justifications.' In conceiving human dignity not only as a 'defensive and individual right', but also as an '*objective value* when certain behavior has humiliating significance without violating the rights of a specific individual', *Hörnle/Kremnitzer* for example affirm that one cannot 'fully grasp the extent of the wrong caused by rape [...] without taking into account the aspect of human dignity.' It is the violation of human dignity that justifies—or so I would understand the paper—this offense, and its relatively high punishment range.

Methodologically speaking, this is a striking line of argument. After all, human dignity—the right of rights in German constitutional law, which shines "on the top of the ladder"[31] and which must never be infringed upon by any German public authority—can[32] be turned against one individual (for example the potential rapist, who faces policing, criminal prosecution and incarceration) for the sake of another (that is, the potential rape victim, who is backed by the state's possibility to police and prosecute the actions of another).[33] This is illustrative of the complex emanation of the dialectics of rights, which arises in multi-polar relations of rights[34] (that is, not bi-polar, individual vs. state, but rather complex, individual and/vs. individual etc. and/vs. state), where we find possible conflicts of rights that are moderated by the state.

Other than posited by *Hörnle/Kremnitzer,* however, I do not think that '[r]eferences to human dignity as an objective value are categorically different from

[30]Kremnitzer and Hörnle (2011), p. 132.

[31]Kremnitzer (2014), p. 116.

[32]I am not claiming that the offensive dimension of rights, or their objective dimension, or possible positive obligations of the state, necessarily result in the coercion of an individual on part of the state. But coercion is a possibility. For a similar disclaimer, see Lazarus (2012a), p. 146. For an attempt to instrumentalize positive obligations to bolster rehabilitation as the aim of punishment, see Meijer (2017), p. 145 et seq.

[33]One could also "state the obvious"—namely that under the dialectic of rights the state should impose criminal liability for murder or theft as these are meant to protect core rights of the victims (life and property). But then: Life and property are "below" human dignity in German constitutional law. What is more, the dialectic of rights only implies that the state *can* impose criminal liability, not that it should or even must do so. For example, property is something that the state can and has to regulate (e.g. under Art. 14 of the German Constitution) so that the state could decriminalize certain theft offenses (think about "stealing" food that was thrown away by super markets; note that this throwing away does not mean that the supermarket gives up its property under German civil law).

[34]See inter alia Isensee (2000), marginal number 83 et seq.

references to human dignity as an individual right.' Or more generally speaking, I do not consider the subjective and the objective dimension of rights to be categorically different. Rather, once multi-polar rights relations enter the equation, the freedoms and liberties of various individuals need to be weighed and balanced against each other (ideally, many would call for an equilibrium of freedom and liberties).[35] Under a rights-based normative order of complex social settings, then, the shield and the sword function of rights are but flip-sides of the same coin.[36] The same holds true for rights as shields and as swords, or negative rights and positive obligations. All of these antinomies bespeak the inherent dialectic of rights, which potentially fight for *and* against individual freedoms and liberties, and against and for public power.

In this respect, it is crucial to note that while rights as shields are at least conceptually[37] placed in(to) the hands of the individual who encounters public coercion (that is, into the hands of the potential rapist, who stands trial), rights as swords are wielded by the state for the benefit of other individuals (that is, by the state criminalizing, policing and prosecuting rape for the benefit of the potential rape victim). Rights as swords are hence not 'self-executing', but rather necessarily mediated through state action.[38] This is why the punitive powers of the state are both limited and unlimited by the dialectics of rights. Rights as shields restrain the state, but rights as swords expand the intrusive powers of the state, at least of the one claiming a monopoly on violence or a monopoly on penal powers; this holds especially true in the administrative or welfare state.[39]

All this holds true for crimes that address and resolve (in one way or another) multi-polar rights relations, i.e. where there is a possible conflict between shields (of possible offenders against state coercion) and swords (of possible victims against other citizens). Crimes that do not protect the rights of others, but rather collective or common goods (think about the protection of state institutions or the environment), are seemingly not covered by this framework. Yet they can be brought back under this framework if said collective or common goods are cast as objective fusions of subjective rights (e.g. most notoriously the right to security).

3.2 *Brief Examples from German and European Constitutional Criminal Law*

I am *not* claiming that the dialectic of rights is a defining feature or a necessary attribute of rights as such, one that we can discern universally, and one that

---

[35]See Barak (2012), p. 350 et seq.

[36]Cf Alexy (1996), p. 81.

[37]Only conceptually so, as it are public authorities that need to realize protective rights for the individual.

[38]See Dreier (2013), marginal number 102.

[39]In this respect, cf the highly instructive reflections by Chiao (2018), esp. 111 et seq.

inevitably leads to the re-forging of rights as shields into rights as swords (on a brief critique of this Marxian position see infra Sect. 3). At this stage, we can simply use the dialectic of rights as an analytical tool for examining the "dig-sites" of constitutional criminal law(s) (see infra Sect. 2). So here are some (indeed only very few and brief, but illustrative) comparative examples from German and European constitutional criminal law, where the scales are currently turned from the defensive (rights as shields) to the offensive function of rights (rights as swords; rights as an expression of an objective order, and so on).

In continuing (see infra Sect. 1) with the German right to human dignity and the principle of individual guilt, the (in-)famous 2013 judgment of the German Federal Constitutional Court (GFCC) on plea bargaining[40] is particularly insightful about the dialectic of rights. The GFCC had to adjudge whether the—rather limited, especially when compared to the situation for example in the USA—German procedural regulation on plea bargaining was reconcilable with the notion of individual guilt. The GFCC, in a joint decision, went at length to ascertain that '[t]he principle of individual guilt enshrined in the Basic Law (*Grundgesetz*—GG) and the related duty to ascertain the substantive truth, as well as the principle of fair trial in accordance with the rule of law, the presumption of innocence, and the court's duty to maintain neutrality make it impermissible to allow parties to the proceedings and the courts to freely determine how to ascertain the truth, how to apply the law to the facts so established, and what sentences to impose.' Nevertheless, in navigating a typical German constitutional compromise, the GFCC also found that 'the legislature is not *a priori* precluded from permitting plea bargains to simplify proceedings. It must, however, take adequate precautions to ensure that the constitutional requirements continue to be met.' And since, at the time of the judgment, the legislature had taken these adequate precautions in the eyes of GFCC, it managed to declare the German regulation of plea bargains constitutional, and in compliance with the principle of human dignity.[41]

More telling than these operative parts of the decision are its backgrounds and especially how Justice Landau, in his academic capacity, interpreted the passages that he managed to slip into the judgment in his role as the rapporteur of the case at the GFCC. It is an open secret that the GFCC is very careful (and crafty) in its selection of constitutional complaints that it brings to fully elaborated judgement. In the decision at hand, the GFCC selected constitutional complaints from defendants that suffered from the pressures of plea bargaining. In one, particularly drastic case, the presiding judge had instructed—very summarily speaking—the defendant that there were essentially three possible outcomes of his case, an acquittal, a sentence for one or two cases of aggravated robbery with a minimum term of imprisonment of three years in each case following contested proceedings, or probation for all

[40]BVerfGE (Decisions of German Federal Constitutional Court) 133, 168. An English translation is available online at https://tinyurl.com/4p83o2cf (last visited 22 February 2021).

[41]On the foregoing, and the quotes, see the English translation of the judgment, supra note 41, holdings 1 to 3.

indicted offenses, as the court would consider them as of minor gravity if the defended decided to make a confession that dispensed with the need to have a full trial (with the taking of evidence and so on). After a short 85-minute break, a court instruction that the defendant better decide quickly, and counsel's advice about the possibility of being 'arrested in the courtroom' if he did not accept the proposed plea bargain, the defendant confessed by simply confirming the terms of the indictment, and all parties to the proceedings waived their right to call witnesses. Here, the shield function of the rights of defendant (the guilt principle as the requirement to establish historical truth; the presumption of innocence; the neutrality of the court) can indeed be called into action against the plea deal. After all, or so the GFCC held, it is a principle of German constitutional criminal law 'that guilt is a prerequisite for every punishment' as the right to human dignity 'defines the understanding of the nature of punishments and the relationship between guilt and atonement.' Punishment, or so the GFCC went on to define, 'sanctions the offender for having violated social ethics.'[42]

It is this last sentence that opens up the dialectic of rights. For do not such violations of social ethics require ample punishment? And is this requirement to punish in an ample way reconcilable with plea bargaining? This was what Justice Landau was evidently also concerned about, namely that the guilty can incur too much of a punishment discount by agreeing to a plea bargain. Justice Landau later published academic comments on the very judgment that he helped render, where he explained that 'guilt constitutes and limits punishment'[43] as the '[t]he "barrel" of guilt has a lid and a bottom: In the same way as the lid must not be exceeded, the bottom of rendering a punishment appropriate to the guilt must not be undercut.'[44] In this way, the defensive concept of 'no punishment without guilt' (*nulla poena sine culpa*), which limits penal powers and which German constitutional criminal law attributes in no small amount to the principle of human dignity, is complemented by the offensive 'no guilt without punishment' (*nulla culpa sine poena*). If this reading of the principle of individual guilt were to carry the day in German constitutional criminal jurisprudence, and this is very much open for debate,[45] it would perpetuate and even petrify current public penal powers. For the democratic legislator would be disallowed—as a matter of protecting (sic!) human dignity—from introducing more far-reaching plea-bargaining or indeed discretion in (not) holding the guilty to account. This illustrates that the dialectic of rights is not only about individuals and "the" state, but also about the institutional separation of powers between various

[42]See BVerfGE, supra note 41, para 54.

[43]Landau (2015), p. 667, my translation of: "Schuld wirkt strafbegründend und straflimitierend."

[44]Landau (2015), p. 248, my translation of: "Das 'Fass' der Schuld hat also einen Deckel und einen Boden: Sowenig wie der Deckel überschritten werden darf, darf auch der Boden des schuldangemessenen Strafens nicht unterschritten werden."

[45]For a warning against reading the principle of individual guilt as a constitutional acceptance of *nulla culpa sine poena* in Germany cf Kaspar (2014), p. 279 et seq.

state actors (in the case at hand between the GFCC interpreting the human dignity and parliament having to heed this interpretation).[46]

Of course, plea bargaining is a delicate field. And of course, it entails that the innocent can be "incentivized" to plead guilty. But analytically speaking, and this is all that I intend to highlight, even the *nulla poena sine culpa* principle can be flipped from a defensive concept (that e.g. protects the innocent from being coerced into pleading guilty) into an offensive concept that perpetuates or increases the penal powers of the state, where the state is not a monistic, but a multi-layered actor.

The dialectic of rights also appears prominently in the jurisprudence of the ECtHR and its doctrine of so-called positive obligations,[47] that is duties that are rooted in the rights and freedoms of the ECHR and that require the contracting states to develop a strong criminal law arm to wield rights as swords. There is no need to explore the doctrinal background of these protective duties (esp. its roots in the doctrine of horizontal effect). Suffice it to recall what *Baroness Tulkens*[48]—then, as today, Vice-President of the ECtHR—laid out in 2011, namely that '[p]reviously conceived solely as "brakes" on state power and limits on repression, rights and freedoms may today be viewed, at the same time, as a driving force for intervention and as justification for states' deployment of their power, in particular that of coercion.' Indeed, as she continued to explain, the ECtHR has developed a 'large number of both diverse and subtle requirements, which may be noted at each stage of the criminal law process: criminalization in primary legislation (that is, the definition of proscribed conduct), interpretation of the criminal law, prosecution policy, the form of prosecution, the availability and choice of investigative measures to clarify the facts in issue, the classification by the courts of conduct being punished, sentencing and, last but not least, execution of the sentence.' Positive obligations, then, formulate duties on the state to criminalize, prevent and repress, especially by means of policing and prosecution, individual conduct that is potentially harmful to the freedoms and liberties of other individuals.

A recent addition to this impressive list of positive obligations in the field of criminal law and justice is cooperation in criminal matters. Once considered the apex of sovereign political power, the ECtHR now draws on the rights and freedoms of the ECHR to induce (of course under many requirements and conditions) its party states into cooperating internationally to guarantee an effective administration of criminal justice. To quote *in extenso* from a recent decision of the Strasbourg court:

> [I]n interpreting the Convention regard must be had to its special character as a treaty for the collective enforcement of human rights and fundamental freedoms. This collective character may, in some specific circumstances, imply a duty for Contracting States to act jointly and to cooperate in order to protect the rights and freedoms they have undertaken to secure within their jurisdiction. [...] In cases where an effective investigation into an unlawful killing

---

[46]In my humble opinion, it is necessary to introduce the "separation of powers" (or rather their mutual checks & balances) into criminal law theory and doctrine. See Burchard (2019), p. 639 et seq.

[47]See inter alia Florczak-Wątor (2017), p. 39 et seq.

[48]Tulkens (2011b), p. 583 et seq.

> which occurred within the jurisdiction of one Contracting State requires the involvement of more than one Contracting State, the Court finds that the Convention's special character as a collective enforcement treaty entails in principle an obligation on the part of the States concerned to cooperate effectively with each other in order to elucidate the circumstances of the killing and to bring the perpetrators to justice. [...] Such a duty is in keeping with the effective protection of the right to life as guaranteed by Article 2. Indeed, to find otherwise would sit ill with the State's obligation under Article 2 to protect the right to life, read in conjunction with the State's general duty under Article 1 to 'secure to everyone within [its] jurisdiction the rights and freedoms defined in [the] Convention', since it would hamper investigations into unlawful killings and necessarily lead to impunity for those responsible. Such a result could frustrate the purpose of the protection under Article 2 and render illusory the guarantees in respect of an individual's right to life. The object and purpose of the Convention as an instrument for the protection of individual human beings require that its provisions be interpreted and applied so as to make its safeguards practical and effective.[49]

This quote aptly summarizes the background and the current drift of the dialectic of rights in European constitutional criminal law, namely towards an effective criminal justice apparatus that counters impunity for serious crimes so as to strengthen the "protection" of the freedoms and liberties by means of criminal law and its effective administration. Rights, then, are no longer only limitations on state action, but demand state action for certain individuals, even if this invades the very rights of other individuals. Put differently, rights as positive obligations turn into entitlements to restrict individual freedoms and liberties (namely those of possible offenders).

The development of positive obligations of the state in the context of the administration of criminal justice is not reserved to the ECtHR.[50] It also features prominently in the jurisprudence of the GFCC,[51] which can draw on a long general doctrinal tradition of so-called rights-based protective duties ("grundrechtliche Schutzpflichten").[52] In a most recent decision, on 25 October 2019,[53] the GFCC has now started to suggest (possibly as a "test balloon") an aggregate "fundamental right to the effective administration of criminal justice" ("Grundrecht auf effektive Strafverfolgung"). This—so the GFCC held—relates to serious crimes against life, physical integrity, sexual self-determination and the freedom of the person, in the case of crimes against victims who are in a special relationship of care with the

[49]ECtHR (2019) *Güzelyurtlu and others v Turkey and Cyprus*, App no 36925/07, 29 January 2019, para 232 et seq.

[50]A general account of positive constitutional rights is offered by Barak (2012), p. 422 et seq., who advances a two-partite definition: "First, the government has to proactively ensure that individuals are able to exercise their constitutional rights. Thus, for example, the government must protect demonstrators of political speech from a hostile crowd. The second element is the state's duty to prevent other individuals from limiting constitutional rights."

[51]See inter alia BVerfGE 39, 1 (41 ff) - Schwangerschaftsabbruch I, and BVerfGE 88, 203 (251 ff) - Schwangerschaftsabbruch II.

[52]Many German scholars consider protective duties as the concept central to the objective dimension of fundamental rights (that we saw supra Sect. 3.2). On protective duties and the objective dimension of fundamental rights see Dreier (2013), with further references.

[53]BVerfG 25.10.2019 - 2 BvR 498/15 (my translations).

public authorities and in the case of crimes committed by public officials. For in such crimes, German constitutional law—in the eyes of the GFCC—"obliges the state to protect and promote the life of the individual and to protect him or her from unlawful interference by third parties where the persons entitled to fundamental rights are themselves not in a position to do so." This positive obligation implies, as the GFCC clarified, the right of one individual to demand criminal actions (investigations, prosecutions and so on) by the state and its agents against other individuals. Here, then, the dialectic of rights comes full circle, by empowering one individual to draw on the defensive side of her or his rights to demand (in court and so on) that the state uses the offensive side of these very rights against another individual, thereby intruding into her or his freedoms and liberties.[54]

3.3 *Brief Critique of Marx's Critique of Rights*

There are many more examples[55]—including from the Interamerican Court of Human Rights[56]—of the dialectic of rights and how it forges rights as shields into rights as swords. But the way that the "fundamental right to the effective administration of criminal justice" pits individuals against each other under the auspices of a rights-based promise of security and protection calls for a brief evaluation (and counter-critique) of one of the most fundamental challenges to the institution of rights: *Marx's* critique of the human and fundamental rights of his time.

Marx voiced his critique of rights in his (in-)famous 1843 piece "On the Jewish Question", and one cannot fail to be deeply shaken and upset by the spite of *Marx's* language and his apparent anti-Jewish prejudices. Yet taking this, as difficult as it is, out of the equation in a Neo-Marxian reading, as it is inter alia suggested by *Menke,*[57] or *Loick,*[58] one indeed finds two powerful general points of critique that need to be addressed: *Firstly*, that rights ultimately exalt security as 'the supreme social concept of civil society, the concept of the police, the concept that the whole

[54]Again, this is but a descriptive account of the dialectic of rights as we can observe it in constitutional criminal law as it develops in the jurisprudence of the GFCC and the ECtHR. This account is to shed light on the transforming image of public penal power (see Sect. 4 below). These transformations, in turn, need careful considerations, as they cater to a real expansion of criminal law and criminal justice that is fueled by a rhetoric of ideal rights and their balancing. Because of this expansionist consequences, I hesitate to embrace the argument that it is valid to argue, from a philosophical analysis of life or property, that my right to life and property creates a positive duty on the state to have an effective, impartial etc., system of investigation and prosecution limited by rights of investigated and accused persons. Or more on point: I challenge this as ideal(ized) arguments (in favor of protective duties) have to account for their real-life consequences (which may, and today: do result in the expansion of criminal law and criminal justice).

[55]Paradigmatically see Ashworth (2013), p. 173 et seq.

[56]See e.g. Basch (2007), p. 195 et seq.; Lavrysen (2014), p. 94 et seq.

[57]See Menke (2009).

[58]See Loick (2013), p. 300 et seq.

society exists only to guarantee for each of its members the preservation of his person, his rights, and his property.'[59] And *secondly*, that many rights (such as the right to property) are but 'right[s] of self-interest. This individual freedom and its application as well constitute the basis of civil society. It lets every man find in other men not the realization but rather the limitation of his own freedom.'[60]

Both points of critique focus on how—in the eyes of *Marx*—a liberal polity manages to indoctrinate human beings into complying with its capitalist ideologies, namely by affording them rights. What was originally thought of as a vehicle for human beings to formulate elementary demands against their polity, is turned into an instrument of that very polity to shape and determine the roles and forms of its residents.[61] Rights cast human beings into separated and egoistic individuals, who are publicly tied together by security concerns (police), rather than by mutual sociality, and who in striving to secure "their" individual freedoms and liberties are thereby alienated from each other and a joint political sphere. Rights, in a Marxian or Neo-Marxian reading, do not limit and contain the (police) powers of the state, but rather cause, generate and legitimize the latter. After all, mutually alienated and egoistic individuals necessarily require the state to protect their freedoms and liberties against each other, thus emboldening the security powers of the state rather than curtailing them.[62]

Although it is tricky and also perilous to cite *Marx* (even more so approvingly) in our academic circles, one cannot fail to notice a certain match between *Marx's* past diagnoses and today's jurisprudential use of rights in German and European constitutional criminal law. Think about how the ECtHR binds its contracting states to establish an effective criminal justice system by way of its long list of corresponding positive obligations, or how the GFCC now argues in favor of a "fundamental right to an effective administration of criminal justice" (infra Sect. 2). With history repeating itself, it comes as little surprise that as of today a general constitutional "right to security"[63] is resurfacing not only in German[64] and European[65] discussions on criminal law and justice but worldwide.[66] Moreover, it is telling that German doctrine considers fundamental rights and its related protective duties as the seat of the state's foundational objective ("Staatsziel") to provide public peace and security ("innere Sicherheit").[67] And it is similarly telling that German constitutional doctrine applies protective duties only to cases of private interventions into the freedoms and

[59]Marx (1967), p. 236.

[60]Ibid.

[61]Loick (2013), p. 305.

[62]Ibid, p. 303.

[63]On "protective duties and the right to security" see also Lazarus (2012a), p. 136.

[64]See inter alia Isensee (1983); Isensee (2000), marginal number 19 et seq.

[65]See generally Art. 5 ECHR and Art- 6 EU Charter of Fundamental Rights, which both stipulate a right to "liberty and security".

[66]See e.g. Lazarus (2012b), pp. 87–106.

[67]See Götz (2006), marginal number 24.

liberties of others, while not applying them for example to (warding off the effects of) natural catastrophes.[68] Security and separating individuals, then, feature prominently in German theories about fundamental rights. And one could even say that one finds the tendency to govern not through crime directly, but through rights and the penal powers they entail.[69]

But this does not mean that *Marx's* original or the current Neo-Marxian critique of rights—and more importantly: its underlying social and political philosophy—is warranted. To the contrary! It merely means that this critique holds at least some analytical (not normative) water when applied to the current practices of rights in constitutional criminal law. What this critique fails to account for, to cut a very long story extremely short, is the dialectic of rights. The dialectic of rights bespeaks their normative openness; their potential to be used in one or another way, for the proverbial good or bad. Even in the "Dialectic of Enlightenment", where Horkheimer and Adorno famously—and depressingly so—linked the undercurrents of Western enlightenment to the horrors of השואה, the workings of this dialectic are not cast as an inevitability, as necessarily tipping (and shattering) to the atrocious. So, it is not the dialectic of rights as such that one should be critical of; neither should one prematurely condemn that rights are being re-forged from shields into swords in constitutional criminal law. What one should question, though, is what drives these developments socially and politically. One needs to identify, explain and understand these underlying social and political developments so as to seriously reflect upon them (that is, to reject or justify them).

4 The Transforming Image of Public Penal Power

There are many causes (not reasons) that may help us in explaining and understanding (not justifying) just why the dialectics of rights today leans towards forging rights into swords in German and European constitutional criminal law, and indeed towards sharpening these swords to effectively protect individual freedoms and liberties by means of a robust administration of criminal justice. What is more, these causes point to different, at times even contradictory general phenomena (like partial withdrawals of the state from the production of security, and a surge of state activity in this area to symbolically demonstrate its capabilities to act).[70] In this contribution, I can only (and merely summarily at that) focus on one driving force

68 This is disputed, but advanced e.g. by Dreier (2013), marginal number 104.

69 This might not be surprising after all, especially for those who think that the philosophical foundations of modern liberal democracy (from Hobbes and Lock onwards) were founded on the right to security, which is the prime justification for the State and its prime duty is to protect security. But it is surprising for those who view fundamental rights (*sans* the right to security) as means to restrict, not to legitimize state powers.

70 See generally Puschke and Singelnstein (2018).

behind the current tipping of the dialectic of rights: the transforming image of public penal power, which advocates the offensive function of rights rarely justify.

Again, *Mordechai Kremnitzer* is well versed in addressing images of public penal power as they lurk in the shadows of legal argumentation. In his review essay (co-authored with *Liat Levanon*) of *Richard Posner's* controversial book "Not a Suicide Pact: The Constitution in a Time of National Emergency", *Mordechai Kremnitzer* in 2009 diagnosed that "[w]hen he recommends permitting torture, Posner gives the government and the executives plenty of credit. A very high level of trust in decision-makers is a precondition for permission to torture, as torture is undoubtedly the most abhorrent means that can be used against the individual. However, Posner does not provide us with any justification for deserting the general suspicion toward the government and for abandoning any care in assigning it such significant powers." Substantively, I cannot agree more with *Mordechai Kremnitzer's* and *Liat Levanon's* well-reasoned conclusion that "governments and executives cannot be trusted with torture".[71] But that is not the issue here. More important for my purpose is the attention given to the design of public power and authority, and its (in *Posner's* case, lack of) justification. This political turn also features in *Kremnitzer's* empirical analysis of proportionality judgments in action. After all, the analysis concludes that the highly vague nature of proportionality judgments "may support the argument that balancing should be relegated to the political domain",[72] rather than to judges. The general lesson that I take from this is that when addressing public penal power, one must not treat it as monolithic (esp. as "the state"), but rather as an incrementally developing arrangement of various actors. Bearing this in mind, here are but a few reflections about why perceptions of public penal powers are changing and how this drives the dialectics of rights towards re-forging rights into swords.

Most fundamentally, the state—or more generally speaking: public penal power—is increasingly no longer met with suspicion, as it is no longer considered the primary peril for individual freedoms and liberties. Rather, the state (or other jurisdictions with public authority, such as the European Public Prosecutor's Office or international criminal courts) now appears as the principal guarantor of these very freedoms and liberties. Therefore, the state needs to develop a strong and efficient administration of criminal justice to safeguard the rights of its citizens against attacks from other individuals. For example, in affirming the turn to positive obligations by the ECtHR, it has been stipulated (not fully explored, let alone justified): 'Nowadays, in a democratic State ruled by law, it is usually private parties that kill individuals, interfere with their private and family life, limit their freedom to express opinions, and disrupt peaceful assemblies. Consequently, an expectation took root that State Parties to the [ECHR] would protect the rights of individuals against the actions of other individuals.'[73] Another explanation of the current turn to positive obligations

[71] Kremnitzer and Levannon (2009), p. 255.

[72] Sulitzeanu-Kenan et al. (2016), p. 379.

[73] Florczak-Wątor (2017), p. 41.

and protective duties, including the creation of a fundamental right to an effective administration of criminal justice (supra Sect. 2), is that the "state as such" may no longer be considered the primary threat to the freedoms and liberties of its citizens, but rather "the biased or partisan state" that colludes or sides with one set of individuals to threaten the freedoms and liberties of other individuals.

Of course, since *Hobbes*, the two-edged setup of public powers—the state as a threat to individual freedoms and liberties; and the state as the guarantor of security, which is necessary so that individuals can enjoy these very freedoms and liberties—lies at the heart of almost all theories of the modern state. What is striking, however, is how easy it is today—to turn *Mordechai Kremnitzer's* critique of *Posner* into a more sweeping statement—to relinquish notions of general suspicion toward public penal power.

The doctrinal *modus operandi* to do so (indeed a *modus operandi* that at least exerts a powerful rhetorical pull towards more rights-based criminalization, prevention, policing, and prosecution) we have seen before in our brief analysis of the dialectic of rights. The security paradigm does *not* become predominant plain and simple; security is *not* merely cast as an overall precondition for individuals to enjoy their freedoms and liberties. Rather, security in general and public penal power in particular (as it is meant to ensure security both by the prevention,[74] as well as by the repression, of crime) are argued to be the direct and individualized realization of individual freedoms and liberties. (Think about the fundamental right to an effective administration of criminal justice, which repressively enforces criminal offenses that promise to prevent the violation of fundamental rights like those to life, physical integrity, sexual self-determination, and the freedom of the person; see supra Sect. 3.2). It is this rights-centered and rights-argued emanation of public penal power that draws liberal minds in and lets them abandon care in assigning significant powers to the state. For security is there no longer to realize hegemonical state domination, but to serve and protect individual freedoms and liberties; and these freedoms and liberties, in turn, are still powerfully reminiscent of a commonwealth curtailed and hedged by rights.

But this reconstruction prompts warnings that caution against the new liberal (rights-orientated) desire for criminal law and justice. At least rhetorically, the assertion of rights to demand coercive action by the state to criminalize, prevent, police, and prosecute violations of freedoms and liberties implies a real risk of coercive overreach.[75] All the more so, as in inegalitarian orders, both the privileged *and* the disenfranchised can assert their rights to expand public penal powers for their protection (to preserve the status quo, or to overcome it).[76] Social and political conflicts or conflicts about colliding interests, then, can be recast as conflicts of

[74]On the relation between security and prevention, and the paradox of prevention, which resembles in many instances the dialectic of rights, see Zabel B (2018) Das Paradox der Prävention. Über ein Versprechen des Rechts und seine Folgen. In: Puschke and Singelnstein (2018), p. 55 et seq.

[75]As already criticized by Lazarus (2012a), p. 151 et seq.

[76]See generally Brown (2000), p. 232.

multi-polar rights, and these conflicts can be carried out by means of a rights-based expansion and intensification of public penal power. This overburdens[77] and de-mystifies rights, because they can no longer be upheld as a liberal institution, which is apparently a-political itself or the legal interpretation of which is supposedly a-political, but juridical in nature. What is more, a rights-based expansion and intensification of state penal power are particularly difficult to criticize, as it seems to be without a justificatory alternative.[78] For who would seriously oppose the notion that for example rape infringes upon the human dignity of the victim, thus justifying the harsh criminalization and prosecution of such atrocious behavior? And would this be opposed even if it leads to the "Kantian" impasse that he who commits a criminal offense places himself outside society, and hence can (or even must?) be treated accordingly?[79] (For example: Why not treat the convicted rapist, who has been proven beyond a reasonable doubt to have treated his victim not as a fellow human being, but as a mere object, as an a-social violator of human dignity?) Finally, re-forging shields into swords under the dialectic of rights in order to expand and intensify public penal powers plays into suppressing the "dark side of criminal law"; that is, into suppressing that the actual administration of criminal law and justice is a social institution, which often proceeds in selective as well as reductionist and dysfunctional manners.[80]

Of course, to finally introduce a comparativist disclaimer, my previous reconstructions and warnings only work (doctrinally and rhetorically so) if certain ideological preconceptions and perceptions about social, political and legal preconditions are met. For example: Where there is widespread libertarian resistance against an increase of state powers, or where the state arbitrarily invades upon individual freedoms and liberties in the everyday administration of criminal justice, it is unlikely that an expansion and intensification of public penal power based on the protection of individual rights will incur much doctrinal momentum and rhetorical sway.[81] Conversely, where the state (geographically, and as concerns certain subfields of criminality like terrorism) is needed to guarantee security plain and simple, there will likely be no need to bolster security regulations by means of the dialectic

[77]Rusterberg (2014), p. 107.

[78]On a comparable problem, see Brown (2000), p. 232.

[79]Cf Kant (1996), p. 335: "As a co-legislator in dictating the penal law, I cannot possibly be the same person who, as a subject, is punished in accordance with the law; for as one who is punished, namely as a criminal, I cannot possibly have a voice in legislation (the legislator is holy)"; also cf 6:331: "A transgression of public law that makes someone who commits it unfit to be a citizen is called a *crime* (*crimen*) simply but is also called a public crime (crimen publicum); so the first (private crime) is brought before a civil court, the latter before a criminal court."

[80]As rightly argued by Kölbel (2019), p. 257.

[81]Paradigmatically, cf Jackson v City of Joliet (1983) 715 F.2d 1200, 1203 (7th Cir.), cert. denied, 465 U.S. 1049. There, Judge Posner held that the US Constitution "is a charter of negative rather than positive liberties. [...] The men who wrote the Bill of Rights were not concerned that Government might do too little for the people but that it might do too much to them. The Fourteenth Amendment, adopted in 1868 at the height of laissez-faire thinking, sought to protect Americans from oppression by state government, not to secure them basic governmental services."

of rights. This explains why I took my examples from German and European constitutional criminal law, why they pertained to everyday serious crime like, sadly, rape or homicide (see infra Sects. 3.1 and 3.2), and why I cautioned against understanding constitutional criminal law in an ubiquitous way (see infra Sect. 2).

In order to dissect the jurisprudential turn towards rights as swords in German and European constitutional criminal law as regards everyday serious crime, then, one needs to identify, discuss and rationalize the underlying preconceptions and perceptions about why public penal power is supposedly not so much a serious threat to, but rather a means to realize, individual freedoms and liberties. For reasons of time and space, I can only resort to name-dropping in this respect: First, a (genuine or instrumental) belief in democracy and, more concretely, parliamentary rule smothers anxieties about public penal power.[82] After all, don't "we" as the people rule for the good of the people in a democracy *per definitionem*?—Second, the supposed humanization of criminal law and justice (for example, when compared to the cruel and unusual modes of punishments of darker times), as well as its rights-based rationalization and legalization, also lessens concerns about the use of criminal law and its administration.[83] After all, aren't we just talking about criminal fines or imprisonment, and just about perpetrators who enjoy human dignity and many procedural rights? These rhetorical questions imply that, paradoxically, the fact that we no longer (rightly!) quarter people and arm them with defense rights, etc., can contribute to the increase of public penal powers because such powers can be justified because they treat defendants humanely and in accordance with their defense rights.[84]—Third, the state as a threat to individual freedoms and liberties finally also loses its sting if other threats are perceived as graver in nature. Those who are threatened can hence call on the state by asserting their particular rights to protect them from this graver threat by means of affirmative penal state action. This relates to minorities and the disenfranchised that call for the affirmation of their particular way-of-life or their state-sponsored emancipation (think about the "lucha contra la violencia machista" in Spain). But it also relates to majorities and the privileged that call on the state to stand up against "fearsome" discrete societal forces, especially if these discrete societal forces appear more powerful than the state (think about the "rise" of powerful transnational corporations, and the way the fight against white collar crime is justified today)[85] or if said discrete societal forces appear to threaten a general way-of-life (this is where the criminology of others comes into play).[86]

---

[82]On the delicate relationship between democracy and criminal law see inter alia Ferdinand Gärditz (2015), p. 49 et seq.

[83]Also see Franz Streng, indirectly reported by Schuhmann and Zabel (2011), pp. 828 and 830; Ferdinand Gärditz (2010), pp. 332–333; Kindhäuser (2017), p. 383 et seq.

[84]Ibid, Kindhäuser (2017), p. 382 et seq.

[85]See inter alia Naucke (2012), p. 10 et seq.; Schünemann (2010), p. 80 f.

[86]Garland (1996), p. 461 et seq.

5 Outlook

This is where things get really interesting—and where I have to stop. For exploring which preconceptions and perceptions about social and political contexts and conditions—as they fuel the dialectic of rights in German and European constitutional criminal law—are sociologically correct or normatively justified is no small feat and not one that should be taken on lightly. This paper has only sought to illustrate that such explorations are warranted. It sought to establish that the dialectic of rights is a valuable analytical tool to scrutinize constitutional criminal law and its justificatory practices in order to bring to the fore that turning to foundational questions about the social and political setup of public penal power is a worthwhile endeavor to critically appreciate the new liberal desire for the expansion and intensification of criminal law. With great admiration and respect, I dedicate these—as I know, very preliminary and tentative—thoughts to *Mordechai Kremnitzer*, and hope that they find his interest and that they are somewhat reminiscent of his constant quest to build bridges, between criminal and constitutional law, between theory and practice, and between individual and social/political philosophy. *Ad multos annos!*

References

Alexy, R. (1996). *Theorie der Grundrechte* (p. 420 ff). Baden-Baden: Nomos.

Ashworth, A. (2013). *Positive obligations in criminal law* (p. 173 et seq). Oxford: Hart.

Barak, A. (2012). *Proportionality: Constitutional rights and their limitations* (p. 350 et seq). New York: Cambridge University Press.

Basch, F. F. (2007). The doctrine of the Inter-American Court of Human Rights regarding states' duty to punish human rights violations and its dangers. *American University International Law Review, 23*, 195.

Bascuñán Rodríguez, A. (2007). Derechos fundamentales y derecho penal. *Revista de Estudios de la Justicia, 9*, 47.

Brown, W. (2000). Suffering rights as paradoxes. *Constellations, 7*, 230.

Burchard, C. (2016). Strafverfassungsrecht – Vorüberlegungen zu einem Schlüsselbegriff. In K. Tiedemann et al. (Eds.), *Die Verfassung moderner Strafrechtspflege. Erinnerung an Joachim Vogel* (p. 28 et seq). Baden-Baden: Nomos.

Burchard, C. (2019). Die strafverfassungsrechtliche Verpflichtung (Art. 103 Abs. 2 GG) des Gesetzgebers, das Wesentliche der Rechtfertigungsgründe selbst zu regeln. Zugleich ein Debattenbeitrag zu Whistleblowing und Investigativjournalismus. *Strafverteidiger, 9*, 637.

Chakravorty Spivak, G. (1993). *Outside in the teaching machine* (p. 44 et seq). New York: Routledge.

Chiao, V. (2018). *Criminal law in the age of the administrative state* (p. 144 et seq). New York: Oxford University Press.

Currie, D. P. (1986). Positive and negative constitutional rights. *The University of Chicago Law Review, 53*, 864.

Dreier, H. (2013). Vorbemerkungen. Allgemeine Grundrechtslehren. In H. Dreier (Ed.), *Grundgesetz Kommentar* (Vol. I, 3rd ed.). Tübingen: Mohr Siebeck.

Ferdinand Gärditz, K. (2010). Strafbegründung und Demokratieprinzip. *Der Staat, 49*, 331.

Ferdinand Gärditz, K. (2015). *Staat und Strafrechtspflege. Braucht die Verfassungstheorie einen Begriff von Strafe?* (p. 49 et seq). Paderborn: Ferdinand Schöningh.

Florczak-Wątor, M. (2017). The role of the European Court of Human Rights in promoting horizontal positive obligations of the state. *International and Comparative Law Review, 17*, 39.
Fredman, S. (2008). *Human rights transformed: Positive rights and positive duties*. Oxford: Oxford University Press.
Garland, D. (1996). The limits of the sovereign state. *The British Journal of Criminology, 36*, 445.
Geneuss, J. (2017). Directory authority: Fertilising international criminal tribunals' human rights standards with European Court of Human Rights' case law. In P. Lobba & T. Mariniello (Eds.), *Judicial dialogue on human rights. The practice of international criminal tribunals* (pp. 40–55). Leiden: Brill Nijhoff.
Ghanayim, K., & Kremnitzer, M. (2014). Mistaken identity and error in performance: A transferred malice. *Criminal Law Quarterly, 61*, 329.
Götz, V. (2006). § 85 Innere Sicherheit. In J. Isensee & P. Kirchhof (Eds.), *Handbuch des Staatsrechts* (Vol. IV). Heidelberg: C.F. Müller.
Hassemer, W. (2004). Strafrecht in einem europäischen Verfassungsvertrag. *ZStW, 116*, 303.
Heinrich Rupp, H. (1976). Vom Wandel der Grundrechte. *Archiv des öffentlichen Rechts, 101*, 161.
Hörnle, T. (2014). Theories of criminalization. In D. Dubber & T. Hörnle (Eds.), *The Oxford handbook of criminal law* (p. 678).
Isensee, J. (1983). *Das Grundrecht auf Sicherheit. Zu den Schutzpflichten des freiheitlichen Verfassungsstaates*. Berlin: De Gruyter.
Isensee, J. (2000). § 111 Das Grundrecht als Abwehrrecht und als staatliche Schutzpflicht. In J. Isensee & P. Kirchhof (Eds.), *Handbuch des Staatsrechts der Bundesrepublik Deutschland* (Vol. V, 2nd ed.). Heidelberg: C.F. Müller.
Jahn, M. (2016). Strafverfassungsrecht: Das Grundgesetz als Herausforderung für die Dogmatik des Straf- und Strafverfahrensrechts. In K. Tiedemann et al. (Eds.), *Die Verfassung moderner Strafrechtspflege. Erinnerung an Joachim Vogel* (p. 63 et seq). Baden-Baden: Nomos.
Kant, I. (1996). *Kant: The metaphysics of morals* (trans and ed Gregor, M.) (Vol. 6, p. 335). Cambridge: Cambridge University Press.
Kaspar, J. (2014). *Verhältnismäßigkeit und Grundrechtsschutz im Präventionsstrafrecht* (p. 279 et seq). Baden-Baden: Nomos.
Kindhäuser, U. (2017). Straf-Recht und ultima-ratio-Prinzip. *Zeitschrift für die gesamte Strafrechtswissenschaft, 129*, 382.
Kölbel, R. (2019). Die dunkle Seite des Strafrechts. *Neue Kriminalpolitik, 31*, 249.
Kremnitzer, M. (1993). Constitutional principles and criminal law. *Israel Law Review, 27*, 84.
Kremnitzer, M. (1999). Constitutionalization of substantive criminal law: A realistic view. *Israel Law Review, 33*, 720.
Kremnitzer, M. (2008). Is the subjective mental element superfluous. *Criminal Justice Ethics, 27*, 78.
Kremnitzer, M. (2014). Is proportionality an effective protector of human rights: Proportionality and constitutional culture by Moshe Cohen-Eliya, Iddo Porat - A critique. *Jerusalem Review of Legal Studies, 10*, 111.
Kremnitzer, M., & Hörnle, T. (2011). Human dignity and the principle of culpability. *Israel Law Review, 44*, 115.
Kremnitzer, M., & Levannon, L. (2009). Not a suicide pact: A comment on preventative means in general and on torture in particular. *Israel Law Review, 42*, 248.
Landau, H. (2015). Die jüngere Rechtsprechung des Bundesverfassungsgerichts zu Strafrecht und Strafverfahrensrecht. *Neue Zeitschrift für Strafrecht, 12*, 665.
Lavrysen, L. (2014). Positive obligations in the jurisprudence of the Inter-American Court of Human Rights. *Inter-American & European Human Rights Journal, 7*, 94.
Lazarus, L. (2012a). Positive obligations and criminal justice: Duties to protect or coerce? In J. Robert & L. Zedner (Eds.), *Principles and values in criminal law and criminal justice* (pp. 135–155). Oxford: Oxford University Press.

Lazarus, L. (2012b). The right to security – Securing rights or securitizing rights. In R. Dickinson et al. (Eds.), *Examining critical perspectives on human rights* (pp. 87–106). Cambridge: Cambridge University Press.

Loick, D. (2013). Abhängigkeitserklärung. Recht und Subjektivität. In D. Loick & R. Jaeggi (Eds.), *Nach Marx. Philosophie, Kritik, Praxis* (p. 300 et seq). Berlin: Suhrkamp.

Marx, K. (1967). On the Jewish question. In D. L. Easton & K. H. Guddat (trs and eds), *Writings of the young Marx on philosophy and society* (p. 236). New York: Doubleday.

Meijer, S. (2017). Rehabilitation as a positive obligation. *European Journal of Crime, Criminal Law and Criminal Justice, 25*, 145.

Menke, C. (2009). Subjektive Rechte und Menschenwürde. Zur Einleitung. Trivium 3

Naucke, W. (2012). *Der Begriff der politischen Wirtschaftsstraftat. Eine Annäherung* (p. 10 et seq). Münster: LIT Verlag.

Puschke, J., & Singelnstein, T. (Eds.). (2018). *Der Staat und die Sicherheitsgesellschaft*. Wiesbaden: Springer.

Rusterberg, B. (2014). Subjektives Abwehrrecht und objektive Ordnung. In T. Vesting et al. (Eds.), *Grundrechte als Phänomene kollektiver Ordnung* (p. 87). Tübingen: Mohr Siebeck.

Schuhmann, A., & Zabel, B. (2011). Diskussionsbeiträge der Strafrechtslehrertagung 2011 in Leipzig. *Zeitschrift für die gesamte Strafrechtswissenschaft, 123*, 827.

Schünemann, B. (2010). Die sog. Finanzkrise - Systemversagen oder global organisierte Kriminalität? In B. Schünemann (Ed.), *Die sogenannte Finanzkrise, Systemversagen oder global organisierte Kriminalität?* (p. 80 f). Berlin: Berliner Wissenschafts-Verlag.

Sulitzeanu-Kenan, R., Kremnitzer, M., & Alon, S. (2016). Facts, preferences, and doctrine: An empirical analysis of proportionality judgment. *Law & Society Review, 50*, 348.

Thorburn, M. (2010). Criminal law as public law. In R. A. Duff & S. P. Green (Eds.), *Philosophical foundations of criminal law* (p. 21 et seq). Oxford: Oxford University Press.

Tulkens, F. (2011a). Human rights as the good and the bad conscience of penal law. In S. Snacken & E. Dumortier (Eds.), *Resisting punitiveness in Europe? Welfare, human rights and democracy* (p. 156 et seq). London: Routledge.

Tulkens, F. (2011b). The paradoxical relationship between criminal law and human rights. *Journal of International Criminal Justice, 9*, 577.

Viganò, F. (2014). La arbitrariedad del no punir. Sobre las obligaciones de tutela penal de los derechos fundamentales. *Política criminal, 9*, 428.

Vogel, J. (2014). *Kriminalpolitikwissenschaft* und Europäische *Kriminalpolitik*. In M. Heger, B. Kelker, & E. Schramm (Eds.), *Festschrift für Kristian Kühl zum 70. Geburtstag* (p. 635). München: C. H. Beck.

Vormbaum, T. (1995). "Politisches" Strafrecht. *ZStW, 107*, 747.

Crime, Guilt and Punishment: Dignifying Criminal Law

Mohammed S. Wattad

1 Introduction

The recent heyday decades of Western nations have provided a trend of constitutionalism, whereby fundamental human rights are highly protected. In 1949, it was the Germans who adopted the *Grundgesetz* (the Basic Law for the Federal Republic of Germany), considering the right to dignity inviolable and inalienable.[1] In 1950, the European nations have concluded the European Convention on Human Rights, demonstrating high sensitivity toward the human being, prohibiting all kinds of servitude, slavery, torture, as well as inhuman or degrading treatment or punishment.[2] In 1982, Canadians have solemnly declared the establishment of the Charter of Rights and Freedoms, preserving human dignity by prohibiting all kinds of humiliation by means of discrimination.[3] This was also the path that Israelis took in 1995 by granting Basic-Law: Human Dignity and Liberty of 1992 a constitutional

Research Fellow, the International Center for Health, Law and Ethics, Haifa University (Israel). I would like to dedicate this article to my mentor Prof. Mordechai Kremnitzer, a man of dignity and values, to whom I owe a lot.

[1]Grundgesetz fur die Bundesrepublik Deutschland (Basic Law, GG). Art. 1(2). Translation at https://www.gesetze-im-internet.de/englisch_gg/englisch_gg.html.

[2]Council of Europe (1988) the Convention for the Protection of Human Rights and Fundamental Freedoms (European Convention on Human Rights) as amended by Protocol No. 11. In Council of Europe Treaty Series 155. Articles 3 and 4.

[3]Canadian Charter of Rights and Freedoms (1982) s 7, Part 1 of the Constitution Act 1982. Article 15.

M. S. Wattad (✉)
Zefat Academic College, Safed, Israel

K. Ghanayim, Y. Shany (eds.), *The Quest for Core Values in the Application of Legal Norms*, https://doi.org/10.1007/978-3-030-78953-4_4

status,[4] thus treating human dignity[5] as the mother of many unlisted human rights, such as equality and freedom of expression. In 1996, the Republic of South Africa established its own constitution, granting the right to dignity a place of honor as an inherent right of every person.[6] Finally, the English People agreed to incorporate the mechanism of the European Convention on Human Rights into English law by adopting the Human Rights Act in 1998.

Unlike Robinson Crusoe,[7] Kafka[8] needs human rights. Human rights are the rights of a person as a part of society; and as such, they are limited by the rights of others and the needs of society. Both the scope and limits of human rights are derived from the constitutional dialect, which is close to the sentiments of human dignity. Criminal punishment represents the harshest means of limiting human rights for purposes of, *inter alia*, preserving public order and preventing severe manifestations of immorality. Correctly observed by the Utopian legal system, criminals are human beings in the first place, and for that they must be treated with dignity, as active subjects, and not as someone who is acted upon. Due to the serious nature of criminal punishment, prohibiting certain acts by criminal means requires special justification.

Substantive criminal law seeks to strike a balance between the offender's rights and society's interest in public order. The requirement of guilt is as essential a part of the substantive criminal law as the justification for the criminal punishment. It treats an individual as a person, with dignity as a subject, and not an object. Criminal law is obviously about the definition of crimes, the procedures for establishing guilt, and the fixing of fair and appropriate punishments. Conceptually speaking, a crime is a violation of norms of socially required conduct (wrongdoing) that can be fairly attributed to a responsible person (the finding of guilt). The guilt requirement embraces both the criminal wrongdoing and the mental state upon which the wrongdoing was committed. As such, just punishment, seeking to impose punishment fairly and justly—as well as demonstrating high sensitivity toward the various possible degrees of wrongdoing and mental states—presupposes a finding of guilt beyond a reasonable doubt. Only by recognizing the criminal guilt requirement as a constitutional principle can we clarify our path toward punishing the guilty and acquitting the innocent.

Constitutional law cuts straight to the heart of the criminal law, where human rights are most likely to be violated. It cuts even more directly to the core of substantive criminal law, which purports to define the meaning of crime, and clarifies the perplexing borders between acts that should be penalized and acts that are subject to other social reactions. Substantive criminal law is the balance between the offender's rights and society's interest in public order. In particular, it is a

[4]Civil Appeal (The Supreme Court of Israel) 6821/93 Bank Hamezrahee Ha-Meuohad v. Megdal Kfar Shetufey (1993) 49(4) P.D. 221.

[5]Article 4 of the Basic Law.

[6]Constitution of the Republic of South Africa (1996) Act 108 of 1996. Article 10.

[7]Defoe (1994).

[8]Kafka (1956).

concept of guilt, not the accused's feeling of guilt, but the guilt attributed to him upon his wrongdoing. The guilt requirement is an essential part of substantive criminal law as the justification for the criminal punishment; it treats an individual as a person.

The right to dignity plays an important role in constitutional law and in criminal law. By definition, constitutional law and criminal law are different fields; their mechanisms are at some level contradictory. Generally speaking, while constitutional law is about rights, criminal law is the law of wrongs; and while constitutional law protects human rights, in principle, criminal law authorizes to limit them. However, both criminal law and constitutional law are driven by the same principles; these are the Utopian principles, *i.e.* they are derived from and driven by human dignity. I shall elaborate on this. The right to dignity not only contributes to our understanding of the nature of criminal punishment, but also to our understanding of the nature of criminal law as an inherent subject of constitutional scrutiny. The right to dignity allows for the argument that criminal law is not mainly a system of violating human rights but rather of preserving them. The constitutional right to dignity is what makes criminal law very close to the sentiments of society. To be protected in their dignity, human beings must be treated as subjects, not as objects.

This article proposes taking substantive criminal law beyond the conventional dogmatic discourse, discussing the nature of substantive criminal law in light of universal fundamental constitutional principles. It suggests that constitutionalizing substantive criminal law is necessary and inevitable, as it brings constitutional models of balance between conflicting rights and interests, and provides the justification for attributing the stigma of guilt to certain acts and inflicting punishment on certain actors. These state practices need to be highly supervised and justified, and that can be best done through constitutional scrutiny. In this article, I seek to inquire into the nexus between constitutional law and substantive criminal law.

2 On Dignity: Constitutionalizing Criminal Law

In U.S. jurisprudence, criminal procedure law has always been viewed as an inherent part of constitutional law,[9] and thus has constantly been subject to constitutional scrutiny.[10] On the other hand, challenging the constitutionality of substantive criminal law has been a saga of hesitation,[11] unlike the case in other western legal jurisdictions, such as Canada and Germany. This issue has been addressed by several

[9]Stuntz (1997), p. 6.

[10]E.g., U.S. Const. amends. IV, V, VI, VIII.

[11]Powell v. Texas (1968) 392 U.S. 514; Robinson v. California (1962) 370 U.S. 660; Lambert v. California (1957) 355 U.S. 225.

scholars of criminal jurisprudence.[12] It has been said that the U.S. Supreme Court is not likely ever to tangle with substantive criminal law.[13] Underlying this criticism is the question what sense does it make to insist upon procedural safeguards in criminal prosecutions if anything can be made a crime in the first place.[14] The argument in U.S. jurisprudence has been that the Constitution of 1787, including the Bill of Rights of 1791, provides no language of substantive criminal law, but rather spells out an array of constitutional safeguards for the law of criminal procedure.[15]

Comparative studies shed light on the importance of constitutionalizing substantive criminal law. Relying on several cognate concepts of human dignity, article 7 of the European Convention on Human Rights of 1950 embodies, in general terms, the principle that only the law can define a crime and prescribe a penalty (*nullum crimen, nulla poena sine lege*).[16] In this context, it is notable that legal philosophy distinguishes between two theories of law:[17] one term is "law," which expresses the idea of laws enacted by an authoritative body; the other term is "Law," which refers to the good and just law, which is binding because it is good and just. Article 7 of the Convention refers to "Law;" *Recht* in German, *droit* in French, and *derecho* in Spanish, but not to "law" (*Gesetz* in German, *loi* in French, and *ley* in Spanish);[18] thus implying the existence of a higher law than the mere legislative enactments, which serves in scrutinizing *inter alia* substantive criminal law. In the same manner, in accordance with Section 7 of the Charter of Rights and Freedoms of 1982,[19] the Supreme Court of Canada has constitutionally scrutinized provisions of the Canadian Criminal Code of 1985 for their compatibility with the principles of fundamental justice,[20] thus holding that its task is not to choose between substantive or procedural content *per se*, but to secure for persons the full benefit of the Charter's protection,[21] while avoiding adjudication of the merits of public policy.[22] The Basic Law for the Federal Republic of Germany (Grundgesetz, GG) of 1949 demonstrates high sensitivity to the inviolable right to dignity (*Würde*),[23] and the right to personal freedom,[24] from which basic principles of criminal law and constitutional law are

[12]Fletcher (1998a), p. 159; Hart (1958), pp. 404–405; Stuntz (1997), p. 6; Dressler and Greenawalt (1999), p. 1532.

[13]Fletcher Fletcher (1998a), p. 12.

[14]Hart (1958), p. 431.

[15]e.g., U.S. Const. amends. IV, V, VI, VIII.

[16]Achour v. France (2006) IV, Eur. Ct. H.R. 268; Kokkinakis v. Greece (1993) Eur. Ct. H.R. 20.

[17]Fletcher (1996), pp. 11–42.

[18]E.K. v. Turkey (2002) Eur. Ct. H.R. 21.

[19]Canadian Charter of Rights and Freedoms (1982) Part I, § 11 of the Constitution Act, 1982, being Schedule B to the Canada Act, c. 11.

[20]Stuart (1995), pp. 249–250.

[21]R. v. Big M Drug Mart Ltd. (1985) 1 S.C.R. 295, 244 ¶ 117 (Dickson J).

[22]Curr v. R. (1972) S.C.R. 889, 899.

[23]Grundgesetz fur die Bundesrepublik Deutschland (Basic Law, GG). art. 1.

[24]Ibid, art. 2.

derived. The German Supreme Court in Constitutional Cases has expressed its position that no act is criminal if the element of wrongfulness is negated by public or private law; it is constitutionally required that no punishment be imposed except on guilty people, and that the punishment be appropriate to the guilt attributed to the offender.[25]

Human dignity has become an important part of the transnational and international vocabulary of constitutionalism and human rights. However, not all constitutions explicitly accord protection to human dignity, *e.g.*, Canada and the United States. One way of recognizing a constitutional right to dignity is through interpretation of the right to equality,[26] or through interpretation of the whole Bill of Rights.[27] Human dignity requires that a person be treated as the world unto himself, and an end unto himself; a free agent, who is capable of developing his body and mind as he wishes.[28] Human dignity is a core component of constitutional jurisprudence in a constitutional system. The core meaning of dignity is that social order must reflect recognition of the equal worth of all persons. Dignity expresses at least the basic meaning of equality. Human dignity might have three central meanings. Yet, at a minimum, it means that social order must reflect recognition of the equality of humankind, for which equality means at least that persons are entitled to equal value and human dignity. It is the initial understanding of all, that men were created equal, namely all are entitled to an equal value. That is, people might be entitled to unequal value only in terms of their qualifications, but not as human beings. As human beings *per se*, they are entitled to equal value, regardless of their color, race, gender and so forth.

Within the constitutional meaning of unlawful discrimination, treating people differently does not necessarily mean an unequal treatment. All it means is differentiation. Unlawful discrimination is treating differently equally qualified persons, and thus, treating unequally, as well as unfairly, those who are entitled and fit to receive equal treatment. However, not every differentiation made between two persons is unlawful discrimination—or we may better use the term unlawful differentiation. Sometimes differentiation is justified due to the differences that exist between two persons. The equality principle is based on relevancies, by which we mean that it is conceivable to differentiate between two persons on the basis of relevant considerations, whilst it is not permissible to do so on the ground of irrelevant consideration. But sometimes, the essence of the differentiation denotes certain stigma against some people.

---

[25]BVerfGE 95, 96–103, 2 BvR 1851/94 (hereinafter "East German Border Guard Case"). https://www.bundesverfassungsgericht.de/SharedDocs/Entscheidungen/DE/1996/10/rs19961024_2bvr185194.html; Poetter S (2009) The Main Leading Cases of Federal Constitutional Court – East German Border Guard (BVerfGE 95, 96). http://www.juraexamen.info/die-wichtigsten-leitentscheidungen-des-bverfg-ddr-mauerschutzen-bverfge-95-96/.

[26]Law v. Canada (Minister of Employment and Immigration) (1999) 1 S.C.R. 497, 507 (Can.); Barak (2006), p. 88.

[27]Griswold v. Connecticut (1965) 381 U.S. 479, 484.

[28]Barak (2006), p. 86.

Criminal law strikes balances between the offender's rights and the society's interest in public order. Constitutional law cuts straight to the core of the criminal law, where human rights are most likely to be infringed. Therefore, constitutionalizing criminal law—particularly substantive criminal law—is necessary and inevitable. It provides a proper justification for attributing the stigma of guilt for certain actions, and ensures that such attribution is highly supervised, if arbitrary punishment is to be avoided. The court must avoid imposing punishment on criminals in an arbitrary manner. In addition, criminal defendants ought to be treated as subjects of the criminal system and not as mere objects. The inalienable right to be treated as an end in itself has serious implications for the articulation of the legal and philosophical justification of criminal punishment. For instance, for a criminal defendant to be an end, he may not be punished solely for the sake of deterrence; if he is so punished, he is being *used* as a means to achieve other goals. This point was articulated by Nils Jareborg, who stated that the threat of punishment is a threat of condemnation and not solely of painful sanction.[29] This is the kind of punishment that embodies sensitivity to human dignity by recognizing the different circumstances, as well as the different states of mind, upon which a crime was committed.

3 Dignifying the Wrongdoing Requirement

In the context of crime and punishment, the wrongdoing requirement reflects the concept of right and wrong as recognized by the community, denoting the moral quality of the act. A criminal offense is an anti-social phenomenon. The wrongfulness of the phenomenon lies in its anti-social harm to a legally protected interest and is the product of the anti-social nature of the act, and of the anti-social nature of the result.

Criminal law must have moral connotation if criminal punishment is to have meaning. The state may not make any conduct a crime. Criminals are first and foremost human beings. As such, they enjoy the right to dignity.[30] Once you treat a human being as a means, rather than an end, you treat them as an object, rather than a subject, and this form of humiliation infringes human dignity. You humiliate a person by ignoring their ability as a human being to distinguish between what is right and wrong, you humiliate a person when you do not distinguish between intentional wrongdoings and accidental ones,[31] and you humiliate a person by ignoring the possibility of negating wrongdoing committed in justified circumstances. To treat a human being as a subject, you must consider the person to be capable of a rational choice, because when you treat a human being as an inanimate object, your

---

[29]Compare Jareborg (1988), pp. 76–78; Smith and Hogan (1996), pp. 4–5.

[30]Fletcher (1998b), p. 43; Kant (1949), p. 46; Fletcher (1984), p. 171.

[31]Ibid, p 59.

responses to the human being are determined not by their choices, but yours, in disregard of or with indifference to theirs.

Criminal liability is the most draconian form of condemnation by society, and may result in a sentence which amounts to a severe deprivation of the liberties of the offender.[32] H.L.A. Hart once asked why certain kinds of actions are forbidden by law and so made crimes or offenses.[33] Fyodor Dostoevsky has passionately expressed the view that society is morally justified in punishing people simply because they had done wrong.[34] It goes without saying that criminal law is not about the law of rights, but rather about the law of wrongs, namely about the prevention of the kind of negative actions which society rejects. Criminalizing an act is to declare the act not merely an undesirable act but as one that must not be done, "to institute a threat of punishment to supply a pragmatic reason for not doing it, and to censure those who nevertheless do it."[35]

The question remains, what kind of acts may the legislature criminalize? Criminal law is the law of public wrongs,[36] those which endanger the common wealth and not just an individual person, crimen publicum,[37] or as called in old Roman law delicta publica.[38] Conceptually speaking, a crime is a violation of norms of socially-required conduct under a particular recognized mental state. Let us call the violation of norms of required conduct wrongdoing; in which case a crime is the commission of wrongdoing to which a certain mental state is attached. A criminal offense is an anti-social phenomenon. "The chief concern of the criminal law is seriously anti-social behavior."[39] Criminal law is a mechanism of formal and normative recognition of social perceptions. Criminal liability carries the strong implication of "ought not to do"; which marks the special social significance of criminal censure that requires a clear social justification. The wrongness of the phenomenon lies in its anti-social harm to a legally protected interest, and is the product of the anti-social nature of the act, and of the anti-social nature of the result. Being punished for a crime is different from being subject to public regulation. Even in the absence of other means of social control available to achieve the same ends, criminal prohibition must be the last means, and the alternative of doing nothing must still be considered.

Criminal acts may be one of two basic types: (1) public wrongs, and (2) moral wrongs. The obvious starting point of any discussion of criminalization is the harm principle, which suggests that crimes are generally acts which have a particularly harmful effect on the public and do more than interfere with merely private rights.[40]

---

[32]Ashworth (1995), p. 3, 83.

[33]Hart (1968), p. 157.

[34]Dostoevsky (1993).

[35]Ashworth (1995), p. 22.

[36]Blackstone (1769), pp. 4–5.

[37]Kant (1965), p. 140.

[38]Bishop (1892), p. 16.

[39]Ashworth (1995), p. 40.

[40]Mill (1859), p. 15; Cf. Feinberg (1988a), p. 124.

In other words, "crime is crime because it consists of wrongdoing which directly, and in serious degree threatens the security or well-being of society, and because it is not safe to leave it redressable only by compensation for the party injured."[41] This has been articulated by John Stuart Mill, who formulated the harm principle as "the only purpose for which power can be rightfully exercised over any member of a civilized community, against his will"; namely preventing harm to others.[42]

However, there are offenses meant to punish conduct simply because it is wrong in itself. In the early days, this concept was limited to the most outrageous and immoral acts, *e.g.*, murder, robbery, rape etc., *mala in se*.[43] But the test of morality is obviously of no great help today, because many acts are prohibited on the grounds of social expediency, or at least not just because of their immoral nature, *mala prohibita*.[44] To demonstrate the problematic features of *mala in se* crimes, I shall consider some examples. The prohibitions against sodomy and obscenity have been justified by their arguably intrinsic wrongful natures. This has gradually changed as movements fighting for gay rights have sprung up. Another example concerns lying; which, although intrinsically immoral, in itself is not a crime. For lying to become a crime, it has to be associated with some extra features, such as lying-in court under oath, which is a crime not because of the intrinsic wrong associated with lying, but rather because of the likely consequences of false judgment.

Coming to address *mala in se* offenses, fundamental principles of criminal law theory must be considered. There is intuitive appeal in the idea that criminal wrongs are typically more serious than their civil counterparts; sufficiently serious that the state is empowered to step in and regulate them directly. The public as a whole has an interest in their prevention and prosecution. Community norms and views determine the contents of the criminal prohibition. The main purpose of the criminal law is to prohibit conduct which a sufficiently strong part of the community feels or believes is harmful to its interests, its safety, its social stability, and which the community repudiates. The general purposes of the provisions governing the definition of offenses in the American Law Institute's Model Penal Code section 1.02 might be taken as a statement of the proper objectives of the substantive law of crime in a modern legal system. The purposes are: (1) to forbid and prevent conduct that unjustifiably and inexcusably inflicts or threatens substantial harm to individual or public interests, (2) to subject to control persons whose conduct indicates that they are disposed to commit crimes, (3) to safeguard conduct that is without fault from condemnation as criminal, (4) to give fair warning of the nature of the conduct declared to be an offense, and (5) to differentiate on reasonable grounds between serious and minor offenses.

The question of criminalizing intrinsic wrongs has always challenged mankind. Deontologists argue that the fact that the wrongdoing is an action that does not

[41]Smith and Hogan (1996), p. 17; Eser (1966), p. 346.

[42]Mill (1859), p. 9.

[43]Fletcher (2000), p. 456, 458, 472, 473; Simester and Sullivan (2002), p. 2.

[44]Green (1997), p. 1570.

respect the person's worth is what makes it wrong.[45] Among the principal legal problems of *mala in se* offenses is their uncertain nature. The meaning that should be given to a criminal legal norm is not fixed for eternity, but rather it is a part of life; and life changes.[46] "The life of law is renewal based on experience and logic, which adapt law to the new social reality."[47] Criminal norms must be of great level of clarity and certainty if they are to avoid vagueness. The due process principle requires that all criminal prohibitions must provide fair notice to persons before making their activity criminal.[48] However, morality is intrinsically uncertain and debatable, and therefore for an immoral act to be criminalized it must have extra characteristics of outrageousness; this should be the immorality that shocks people's minds and consciousness *e.g.*, incest or obscenity. In addition, for these immoral acts to be criminalized, they must violate nearly universally shared views about morality.

It is, however, my view that morality can be enforced by criminal means, but not always. No conduct should be defined as criminal unless it represents a serious threat to society, and unless the act cannot be dealt with effectively through other social or legal means. Immoral acts are indeed wrongs, but not necessarily punishable wrongs. There must be an intrinsic common quality to distinguish the criminal from the non-criminal.[49] It might be true that law and social morality will constrain much of the same behavior, but this does not mean that the law will enforce every aspect of morality.[50] Criminal law is a crude instrument, requiring findings of uncertain facts, with rules backed by a limited arsenal of coercive sanctions.

Right and wrong are, paradigmatically, contradictory concepts. In a constitutional democracy, *e.g.*, the United States, Israel, South Africa, Germany, and Canada, legal norms are reflective of the will of the people and for the good of the people. The laws of any society must be acceptable to the general moral sense of the community if they are to be respected and enforced. A total departure from morality will bring horrific consequences.[51] By nature, society suffers from diversity. In order to avoid any abuse of minority views by the majority, it is important to consider the will of society in light of higher values of constitutionalist nature, which guarantee that all members of society are able to exercise their rights in an equal manner, thus being treated with dignity, as ends rather than means. This however does not resolve the problem of imposing on the minority the moral sensibilities of the majority; yet does it guarantee, as I shall elaborate on later in this paper, the existence of a mechanism of judicial scrutiny that aims to guarantee the existence of a proper justification for such imposition and that it be done in proportionate manner.

---

[45]Murphy (1988), p. 25.

[46]Barak (2006), p. 9.

[47]Ibid, p. 4; cf. Holmes (1881), p. 1.

[48]Colautti v. Franklin (1979) 439 U.S. 379.

[49]Shoham (1970), p. 47.

[50]Greenawalt (1995), p. 710.

[51]Bishop (1892), p. 19.

However, there are many controversial conducts, and their classification between right and wrong is a matter of perspective. In this regard, I shall consider two important principles. First, what society views as a wrong is not necessarily a punishable wrong. For a wrong to be punishable, it must, first and foremost, meet fundamental principles of criminal law theory. Second, among the fundamental principles of the theory of criminal law are clarity, certainty, and stability; as a concept of due process of law, as well as fair and just warning.[52] If doubts exist about the wrongful nature of a certain conduct, or about its criminal features, the actor should be afforded the benefit of the doubt. The general prohibition against retroactive criminal legislation, *ex post facto* laws, provides some guidance in understanding this third consideration. The principle is also expressed in the Latin maxim *nullum crimen, nulla poena sine lege*, there is no crime, no punishment, without prior legislative warning.[53] The basic principle is that individuals have a right to know what the law is at the time they are said to violate it, and therefore the law, *i.e.*, the criminal prohibition, has to be as clear as possible, as narrow as possible, and as definitive as possible. Individuals do not have a right to know what could make utilitarian differences in their choice to engage in an action or not. Rather, they have a right to know that which could make a moral difference in their choice to engage in an action or not.

Society's perspective has had a very significant role in the history of criminal law development, referred to as the "social protected interest."[54] The socially protected interest concept is the legitimacy for every criminal prohibition. A conduct may not be criminalized solely because the legislature has decided so, unless the conduct, first and foremost, conflicts with the general public consciousness and values. Albeit, criminal law is not required to embrace all social views and conducts. The socially protected interest has to be of great importance, to the extent that it may not be sufficiently protected except by the coercive tools of criminal law. In seeking to articulate a criminal prohibition, it is accordingly necessary to: first, locate the socially protected interest; second, clarify the concrete substance of this social protected interest; and third, decide whether the particular social protected interest deserves and requires protection by criminal means, namely, examining less intrusive means, such as civil law and administrative law.[55]

I have already addressed the harm principle as a primary basis for criminalizing certain actions. However, one must not confuse Mill's harm principle[56] as a basis for penal legislation with the offense principle. Joel Feinberg has tried to account for our shared understanding of the conceptual distinction between the two principles.[57] In his view, the harm principle supports penal legislation as a means of preventing harm

[52]Fletcher (2000), pp. 569–573.

[53]Fletcher (1998b), p. 12.

[54]Fitzgerald (1966), pp. 123–124.

[55]Eser (1966).

[56]See supra text accompanying note 41.

[57]Feinberg (1988b), pp. 1–3.

to other persons, in the absence of other means of equal effectiveness at no greater cost to other values. Unlike the harm principle, the offense principle suggests that: "[i]t is always a good reason in support of a proposed criminal prohibition that it is probably necessary to prevent serious offense to persons other than the actor and would probably be an effective means to that end if enacted."[58] This conceptual distinction contributes to our understanding of the basic difference between the two principles as basis for penal legislation.

Not every offense to others causes harm, for offense is a less serious thing than harm.[59] As Fienberg explains, the word "offense" has two possible meanings; one refers to a miscellany of disliked mental states, and the other concerns those states only when caused by the wrongful conduct of others. In Fienberg's view, only the second meaning is intended in the offense principle to be parallel to the harm principle. That is, an extreme offense can cause harm to a person "who becomes emotionally upset over the offense, to the neglect of his real interest. But the offended mental state in itself is not a condition of harm."[60]

Considering the nature of the harm principle as a basis for penal legislation, one may wonder if the offense principle can serve as a basis for such legislation. It has already been said that consequences of offense are not as serious as those of harm, and therefore, generally speaking, the law should not treat offenses and harms as if they are of the same degree of seriousness; for instance, in the event there exists other means of regulation, which afford the same degree of effectiveness, the law should avoid controlling offensiveness by means of criminal law.[61] This is not to suggest that criminal law should neglect offense to others altogether; however, other alternative effective means must be considered before adhering to criminal law, such as "licensing procedures that depend on administrative suspension of license as a sanction."[62]

As I have initially provided, the fact that a particular criminal prohibition meets the fundamental principles of criminal law does not mean it is a constitutional prohibition. This has been my initial argument: A punishable wrong is not a valid crime unless it is constitutional. The constitutionality of any criminal prohibition is required in light of the coercive nature of criminal law. As I have already argued, constitutional law strikes a balance between constitutional rights and other important social interests. Criminal law is about limiting rights, but constitutional law is about their protection. Constitutional law guarantees that criminal law limits human rights in a proportionate manner.

From a constitutional point of view, the question is: what kind of acts may the legislature criminalize? This question has been largely addressed in the legal

[58] Ibid, p. xiii.

[59] Ibid, p. 2.

[60] Ibid, p. 3.

[61] Ibid, p. 25.

[62] Ibid.

literature, and I wish to highlight two primary approaches.[63] The first approach suggests that any criminalization punishable by imprisonment or an aggravation of the punishment for an existing crime, establishes an infringement to the right to liberty.[64] The second approach asserts that constitutionalizing substantive criminal law is possible only when the constitution provides a clear permission to do so. The mere fact that a constitution includes a chapter on human rights does not make it self-evident that constitutional scrutiny applies to the criminal responsibility (liability).[65] This has been the argument, primarily in the context of the United States, where it has been contended that the U.S. Constitution provides no language of substantive criminal law; put in the words of Justice Antonin Scalia: "the Court has *never* held that the Constitution forbids the execution of a convicted defendant who has had a full and fair trial but is later able to convince a habeas court that he is "actually" innocent."[66]

In this article, I endorse the first approach, though I seek to widen it, applying it to all criminalization measures, not only when criminalization is punishable by imprisonment.[67] It is my argument that classifying certain types of conduct as wrongs undermines, confines and infringes, constitutionally protected rights, most notably the right to liberty. As soon as a prohibition is in force, it touches either on special guarantees of freedom or on the general freedom to do or not to do what one wants to. As such, a prohibition has to be constitutionally justified without reference to what type of sanctions may be imposed for violating the prohibition.[68]

However, insofar as constitutional law is concerned it might be asserted that limiting the right to liberty is not the chief concern, but rather the right to dignity, which is relevant in the context of criminalizing a particular conduct like adult incest, thus turning a normative person into a criminal, including condemning and denouncing him by the community by attributing him the Mark of Cain. Such condemnation, even if no sanction of imprisonment is involved, still concerns constitutional law in relation with the right to dignity.[69] This kind of infringement must be highly scrutinized, and should be justified. Constitutional scrutiny is the kind of balance that is drawn between rights and punishable wrongs, and it reflects the inherent non-absolute nature of constitutional rights.

As for the appropriate formula for constitutional scrutiny over criminalization, it is notable that the leading discussion on this matter is that of countries like Germany,

---

[63]For a comprehensive study on the various approaches, see Bendor and Dancig-Rosenberg (2016), p. 325 (Isr.) (Hebrew).

[64]e.g., CA 4424, 4713, 4779/98 Selgado v. The State of Israel (2002) IsrSC 56(5) 529, 539–41 (Isr.) (Barak, C.J.); Roach (2011), p. 91. For other approaches in between, see Gur-Arye and Weigend (2001), pp. 77–80.

[65]Selgado (2002) IsrSC 56(5) 529, at 551–62 (Strasberg-Cohen, J.).

[66]See In re Davis, 557 U.S. 1, 2 (2009). See also Fletcher (2010), p. 330.

[67]Compare Kremnitzer (1993), p. 86; Stribopoulos (1999), p. 227.

[68]Langodny (2011), pp. 764–765.

[69]e.g., Lawrence v. Texas (2003) 539 U.S. 558, 575.

Canada, and Israel, which include in their constitutional systems different variations of limitation clause, whereby the conditions for justifying infringements of constitutional rights are set forth, *inter alia*, that for a crime to be constitutionally justified, it must meet three cumulative criteria: (1) the criminal prohibition must befit the values of a constitutional democracy; (2) the prohibition must be undertaken for a proper purpose; and (3) the criminalization must be done in proportionality, namely, the legislature must scrutinize and fine tune even the details of its action, and consider the myriad of potential alternatives, to determine the least offensive means. Underlying this kind of proportionality principle is the promise that rights may not be infringed to a degree that is greater than necessary.

Criminal prohibitions infringe rights otherwise constitutionally protected, so that such an infringement must be highly justified by the fundamental values of constitutional democracy, which justify legal rules and are the reason for changing them when necessary.[70] I shall reiterate what I have already stated on the nature of a constitutional democracy. In a constitutional democracy, the constitution serves a form of safeguard and minority human rights protector. Constitutional democracy must protect the liberties and autonomy of the individual and guarantee his ability to exercise his liberties in peaceful means, thus viewing the individual as a free person, capable of developing his character in accordance with his free will as well as his free choice.[71]

The rule of law plays an important role in locating the 'values of a constitutional democracy.' Correctly observed by Dworkin, we must not be satisfied with a 'rule-article conception' of the rule of law,[72] rather it must be extended to the "right conception" of the rule of law, which means guaranteeing fundamental values of human rights, with a proper balance between these and the other social values supporting the existence of the state and public welfare, such as certainty and stability in interpersonal arrangements, and values of proper conduct, such as reasonableness, fairness,[73] and good faith.[74]

The values of constitutional democracy require that the legislature may not limit rights except for a proper purpose, which fulfils the promise of these values, namely, enabling the individual to exercise his autonomy and liberties by peaceful means. The proper purpose according to which the legislature may criminally prohibit certain conduct may not be articulated arbitrarily, but rather with due process and in an equal manner. Generally speaking, constitutional law is very generous in accepting purposes advanced by the legislature. Only a very few purposes, particularly those which stand in contrast with the basic pillars of the values of a constitutional democracy, can make a law constitutionally invalid.

---

[70]Barak (2006), p. 57.

[71]E.g., Lawrence, 539 U.S. at 558, 567.

[72]Dworkin (1990), p. 11.

[73]Barak (2006), p. 58.

[74]Summers (1982), p. 810.

The rule of law means the guaranteeing of fundamental values and human rights, with a proper balance between these and the other needs of society.[75] Proportionality mandates that a prohibition must be in adequate relation to the special importance and meaning of the particular constitution at stake.[76] Limitations on the rights and freedoms must be proportionate to the specific needs on which they are predicated. Proportionality means that all rights at stake must be considered and balanced against each other and against other proper purposes, and that the least restrictive means available is taken.[77]

Proportionality consists of three sub-tests:[78] (1) rational connection, which requires a rational link between the means employed and the goal the legislature wishes to accomplish; namely, there must be reasonable grounds for expecting the legislation to be effective in achieving it objective; (2) least intrusive means, which requires that of the range of means that can be employed to accomplish the goal, the legislature must employ the least harmful means; namely, the legislation must limit the right no more than is necessary in order to achieve its objective; and (3) strict proportionality, which demands that the harm caused to the individual by the means employed, must be in appropriate proportion to the benefit stemming from it; in other words, the costs of the limitation must not exceed the benefits to be gained from achieving the objective.

4 Dignifying the Principle of Guilt

Guilt is a unique feature of criminal law.[79] Criminal law may not punish but only guilty[80] people,[81] for which only a guilty person could generate a unifying perspective on criminal liability.[82] Guilt means that the criminal actor has been condemned, personally, by the community for his wrongdoing, and thus is blameworthy.[83] The requirement for wrongdoing (*le mal* in French, *Maa'seh Ra'* in Hebrew, *khataa'* in Arabic) is the basic element in constituting criminal guilt.[84] In the absence of

[75]Barak (2006), pp. 55–56.

[76]E.g., East German Border Guard Case, BVerfGE 67 at 151, 173.

[77]Donald and Howard (2015), p. 18.

[78]R. v. Oakes (1986) S.C.R. 103 (Can.).

[79]Fletcher (2002), pp. 77–78.

[80]Fletcher (2000), p. 532.

[81]I mean only those who could fairly be blamed for wrongdoing.

[82]Davis v. United States (1895) 160 U.S. 469, 485–486; Fletcher (2000), p. 536.

[83]Crimes are public wrongs, for in addition to the particular victim the public as a whole is injured in its sense of security and well-being.

[84]Fletcher (1998b), p. 77.

wrongdoing, there can be no room for finding someone guilty, and subject him to community condemnation, since there is nothing to condemn him for.[85] For the actor to be responsible, an attribution of the wrongdoing ought to be established.[86] Attribution,[87] in the substantive sense, means holding the offender responsible for the crime.[88] If wrongdoing is imputed to the actor, he is 'responsible' or 'blameworthy,'[89] and community condemnation would then justify imposing a punishment.[90] Therefore, the guilt requirement justifies imposing criminal punishment on the actor upon the establishment of criminal responsibility, which grounds all criminal prosecutions. Without the establishment of guilt, the constitutional obligation of fair and just punishment cannot be achieved. If this has been true for German, Canadian, and Israeli law, as well as the European Convention on Human Right, it may also hold true for American law.

In the context of crime and punishment, the guilt requirement plays an important role as an outgrowth of the right to human dignity. It embraces both the criminal wrongdoing and the mental state upon which the wrongdoing was committed. As such, the due process principle, seeking to impose punishment fairly and justly, as well as demonstrating high sensitivity toward the various possible degrees of wrongdoing and mental states, requires that punishment not be imposed but only upon the establishment of guilt. That is, upon the establishment of an ultimate calculation of the severity of the wrongdoing and mental state. Only after this, can criminal defendants be treated as human beings, namely as subjects—not objects. If substantive criminal law is merely about the finding of crime versus no-crime, without a need to establish guilt, then such a criminal system would allow punishment to be imposed solely on the basis that the commission of the crime by the offender was proved. This kind of criminal system shows no sensitivity toward the difference between a complete criminal act and *e.g.*, a wrongdoing that can be justified, and thus negated, as an act of self-defense. For such a criminal system there is no issue of blameworthiness for once the commission of wrongdoing is proven, there might be no allowance for the argument that the offender should not be blamed for acting under overriding circumstances, such as duress. Finally, for this kind of a criminal system it makes no difference if the criminal commission was driven by a factual or a legal mistake. Ignoring these kinds of differences is nothing but the classic understanding of how criminal defendants can be treated as objects and thus humiliated. For a criminal system to avoid this, it is required that punishment not be imposed solely on the basis that a criminal wrongdoing was committed.

---

[85]The wrongdoing is reflected by the harm caused by the criminal actor to the legal-social order, namely violating a particular protected interest. On the notion of harm as wrongdoing. See Feinberg (1984), pp. 105–125.

[86]Fletcher (1998b), p. 213.

[87]Or 'imputation.' See Robinson (1997), pp. 279–377.

[88]On 'criminal responsibility,' see Brandt (1960), pp. 106–115.

[89]Fletcher (1998b), pp. 81–82.

[90]On 'punishment,' Feinberg (1960), pp. 152–167; Fletcher (1987), p. 551 n.78.

Criminal punishment ought to be imposed only after the establishment of criminal guilt, as part of the right to human dignity.

Kafka's *The Trial*[91] represents two complicated issues. One addresses the meaning of guilt, and the other challenges the 'finding of guilt.' Guilt is a legal-social theory, which targets the actor.[92] The concept is rooted in the Old English word *gylt*. Guilt is a concept which might be understood only within a particular context: In itself, I do not really know what it means. The context under which it is discussed provides the concept with its primary content. I may talk about guilt as the "delinquency or failure in respect to one's duty;"[93] we may also understand guilt within the various contexts in which it appears in the Bible. We may even understand guilt as a theory of morality, and then distinguish between morality as a universal philosophy and morality as a normative concept as acknowledged by the legislature. However, the concept of guilt has been among the richest words of our criminal theory lexicon. Criminal guilt is generated by violating the normative expectation that the criminal actor respect the law. This expectation relies on the human being's mental ability to act in accordance with the legal order, and this is the basis for community condemnation upon a violation of a particular socially protected interest. The 'mental ability' or *mens rea* requirement is a fundamental component of the guilt requirement—it is the minimum requirement for establishing criminal guilt. Denying the actor's mental ability to obey the rules of the law means ignoring his qualifications as a human being.[94]

In other words, guilt is required in order to measure the severity of the condemnation that the community ought to direct toward the criminal upon violating norms of correct conduct (wrongdoing). Ignoring such a measure would render criminal condemnation arbitrary, thus violating the criminal's right to due process of law. Treating all criminal defendants equally, regardless of the mental state upon which each had committed their wrongdoing, shows a clear ignorance of the human capacity to make a rational choice. This is treating the criminal as an object and accordingly infringing his right to dignity. Guilt is the barometer by which criminal responsibility should be established and community condemnation rendered accordingly.[95] This is a vital requirement of the due process principle. Guilt concerns measuring the different degrees of wrongdoing, and accordingly attributing to the actors the compatible magnitude of condemnation in a fair manner.[96] This is what keeps the law in close touch with the sentiments of the community.

[91]Kafka (1956), p. 209.

[92]On the meaning of moral guilt, see Fletcher (1998b), p. 99.

[93]Babcock Gove (1993).

[94]Wendell Holmes (1963), p. 3.

[95]E.g., Nozick (1981a), p. 363.

[96]Ashworth (1995), p. 86.

5 Dignifying the Concept of Punishment

Criminal law is not solely about the crimes. It is also about punishing criminal defendants for committing crimes, and violating certain protected interests of the community. Criminal law provides the legal tools for preserving the social order by adhering to a condemnatory technique as reflected through the imposed punishment. This raises a fundamental philosophical question about theories of criminal punishment. We already saw that criminal responsibility brings community condemnation; that is, the conviction for committing a crime means that the community condemns the offender for violating particular protected interests of the community. Perhaps this was more elegantly articulated by Ashworth: "Criminal liability is the strongest formal condemnation that society can inflict, and it may also result in a sentence which amounts to a severe deprivation of the ordinary liberties of the offender."[97] The question then becomes: What links criminal responsibility to criminal punishment? In what sense is punishment deserved and what purpose does its infliction serve? To answer these questions, this article shall outline in general terms a theory of punishment, one that complies with the principal rule that a criminal ought to be treated as a subject of the criminal system, not an object.

The due process principle—associated with the right to dignity—plays several important roles in the context of criminal punishment; two of them are important for our concerns: (1) the purpose of the criminal punishment, namely punishing criminals for criminal wrongdoing they have committed; and (2) the justification for criminal punishment, namely the prohibition on imposing criminal punishment except upon the finding of guilt.

Punishment is an inherent component of criminal law theory.[98] The question why we punish remains in large dispute and the subject of intensive scholarly debate in the literature.[99] Philosophical discussions on punishment deal with the significant questions of whether or not societies ever have the right to punish, and if they do, under what conditions, to what degree, and in what manner.[100] Henceforth, I seek to outline, in general terms, a theory of punishment, composed of two complementary components, premised upon the argument is that criminal punishment might be justified under the following two complementary factors: (1) retributive punishment; and (2) criminal responsibility, which provides community condemnation for the person who violated norms of the correct conduct of the community (wrongdoing). I shall shortly elaborate on both factors. At this stage, it is worth noting that ultimately, understanding the notion of condemnation under the retributive theory of punishment, and within the due process principle, requires that criminal punishment be imposed on the basis of the establishment of guilt, by which criminal punishment can be justified, as a just and fair punishment.

---

[97] Ibid, p. 1.

[98] Simester and Sullivan (2002), p. 3.

[99] Ibid, pp. 20–21.

[100] E.g., Rawls (1973), p. 83.

Let us step back to the basic principles of criminal law: Criminal defendants ought to be treated as subjects of the criminal system and not as a means in order to achieve other goals. That is, "judicial punishment... must in all cases be imposed on the offender only on the ground that he [the criminal defendant] has committed a crime; for a human being can never be manipulated merely as a means to the purposes of someone else and can never be confused with the objects of the Law of things."[101] The inalienable right to be treated as an end has serious implications for the articulation of the legal and philosophical justification for criminal punishment. For instance, for a criminal defendant to be an end, he may not be punished solely for the sake of deterrence; if he is so punished, he is being *used* as a means to achieve other goals. This point was articulated by Nils Jareborg, who stated that the threat of punishment is a threat of condemnation and not solely of painful sanction.[102] This is the kind of punishment that embodies sensitivity to human dignity by recognizing the different circumstances, as well as the different states of mind, upon which a crime was committed. Condemnation is the community's reaction to the violation of the social order, namely the violation of certain protected interests of the community, which is expressed through the denouncing of the criminal defendant by the community. Therefore, and for the dignity of all criminal defendants, we—the community—may not denounce all criminal defendants alike, for if we do, not only do we humiliate them as objects, but we also violate their right to due process by imposing community condemnation arbitrarily. Therefore, for a criminal punishment to be constitutional, it must be imposed on the criminal defendant because of the wrongdoing committed by him. Furthermore, the court must avoid imposing punishment on them in an arbitrary manner.

Put otherweise: punishment is meted out for a wrong.[103] Punishment is an attempt to demonstrate to the wrongdoer that his act was wrong, not only to recognize the act as wrong, but to show him its wrongfulness by bringing him to realize the nature of what he has done.[104] For a person to be treated as an end, and for a punishment to be justified at all, the criminal's act must be that of a responsible agent, namely, it must be the act of one who could have kept the law which one has broken. And at the sentencing stage, the punishment must bear some sort of a relation to the act.[105] The threat of punishment is not only a conditional threat of a painful sanction, but also an official expression of how negatively different kinds of actions or omissions are judged. Condemnation is the community's reaction to the violation of the social order, namely the violation of certain protected interests of the community. For the dignity of all criminals, the community may not denounce all criminals in the same manner, for if the community so does, not only does the community humiliate them as objects, but the community also violates their right to due process by imposing

[101] Kant (1965), p. 100 (parenthesis added).

[102] Jareborg (1988), pp. 44–46, 76–78.

[103] Simester and Sullivan (2002), p. 4.

[104] Nozick (1981a), pp. 366, 370.

[105] Hart (1968), p. 160.

community condemnation so arbitrarily. This is what I consider to be constitutional punishment.[106]

However, if guilt is the barometer for community condemnation and denunciation, and if the criminal defendant puts himself out of the community by virtue of his wrongdoing, is there a way back for him? The absence of such a way for the criminal defendant to reenter the community would again violate his right to dignity, and treat him as an object, by ignoring the criminal's ability to establish a rational choice to comply with the social order, rules, and norms, and to reenter the right path of correct conduct. I support a theory of retribution which requires proportionate punishment in accordance with the seriousness of an offense. The fundamental aim is not to inflict suffering on offenders but to reassert the existence of the moral order that governs human life. This might also be achieved by bringing all criminals back to the community as exemplary persons. Thus, a retributive theory which treats criminals as ends and not means supports restoring offenders into the community.

The retributive theory suggests punishing offenders not merely for wrongdoing, but also linking punishment to the categorical imperative that I respect persons and treat them accordingly. *Retribution* means in Latin *retribuo*, namely, 'I pay back.' It is also found in the German term *vergeltung*, 'to pay back,' 'return,' 'repay,' or 'recompense.'[107] In the Kantian theory that Man has a duty of self-esteem. The idea is that because it was associated with shame and rejection attributed by the community, punishment could bring the criminal up short and force him to reconsider his life in the light of society's condemnation of his actions. Accordingly, the retributive theory suggests that the appropriate punishment is understood as the appropriate desert of a responsible guilty agent. The retributive view is that 'people deserve punishment for their wrongful acts,' but the degree of the punishment must be in accordance with the magnitude of their criminal responsibility, regardless the possible deterrent effect.[108]

However, one may plausibly argue that criminal punishment is not grounded solely in the theory of retribution. Though I may oppose this argument, any punishment—under any theory other than this a advocated approach—still may not be imposed arbitrarily if the guilt requirement is to comply faithfully with the right to human dignity and the due process principle.

---

[106]Ripstein (1999), pp. 140–141.

[107]It is remarkable that the German term for guilt is schuld. The German word associated with schuld is verschulden, which means debt, indebted, under obligation, and be blamed. Alike, the German term for retribution is vergeltung, which means to pay back or to repay.

[108]Nozick (1981b), pp. 60–61.

6 Epilogue: Instead of Conclusions

Inquiring into the meaning of criminal law is a delicate process; the smallest mistake at the beginning will lead to great errors at the end. Like a puzzle, criminal law consists of very sophisticated pieces and it may not be comprehended unless each piece is put in its place, and in the face of perplexity, order must be invoked. For the whole puzzle to be completed and arranged, the contours of the puzzle's structure must be first understood. In this article I sought to address this kind of normative grammar and its logic, endeavoring to clarify the meaning of each piece as well as its location in the puzzle. I have viewed criminal law theory as standing on three tenets—namely, crime, guilt and punishment—which if well understood may clarify other important dogmas of the theory of crime and punishment.

By definition, constitutional law and criminal law are different fields, despite some clear overlap. Each represents a different discipline which has its own way of thinking and arguing, and in principle their mechanisms are contradictory. Generally speaking, while constitutional law is the law of rights, criminal law is the law of wrongs; and while constitutional law protects and balances human rights, criminal law protects and infringes them. However, both criminal law and constitutional law are driven by the same core principles; they are derived from and driven both by the right to dignity, which plays an important role in constitutional law, and a more important one in criminal law. Criminals are human beings; as such they enjoy the right to be treated with dignity.

A sophisticated comparison between constitutional law and criminal law allows for a distinction between dogma and skepticism. In the context of legal theory, dogmatic disciplines are driven by a set of beliefs, some of which are accepted without argument. Obviously, these are not arbitrary beliefs, but rather based on reason, methodology and doctrine; they are not about fiction. However, dogma suggests paying no attention to evidence or other opinions. At the extreme opposite end, skepticism is a prominent feature of the constitutional discipline. "But how will I find such a belief?" René Descartes once asked, and he answered, "by the method of doubt."[109] Constitutional law is chiefly characterized by skepticism, thus suggesting a very cautious methodology; it is a questioning approach towards what might be considered as a dogma by criminal law. Skepticism doubts the nature of right and wrong and requires not only reasoning but substantial evidence. For this discipline, dogmas of the past might not be relevant for the present.[110] Constitutionalizing the substantive criminal law allows for a very delicate interaction between constitutional law and criminal law; it allows for a peculiar observation on the interplay between dogma and skepticism.

[109] See generally Descartes (1641).

[110] As Abraham Lincoln said during a speech, he delivered to the U.S. Congress on December 1, 1862, "The dogmas of the quiet past are inadequate to the stormy present." Lincoln (1953), p. 537.

References

Ashworth, A. (1995). *Principles of criminal law* (Vol. 3, 2nd ed., p. 83). Clarendon Press.

Babcock Gove, P. (Ed.). (1993). *Webster's third new international dictionary* (p. 1009). Springfield, MA: Merriam-Webster.

Barak, A. (2006). *The judge in a democracy* (p. 88). Princeton, NJ: Princeton University Press.

Bendor, A., & Dancig-Rosenberg, H. (2016). Averout Pliliout v-Zkhoyut Hukatout [criminal offense and constitutional rights]. *Mishpat U-Mimshal [Law and Government], 17*, 325.

Bishop, J. P. (1892). *New commentaries on the criminal law* (8th ed., p. 16). Chicago: T.H. Flood and Company.

Blackstone, W. (1769). *Commentaries on the laws of England* (pp. 4–5). Oxford: Clarendon Press.

Brandt, R. B. (1960). The conditions of criminal responsibility. In C. J. Friedrich (Ed.), *Responsibility* (pp. 106–115). New York: Liberal Arts Press.

Defoe, D. (1994). *Robinson Crusoe*. London: William Taylor.

Descartes, R. (1641). *Meditations on first philosophy* (Donald A. Cress, Trans.). 1993, Hackett Publishing Company, Inc.

Donald, A., & Howard, E. (2015). *The right to freedom of religion or belief and its intersection with other rights*. ILGA-Europe, Res. Paper, p. 18. https://www.ilga-europe.org/sites/default/files/Attachments/the_right_to_freedom_of_religion_or_belief_and_its_intersection_with_other_rights_0.pdf.

Dostoevsky, F. (1993). *Crime and punishment* (R. Pevear & L. Volokhonsky, Trans.). New York: Alfred A. Knopf.

Dressler, J., & Greenawalt, K. (1999). Criminal responsibility, and the supreme court: How a moderate scholar can appear immoderate thirty years later. *Notre Dame Law Review, 74*, 1507.

Dworkin, R. (1990). *A bill of rights for Britain* (p. 11). London: Chatto & Windus.

Eser, A. (1966). The principle of 'harm' in the concept of crime. *Duo Law Review, 4*, 345, 346.

Feinberg, J. (1960). On justifying legal punishment. In C. J. Friedrich (Ed.), *Responsibility* (pp. 152–167). New York: Liberal Arts Press.

Feinberg, J. (1984). *The moral limits of the criminal law: Harm to others* (pp. 105–125). New York: Oxford University Press.

Feinberg, J. (1988a). *The moral limits of the criminal law: Harmless wrongdoing* (p. 124). New York: Oxford University Press.

Feinberg, J. (1988b). *The moral limits of the criminal law: Offense to others* (pp. 1–3). New York: Oxford University Press.

Fitzgerald, P. J. (1966). *On Jurisprudence* (12th ed., pp. 123–124). London: Sweet & Maxwell.

Fletcher, G. P. (1984). Human dignity as a constitutional value. *University of Western Ontario Law Review, 22*, 171.

Fletcher, G. P. (1987). Law and morality: A Kantian perspective. *Columbia Law Review, 87*, 533.

Fletcher, G. P. (1996). *Basic concepts of legal thought* (pp. 11–42). Oxford University Press.

Fletcher, G. P. (1998a). The meaning of innocence. *University of Toronto Law Journal, 48*, 157.

Fletcher, G. P. (1998b). *Basic concepts of criminal law* (p. 43). New York: Oxford University Press.

Fletcher, G. P. (2000). *Rethinking criminal law* (p. 456). New York: Oxford University Press.

Fletcher, G. P. (2002). *Romantics at war: Glory and guilt in the age of terrorism* (pp. 77–78). Princeton, NJ: Princeton University Press.

Fletcher, G. P. (2010). The relevance of law to the incest taboo. In F. Herzog & U. Neumann (Eds.), *Festschrift für Winfried Hassemer* (p. 321). Heidelberg: C.F. Müller.

Green, S. P. (1997). Why It's a crime to tear the tag off a mattress: Overcriminalization and the moral content of regulatory offences. *Emory Law Journal, 46*, 1533.

Greenawalt, K. (1995). Commentaries: Legal enforcement of morality. *Journal of Criminal Law and Criminology, 85*, 710.

Gur-Arye, M., & Weigend, T. (2001). Constitutional review of criminal prohibitions affecting human dignity and liberty: German and Israeli perspectives. *Israel Law Review, 44*, 63.

Hart, H. L. A. (1968). *Punishment and responsibility* (p. 157). New York: Oxford University Press.

Hart, H. M., Jr. (1958). The aims of the criminal law. *Law and Contemporary Problems, 23*, 401.
Holmes, O. W., Jr. (1881). *The common law* (p. 1). Boston: Little, Brown, and Co.
Jareborg, N. (1988). *Essays in criminal law* (pp. 44–46). Stockholm: Almqvist and Wiksell International.
Kafka, F. (1956). *The trial* (W. Muir & E. Muir, Trans.). New York: Modern Library.
Kant, I. (1949). *Fundamental principles of the metaphysics of morals* (p. 46). New York: Bobbs-Merrill Co.
Kant, I. (1965). *The metaphysical elements of justice* (J. Ladd, Trans.) (p. 100). New York: Bobbs-Merrill Co.
Kremnitzer, M. (1993). Constitutional principles and criminal law. *Israel Law Review, 27*, 84.
Langodny, O. (2011). Basic rights and substantive criminal law: The incest case. *University of Toronto Law Journal, 61*, 761.
Lincoln, A. (1953). Annual message to congress. In R. P. Basler et al. (Eds.), *Collected works of Abraham Lincoln* (p. 537). New Brunswick, NJ: Rutgers University Press.
Mill, J. S. (1859). *On liberty* (p. 15). London: Longman, Roberts, & Green Co.
Murphy, J. (1988). Forgiveness and resentment. In J. Murphy & J. Hampton (Eds.), *Forgiveness and mercy* (p. 25). Cambridge: Cambridge University Press.
Nozick, R. (1981a). *Philosophical explanations* (p. 363). Cambridge: Harvard University Press.
Nozick, R. (1981b). *Anarchy, state, and utopia* (pp. 60–61). New York: Basic Books.
Rawls J (1973) Punishment as a practice. In: Murphy JG (ed) Punishment and rehabilitation. Wadsworth Pub., Belmont, CA, p 83.
Ripstein, A. (1999). *Equality, responsibility and the law* (pp. 140–141). Cambridge: Cambridge University Press.
Roach, K. (2011). The primacy of liberty and proportionality, not human dignity, when subjecting criminal law to constitutional control. *Israel Law Review, 44*, 91.
Robinson, P. (1997). *Criminal law* (pp. 279–377). Aspen: Aspen Law & Business.
Shoham, G. S. (1970). *The mark of cain: The stigma theory of crime and social deviation* (p. 47). Jerusalem: Israel University Press.
Simester, A. P., & Sullivan, G. R. (2002). *Criminal law: Theory and doctrine* (p. 2). Oxford: Hart.
Smith, J., & Hogan, B. (1996). *Criminal Law* (8th ed., pp. 4–5). Butterworths Law.
Stribopoulos, J. (1999). The constitutionalization of "fault" in Canada: A normative critique. *Criminal Law Quarterly, 42*, 227.
Stuart, D. (1995). *Canadian criminal law* (3rd ed., pp. 249–250). Toronto: Carswell.
Stuntz, W. J. (1997). The uneasy relation between criminal procedure and criminal justice. *Yale Law Journal, 107*, 1.
Summers, R. S. (1982). The general duty of good faith – Its recognition and conceptualization. *Cornell Law Review, 67*, 810.
Wendell Holmes, O. (1963). *The common law* (p. 3). Cambridge: The Belknap Press of Harvard University Press.

Part II
Core Values in Criminal Law

Criminal Law in Multicultural Societies

Tatjana Hörnle

1 Cultural and Religious Diversity

Like many other societies, German society is becoming socially, culturally, and religiously more diverse. What was once described as a "leveled middle-class society" (not only economically, but also culturally) no longer exists.[1] A panoply of political, economic, technological, and cultural developments have led to polarization, fragmentation, and fractures.[2] In this article, which I dedicate to my colleague and friend Mota Kremnitzer, I will focus on issues that are related to one aspect of the whole complex mosaic, namely, cultural diversity. Immigration is one factor (among many) that contributes to religious and cultural pluralization. Given the political and social situations in many of the countries from which immigrants come (and will come), it is safe to assume that the multicultural composition of German society will become more pronounced. This includes religious diversity: for 2017, the share of Muslims in the population was estimated at 6.1%; for the year 2050, a share of 11% to 14% can be expected.[3] It would, however, be misleading to concentrate only on religious affiliations. Culture is a much wider concept than religion. Within the limited scope of this article, it is not possible to describe the

[1] The sociologist Helmut Schelsky coined the famous expression "nivellierte Mittelstandsgesellschaft" to describe German society in the middle of the twentieth century, see Schelsky (1965), pp. 331–336.

[2] Reckwitz (2019a), pp. 63–133; Mau (2019); for the U.S., see Levin (2017); for the UK, see Goodhart (2017).

[3] See Pew Research Center (2017) Europe's Growing Muslim Population, pp. 4, 5. https://www.pewforum.org/2017/11/29/europes-growing-muslim-population/.

T. Hörnle (✉)
Max Planck Institute for the Study of Crime, Security and Law, Freiburg, Germany
e-mail: t.hoernle@csl.mpg.de

K. Ghanayim, Y. Shany (eds.), *The Quest for Core Values in the Application of Legal Norms*, https://doi.org/10.1007/978-3-030-78953-4_5

many different meanings of the term "culture".[4] I will rely on the notion of culture as a "toolbox" that provides norms, guidelines, practices, and routines for all kinds of human activities.[5]

Cultural diversity and its impact on law and legal practices can be analyzed from several different perspectives: descriptive, comparative, and normative. Obviously, the first step must be to obtain a sufficiently clear picture by describing the phenomena. Legal sociology, anthropology, and criminology analyze how cultural diversity develops and how it impacts criminal behavior, cultural justifications of such behavior, and reactions by criminal justice systems, for instance, sentence severity. A legal comparative approach would map how various legal systems respond to challenges that appear in multicultural environments. Neither the descriptive nor the legal comparative perspective will be taken in this article. Instead, the focus will be on foundational normative questions that can and need to be asked independent of the positive criminal law in a given legal system: How *should* legislatures and courts respond to increasing cultural diversity? After discussing general principles for criminalization (below Sect. 2), I will take up two examples: whether defamation of religions should be a criminal offense (below Sect. 3) and how to grade the seriousness of so-called honor killings and killings in the context of blood feuds (below Sect. 4).

2 Criminalizing Conduct in Multicultural Societies: Should Legal Moralism Be Revived?

What kinds of general considerations should guide policy decisions regarding the criminalization (or de-criminalization) of conduct? Legal moralism, a traditional and (at least seemingly) uncomplicated approach, demands or allows criminalization for conduct that is incompatible with moral norms. In recent decades, legal moralism has not been very popular. After the famous English debate between Lord Devlin and Hart in the 1950s,[6] the *Zeitgeist* favored liberal positions. Nevertheless, some prominent authors in criminal law theory, for instance, Michael Moore, continue to rely on legal moralism.[7] Antony Duff recently published his *opus magnus* on criminalization theory, which defends a moderate version of legal moralism. His basic idea is that not every justified claim of moral wrongness supports a criminal prohibition but that for a subset of morally objectionable behavior a *prima facie* reason to criminalize can be assumed. His master principle reads: "A. We have reason to criminalize a type of conduct if, and only if, it constitutes a public wrong. B. A type of conduct constitutes a public wrong if, and only if, it violates

[4]For a succinct analysis of the different meanings, see Reckwitz (2019b), pp. 29–61.

[5]For the notion of culture as toolbox, see Swidler (1986), pp. 273–286.

[6]Devlin (1959) and Hart (1963).

[7]See Moore (2017), pp. 441–463.

the polity's civil order."[8] Not all moral wrongs are, in his analysis, public wrongs that violate the polity's civil order—some are only private moral wrongs. For the example I will discuss below (Sect. 3), defamation of religions, it could be argued that public statements (other than private conversations) that express a serious degree of intolerance and resentment are public wrongs.

In my own writings about criminalization theory, I have always expressed skepticism about legal moralism and favored the classical liberal approach, relying on criteria similar to those Joel Feinberg proposed in his groundbreaking work "The Limits of the Criminal Law."[9] The decisive questions should, in my view, be the following: Does this kind of behavior violate the rights of other persons?[10] Can another person claim an individual defensive right (an *Abwehrrecht* in the terminology of German constitutional law)? Does the conduct in question harm or endanger important collective interests in the maintenance of essential goods, services, or organizational structures?[11] According to this scheme of analysis, there is a *prima facie* reason to criminalize conduct if it violates the rights of others or if it endangers important collective interests; there is no such reason, however, for conduct that merely transgresses moral norms.

In the contemporary world, liberal criminal law theorists are again forced to engage with legal moralism, because in public discourses certain moral demands play an important role. For instance, it has become common to demand that the state vigorously combat expressions of disrespect, intolerance, and hate in social media.[12] Under certain conditions, for extreme cases, it can be argued that disrespectful and hateful speech violates the rights of other persons, such as the right to human dignity or the right not to be brought into physical danger by incitement to violence.[13] However, it would not be plausible to equate every instance of disrespect and intolerance with a violation of the rights of individuals. Calls for state action against signs of disrespect and intolerance attest to growing worries that civil society is no longer capable of effectively implementing and enforcing standards of interpersonal decency. As can be seen from this example, the content of moral demands has changed. The focus is no longer on sexual immorality, traditionally an important concern for legal moralists. Today, demands for prohibitions concentrate on derogatory statements.

Perhaps the rejection of legal moralism needs to be reconsidered. In more homogeneous societies, it is easier to argue that moral education should not be the

[8]Duff (2018), pp. 275, 277.

[9]See Feinberg (1987, 1988, 1989, 1990).

[10]Hörnle (2005).

[11]Collective interests in this sense are independent of what persons consider a good life according to their cultural environment and personal lifestyle. Everybody relies, for instance, on efficient, corruption-free administrations, reliable monetary systems, and a physical environment that is not hazardous to one's health.

[12]See, for instance, the newest German law to fight right-wing extremism and hate crimes from March 30, 2021, Bundesgesetzblatt I p. 441.

[13]See Hörnle (2005), pp. 285–302.

task of the state but rather should be entrusted to other means of social control. With dwindling shared social institutions, the criminal law might be indispensable to entrench norms of conduct in the conscience and habits of human beings. For a full analysis of this thought, it would be necessary to pay full attention to the factual premises behind it, which is not possible here. One could, for example, question whether "multicultural" really means less shared moral commitments, arguing that sweeping pessimistic assumptions about moral life and moral education in multicultural environments are not convincing. It is likely that some culturally and religiously diverse communities share similar moral norms in their respective toolboxes of narratives and practices. However, it is likely that there is no universal story to be told. It would require a nuanced analysis of case studies to unravel the interactions of social fragmentation, immigration, and cultural heterogeneity and to assess the impact on shared moral commitments. I presume that it is not a multitude of cultural toolboxes *as such* that creates problems but the *combination* of cultural diversity with social and economic fragmentation. Under these conditions, it does not seem far-fetched to assume detrimental effects on moral norms and practices that are necessary for a civilized coexistence.[14]

For criminal law theorists, the essential question is whether the criminal law should compensate for civil society's weakening centripetal forces and enforce essential standards of tolerance and human decency. I am still more sympathetic to the alternative, arguing that in fragmented societies it becomes even more important to rely on a parsimonious, not morally ambitious criminal law. One argument in support of the parsimonious use of criminal law is the limited nature of resources. We can safely assume that the demand for financial resources (and, in aging societies, qualified personnel) exceeds the supply. Money spent on the criminal justice system is not available for other pressing needs.[15] This makes it mandatory to allocate resources with a clear eye to priorities. In the context of criminal law, this means focusing on severe violations of the rights of individuals and on serious threats to important collective interests. Also, from the perspective of social psychology, it might not be a good idea to rely on the criminal law to civilize human conduct. In fragmented societies, moral indignation is a rather widespread response, with spirals of strong emotional reactions and counterreactions. Part of the problem can be a tendency towards self-righteousness and blaming "the other". Having the criminal law on one's side might enhance such tendencies towards moralistic exclusions of others, while for these others the application of criminal law will, in turn, intensify their resentment and anger.

To summarize: Criminal law theorists should pay attention to the degree of fragmentation experienced in multicultural societies. It is not *prima facie*

[14]Another question then is whether criminal law is needed to implement essential norms of conduct. Obvious alternatives are other institutions run or supervised by the state—schools, in particular. Again, the complicated question of what works cannot be tackled here. It must suffice to express some doubts as to whether schools can effectively entrench moral standards—assuming that moral dispositions depend primarily on long term, affective influences by families and peer groups.

[15]For similar considerations, see Chiao (2018), pp. 99–101.

unreasonable to reconsider a more extensive criminal law if a shrinking moral consensus and group egoism call for the reinforcement of moral norms. In the end, however, I do not propose the revival of legal moralism.

3 Defamation of Religions

From general considerations about the most convincing framework for criminalization I now turn to an example: Should contemporary multicultural states retain (or perhaps introduce) criminal laws against the defamation of religions?

German law includes such a prohibition in § 166 German Criminal Code (StGB):

(1) Whosoever publicly or through dissemination of content (§ 11 Abs. 3) defames the religion or ideology of others in a manner that is capable of disturbing the public peace, shall be liable to imprisonment not exceeding three years or a fine.
(2) Whosoever publicly or through dissemination of content (§ 11 Abs. 3) defames a church or other religious or ideological association within Germany, or their institutions or customs in a manner that is capable of disturbing the public peace, shall incur the same penalty.[16]

A similar offense definition was part of the Criminal Code of the German Empire (*Reichsstrafgesetzbuch*) of 1871, a definition whose historical roots reach back to the Middle Ages.[17] The original logic was to protect God against defamation. This rationale requires belief in the existence of God, in His caring about human beings' words, and in the resulting need to avert His wrath. Contemporary criminal laws in states that explicitly emphasize their religious affiliation, such as the Islamic Republic of Pakistan, have extensive anti-blasphemy laws with non-trivial punishments.[18] In modern constitutional states, protecting God or protecting humans against God's wrath is no longer considered an appropriate justification for criminal punishment.[19] International bodies committed to the protection of human rights have criticized anti-blasphemy laws,[20] and several countries have repealed them, for instance,

[16]A translation of the StGB (used here) can be found on a website provided by the German Federal Ministry of Justice and Consumer Protection. https://www.gesetze-im-internet.de/englisch_stgb/. For discussion of the German law, see Cornils (2017), pp. 358–388.

[17]For the history of § 166 StGB, see Pawlik (2007), pp. 411–428; Stübinger (2015), pp. 573–585.

[18]See Rumi (2018), pp. 319–339.

[19]To demarcate the non-metaphysical quality of human rights and laws, Art. 4 German Basic Law and § 166 StGB include the hard-to-translate *Weltanschauungen* ("ideologies" in the translation of § 166 StGB cited above). This was, however, a symbolic move. In my research on § 166 StGB, I have not once seen a case involving *Weltanschauungen*.

[20]Hill and Sandberg (2017), pp. 115–116.

England and Wales (2008),[21] the Netherlands (2014),[22] Norway (2015),[23] Denmark (2017),[24] and Canada (2018).[25]

Reforms were discussed in Germany, too. In my report for the German Lawyers' Association (*Deutscher Juristentag*) in 2014, I proposed a repeal of § 166 StGB[26]—to no avail (59 votes against, 21 votes for).[27] One argument for the abolitionist camp could point to the fact that the norm is largely symbolic. Convictions are rare: in 2016, 14 persons were convicted; in the year 2017, only 10.[28] However, this is not the most convincing argument in support of my proposal. First, it is hard to predict how the number of registered offenses will evolve. Second, the fact that the criminal justice system does not have to deal with a large number of offenses of a certain type does not tell us much about the importance and legitimacy of the underlying norms of conduct. Criminal laws are more than *carte blanche* to prosecute: their main function is to inform citizens about what the law expects from them, and the fact that prosecutors and courts do not see many contraventions might be an indication that norms of conduct are working very well.

One could also argue that there is no need to repeal § 166 StGB because the German courts seem to handle the prohibition in a sensible way. From a pragmatic point of view, the law on the books is harmless as long as the courts value freedom of speech and freedom of the arts. Commentaries to the German Criminal Code emphasize that the description of speech as "defamatory" must take speakers' constitutional rights into account.[29] Accordingly, for instance, the Higher Administrative Court (*Oberverwaltungsgericht*) of Berlin-Brandenburg ruled that a display of Muhammad caricatures was not defamatory.[30] However, even if in the majority of complaints freedom of speech and freedom of art are given decisive weight, the question remains of how the punishment of offenders can be justified in the few cases that do end in a criminal conviction. The rationale of a criminal prohibition needs scrutiny, independently of how many persons are in fact punished.

---

[21] § 79 Criminal Justice and Immigration Act 2008. See Howard (2017), pp. 595–618.

[22] See Janssen (2017), pp. 619–641.

[23] Årsheim (2017), pp. 553–575.

[24] See The Guardian (2017) Denmark scraps 334-year-old blasphemy law. https://www.theguardian.com/world/2017/jun/02/denmark-scraps-334-year-old-blasphemy-law.

[25] Repealed in 2018 by Bill C-51 (An Act to amend the Criminal Code and the Department of Justice Act and to make consequential amendments to another Act). https://www.parl.ca/DocumentViewer/en/42-1/bill/C-51/royal-assent.

[26] See Hörnle (2014), C42; Hörnle (2015), pp. 293–297.

[27] Beschluss des Deutschen Juristentages v. 18.09.2014, Abteilung Strafrecht. http://www.djt.de/fileadmin/downloads/70/djt_70_Beschluesse_141202.pdf (Stand: 22.6.2015), p. 11. The majority argued that the norm exhibits an important value-shaping function that provides religious minorities with a feeling of existential security.

[28] Statistisches Bundesamt, Strafverfolgung (Fachserie 10 Reihe 3), Tab. 2.

[29] Hörnle (2017), § 166 Rn. 15; Bosch and Schittenhelm (2019), § 166 Rn 9.

[30] Oberverwaltungsgericht Berlin-Brandenburg, Aug. 17, 2012 - OVG 1 S 117.12.

If legal moralism were to be chosen as the general principle for criminalization, it would not be difficult to justify the existence of a norm like § 166 StGB for core cases. It is morally reprehensible to use words that are rude and insulting even from an agnostic observer's perspective (beyond religious believers' hurt feelings).[31] Nevertheless, for those who are critical of legal moralism, moral faults are not sufficient to justify criminal punishment. The next question, then, is whether defamatory remarks against a religion, church, or other religious organization violate the rights of individuals. German constitutional lawyers argue that § 166 StGB supports Art. 4 I, II German Constitution (the basic right that protects freedom of religion).[32] This is a debatable proposition. Typical acts that fall under § 166 StGB do not impede members of the religion in the exercise of or the commitment to their religion.[33] Consider defamatory remarks in a film or comments published somewhere on the Internet: hurtful for members of the attacked religion (if they notice it) but not an obstacle to peaceful congregation, prayer, etc.[34]

Perhaps yet another individual right—one that is not explicitly mentioned in the German constitution—is at stake. When discussing the subject of multiculturalism, political scientists have emphasized the interest of protecting identity,[35] and criminal law theorists argue that § 166 StGB protects identity and claims for recognition (*Anerkennungsrechte*).[36] In discussing this argument, two ways in which defamatory statements can relate to the adherents of the religion should be distinguished. First, the statement can address persons directly, such as explicitly claiming that all followers of a certain religion are "idiots" or whatever the invective might be. For these cases, it is necessary to discuss whether insult should be a criminal offense and how insults against larger groups of persons should be treated.[37] Often, however, blasphemous remarks are not directed at human beings alive today; rather, they mock religious narratives, holy figures who are long dead (or who might never have existed), or religious customs. This creates a gap between the content of the verbal attack and the claim of a living person to be the victim of an offense. The crucial

[31] Of course, there are borderline cases even from the moral perspective. How much tact is necessary if the speaker is motivated by an understandable motive to make the world a more rational place or the intention to help what she sees as the victims of religious abuse? Similar difficult questions as in legal assessments regarding freedom of speech would arise, as a matter of correct moral judgments, in the context of a legal moralism approach to criminalization.

[32] Waldhoff (2010), D 162.

[33] Another provision in the German Criminal Code does indeed protect religious freedom: It is a criminal offense to disturb the exercise of religion (§ 167 StGB), for instance, by interrupting religious ceremonies.

[34] In the same way, the freedom of artistic expression is not impinged when a newspaper reviews an exhibition in an annoyingly ignorant manner. A journalist's lack of understanding does not make it impossible or more difficult for art lovers to visit the exhibition or for the artist to paint in the future.

[35] Taylor (1994), pp. 25–74.

[36] Pawlik (2007), pp. 421–428; Seelmann (2012), p. 181.

[37] For the latter discussion in German criminal law doctrine, see Zaczyk (2017). Vorbemerkungen zu den §§ 185 ff., Rn. 27–36.

question is whether an individual's religious commitment creates the right to have her identity recognized and respected. German philosophers in the nineteenth century, most notably Hegel, put the notion of recognition (*Anerkennung*) at the heart of their writings.[38] Contemporary German philosophers continue this tradition,[39] with a rather ambitious concept of recognition that is more demanding than mere tolerance.[40] Other authors raise doubts about the celebration of group-based identities.[41]

For our discussion, we do not need to address the complexity of identities in multicultural societies,[42] or the general normative ideal of recognizing others. Criminal law theory addresses the narrower question of which psychological needs and ethical demands justify criminal prohibitions and punishment. Acknowledging identity rights in this context leads to the question of why only the religious aspects of personal identity should be protected. Strong forms of identification exist beyond the celestial domain (e.g., with ethnic groups or families, with sports teams, or the LGBT movement). Using the criminal law to protect all forms of strongly felt identification with a group could hardly be reconciled with the notion of parsimony. Also, a strong focus on individual identities could lead to consequences that are detrimental to living together in fragmented societies. Reinforcing a culture of "feeling aggrieved" means affirming psychological dispositions that aggravate rather than ameliorate problems. The German cultural sociologist Andreas Reckwitz, in his most recent book, analyzes the paradoxes created by a "culture of emotions."[43] In multicultural societies, it seems preferable to promote a relaxed attitude towards identity claims and a stoic stance when confronted with provocations by others, rather than the emotional reaction that insists on state intervention if others behave in a disrespectful way. I am aware that this proposition might seem rather alien to many participants in our contemporary discourses who tend to insist on "more respect!". From a normative point of view, or at least from the perspective of criminalization theory, however, I think that there are good reasons to be chary in the acknowledgement of identity rights.

We still need to discuss another line of arguments. The most common justification for § 166 StGB involves the protection of public peace (*öffentlicher Friede*).[44] Defamation of religion might entail more than disrespect and hurt feelings for religious persons—it can put into motion events that result in violent attacks and killings. Remember the massacre in the offices of the satirical newspaper Charlie Hebdo in Paris 2015, where, in revenge for the dissemination of Mohammed caricatures, twelve people were killed. The problem with the "public peace"

[38]For a comprehensive description of the traditions established by Fichte and Hegel, see Siep (2014).

[39]Honneth (2003, 2018).

[40]For the distinction between recognition and tolerance, see Forst (2006), pp. 78–83.

[41]Appiah (1994), pp. 149–163.

[42]See Appiah (1994).

[43]Reckwitz (2019c), pp. 203–238.

[44]See Bosch and Schittenhelm (2019), Vor §§ 166ff. Rn. 2.

approach is the attribution of possible consequences. Even if it can plausibly be assumed that some defamatory statements create the risk of emotional uproar and retaliatory violence (although this will not always be the case), the question of who should be assigned responsibility for such (possible) events remains.[45] Attribution of responsibility must be distinguished from causation. German criminal law doctrine emphasizes that a causal link between act and harm is a necessary but not a sufficient condition for criminal liability.[46] Similar conclusions can be drawn for the creation of a risk. If the realization of actual harm is not a matter of random events but rather depends on a third party's serious wrongful acts, ultimate responsibility for the situation should be limited to this third party.[47] Attributing (real or potential) violence to speech acts is not problematic when they include a direct call for violence. For instance, the offense of *Volksverhetzung* (incitement to hatred) consists in calling for violent or arbitrary measures against a national, racial, or religious group or a group defined by their ethnic origins (§ 130 para. 1 alt. 2 StGB). Under such conditions, the speaker can be held responsible for the risk of violent outcomes. Typical cases of defamation of religion are, however, different. Often, the person in danger is the person who defamed the religion herself. Should Stéphane Charbonnier, one of the cartoonists shot in the Charlie Hebdo massacre, have been punished for drawing caricatures of Mohammed? Proponents of the "public peace" explanation might respond that it is virtually impossible to predict exactly who will fall victim to vengeful violence (the Paris terrorists also killed several persons who did not belong to Charlie Hebdo). Nevertheless, the difference in the degree of blameworthiness is noteworthy when comparing persons who are rude about religions with those who physically attack others. The criminal law should focus on the latter.[48]

Criminal punishment for blasphemous speech that might trigger acts of revenge also has the curious effect of treating major religions unequally. A criminal court in Berlin recently held that defamation of the Catholic Church does not endanger the public peace. The relevant statement was certainly dramatic (it labelled the Catholic Church a "children-fucking sect"),[49] but it was perfectly logical to deny the existence of danger to the public peace because it is indeed unlikely that today's German Catholics would respond in a violent way. At the same time, the existence of fanatical groups within the heterogeneous religion of Islam has the paradoxical side effect of ensuring that the confession as a whole is protected as a matter of public peace. The state should not, however, tacitly support fundamentalists by only protecting religious feelings if the religion includes extremist groups.

---

[45] For this point, see also Cornils (2017), p. 371.

[46] Roxin (2006), § 11.

[47] See Hörnle (2005), pp. 185–193, 346–347; Rox (2012), pp. 231–232.

[48] Simple prohibitions might be justifiable (in police law, for example, preventing the screening of a movie with blasphemous content if violent demonstrations are expected). Criminal punishment is, however, a different matter.

[49] *Amtsgericht* Tiergarten, Feb. 6, 2012 – (263b Ds) 224 Js 3745/11 (228/11), 263b Ds 228/11.

And yet another problem with punishing persons for risks resulting from anti-religious statements is the effect on freedom of speech. Freedom of speech becomes particularly important if the speaker is not driven by resentment but wishes to communicate facts. There is, however, no perfect match between the value of sober criticism and the intensity of emotional and violent reactions. Risks might even be particularly high if the statement speaks the truth. Consider religious sects led by leaders who financially, emotionally, and sexually exploit their followers under the guise of being directed by divine commands. For the faithful, confrontation with the truthful statement that their leader is not receiving divine commands—but is rather a swindler and charlatan—can be particularly hurtful and drive them towards revenge.

To sum up: It is impossible to justify § 166 StGB and similar norms in other legal systems with the urgency and stringency that should be the benchmark for prohibitions in criminal law.

4 Assessing the Seriousness of Offenses: Should Cultural Backgrounds Be Considered?

In multicultural societies, offenders sometimes opine that their actions either were justified or should be punished less severely because they were motivated by cultural or religious influences. Returning to the example of the Paris attacks: If the murderers had survived, should their sentences have been mitigated due to their cultural socialization and their (at least superficially) religiously-tinted motives? Other disputed cases are so-called honor killings—where offenders claim to have acted out of a desire to "restore family honor", with this family honor based on cultural guidelines in patriarchal societies that place restrictions on the sexual conduct of women,[50] and revenge killings carried out in the course of blood feuds between families. In the discussions about "cultural defenses", the term "defense" is sometimes used to express the notion that the legal system must somehow process cultural influences as a matter of being fair to offenders.[51] The point I would like to make is that broad references to fairness or justice are not sufficient in the context of criminal law. Exemptions from criminal liability and mitigations must tie in with the criminal law categories of wrongfulness and guilt (Unrecht und Schuld).[52]

The internal logic of criminal law is often not appreciated by authors from the disciplines of philosophy or cultural theory. For example, the German philosopher Otfried Höffe calls for criminal courts to give equal weight to offenders and victims in typical cultural conflicts.[53] Such a "balancing of interests" does not sufficiently

[50]See Oberwittler and Kasselt (2011), p. 23.

[51]Dundes Renteln (2005), p. 48.

[52]For this point, see also Lernestedt (2014), pp. 15–46.

[53]Höffe (1999), p. 97.

account for the structures of the criminal law. Ethnologists have demanded that judges always be provided with ethnological reports so that they can better understand the crime.[54] However, from the legal perspective, the history of criminal offenses is relevant only as far as it plays a role within the legal categories of criminal wrongdoing (*Unrecht*) or guilt (*Schuld*). Not only for practical reasons (time and resources) but also for conceptual reasons, it is not the task of courts to elucidate *all* cultural, social, psychological, etc. details behind a criminal offense without asking for their relevance in a legal sense.

Legal scholars agree that cultural customs and norms could not amount to a full justification;[55] at most, *mitigating circumstances* can be discussed. German courts have on occasion granted mitigations on the basis of offenders' "cultural otherness" or their "Islam-based values",[56] or they have treated angry and emotional situations as the result of cultural conflicts.[57] Mostly, appellate courts apply more restrictive criteria, demanding that beliefs and patterns of behavior be considered mitigating only if such mitigations are in harmony with the legal system in the offender's country of origin.[58] However, this is not a convincing approach. In failed states or states with limited effective central state power, the formal national legal order can be meaningless as far as the cultural socialization of individuals and the mechanism of social control in these societies are concerned.[59] And for offenses committed after migration, it is hard to see why assessments should rely on the formal law of the state where the offenders (or their parents) were born or lived previously.

From the perspective of criminal law theory, the crucial question is whether an offender's cultural background could possibly affect the degree of wrongdoing or the degree of guilt. One chain of arguments in support of mitigation could focus on the biographies of offenders (their upbringing in different cultural environments, see below Sect. 4.1). This approach requires tracking individuals' lives way into the past. An alternative approach asks if motives present at the time of the criminal act might provide grounds for the mitigation of punishment (see below Sect. 4.2).

4.1 Relevance of Offenders' Socialization

For the longitudinal approach, the central idea is that long-term immersion in certain cultural environments can make it more difficult for people to adapt their behavior to the norms in the country of immigration, even if they are cognitively aware of these norms; this is particularly true if the cultural training took place during crucial phases

---

[54] Dundes Renteln (2010), p. 803.

[55] Hassemer (1999), pp. 163–164; Valerius (2011), p. 170; Pohlreich (2009), pp. 271–285.

[56] *Bundesgerichtshof* (BGH) (2001) 2 StR 276/01, Aug. 29.

[57] *Landgericht* Stuttgart, trial court, mentioned in BGH, 1 StR 307/06, Nov. 7, 2006.

[58] BGH, 1 StR 307/06, Nov. 7, 2006; 1 StR 437/95, Sept. 12, 1995; 5 StR 258/98, June 24, 1998.

[59] For the relevance of informal justice, see Tellenbach (2016), pp. 311–328.

of personal development. A mitigation of punishment might be an appropriate reflection of the lesser degree of personal guilt exhibited by a person whose framework for decision-making was formed by social and cultural influences beyond her control.[60] Such arguments do not apply if criminogenic factors become relevant later in life (such as in the case of Islamist radicalization in a detention center), but the cultural imprinting of childhood and adolescence might matter. "Foreign socialization" has played an occasional role in criminal court decisions. For instance, in a case before the *Landgericht* Leipzig, the defendant was charged with throwing his eight-month-old baby out of a multi-story building to punish the mother of the child. The trial court treated the fact that the offender came from Algeria as a mitigating circumstance (a decision that was overturned on appeal).[61]

There are several problems with such arguments. First, they smack of sweeping, unfounded conclusions. In the case mentioned: Which cultural norms in Algeria might support throwing babies out of windows? If the underlying logic is that some cultural environments do not provide sufficient training in controlling emotions and impulses, the question arises of whether this can be empirically tested or whether judges in some cases simply succumb to stereotypes about—for instance—Arab men. "Foreign culture" should not simply be equated with "diminished control".[62]

The second objection is that taking account of an offender's upbringing only in the case of migrants (or their children) disregards the principle of equality before the law. Each person's life is rife with childhood and youthful influences that affect their interactions with others, for instance, how they cope with stressful situations and whether interpersonal conflicts lead to violent reactions. Ingrained behavioral patterns always limit behavioral options. Focusing on the "otherness" of offenders with a migration background creates a dichotomy of "them and us"[63] that neglects the myriad of relevant factors in *all* offenders' personal histories. Sentencing decisions usually do not attempt to trace formative influences from early childhood on (or, more precisely, since conception), because this would clearly be impossible. Rather than drawing superficial pictures of offenders' childhoods if they (or their parents) migrated from another country, courts should admit that it is impossible to identify the influences that shaped the framework for decisions made later in life.

4.2 Relevance of Offenders' Motives

The next issue to be discussed is offenders' motives at the moment of the criminal act. Considering the relevance of motives for wrongdoing and guilt does not

---

[60] See Fabricius (1996), p. 210; Neumann U, Saliger F. In: Nomos Kommentar zum StGB, § 211 Rn. 30a. For a different point of view, see Jakobs (2006), p. 847.

[61] BGH, 5 StR 401/05, Oct. 13, 2005.

[62] Pohlreich (2009), pp. 266–267, 283–285; Erbil (2008), pp. 78–79, 250–251.

[63] Foljanty and Lembke (2014), pp. 304–305.

necessarily require longitudinal explorations of individual biographies. For the types of crimes mentioned at the beginning of this section, we could ask if the motive to restore family honor or the motive to avenge religions or religious figures against slander should be considered a relevant factor for sentencing.

In moral philosophy and in our day-to-day moral discourses, agents' motives are taken into account when assessing how much blame is appropriate for harmful or dangerous acts.[64] Douglas Husak confidently argued that "it is beyond dispute" that "a bad motive might aggravate, or a good motive might mitigate, the severity of the defendant's punishment."[65] Positive criminal law provides ample examples for similar assessments, for instance, German law relies on motives (in the form of "base motives", *niedere Beweggründe*, § 211 StGB) to distinguish between simple homicide and murder. Legal scholars have argued that political and ideological reasons that motivate defendants should be considered as mitigating circumstances.[66] Following this logic, it could be concluded that sentencing judges should make allowances for cultural and religious motives, too, and mitigate sentences—after all, defendants do not follow an egotistical, self-centered motive when they are motivated by political ideologies or cultural norms. For our examples, in most cases, German courts will not follow this line of reasoning. To the contrary, the motivations of offenders involved in honor killings and those of most offenders involved in blood feuds are assessed as base motives.[67]

With regard to motives, two kinds of inquiry should be distinguished. If it is assumed that motives should, in principle, matter for the assessment of crimes, questions arise about how motives such as defending family honor fit into the categories of mitigation and aggravation. A more general, foundational question is whether motives should be considered circumstances of crucial importance for sentencing. Before pondering about the assessment of particular motives, criminal law theory should discuss the general normative significance of motives in more detail. A comprehensive sentencing theory, which in turn must be grounded in a general theory of criminal punishment, cannot be developed here; instead, a brief sketch will have to do. My approach is based on the following assumptions. First, criminal law is an instrument used by the state to fulfill its task of protecting citizens against transgressions by their fellow-citizens.[68] Second, the rationale and structures of state punishment are different from the practices of interpersonal morality.[69]

---

[64] See, for instance, Sverdlik (1996), pp. 327–349.

[65] Husak (1989), p. 3.

[66] Norrie (2014), pp. 171–196.

[67] See BGH, 5 StR 222/19, Sept. 25, 2019; 2 StR 234/16, Feb. 28, 2018. In cases of blood feuds, offenders are sometimes convicted of simple homicide rather than murder. Take, for instance, the trial of the son and wife of a man who had been murdered. The two retaliated by killing a family member of the murderer. The argument for simple homicide was that these defendants had suffered greatly after the death of the father/husband, see BGH, 5 StR 341/05, Jan. 10, 2006. For a description of this judgment, see Kretschmer (2018), pp. 419–421.

[68] See Hörnle (2019), pp. 207–226.

[69] On this point, see also Thorburn (2011), pp. 21–43.

Third, the difference between state punishment and interpersonal morality needs even more attention if one takes into account that the latter has been deeply permeated by Judeo-Christian roots.[70] Our moral practices with their strong interest in wrongdoers' mental states imitate a perspective (God's point of view) that can be understood in the context of its religious background. My plea is to consciously redesign judgments in criminal law rather than simply sticking to interpersonal morality with its religious roots. If the state assesses wrongdoing, the primary focus should be on what defendants have done to other citizens, while the thoughts and emotions that preceded and accompanied a criminal act are less important than what is generally assumed.[71] Consider, for example, provocation. Focusing on offenders' subjective descriptions of their motives, that is, their *feeling* of having been provoked, can be misleading. What should matter is whether the victim's prior conduct was provocative in a way that exceeded the boundaries drawn by law.[72]

A more careful analysis of the relevance of motives is particularly important in highly fragmented multicultural societies for at least two reasons. First, with declining social cohesion, there is an even more pressing need to emphasize the (limited) core of legal norms of conduct and the essential obligations, duties, and rights that citizens have to respect in their relation to others and the collective of all citizens. The purpose of criminal convictions is to affirm *the most basic standards*, and if criminal prohibitions match these basic standards, the message should not be distorted by emphasizing personal backgrounds and personal motives. Second, the more diverse the cultural subgroups are, the more difficult it becomes to achieve consensus on which motives and emotions should be categorized as "good" and which as "bad". This has always been evident with regard to political motives, but the same can be said for cultural values. In fragmented societies, criminal courts should refrain from generously referring to moral judgments that are not part of the legal norms of conduct—judges should be aware that there is no uniform moral community beyond their courtroom.[73]

What conclusions could be drawn for the examples mentioned at the beginning of this section? The common denominator of so-called honor killings, blood feuds, and

---

[70]For the relevance of guilt (*Schuld*) in theological writings, see Maihold (2005), pp. 109–121.

[71]This statement invites the objection that psychological phenomena *must* matter, for instance, those that make up the difference between intent and recklessness. My brief answer would be that to explain the significance of intent for the assessment of wrongdoing, it is not the mental state *as such* that matters but its meaning from a victim's perspective. First, intentional acts are typically more brutal, more destructive, or more dangerous for victims. Second, attacking another person (or collectives of citizens) with the intention of inflicting harm signifies a practical attitude towards the victims that deserves some additional blame, see Duff (2009), Chap. 7.

[72]Grünewald (2010), pp. 228–261.

[73]These considerations are not meant to propose moral relativism or moral nihilism. Within the realm of morals and ethics, it is of course an important task to consider which personal virtues and moral requirements are particularly important in fragmented multicultural environments, and we should rely on such considerations in schools and for other mechanisms of social control. My point is more limited: state punishment should be more restrained and should not be utilized for the purpose of affirming and enforcing interpersonal morality.

attacks after religious defamations is the claim of offenders that they were forced to take revenge or to exact punishment for the prior misconduct of the victim. The fact that retaliatory actions are supported or demanded by an offender's cultural environment should not, according to my analysis, give us reason to mitigate the sentence. This does not mean that offenders' explanations and their emotions, such as anger or despair, never matter. They can be taken into account under one condition: The crucial filtering question should be whether the victim had committed a legal wrong against the offender.[74] In typical cases of honor killings, the female victims could not have been accused of wrongdoing. Notions of "female chastity and female honor" are not part of our legal systems, and having a sexual relationship is not a legal wrong. Also, in traditional constellations of blood feuds that call for the killing of *any* male member of a family, the person who is ultimately killed has not necessarily wronged the offender. If, however, the criminal act at issue was committed in response to a serious legal wrong previously inflicted on the offender by the victim, this previous wrong counts as a sentencing factor with (moderate) mitigating impact. For this assessment, it is not necessary to refer to cultural backgrounds of whatever kind. From a legal point of view, there is no difference between a German mother shooting the man who sexually abused and killed her child,[75] and a Turkish husband shooting the man who raped his wife.[76]

One last point deserves our attention: the question of whether for certain motives punishment should be *aggravated* to reaffirm legal values. If the relevant circumstances objectively increase the wrong done to the victim, such as the physical cruelty of the act or the presence of insults in addition to a physical attack, this should be taken into account. The point is additional wrongdoing; thus, it is not necessary to point to legal values as an *additional* sentencing consideration. The interesting cases are those in which offenders' motives do not show up in the form of additional harm to the victims in comparison to differently motivated killings. In the case of so-called honor killings of women: Should sentences be higher as compared to the otherwise similar killing of a female victim for reasons not related to issues of honor? One could argue that more severe sanctions for honor killings affirm the equality of men and women as a constitutional value. Such arguments take the legal point of view I propose. Nevertheless, I remain skeptical of treating certain motives

---

[74]It should be mentioned that German courts take a somewhat different approach. In deciding about base motives (i.e., motives that turn simple homicide into murder), they also proceed from the assumption that filtering criteria are necessary in order to determine whether or not anger, jealousy, and other strong emotions constitute "base motives", see BGH, 3 StR 481/83, Jan. 25, 1984; 2 StR 349/08, Oct. 29, 2008; 2 StR 5/13, July 30, 2013. In the next step, however, the courts apply vague moral categories rather than taking the strictly legal point of view (assessing victims' prior wrongdoing) that I advocate.

[75]A famous case in Germany was the trial of a woman, Marianne Bachmeier, who (in the courtroom) shot the defendant who was accused of sexually abusing and killing her daughter. Bachmeier was convicted of simple homicide, received a sentence of six years, and was released after spending three years in prison. https://www.welt.de/vermischtes/article1725386/Die-Rache-der-Marianne-Bachmeier.html.

[76]BGH, GSSt 1/81, May 19, 1981.

as aggravating circumstances. Criminal law judgments should be designed to clearly delineate the wrongdoing, which consists in the intentional attack on another human being. In cases of honor killings, the crucial point is not to acknowledge cultural norms that reflect anti-constitutional norms and attitudes. If this condition is met, and if what is objectively serious wrongdoing is flagged as such, there is no need for additional value judgments that obscure the clarity and simplicity of blame for the intentional killing of another human being.

5 Summary

The fact that societies are becoming more multicultural and fragmented should not prompt us to give cultural backgrounds greater relevance for decisions about criminalization and the assessment of crimes. On the contrary, my proposal is to assign less importance to cultural factors and to design parsimonious criminal laws with relatively simple criteria for assessing the seriousness of crimes. A parsimonious criminal law emphasizes the most basic rights and duties that citizens have vis-à-vis one another, such as the right not be intentionally attacked by another citizen. Although we can observe a tendency towards legal moralism among lawmakers, modern states should resist the temptation to use the criminal law as a substitute for moral consensus or as a means for moral education. Moral judgments should be avoided not only when deciding which conduct should be prohibited but also when courts assess the seriousness of criminal acts. These assessments should reflect what offenders (and sometimes also the later victims) have done (to each other) and should adopt a legal point of view rather than applying moral postulates.

References

Appiah, K. A. (1994). Identity, authenticity and survival: Multicultural societies and social reproduction. In A. Gutmann (Ed.), *Multiculturalism* (pp. 149–163). New Jersey: Princeton University Press.

Årsheim, H. (2017). Giving up the ghost: On the decline and fall of Norwegian anti-blasphemy legislation. In J. Temperman & A. Koltay (Eds.), *Blasphemy and freedom of expression. Comparative, theoretical and historical reflections after the Charlie Hebdo Massacre* (pp. 553–575). Cambridge: Cambridge University Press.

Bosch, N., & Schittenhelm, U. (2019). § 166. In *Schönke/Schröder, Strafgesetzbuch* (30th ed.).

Chiao, V. (2018). *Criminal law in the age of the administrative state*. New York: Oxford University Press.

Cornils, M. (2017). Legal protection of religion in Germany. In J. Temperman & A. Koltay (Eds.), *Blasphemy and freedom of expression. Comparative, theoretical and historical reflections after the Charlie Hebdo Massacre* (pp. 358–388). Cambridge: Cambridge University Press.

Devlin, P. (1959). *The enforcement of morals*. London: Oxford University Press.

Duff, R. A. (2009). *Answering for crime*. Oxford: Hart Publishing.

Duff, R. A. (2018). *The realm of criminal law*. Oxford: Oxford University Press.

Dundes Renteln, A. (2005). The use and abuse of cultural defense. *Canadian Journal of Law and Society, 20*, 47–67.

Dundes Renteln, A. (2010). The cultural defense: Challenging the monocultural paradigm. In M. C. Foblets et al. (Eds.), *Cultural diversity and the law* (pp. 791–817). Brüssel: Bruylant.
Erbil, B. (2008). *Toleranz für Ehrenmörder? Soziokulturelle Motive im Strafrecht unter besonderer Berücksichtigung des türkischen Ehrbegriffs*. Berlin: Logos Verlag.
Fabricius, D. (1996). Anmerkung, Strafverteidiger, 209–211.
Feinberg, J. (1987). *Harm to others*. New York: Oxford University Press.
Feinberg, J. (1988). *Offense to others*. New York: Oxford University Press.
Feinberg, J. (1989). *Harm to self*. New York: Oxford University Press.
Feinberg, J. (1990). *Harmless wrongdoing*. New York: Oxford University Press.
Foljanty, L., & Lembke, U. (2014). Die Konstruktion des Anderen in der "Ehrenmord"-- Rechtsprechung. *Kritische Justiz, 47*, 299–315.
Forst, R. (2006). Anerkennung und Toleranz. In C. Augustin et al. (Eds.), *Religiöser Pluralismus und Toleranz in Europa* (pp. 78–83). Wiesbaden: VS Verlag für Sozialwissenschaften.
Goodhart, D. (2017). *The road to somewhere. The new tribes shaping British politics*. Penguin Books.
Grünewald, A. (2010). *Das vorsätzliche Tötungsdelikt*. Tübingen: Mohr Siebeck Verlag.
Hart, H. L. A. (1963). *Law, liberty and morality*. Stanford: Stanford University Press.
Hassemer, W. (1999). Vielfalt und Wandel eines internationalen Strafrechts. In O. Höffe (Ed.), *Gibt es ein interkulturelles Strafrecht? Ein philosophischer Versuch* (pp. 157–180). Berlin: Suhrkamp.
Hill, M., & Sandberg, R. (2017). The right to blaspheme. In J. Temperman & A. Koltay (Eds.), *Blasphemy and freedom of expression. Comparative, theoretical and historical reflections after the Charlie Hebdo Massacre* (pp. 114–133). Cambridge: Cambridge University Press.
Höffe, O. (1999). *Gibt es ein interkulturelles Strafrecht? Ein philosophischer Versuch*. Berlin: Suhrkamp.
Honneth, A. (2003). *Kampf um Anerkennung. Zur moralischen Grammatik sozialer Konflikte*. Berlin: Suhrkamp.
Honneth, A. (2018). *Anerkennung: Eine europäische Ideengeschichte*. Berlin: Suhrkamp.
Hörnle, T. (2005). *Grob anstößiges Verhalten. Strafrechtlicher Schutz von Moral, Gefühlen und Tabus*. Frankfurt: Klostermann Verlag.
Hörnle, T. (2014). *Kultur, Religion, Strafrecht – Neue Herausforderungen in einer pluralistischen Gesellschaft*. München: C. H. Beck Verlag.
Hörnle, T. (2015). Bekenntnisbeschimpfung (§ 166): Aufheben oder Ausweiten? *Juristenzeitung, 70*, 293–297.
Hörnle, T. (2017). § 166. In W. Joecks & K. Miebach (Eds.), *Münchener Kommentar zum StGB* (3rd ed.). C.H. Beck.
Hörnle, T. (2019). The role of victims' rights in punishment theory. In A. Bottoms & A. du Bois-Pedain (Eds.), *Penal censure: Engagements within and beyond desert theory* (pp. 207–226). Oxford: Hart.
Howard, E. (2017). Freedom of expression, blasphemy and religious hatred. In J. Temperman & A. Koltay (Eds.), *Blasphemy and freedom of expression. Comparative, theoretical and historical reflections after the Charlie Hebdo Massacre* (pp. 595–618). Cambridge: Cambridge University Press.
Husak, D. (1989). Motive and criminal liability. *Criminal Justice Ethics, 8*, 3–13.
Jakobs, G. (2006). Die Schuld der Fremden. *ZStW, 118*, 831–854.
Janssen, E. (2017). The rise and fall of the offence of blasphemy in the Netherlands. In J. Temperman & A. Koltay (Eds.), *Blasphemy and freedom of expression. Comparative, theoretical and historical reflections after the Charlie Hebdo Massacre* (pp. 619–641). Cambridge: Cambridge University Press.
Kretschmer, B. (2018). Blutrache: Selbstjustiz als Mordmerkmal. In S. Barton et al. (Eds.), *Festschrift für Fischer* (pp. 415–429). München: C.H. Beck Verlag.
Lernestedt, C. (2014). Criminal law and "culture". In W. Kymlicka et al. (Eds.), *Criminal law and cultural diversity* (pp. 15–46). Oxford: Oxford University Press.

Levin, Y. (2017). *The fractured republic: Renewing America's social contract in the age of individualism*. New York: Basic Books.
Maihold, H. (2005). *Strafe für fremde Schuld?* Köln: Bohlau Verlag.
Mau, S. (2019). *Lütten Klein: Leben in der ostdeutschen Transformationsgesellschaft*. Berlin: Suhrkamp Verlag.
Moore, M. (2017). Legal moralism revisited. *San Diego Law Review, 54*, 441–463.
Norrie, A. (2014). *Crime, reason and history. A critical introduction to criminal law* (3rd ed.). New Jersey: Cambridge University Press.
Oberwittler, D., & Kasselt, J. (2011). *Ehrenmorde in Deutschland*. Köln: Luchterhand Verlag.
Pawlik, M. (2007). Der Strafgrund der Bekenntnisbeschimpfung. In M. Hettinger et al. (Eds.), *Festschrift für Wilfried Küper* (pp. 411–428). Heidelberg: C.F. Müller Verlag.
Pohlreich, E. (2009). *"Ehrenmorde" im Wandel des Strafrechts*. Berlin: Duncker & Humblot.
Reckwitz, A. (2019a). Von der nivellierten Mittelstandsgesellschaft zur Drei-Klassen-Gesellschaft: Neue Mittelklasse, alte Mittelklasse, prekäre Klasse. In A. Reckwitz (Ed.), *Das Ende der Illusionen. Politik, Ökonomie und Kultur in der Spätmoderne* (pp. 63–133). Berlin: Suhrkamp Verlag.
Reckwitz, A. (2019b). Kulturkonflikte als Kampf um die Kultur: Hyperkultur und Kulturessenzialismus. In A. Reckwitz (Ed.), *Das Ende der Illusionen. Politik, Ökonomie und Kultur in der Spätmoderne* (pp. 29–61). Berlin: Suhrkamp Verlag.
Reckwitz, A. (2019c). Erschöpfte Selbstverwirklichung: Das spätmoderne Individuum und die Paradoxien seiner Emotionskultur. In A. Reckwitz (Ed.), *Das Ende der Illusionen. Politik, Ökonomie und Kultur in der Spätmoderne* (pp. 203–238). Berlin: Suhrkamp Verlag.
Rox, B. (2012). *Schutz religiöser Gefühle im freiheitlichen Verfassungsstaat*. Tübingen: Mohr Siebeck.
Roxin, C. (2006). *Strafrecht Allgemeiner Teil* (Vol. 1, 4th ed.).
Rumi, R. (2018). Unpacking the blasphemy laws of Pakistan. *Asian Affairs, 49*, 319–339.
Schelsky, H. (1965). Die Bedeutung des Schichtungsbegriffs für die Analyse der gegenwärtigen deutschen Gesellschaft. In H. Schelsky (Ed.), *Auf der Suche nach Wirklichkeit* (pp. 331–336). Düsseldorf/Köln: Eugen Diederichs Verlag.
Seelmann, K. (2012). Was schützt der liberale Rechtsstaat? In T. Gutmann et al. (Eds.), *Von der religiösen zur säkularen Begründung staatlicher Normen* (pp. 171–182). Tübingen: Mohr Siebeck Verlag.
Siep, L. (2014). *Anerkennung als Prinzip der praktischen Philosophie: Untersuchungen zu Hegels Jenaer Philosophie des Geistes*. Hamburg: Felix Meiner Verlag.
Stübinger, S. (2015). Der Tatbestand der Bekenntnisbeschimpfung (§ 166 StGB) als Herausforderung der Rechtsgutslehre. In P. A. Albrecht et al. (Eds.), *Festschrift für Walter Kargl* (pp. 573–585). Berliner Wiss.-Verl..
Sverdlik, S. (1996). Motive and rightness. *Ethics, 106*, 327–349.
Swidler, A. (1986). Culture in action: Symbols and strategies. *American Sociological Review, 51*, 273–286.
Taylor, C. (1994). Multiculturalism and the politics of recognition. In A. Gutmann (Ed.), *Multiculturalism* (pp. 25–74). New Jersey: Princeton University Press.
Tellenbach, S. (2016). Islamic law, secular law and customary law. In P. Collin (Ed.), *Justice without the state within the state* (pp. 311–328).
Thorburn, M. (2011). Criminal law as public law. In R. A. Duff & S. Green (Eds.), *Philosophical foundations of criminal law* (pp. 21–43). New York: Oxford University Press.
Valerius, B. (2011). *Kultur und Strafrecht*. Berlin: Duncker & Humblot.
Waldhoff, C. (2010). *Neue Religionskonflikte und staatliche Neutralität: Erfordern weltanschauliche und religiöse Entwicklungen Antworten des Staates?* München: C.H. Beck Verlag.
Zaczyk, R. (2017). Vorbemerkungen zu den §§ 185 ff. In U. Kindhäuser et al. (Eds.), *Nomos Kommentar zum StGB* (5th ed.).

Corporate Responsibility in Germany

Thomas Weigend

1 Introduction

I had the good luck of meeting Mota Kremnitzer on many occasions and in different contexts. We discussed problems of the general part, international criminal law, sentencing law, human rights law, and several other topics. Every time we met, I was impressed by Mota's intelligence, sober and rational analysis, and his enlightened, humanistic approach to legal as well as political issues.

One early instance of Mota having a long-lasting effect on my thinking was not a live discussion but an article—a piece he wrote in 2001 together with my good friend Khalid Ghanayim on the criminal responsibility of business enterprises. At the time, I was an editor of the law journal Zeitschrift für die gesamte Strafrechtswissenschaft, where the German version of the article was to appear,[1] and thus had the pleasure of helping to arrange the text for publication in Germany. That was the first time I obtained any detailed information on the concept of corporate criminal responsibility (CCR), which played only an insignificant role in the German debate at the time. I learned about the various models used to explain the existence of CCR (alter ego model, vicarious liability, and corporate fault model),[2] as well as the practical ways of applying the concept in English-speaking countries and in Israel. Contrary to the almost unanimous German view at the time, the authors supported the criminal responsibility of corporations, mainly based on the fact that corporations play a significant role in social and economic life.[3] I have since repeatedly harvested the

[1] Kremnitzer and Ghanayim (2001), p. 539.

[2] For an exposé of this model see Schmitt-Leonardy (2017), p. 71; for a critical assessment, Kölbel (2014), p. 552.

[3] Kremnitzer and Ghanayim (2001), p. 551, 562.

T. Weigend (✉)
Universität zu Köln, Cologne, Germany
e-mail: thomas.weigend@uni-koeln.de

K. Ghanayim, Y. Shany (eds.), *The Quest for Core Values in the Application of Legal Norms*, https://doi.org/10.1007/978-3-030-78953-4_6

fruits of the seed planted by Mota Kremnitzer and Khalid Ghanayim.[4] As it happened, the issue of CCR has in the last decade become a topic of vivacious debate in Germany. I will use this opportunity to pay back part of my debt to Mota by reporting on the current state of that debate and possible future developments.

2 Responsibility of Corporations Under Present German Law

Since the 19th century, criminal responsibility in Germany has been limited to natural persons. In several instances, the introduction of criminal liability for legal persons was discussed,[5] but the arguments against such a measure prevailed. These arguments were mostly theoretical: The main objection was that a legal person cannot act (in a physical sense) and that it cannot make responsible decisions that could be a basis for attributing guilt.[6] There were strong counter-arguments against both of these propositions: the law nowhere requires that criminal liability must be based on an act in a physical sense, and even if such a requirement existed, a corporation could be held to act through its responsible agents; and guilt is a fluid concept that can be attributed to (natural or legal) persons under various conditions, according to any legislature's normative judgments. Still, the German discussion of the matter remained rather inflexible.

The German legislature had indeed devised an intermediate solution that took the pressure off the reform debate: Although corporations cannot be held criminally responsible, since 1968 they can be ordered to pay a fine and their illicit gains can be confiscated whenever a member of the management committed a criminal offense or an administrative infraction, thereby violating a legal obligation of the corporation or generating a financial benefit for the corporation.[7] An infraction may also consist of neglecting to properly select or supervise subordinate staff,[8] so that the company may be held responsible if a low-level employee commits a crime or infraction and his superior could have reduced the probability of the commission of the offense by properly supervising the subordinate. Under administrative infractions law, fines up

[4]See, e.g., Weigend (2008), p. 927; Hoven and Weigend (2018), p. 213.

[5]See the expert reports by Kommission zur Reform des strafrechtlichen Sanktionensystems (2002). In: Hettinger M (ed) Reform des Sanktionenrechts, vol. 3. p. 7. For an overview of the debate see Schünemann and Greco (2021); see also Heine (1995).

[6]For discussion of this argument, see Hirsch (1993); Jäger (2012), p. 43; Großmann (2016), p. 268 et seq.

[7]§ 30 Gesetz über Ordnungswidrigkeiten (Law on Administrative Infractions).

[8]Ibid., § 130.

to 10 million Euro can be imposed on a corporation, and illicit gains can be confiscated.[9]

3 Influence of EU Law

Even with this halfway house between criminal and mere civil responsibility, Germany has become an outlier among European states. Many of them have introduced straightforward criminal responsibility of corporations, at least for some types of offenses.[10] Several Directives of the European Union mandate that Member States provide for responsibility of legal persons for violations of certain criminal laws,[11] but so far, the EU has not specified that responsibility needs to be criminal in a strict sense. For example, Art. 12 of Directive 2011/93 of 13 December 2011 on combating the sexual abuse and sexual exploitation of children and child pornography provides that the Member States

> shall take the necessary measures to ensure that legal persons may be held liable for any of the offences referred to in Articles 3 to 7 committed for their benefit by any person, acting either individually or as part of an organ of the legal person, and having a leading position within the legal person, based on a power of representation of the legal person; an authority to take decisions on behalf of the legal person; or an authority to exercise control within the legal person.

Legal persons shall also be held responsible "where the lack of supervision or control by a person referred to above has made possible the commission, by a person under its authority," of a relevant offense. Art. 13 of the same Directive further requires that legal persons are "punishable by effective, proportionate and dissuasive sanctions, which shall include criminal or non-criminal fines and may include other sanctions", such as exclusion from entitlement to public benefits, placing under judicial supervision, and even "judicial winding-up" of the legal person.[12] The compromise character of the Directive can be gleaned from the use of the word "punishable" (which seems to indicate criminal sanctions) on the one hand and the acceptance of "non-criminal fines" as a sufficient sanction on the other hand. With the majority of Member States of the EU moving toward genuine criminal responsibility of legal persons, in the future the pressure from the EU may mount to impose criminal penalties on corporations for violations of interests protected by the EU.[13]

---

[9]Ibid., §§ 17 and 22. For a critique of the Ordnungswidrigkeiten model, see Kubiciel (2016), p. 178.

[10]For comparative overviews see Vermeulen et al. (2012), p. 31 et seq.; Bedecarratz Scholz (2016).

[11]For a list of such legal instruments, see Referentenentwurf des Bundesministeriums der Justiz und für Verbraucherschutz (2019), pp. 50–51. https://www.steuerberater-center.de/media/VerSanG_RefE.pdf.

[12]For a similar regime of CCR see Council Directive (EU) 2017/1371 of 5 July 2017 on the fight against fraud to the Union's financial interests by means of criminal law. Arts. 6 and 9.

[13]For overviews see Rönnau and Wegner (2014), p. 158; Böse (2016), p. 88; Dannecker and Dannecker (2016), p. 162.

4 Proposals de lege ferenda

It is in this context that in recent years various draft laws have been presented in Germany, all purporting to regulate CCR in a way that goes beyond the present typology of administrative infractions.[14] The first such initiative was taken by the German state of Northrhine-Westphalia in 2013 (cited here as "NRW draft").[15] In 2018, a group of researchers based at the University of Cologne presented a private draft law named Kölner Entwurf (cited as "Cologne draft"),[16] and in 2019 another group of experts published a draft law named Münchner Entwurf ("Munich draft"), which shares the general outlook of the Cologne draft but differs from it in significant respects.[17] In 2019, an unofficial draft law emanated from the Federal Ministry of Justice as the result of lengthy consultations within the Federal government (this draft will be cited as "Ministry draft").[18] This draft was in 2020 superseded by an official government draft,[19] which however has not been accepted by the German parliament. It is nevertheless likely that the topic of CCR will remain on the political agenda after the parliamentary elections of 2021 and that the elaborate drafts that represent the expert opinion of the Ministry of Justice will continue to be the basis fo further debate. For that reason, the following remarks will discuss the Ministry draft and will refer to the earlier drafts for purposes of comparison.

4.1 Scope of Application

According to the Ministry draft, the new statute is to be applicable to private as well as public legal persons, to associations (Vereine) without legal capacity, and to partnerships with legal capacity (rechtsfähige Personengesellschaften).[20] The

[14]For ways of dealing with corporate misconduct outside the criminal law see Schmitt-Leonardy (2013); Jahn et al. (2018), p. 27.

[15]Entwurf eines Gesetzes zur Einführung der strafrechtlichen Verantwortlichkeit von Unternehmen und sonstigen Verbänden of 18 September 2013. After a change of government in Northrhine-Westphalia, the Draft Law was retracted. https://www.landtag.nrw.de/portal/WWW/dokumentenarchiv/Dokument/MMI16-127.pdf. In Germany, the Federation (Bund) is competent for criminal legislation. The States (Länder) may however introduce draft laws through the second chamber of parliament (Bundesrat). The NRW draft was never officially introduced in the Bundesrat but has been discussed extensively. See, e.g., Hoven (2014), p. 19; Löffelmann (2014), p. 185; Zieschang (2014), p. 92; Krems (2015), p. 5; Schnitzer (2016).

[16]Henssler et al. (2018), p. 1. For critical statements, see Kölbel (2018), p. 407; Wohlers (2018), p. 412.

[17]Saliger et al. (2019).

[18]Although the draft has not been officially published by the Ministry of Justice, its text can be found here: https://www.steuerberater-center.de/media/VerSanG_RefE.pdf.

[19]Entwurf eines Gesetzes zur Stärkung der Integrität in der Wirtschaft, Bundesrat Drucksache 440/20 of 7 August 2020.

[20]Ministry draft, supra note 18, § 2 (1) no. 1.

German Federation (Bund) and Länder (states) are exempt from the reach of the new statute, and so are foreign states. Other corporations under public law (e.g., cities) can be liable unless the offence was committed in the course of exerting public authority.[21]

4.2 Character and Purpose of CCR

With regard to the character of corporate responsibility, the Ministry draft avoids taking a clear and straightforward position in favour of "criminal" responsibility and "criminal" punishment of corporations. Instead, the Ministry draft speaks of Verbandsverantwortlichkeit (corporate responsibility) and calls the sanctions to be imposed not penalties (Strafen) but Verbandssanktionen (corporate sanctions).[22] It is not clear whether (and in what respect) sanctioning corporations under the new law is to differ from the present system of treating corporate wrongdoing in accordance with the law of administrative infractions. The choice of terms, as well as the introduction of a separate statute (instead of incorporating CCR into the Penal Code), make it clear, however, that the authors of the draft wish to maintain the distinction between criminal penalties for natural persons (which presuppose individual blameworthiness) and sanctions for corporations,[23] thus avoiding the theoretical difficulty of ascribing criminal blame (Schuld) to legal persons.

The Ministry draft describes the purpose of holding corporations liable as making possible a proportionate (angemessen) sanctioning of corporate crime and at the same time encouraging corporations to implement compliance systems and to undertake internal investigations.[24] The retributive orientation of the Ministry draft is reflected in the list of circumstances determinative of sentences: the main sentencing factors are the seriousness of the offence including its consequences as well as the blameworthiness of the individual whose conduct triggers the corporation's liability.[25] At the same time, the Ministry draft authorizes a reduction of the sentence by half in order to reward the corporation's conducting an internal investigation[26]—a pragmatic compromise that is difficult to reconcile with the draft's overall retributive approach. The Cologne draft differs in its general approach by emphasizing the

---

[21]Ibid., § 5 no. 4. Similar provision in Cologne draft, supra note 16, § 1 (2).

[22]Ibid., § 3.

[23]The same approach has been taken (for pragmatic reasons) by the Cologne draft, supra note 16, p. 9; and the Munich draft, supra note 17, p. 38. By contrast, the NRW draft, supra note 15, p. 8, 10, had introduced „true" criminal responsibility for corporations, calling the offenses Verbandsstraftaten (corporate crimes) and the fines Verbandsgeldstrafen (corporate monetary penalties).

[24]Ministry draft, supra note 18, p. 1.

[25]Ibid., § 16.

[26]Ibid., § 18.

reformative purpose of sanctioning corporations: its system is designed to guide the offending corporation toward (again) becoming a "good corporate citizen".[27]

4.3 Model of Liability

As regards the model of establishing responsibility, the Ministry draft, in line with all other published draft laws and with EU law, implements an extended alter ego model: corporations will be held responsible for criminal acts committed on their behalf by leading personnel (Leitungspersonen). Responsibility is, however, not shifted from the individual to the corporation, but individuals remain (criminally) responsible for their acts and can be sanctioned alongside the corporation. Leading personnel is defined as including officers of the corporation and other persons with legal authority to act on behalf of the corporation, but the definition extends further down the echelon and covers persons responsible for directing an enterprise or plant of the corporation or for controlling the activities of the corporation in a position of leadership.[28] The Ministry draft thus represents a broad understanding of the alter ego model. And it extends responsibility even further: although there is no strict liability of leading personnel for acts of subordinates, the corporation is subject to sanctions for offences committed by its employees on behalf of the corporation if these offences could have been avoided or made significantly more difficult to commit by proper supervision or selection of the employee in question.

Sanctioning of the corporation does not require the actual conviction of an individual and can be imposed even if the identity of the offending leading person or employee has not been established, but it must be proved that a responsible person or an employee acted unlawfully and culpably.[29] In addition, the individual's criminal act must have violated a legal obligation imposed on the corporation or must have enriched (or have been intended to enrich) the corporation.[30] The leading person must have acted in his official capacity in the context of the corporation, but it is no barrier to CCR if he went beyond his authority and/or also acted for his own benefit.[31] There is no limit as to the kind or seriousness of an offence that can trigger corporate liability; the Ministry draft provides for corporate sanctions even if an offence against the person such as murder or assault was committed, and even minor

[27]Cologne draft, supra note 16, p. 8.

[28]Ministry draft, supra note 18, § 2 no. 2.

[29]Ibid., p. 77. For similar proposals, see Cologne draft, supra note 16, § 3 (1); and Munich draft, supra note 17, § 3 (1). With respect to offences committed by employees, § 3 (2) Cologne draft only requires the unlawful commission of the objective elements (actus reus) of a criminal offence. This rule is based on the consideration that a corporation should be held responsible even if one of its employees—who was not properly selected or supervised—did not act culpably, e.g., because he was insane or completely drunk when he committed the unlawful act.

[30]Ministry draft, supra note 18, § 1.

[31]Ibid., p. 77.

criminal offences can lead to corporate liability. However, if a leading person or an employee only committed an administrative infraction (Ordnungswidrigkeit), the new law does not apply; these cases will continue to be treated under § 30 of the Law against administrative infractions (see above).

4.4 Sanctions

All drafts provide mainly for financial sanctions to be imposed on corporations. They also permit the court to refrain from imposing a sanction or to place the corporation on probation. Details differ, however, among the various drafts. The NRW draft as well as the Munich draft would impose a day fine system, as has been introduced for natural persons in 1975.[32] According to the NRW draft, one day fine equals the 360th part of the corporation's annual profit, and the maximum fine is 360-day fines.[33] The Ministry draft and the Cologne draft, by contrast, do not apply the day fine system but provide for the imposition of the fine as a lump sum. According to the Ministry draft, the maximum fine is 10 million Euro if the triggering offence was committed intentionally, and 5 million Euro when it was a negligent offence.[34] However, if the corporation has an average annual turnover of more than 100 million Euros, the fine may be as high as 10 percent of its global annual turnover.[35]

Regardless of whether the fine is calculated as a lump sum or as a multiple of a fictitious day fine,[36] the relevant question is what factors may be used for determining the amount of the fine. The Ministry draft lists several factors, many of them related to the seriousness of the triggering offence and the motives of the individual who committed it.[37] General aggravating considerations are the commission of prior offences attributable to the corporation as well as the fact that a leading person of the corporation personally committed a serious offence.[38] In mitigation, the court is to

[32]See German Penal Code, § 40.

[33]NRW draft, supra note 15, § 6 (4). The calculation of day fines is similar according to Munich draft, supra note 17, § 8 (6), but the maximum would be 720 day fines for the most serious offences (§ 7 (3) Munich draft).

[34]Ministry draft, supra note 18, § 9 (1).

[35]Ibid., § 9 (2). For calculating turnover, the average turnover of the corporation and economically connected corporations within the last three years is taken into account. According to Cologne draft, supra note 16, § 4 (2), the fine may even reach 15 per cent of the corporation's annual turnover. § 7 (1) of the Munich draft, supra note 17, by contrast, sets a general limit of 20 million Euros for any fine. Only if the corporation's annual turnover exceeds 2 billion Euros may a fine of up to 200 million Euros be imposed.

[36]Day fines are said to have the advantage of expressing the relative guilt of the corporation before its ability to pay enters into the calculation; see Munich draft, supra note 17, pp. 58–59.

[37]Ministry draft, supra note 18, § 16 (2).

[38]Ibid., § 3 (2) and § 16 (2) no. 6.

take into account any activities the corporation undertook to prevent corporate crime, its efforts to investigate the triggering offence and to cooperate with the prosecution as well as negative economic consequences of the offence for the corporation.[39] Moreover, the sentence can be significantly reduced as a reward for the corporation's efforts at conducting an internal investigation of the offence in question.[40] This mixed bag of sentencing factors appears to be unrelated to any consistent sentencing theory with regard to corporations; nor does the Ministry draft explain what relative weight is to be given to each of the (possibly conflicting) considerations listed. In that sense, the Ministry draft's sentencing provisions reflect the generally confused (or, put positively: pragmatic) state of sentencing law in Germany. The Cologne draft, by contrast, emphasizes sentencing factors related to the need for bringing about a reform of the corporation, e.g., the existence of a crime-prone structure of the corporation on the one hand and measures taken toward improved compliance and compensation for any damage caused on the other hand.[41]

In order to prevent corporations from escaping the consequences of misconduct by changing their legal structure, the Ministry draft provides that any fine imposed on the corporation may also be enforced against any entity that has succeeded the offending corporation or has acquired the bulk of its assets.[42] According to the Ministry draft, the general rules on confiscation of the Penal Code[43] apply to the proceeds of any crime attributable to a corporation; depriving the corporation of illicit gains is therefore not a purpose of the fine but will be achieved by separate measures.[44]

In addition to fines, the Ministry draft lists a number of other sanctions that may be imposed on corporations. The most serious and at the same time the most controversial sanction is the dissolution of the corporation.[45] According to § 14 of the Ministry draft, the court may dissolve the corporation if such dissolution is foreseen by law,[46] if the corporation's leading persons obstinately committed serious offences on the corporation's behalf and if there exists a risk that further serious offences will be committed in the future if the corporation continues to exist. This clause appears to be directed especially against corporations serving organized crime.[47]

[39]Ibid., § 16 (2) nos. 6–8.

[40]Ibid., § 18.

[41]Cologne draft, supra note 16, § 3 (3).

[42]Ministry draft, supra note 18, §§ 6 and 7.

[43]German Penal Code, §§ 73-76b.

[44]Ministry draft, supra note 18, p. 93.

[45]NRW draft, supra note 15, § 12 contains a similar provision, whereas the Cologne and Munich drafts do not provide for the dissolution of the corporation as a criminal sanction. Due to broad criticism of this aspect of the Ministry draft, the final draft introduced into parliamentary debate did not contain any provision on dissolution as a sanction.

[46]Legal persons of public law and religious corporations cannot normally be dissolved by a criminal court.

[47]Ministry draft, supra note 18, pp. 90–91.

Because heavy fines can jeopardize the survival of a corporation and thus cause severe consequences for employees, creditors, and shareholders, the draft laws provide for several options for avoiding or limiting such consequences while at the same time encouraging the corporation to conduct its business lawfully in the future. The least intrusive measure of this kind is the deferral (with a view toward eventual dismissal) of the case by the prosecutor or by the trial court on the condition that the corporation fulfils certain obligations.[48] Such obligations can consist of compensating the victims for harm suffered, making a payment to the State, and implementing certain measures in order to prevent further offences.[49] The prosecutor or court may demand that the corporation prove the implementation of any required compliance measures by an affidavit of an outside expert. If the corporation fulfils the obligations imposed within a given period of time (which may not exceed two years), the prosecutor or court dismisses the case against the corporation.

A similar effect as with deferred prosecution can be reached by imposing a conditional fine. According to § 10 of the Ministry draft, the trial court, after finding that an offence attributable to the corporation has been committed, may pronounce a formal warning and determine a fine but suspend its imposition for a period of up to 5 years.[50] The court may at the same time impose the same obligations as the ones mentioned above. If the corporation fulfils the obligations, it faces no further sanction; if the conditions are not met, the court imposes the pre-determined fine.[51] This least incisive sanction shall be used only if special considerations make it unnecessary to (immediately) impose a fine and if it is to be expected that the warning, in combination with any obligations imposed, is sufficient to prevent further wrongdoing attributable to the corporation. If the stringent preconditions of § 10 Ministry draft are not met but payment of the entire fine is not regarded as necessary for preventing further offences, the court may suspend part of the fine under the same conditions and with the same possible obligations as described above.[52] If there exists a large number of victims, the court may, as an additional sanction, order the publication of the conviction of the corporation.[53]

[48]Ibid., § 37. This option resembles Deferred Prosecution Agreements as practiced in the United States. However, the Ministry draft also permits the trial court to conditionally dismiss a case—with the consent of the prosecuting agency as well as the corporation—even after an indictment has been filed and trial has started; § 37 (3) Ministry draft.

[49]Ibid., §§ 12 (2) and 13 (2).

[50]NRW draft, supra note 15, § 7 and Munich draft, supra note 17, § 14 provide for similar schemes of a warning with a suspended fine. The Cologne draft does not provide for this option but only for conditional suspension of part of the fine; Cologne draft, supra note 16, § 5. § 5 (4) Cologne draft additionally provides for the appointment of a monitor who gives the corporation guidance and reports to the court on the implementation of compliance measures.

[51]A similar scheme exists for individual offenders (Germany, Penal Code, § 59).

[52]Ministry draft, supra note 18, § 11.

[53]Ibid., § 15.

On the whole, the sanctioning system is designed to afford the corporation incentives for cooperating with the prosecution and especially for making credible and verifiable efforts towards implementing effective compliance measures. Both the prosecutor and the court may design conditions to promote that goal. On the other hand, the threat of heavy fines is to work as a strong motivation for the leaders of the corporation to avoid further wrongdoing.

4.5 Procedural Issues

Even in the present context of non-criminal administrative infractions, the involvement of legal persons as participants in the process leads to problems and open questions, in particular regarding the question as to what extent procedural rights afforded to individuals—such as the right not to incriminate oneself—also apply to legal persons.[54] Present statutory law has little to say on this and limits itself to declaring that legal persons may take part in the process—through their representatives—to the extent that their liability is at issue.[55] If CCR is to be introduced in German law, any statute would have to deal with a host of procedural issues[56] that cannot be resolved simply by applying the rules of criminal procedure law designed for natural persons.[57] All drafts discussed here, therefore, have sections dealing with procedural questions.

One important issue concerns the question of whether the public prosecutor is obliged to investigate CCR and to bring cases to trial if there is sufficient evidence for holding the corporation liable. Under the presently applicable law on administrative infractions, the prosecutor has full discretion in this matter,[58] which leads to glaring differences as to the intensity of enforcing corporate liability in different parts of Germany. All existing drafts would therefore limit the prosecutor's broad discretion in this regard. § 13 Cologne draft provides for an obligation on the part of the public prosecutor to investigate possible instances of crime attributable to a corporation but leaves a margin of discretion as to whether to file charges. The

---

[54]The Federal Constitutional Court has decided that the right not to incriminate oneself is based on human dignity and therefore does not apply to legal persons; see Bundesverfassungsgericht (1977) 2 BvR 70/75, 2 BvR 361/75, 95 Entscheidungen des Bundesverfassungsgerichts 220, pp. 241–242. For critical discussions, see von Freier (2010), p. 117; Fink (2014), p. 457; Dannecker (2015), p. 370.

[55]German Code of Criminal Procedure, § 444 (1).

[56]For an overview see Drope (2002).

[57]Ministry draft, supra note 18, § 25 declares the general procedural rules, especially those of the Code of Criminal Procedure and the Court Organisation Law (Gerichtsverfassungsgesetz) to be applicable, mutatis mutandis, to the proceedings for sanctioning corporations. To the same effect, Cologne draft, supra note 16, § 14; Munich draft, supra note 17, § 18.

[58]See German Ordnungswidrigkeitengesetz (Administrative Infractions Law), § 30 in connection with § 47 (1).

Ministry draft refers generally to the prosecutor's obligation to investigate and prosecute as imposed by the Code of Criminal Procedure (so-called Legalitätsprinzip),[59] but provides for a long list of instances in which the prosecutor may refrain from demanding sanctions for the corporation. This list includes:

- The offence committed was insignificant and there exists no public interest in prosecuting the corporation;[60]
- there exists a public interest in prosecution, but the corporation can otherwise satisfy this interest by fulfilling certain obligations imposed by the prosecutor (deferred prosecution, see above);[61]
- the offence had serious negative consequences for the corporation so that it would be inappropriate to impose further sanctions;[62]
- the corporation has become insolvent;[63]
- the expected sanction against the corporation is insignificant compared with a sanction that has been imposed or is expected in another case against the corporation;[64]
- it is to be expected that the corporation will be sanctioned sufficiently by a foreign authority.[65]

This list of reasons for dropping a case against a corporation mostly parallels similar provisions of the Code of Criminal Procedure applicable to natural persons in cases of lesser seriousness (Vergehen);[66] but the prosecution of the corporation may be dismissed even if the underlying offence was a felony (Verbrechen).

A special reason for temporarily withholding an investigation and prosecution is the initiative of the corporation to conduct an internal investigation of the matter. If the corporation informs the prosecutor of having started an internal investigation, the prosecutor may (but does not have to) put the official investigation on hold and wait for the outcome of the internal investigation.[67]

---

[59]See German Code of Criminal Procedure, §§ 152, 160, 170 (1). NRW draft, supra note 15, § 14 states that the prosecutor is obliged to take action (einschreiten) with regard to any corporate misconduct unless the law explicitly provides otherwise.

[60]Ministry draft, supra note 18, § 36.

[61]Ministry draft, supra note 18, § 37. For a criticism of this model, see Stuckenberg (2018), p. 331.

[62]Ministry draft, supra note 18, § 38. This provision is similar to § 56 Penal Code, which applies if the offence has resulted in severe hardship for the offender, e.g. a negligently caused traffic accident in which the offender's children died. It is not quite clear, however, to what extent economic consequences of an offence for the corporation (e.g., an obligation to pay damages) qualify for this exception from prosecution.

[63]Ibid., § 40.

[64]Ibid., § 39 (5) in connection with §§ 154 and 154a Code of Criminal Procedure.

[65]Ibid., § 39. In this case, the prosecution may be resumed if the expected sanction abroad is not imposed. For similar provisions, see Cologne draft, supra note 16, § 15; and Munich draft, supra note 17, § 27.

[66]German Code of Criminal Procedure, §§ 153 et seq.

[67]Ministry draft, supra note 18, § 42.

Another difficult and contested issue is the legal position and the representation of the corporation during the investigation and trial. The common position of all drafts is to confer upon the corporation the rights of a suspect/defendant.[68] According to § 28 Ministry draft, the provisions of the Code of Criminal Procedure concerning the suspect/defendant are to be applied mutatis mutandis to any corporation subject to prosecution and sanctions.[69] This rule implies, for example, that the corporation has the right to consult a lawyer at any time (§ 137 Code of Criminal Procedure).[70] According to the Cologne and Munich drafts, the participation of a lawyer is obligatory for any sanctioning proceeding directed against a corporation.[71]

The fact that the corporation is afforded the legal position of a suspect implies that its representatives have the right to remain silent with respect to the allegations throughout the proceedings directed against the corporation, and even in other legal proceedings.[72] § 50 Ministry draft makes an exception from that rule, however, with regard to the corporation's annual turnover, which is determinative of the maximum sanction to be imposed on large corporations (cf. § 9 (2) Ministry draft). It is difficult to explain this exception on principled grounds;[73] one might argue, however, that the corporation lacks a constitutional right to silence,[74] hence the legislature may impose limited obligations of disclosure.

Since the corporation itself cannot speak, its right to make statements or to remain silent will be exercised by its legal representatives, i.e., the persons authorised to act on behalf of the corporation according to the applicable rules of private and commercial law.[75] Natural persons who are subject to an investigation for (or have been convicted of) the offences giving rise to holding the corporation liable are excluded from representing the corporation, regardless of whether their personal

[68]The German term Beschuldigter is applicable both before and during trial, even though § 157 Code of Criminal Procedure reserves the term Angeklagter for a suspect against whom a trial date has been set.

[69]For similar provisions, see Cologne draft, supra note 16, § 17; and Munich draft, supra note 17, § 22.

[70]See Munich draft, supra note 17, § 23 (1).

[71]Cologne draft, supra note 16, § 19 (1); Munich draft, supra note 17, § 23 (3). Ministry draft, supra note 18, p. 110, by contrast, would apply the rules on „necessary defence“ in § 140 Code of Criminal Procedure, which permit the defendant to defend himself without a lawyer unless the trial concerns a serious crime.

[72]Ministry draft, supra note 18, § 34; Cologne draft, supra note 16, § 17 (1) provides that the representatives of the corporation may remain silent and may withhold any active participation in the investigation of the matter.

[73]The Ministry draft, supra note 18, p. 123 does not even attempt to give such an explanation except to point out that a similar obligation exists in German anti-trust law.

[74]Bundesverfassungsgericht (1977) 2 BvR 70/75, 2 BvR 361/75, 95 Entscheidungen des Bundesverfassungsgerichts 220, pp. 241–242.

[75]See Ministry draft, supra note 18, § 29 (1); Cologne draft, supra note 16, § 16 (1); Munich draft, supra note 17, § 21 (2).

case is tried jointly with that of the corporation. If every person authorised to represent the corporation is thus excluded from representing it, the court will appoint a special representative that exercises the corporation's procedural rights.[76]

Until recently, the concept of internal investigations of possible corporate crime was unknown in Germany. That has changed in the wake of investigations against large German companies conducted by American law enforcement agencies.[77] Since 2010, issues of compliance and internal investigations have been discussed intensively in German practice and legal literature.[78] It is therefore not surprising that draft laws dealing with the prosecution of corporate misconduct also cover the issue of internal investigations. The Cologne draft conceives of internal investigations as interviews conducted by lawyers hired by the corporation on its behalf for the purpose of gathering information on possible violations of the law and for the preparation of the corporation's legal defence in a prosecution. As a consequence, the Cologne draft regards the information obtained by the investigating lawyers as confidential, grants the lawyers a testimonial privilege, and exempts written records of interviews conducted with employees from seizure by law enforcement.[79] Nothing disclosed by an employee in the course of an internal investigation can be used against the employee in a criminal prosecution.[80]

The concepts of internal investigations proposed by the Ministry draft and the Munich draft[81] differ significantly from that of the Cologne draft. The Ministry draft regards internal investigations as measures undertaken by the corporation in the interest of law enforcement; such investigations may therefore be the basis of significant mitigation of punishment.[82] In order to earn the prospect of mitigation,[83] the corporation must, however, comply with a number of conditions. Most impor-

---

[76]Ministry draft, supra note 18, § 30 (1); Cologne draft, supra note 16, § 16 (1) 3rd sent. Munich draft, supra note 17, § 21 (2) 3rd sent, proposes that the corporation nominate an independent lawyer as its representative.

[77]For an overview of the 2006 investigation of Siemens by the SEC see SEC (2006) Investigation into Siemens AG's Activities in the U.N. Oil-for-Food Program. http://fcpa.stanford.edu/investigation.html?id=257. See also Jahn (2009), p. 41.

[78]See, e.g., Momsen (2011), p. 508; Knauer and Gaul (2013), p. 192; Kuhlen (2013), p. 1; Zerbes (2013), p. 551; Anders (2014), p. 329; Kasiske (2014), p. 262; Kruse (2014); Theile et al. (2014), p. 803; Rotsch (2015); Knierim et al. (2016); Krug and Skoupil (2017), p. 2374; Veit (2018); Küster (2019); Nienaber (2019).

[79]Cologne draft, supra note 16, § 17.

[80]Ibid., § 17 (3).

[81]The extensive regulations on internal investigations in Munich draft, supra note 17, §§ 33–39 cannot be discussed at length here. Their main feature is an 'independent' investigation conducted by a lawyer in cooperation with the prosecution (§ 34 Munich draft).

[82]Ministry draft, supra note 18, § 19 provides that if the court grants a mitigation there is no minimum sanction and the applicable maximum sanction is reduced by 50%.

[83]According to Ministry draft, supra note 18, § 18 (1) the court may grant mitigation if all conditions of an internal investigation have been fulfilled.

tantly, the internal investigation must have contributed significantly to factfinding (Aufklärung) on the relevant offences, and the corporation and its agents must have cooperated with the prosecution without interruption and limitation (ununterbrochen und uneingeschränkt).[84] The persons who conduct the internal investigation must moreover turn over to the prosecution all relevant documents generated in the course of the internal investigation as well as a final report on its results.[85] The Ministry draft also emphasises that the internal investigation must be conducted with full respect of the rights of individuals concerned: investigators must therefore inform anyone questioned that they have the right to the assistance of a lawyer or a member of the Workers' Council (Betriebsrat), that they may refuse to answer questions if they could incriminate themselves, and that anything they say may later be used against them in a criminal proceeding.[86] Despite this seemingly broad array of rights, employees subject to an internal investigation are in a difficult position: they may under applicable labour law be obliged to cooperate in any investigation conducted by their employer and to answer questions truthfully; and they have no protection against the use of their responses for convicting them in a later trial.[87] In order to make sure that a prosecution-friendly internal investigation is not contaminated by defence interests, the Ministry draft provides that mitigation of the sanction may only be granted if the internal investigation was not conducted by the corporation's defence lawyer.[88]

The Ministry's concept of an internal investigation seems to have been informed by United States practices in this regard. The carrot of potential mitigation of the eventual sanction is used for goading the corporation toward full and active cooperation, at its own cost, with the prosecution and thus for collecting and delivering the evidence for its conviction. The corollary is, of course, that any corporation under suspicion that prefers not to present all internal information to the prosecution will be heavily penalised at the sentencing stage. And even if the corporation conducts an internal investigation and cooperates with the prosecution in good faith, this may be to no avail if the court determines that the results did not "significantly" contribute to finding the truth.

[84]Ibid., § 18 (1) nos. 1 and 3.

[85]Ibid., § 18 (1) no. 4. The Ministry draft also proposes to amend § 97 (1) no. 3 Code of Criminal Procedure in order to clarify that any documents emanating from an internal investigation may be seized from a lawyer's office unless the lawyer obtained these documents while being the suspect's defence lawyer; for the background of this amendment see Ministry draft, pp. 136–137.

[86]Ministry draft, supra note 18, § 18 (1) no. 5.

[87]Cologne draft, supra note 16, § 18 (3), by contrast, provides that nothing an employee says in the course of an internal investigation may be used as evidence against him or her in a criminal trial unless the employee consents.

[88]Ministry draft, supra note 18, § 18 (3) no. 2.

5 Conclusion

Germany has undertaken significant steps toward introducing its own version of corporate criminal responsibility. A close look at the draft law written in the Ministry of Justice, however, reveals the lack of a clear and consistent concept underlying this effort. Liability of corporations for the misconduct of their leading personnel (including not properly supervising subordinates) is located somewhere between criminal law and mere administrative law; sanctions have mainly retributive elements but can be withheld, in whole or in part, for reasons of special prevention and in particular for the purpose of encouraging the corporation's cooperation in its own conviction. The corporation is formally granted a right not to incriminate itself, but lack of full cooperation with the prosecution can result in a significantly more severe sentence. Likewise, the rights of employees in internal investigations are formally respected but are neglected in practical terms.

The question remains whether a legitimate surplus in retributive or preventive terms flows from holding corporations criminally responsible, beyond the mere symbolism of attaching the "criminal" label to them.[89] In practical terms, it may well be sufficient to deprive corporations of any gains obtained from the criminal conduct of their managers and employees and to hold them financially responsible for any fines due and not enforceable against individual members of the corporation because internal responsibility had not been clearly allocated.[90] Yet, if it is deemed politically advisable to introduce a regime of CCR (or something analogous), legislatures should build the system of responsibility on a clear and consistent concept. They should also make sure that applicable procedural rules reflect the principles of due process and fair trial. The half-hearted solutions proposed by the German Ministry draft do not meet this standard. In that regard, the fact that the draft was stopped in parliament opens up a welcome opportunity to rethink the issue of CCR and to work on a more coherent lgal concept.

References

Anders, R. P. (2014). Internal Investigations. *Zeitschrift für Wirtschafts- und Steuerstrafrecht, 33*, 329.

Bedecarratz Scholz, F. J. (2016). *Rechtsvergleichende Studien zur Strafbarkeit juristischer Personen*. Zürich: Nomos.

[89]For critical statements as to the necessity of CCR in Germany see von Freier (1998); Murmann (2019), p. 69 et seq.

[90]Cf. Swiss Penal Code, Art. 102 (1): "If a felony or misdemeanour is committed in an enterprise in the course of its business and in the framework of its purpose, and if this offence cannot be attributed to a natural person due to a defaultive organisation of the enterprise, the felony or misdemeanour is attributed to the enterprise" (and a fine will be imposed on the enterprise). For criticism of this model, see Pieth (2017), p. 177.

Böse, M. (2016). Das Unternehmensstrafrecht im Spiegel völker- und unionsrechtlicher Vorgaben. In M. Jahn, C. Schmitt-Leonardy, & C. Schoop (Eds.), *Das Unternehmensstrafrecht und seine Alternativen* (p. 88). Baden-Baden: Nomos.
Dannecker, C. (2015). Der nemo tenetur-Grundsatz – prozessuale Fundierung und Geltung für juristische Personen. *Zeitschrift für die gesamte Strafrechtswissenschaft, 127*, 370.
Dannecker, G., & Dannecker, C. (2016). Europäische Vorgaben für das materielle und formelle Unternehmensstrafrecht. *Neue Zeitschrift für Wirtschafts-, Steuer- und Unternehmensstrafrecht, 5*, 162.
Drope, K. (2002). *Strafprozessuale Probleme bei der Einführung einer Verbandsstrafe*. Berlin: Duncker & Humblot.
Fink, G. (2014). Gilt nemo tenetur se ipsum accusare auch für juristische Personen? *Zeitschrift für Wirtschafts- und Steuerstrafrecht, 33*, 457.
Großmann, S. (2016). *Liberales Strafrecht in der komplexen Gesellschaft*. Baden-Baden: Nomos.
Heine, G. (1995). *Die strafrechtliche Verantwortlichkeit von Unternehmen*. Baden-Baden: Nomos.
Henssler, M., Hoven, E., Kubiciel, M., & Weigend, T. (2018). Kölner Entwurf eines Verbandssanktionengesetzes. *Neue Zeitschrift für Wirtschafts-, Steuer und Unternehmensstrafrecht, 7*, 1.
Hirsch, H. J. (1993). *Die Frage der Straffähigkeit von Personenverbänden*. Wiesbaden: Springer.
Hoven, E. (2014). Der nordrhein-westfälische Entwurf eines Verbandsstrafgesetzbuchs. *Zeitschrift für internationale Strafrechtsdogmatik, 9*, 19.
Hoven, E., & Weigend, T. (2018). Praxis und Probleme des Verbandsstrafrechts in den USA. *Zeitschrift für die gesamte Strafrechtswissenschaft, 130*, 213.
Jäger, C. (2012). Die Unternehmensstrafe als Instrument zur Bekämpfung der Wirtschaftsdelinquenz. In L. Schulz et al. (Eds.), *Festschrift für Imme Roxin* (p. 43). Heidelberg: C. F. Müller.
Jahn, M. (2009). Ermittlungen in Sachen Siemens/SEC. *Strafverteidiger, 29*, 41.
Jahn, M., Schmitt-Leonardy, C., & Schoop, C. (2018). Unternehmensverantwortung für Unternehmenskriminalität – "Frankfurter Thesen". *Zeitschrift für Wirtschafts- und Steuerstrafrecht, 37*, 27.
Kasiske, P. (2014). Mitarbeiterbefragungen im Rahmen interner Ermittlungen. *Neue Zeitschrift für Wirtschafts-, Steuer- und Unternehmensstrafrecht, 3*, 262.
Knauer, C., & Gaul, M. (2013). Internal Investigations und Fair trial. *Neue Zeitschrift für Strafrecht, 33*, 192.
Knierim, T. C., Rübenstahl, M., & Tsambikakis, M. (2016). *Internal investigations* (2nd ed.). Heidelberg: C F Müller.
Kölbel, R. (2014). Corporate Crime, Unternehmenssanktion und kriminelle Verbandsattitüde. *Zeitschrift für internationale Strafrechtsdogmatik, 9*, 552.
Kölbel, R. (2018). Kriminologischer Kommentar zum Kölner Entwurf eines Verbandssanktionengesetzes. *Neue Zeitschrift für Wirtschafts-, Steuer und Unternehmensstrafrecht, 7*, 407.
Kremnitzer, M., & Ghanayim, K. (2001). Die Strafbarkeit von Unternehmen. *Zeitschrift für die gesamte Strafrechtswissenschaft, 113*, 539.
Krems, K. H. (2015). Der NRW-Entwurf für ein Verbandsstrafgesetzbuch. *Zeitschrift für internationale Strafrechtsdogmatik, 10*, 5.
Krug, B., & Skoupil, C. (2017). Befragungen im Rahmen von internen Untersuchungen. *Neue Juristische Wochenschrift, 70*, 2374.
Kruse, B. (2014). *Compliance und Rechtsstaat*. Frankfurt: PL Acad. Research.
Kubiciel, M. (2016). Die deutschen Unternehmensgeldbußen: Ein nicht wettbewerbsfähiges Modell und seine Alternativen. *Neue Zeitschrift für Wirtschafts-, Steuer- und Unternehmensstrafrecht, 5*, 178.
Kuhlen, L. (2013). Grundfragen von Compliance und Strafrecht. In L. Kuhlen, H. Kudlich, & I. Ortiz de Urbina (Eds.), *Compliance und Strafrecht* (p. 1). Heidelberg: C.F. Müller.

Küster, M. (2019). *Der rechtliche Rahmen für unternehmensinterne Ermittlungen*. Wisbaden: Springer.

Löffelmann, M. (2014). Der Entwurf eines Gesetzes zur Einführung der strafrechtlichen Verantwortlichkeit von Unternehmen und sonstigen Verbänden. *Juristische Rundschau*, 185.

Momsen, C. (2011). Internal Investigations zwischen arbeitsrechtlicher Mitwirkungspflicht und strafprozessualer Selbstbelastungsfreiheit. *Zeitschrift für internationale Strafrechtsdogmatik, 6*, 508.

Murmann, U. (2019). Unternehmensstrafrecht. In K. Ambos & S. Bock (Eds.), *Aktuelle und grundsätzliche Fragen des Wirtschaftsstrafrechts* (p. 57). Berlin: Duncker & Humblot.

Nienaber, L. (2019). *Umfang, Grenzen und Verwertbarkeit compliancebasierter unternehmensinterner Ermittlungen*. Baden-Baden: Nomos.

Pieth, M. (2017). Anwendungsprobleme des Verbandsstrafrechts in Theorie und Praxis. In M. Henssler et al. (Eds.), *Grundfragen eines modernen Verbandsstrafrechts* (p. 177). Baden-Baden: Nomos.

Rönnau, T., & Wegner, K. (2014). Reform des Rechts der Verbandssanktionen. *Zeitschrift für Rechtspolitik, 47*, 158.

Rotsch, T. (2015). Criminal compliance. In *Handbuch*. Baden-Baden: Nomos.

Saliger, F., Tsambikakis, M., Mückenberger, O., & Huber, H. P. (Eds.). (2019). *Münchner Entwurf eines Verbandssanktionengesetzes*. Baden-Baden: Nomos.

Schmitt-Leonardy, C. (2013). *Unternehmenskriminalität ohne Strafrecht?* Köln: Otto Schmidt.

Schmitt-Leonardy, C. (2017). Originäre Verbandsschuld oder Zurechnungsmodell? In M. Henssler et al. (Eds.), *Grundfragen eines modernen Verbandsstrafrechts* (p. 71). Baden-Baden: Nomos.

Schnitzer, A. (2016). *Der Entwurf eines Verbandsstrafgesetzbuches: Rechtspolitische Illusion oder zukünftige Rechtswirklichkeit?* Frankfurt: Peter Lang.

Schünemann, B., & Greco, L. (2021). Vor § 25 notes 21 et seq. In G. Cirener et al. (Eds.), *Strafgesetzbuch. Leipziger Kommentar* (Vol. 2, 13th ed.). Berlin: de Gruyter.

Ständige Deputation des Deutschen Juristentages (Ed.). (1953). *Verhandlungen des 40. Deutschen Juristentages* (Vols. I and II). Tübingen: J.C.B. Mohr.

Stuckenberg, C. F. (2018). "Deferred Prosecution Agreements" – Ein empfehlenswertes Instrument zur Ahndung von Unternehmenskriminalität? In F. Dünkel et al. (Eds.), *Strafrecht, Wirtschaftsstrafrecht, Steuerrecht* (p. 331). München: C. H. Beck.

Theile, H., Gatter, M. J., & Wiesenack, T. (2014). Domestizierung von Internal Investigations? *Zeitschrift für die gesamte Strafrechtswissenschaft, 126*, 803.

Veit, V. (2018). *Compliance und interne Ermittlungen*. Heidelberg: C F Müller.

Vermeulen, G., De Bondt, W., & Ryckman, C. (2012). *Liability of legal persons for offences in the EU*. Antwerpen: Maklu.

von Freier, F. (1998). *Kritik der Verbandsstrafe*. Berlin: Duncker & Humblot.

von Freier, F. (2010). Selbstbelastungsfreiheit für Verbandspersonen? *Zeitschrift für die gesamte Strafrechtswissenschaft, 122*, 117.

Weigend, T. (2008). Societas delinquere non potest? A German Perspective. *Journal of International Criminal Justice, 6*, 927.

Wohlers, W. (2018). Grundlagen der Verbandsverantwortlichkeit. *Neue Zeitschrift für Wirtschafts-, Steuer und Unternehmensstrafrecht, 7*, 412.

Zerbes, I. (2013). Unternehmensinterne Untersuchungen. *Zeitschrift für die gesamte Strafrechtswissenschaft, 125*, 551.

Zieschang, F. (2014). Das Verbandsstrafgesetzbuch. *Goltdammers Archiv für Strafrecht, 161*, 92.

Sanctions for Legal Entities in South American and European Systems of Corporate Criminal Liability

Vincenzo Militello

1 Introduction

The choice of Latin-American systems for a legal comparison in the field of the relationship between "sanctions for the individual and sanctions for the legal entity" is interesting on a double note. It shall enrich the debate on corporate criminal liability with the peculiar theoretical reflections provided through comparative methods.[1]

Firstly, there is an international trend on the countering of white-collar and corporate crimes, moved from a criminal policy point of view by the identification of effective sanctions. However, the reflections on sanctioning profiles are not among the most studied issues within Italian scholarship on corporate criminal liability. Albeit already vast, said scholarship has until now been focusing mainly on the issues of the nature of liability, the structure of the attribution of the crime to

The English version of the text is dedicated to Prof. Mordechai Kremnitizer, who has always made comparison and dialogue between various systems a qualifying profile of his activity. The Italian text was first elaborated for the Conference "Sanctions for the individual and for the legal entity" held in Rome, at the University of Roma La Sapienza, on 25–26 May 2018. I would like to thank for the research assistance Dr. Micaela Raimondo and Dr. Salvatore Orlando (University of Palermo), as well as my colleagues Javier De Luca (Argentina), Miguel A. Girao (Peru), Ricardo Posado Maya (Colombia), and Luciano Nascimento da Silva (Brazil).

[1]Reference is made to that type of comparison in criminal law known as "theoretical": Eser (2017), p. 16, 28 ff., or "basic": Sieber (2006), p. 94.

V. Militello (✉)
University of Palermo, Palermo, Italy
e-mail: vincenzo.militello@unipa.it

K. Ghanayim, Y. Shany (eds.), *The Quest for Core Values in the Application of Legal Norms*, https://doi.org/10.1007/978-3-030-78953-4_7

the legal entity, the criteria founding and excluding liability, the relationship between the two kinds of liability (individual and collective) arising from the crime.[2]

Truly innovative is the consideration given to criminal legal systems of Southern America, both with respect to the Eurocentric direction (especially in German scholarship) of our theoretical tradition on the so-called "general theory of crime,"[3] and with respect to the new and specific sector of corporate liability, developed mainly upon the rich experiences of legal families of common law.[4]

This issue lies within the trend of harmonization processes induced by supranational sources in the field of criminal law. South American countries witnessed a rapid implementation of international instruments foreseeing forms of corporate liability. From this stems the interest to assess the overall trends arising in that continent when implementing internally the supranational indications as to sanctions for legal entities. This interest is even stronger than that towards analysing in depth a single legal system among the South American ones, however peculiar the adopted solutions may be in terms of sanctions chosen and effectiveness.

We then have to take into account the common historical and cultural rooting, albeit in different legal systems, and that all these systems take part in normative harmonization processes stimulated by several regional organizations.[5] The comparison among trends arising in those systems on this topic should not be conducted only with respect to a single legal system, as the Italian one. It would rather be preferable to open the comparison with the corresponding solutions in other European criminal law systems, where corporate liability has become among the most important examples of harmonization. And especially so within the European Union, which can use internal harmonization tools much more stringent than similar ones in South America.

In the following, we shall consider that many South American countries have introduces, in the last two decades, punitive measures towards legal entities, within processes of implementation of supranational norms. Shared norms have been specifically introduced with the aim to counter serious criminal phenomena, such as organized crime, corruption or environmental crimes, whose features and negative effects often possess a transnational dimension.

[2]Among the Italian books published on the issue: Mongillo (2018); De Simone (2012). Less are the published contributions on sanctions: e.g. Guerini (2006), pp. 140–188; Gargani (2006), p. 79 ff. The focus on the foundations of liability is also perceivable at the international level: e.g., within a now extremely vast bibliography, the comparative study Kremnitzer and Ghanayin (2001), p. 539.

[3]See, *e.g.*, Militello (2012), p. 348 ff, p. 352 fn. 20.

[4]The first Italian book after the entry into force of the Italian corporate liability regime opened with a long description of the experience of common law countries: De Maglie (2002), p. 12 ff. (on the US system), p. 145 ff. (on the U.K.), p. 163 ff. (on Australia), p. 177 ff. (on Canada), p. 180 (on the Netherlands). See also Gentile (2009).

[5]*E.g.* Organization of American States (OAS); Union of South American Nations (USAN/UNASUR); Southern Common Market (Mercosur).

In South American criminal law systems, there are still theoretical struggles in accepting the criminal nature of such a liability, especially in countries like Brazil or Argentina where traditional dogmatic scholarship is still strong.

The goal of the present inquiry is to analyse the sanctioning side of such liability, to assess whether its harmonization among the different countries in that context is less developed than the mere acknowledgement thereof. We shall not focus—as the subject matter—on the general issue of the nature of corporate liability. That issue, unless one follows the formal criterion of the formal label chosen by the legislator, is doomed to be influenced by manifold factors, concerning both the requisites to attribute liability and the features of sanctions, as well as the theoretical reflections of the various scholars in each country, which go beyond the scope of the present work.

2 The Basis of Data: The Selection of Criminal Law Systems in South America and in Europe Including Some Type of Corporate Criminal Liability

As always happens in a comparison, we shall firstly identify which materials are to be analysed. This is needed to allow for a proper research on the existing resources, taking into account the primary need to identify a sufficient basis of data to make the assessment significant for the two groups of systems: the South American one, with 14 national States; the European Union, with twice as many States (27, after the notorious—and still ongoing—episode of Brexit) if considered only its "small" meaning corresponding only to the European Union (and not to the wider area of the Council of Europe).

To that end, we deemed it appropriate to adopt an essentially dimensional criterion for South America, even just to avoid extending too broadly the outer boundaries of the present analysis. The adopted criterion refers to the magnitude of population of the countries. The research thus focuses on the following ten States: **Argentina**, **Bolivia**, **Brazil**, **Chile**, **Colombia**, **Ecuador**, **Paraguay**, **Peru**, **Uruguay**, **Venezuela**. We had to exclude the experiences of the legal systems of the four less inhabited States: Suriname, Trinidad and Tobago, Guyana, French Guyana.[6]

The first consideration emerging from the analysis of the considered criminal law systems is the absolute prevalence of States foreseeing sanctions for corporate crimes. This is independent from the *vexata questio* of the nature of corporate

[6]With the exception of this last one, belonging to France as a South American Department, the other three States mentioned in the text have a population of ca. 2.5 million inhabitants, slightly more altogether than the population of the less inhabited capital of the other South American States here considered (i.e. Quito-Ecuador: ca. 2.3 million inhabitants).

liability, labeled as criminal in certain States,[7] and as administrative in others,[8] while others foresee both types of sanction types.[9] Some sort of sanctioning for corporate crimes is foreseen in all considered States, with the sole exception of Uruguay.

A peculiar approach is that of **Bolivia**, where provisions on the matter are left to special laws, outside of criminal codes, although the whole theme recently was the subject matter of a new criminal code, "*codigo do sistema penal,*" which had been approved by Parliament in December 2017 (Ley n.1005 del 15.12.2017), but which has been repealed before its entry into force upon request by the President Evo Morales, after protests erupted in the country against other aspects of the new code (Ley n.1027 del 25.1.2018). In its Title 4 of the General Part (art. 65–78), the "unborn" code would have legislated in detail on legal entities' liability, foreseeing a criminal nature thereof, some attribution criteria and the exemptions possible in case of adoption of compliance programs, besides specific norms on sanctions (art. 71–78). Its contents are highlighted in the present work, albeit underlining the peculiarity of the Bolivian system with respect to other countries, whose current legislation only has been taken into account. Bolivia itself might be interested in such a positivistic approach, since it has legislated on the topic through three special norms, inserted in additional laws to the criminal code in force since 1997.[10]

As to the European context, we have considered sanctions for legal entities in some of the systems foreseeing some kind of corporate criminal liability: **Austria**, **Belgium**, **Denmark**, **Finland**, **France**, **Germany**, **Italy**, **Norway**, **The Netherlands**, **Portugal**, **Sweden**, **Spain**. It is worth noting, on the one hand, that, within the European Union, there are also additional countries with a form of corporate liability for crimes, which had to be excluded because it would not have been possible to

---

[7]Chile, in relation to the offences of terrorism, corruption and money laundering: Ley 20.393 (2009); Ecuador, Codigo Organico Integrado Penal, Chapter V criminal liabiliy of a legal entity, art. 49–50 (2014) sanctions are dealt with in art. 71; Argentina, Régimen de responsabilidad penal para las personas jurídicas por delitos cometidos contra la administración pública y cohecho transnacional, Ley 27.401 (2017) on certain crimes against the public administration: corruption, bribery, influence peddling; activities which are incompatible with public functions. Part of the national scholarship denies the criminal nature of liability, although it is explicitly prescribed by the law.

[8]Colombia, in relation to the offences against the public administration: Ley 1474 (2011); Paraguay, a sanctioning power is given to the Central Bank, Ley 1474 (2011).

[9]For criminal sanctions for environmental crimes in Brazil, see: Brazil, Constitution of The Federative Republic of Brazil, art. 225 (1988), and in Brazil, Lei dos crimes ambientais, Law 9.605 (1998); Brazil, administrative sanctions for corruption crimes, Ley 13.846 (2013); Paraguay and Venezuela, "Ley Orgánica contra la Delincuencia Organizada y Financiamiento al Terrorismo": LOCDOFT, art. 31 and 32.

[10]Bolivia, Código Tributario, Ley N° 2492 - 02.8.2003; Bolivia, Ley de Lucha contra la corrupción, Enriquecimiento Ilícito e Investigaciones de Fortunas "Marcelo Quiroga Santa Cruz", Ley N° 004 - 31.3.2010; Bolivia, Ley de Servicios Financieros, Ley N° 393 - 21.8.2013.

analyse sufficiently the sources of law: *e.g.* Malta, Romania, Slovenia, Slovakia, Hungary, Estonia, Latvia, Lithuania, Czech Republic.[11] On the other side, we decided to include in this analysis on sanctions for legal entities the **United Kingdom, Ireland** and **Switzerland**. As to the first two, the reasons lie in their long traditions on corporate liability, which makes them interesting even though the United Kingdom is leaving the European Union. As to Switzerland, its traditional rejection of corporate liability makes it interesting to study, since many European corporations opted to be based in its territory (e.g. in the chemical and pharmaceutical industry and in the financial and insurance sector).

We shall now consider the different types of sanctions in each legal system, in order to assess whether there might be common grounds and to highlight potential issues of contrast and difference. This shall be done first within each of the two contexts considered and then in a second-level comparison which could allow for further reflections on harmonization processes in the field.

3 The Types of Sanctions in South America

3.1 Monetary Fines

Monetary fines are among the main sanctions of liability regimes for crimes committed by legal entities. They are pivotal in each of the sanctioning systems and thus are tantamount to what deprivation of liberty represents for individuals. Even in South American countries, this trend is confirmed, with the sole exception of Peru. There, the sanction of "multa" (fine) is foreseen among the possible ones in general in the criminal law system (art. 41–44 CP PER); however, weirdly enough, it is not listed among the "measures applicable to legal entities" (in art. 105-105a CP PER).

The other legal systems considered, instead, always include fines as a specific sanction for legal entities. The main difference among them lies in the measuring of the amount of the fine. That might refer either to a sum depending on the financial possibilities of the criminal or to an amount linked to the specific features of the crimes, in particular the undue advantage (however labeled) deriving from the crime.

In the first case, it is interesting to underline that the benchmark is often a fixed amount, predetermined in general on the basis of a minimum monthly salary or to a base salary published by each State and regularly updated. In particular, the fine in **Brazil** hovers between one and three hundred sixty times as much as this benchmark (art. 8, L. 9.605/1998); in **Colombia** between five hundred and two thousand times (art. 34, L. 1474/2011); in **Paraguay** between one hundred and one thousand (art. 94 n. 3, L. 489/1995); in **Ecuador** it depends upon each crime, e.g. for

[11] See the provisions in those criminal systems on corporate liability and criminal organizations in our previous work: Militello (2015). ISBN 978-88-6149-092-5.

environmental crimes between one hundred and three hundred base salaries (art. 258, CP ECU).

A variation of this first model is offered by Chile with the so-called "*multa a beneficio fiscale.*" Its perk is that it uses a different measure unit to assess the amount of the fine, *i.e.* the monthly tax unit, a public measure determined on a monthly basis by the State and used for the payment of taxes and fines (art. 8 n. 4 and 12, Ley 20.393/2009).

Fines in **Argentina** are instead measured on the basis of profits linked to the crime, in an amount that may go between two and five times as much as the profit, including that which could have been obtained by the crime (art. 7 n.1, Ley 27.401/2017). An analogous approach is adopted by **Venezuela**, where the fine is measured upon a fixed amount of equivalence to capital, goods or other things obtained through the crime. This is substantially the same as the function of a confiscation by equivalence as will be seen below (art. 32 n. 5, *Ley Organica contra la Delincuencia Organizada y Financiamiento al Terrorismo*).

3.2 Confiscation

The framework of a shared approach to sanctions for legal entities emerging from monetary fines starts trembling already when it comes to profit confiscation as a specific sanction. Only some of the studied systems foresee confiscation among specific sanctions for legal entities: **Argentina**, **Chile,**[12] **Ecuador, Venezuela**.

It was also foreseen by the "unborn" **Bolivian** *codigo penal*, repealed and never entered into force. In the special laws on the matter foreseeing specific cases of corporate liability, a form of confiscation is included in the 2010 law against corruption and illicit enrichment for the crime of "*Enriquecimiento Ilícito de Particulares con afectación al Estado*" (art. 28). It mandates that goods obtained as a product of the crime shall be given back to the State; it also foresees a fine amounting to a quarter of the net worth of the legal entity.

A peculiar approach, among countries not foreseeing confiscation as an ordinary sanction for legal entities (**Colombia**, **Ecuador**, **Paraguay**, **Peru**) is the **Brazilian** one. They only use confiscation as a sanction for cases where the legal person had been established or mainly used with the aim of allowing, facilitating or concealing the commission of environmental crimes: in that case, the legal entity might be wound up and its net worth is deemed as an instrument of the crime and as such transferred to "*Fundo Penitenciario Nacional.*"

[12]In Chile confiscation is foreseen as accessory sanction: Ley 20.393 (2009) art. 13.

3.3 *Interdictory Sanctions*

Even interdictory sanctions play an important role in the listing of specific sanctions for legal entities. They aim to strike a chord with the corporate interest in granting business continuity. In this field, however, the variety of the choices made by each national system greatly increases. With regard to certain types thereof, it is impossible to identify whether there is a prevalence towards one direction or another.

Thus, there are almost everywhere provisions for the most extreme form: winding-up, dismemberment or definitive interdiction. This is present in all considered systems except **Paraguay**. The specific form varies greatly among different States, with the possibility to deprive the legal entity of its legal personality, as in **Argentina**, **Chile** and **Colombia** (as well as in the "unborn" **Bolivian** code). Instead, the less serious sanction of temporary interdiction or suspension of the activities is only foreseen by five legal systems: **Argentina**, **Brazil**, **Paraguay** (as a *limit to carrying out certain activities* or a *temporary prohibition to dividend distribution*), **Peru** and **Venezuela**. The same number of States, including this time also **Argentina**, **Brazil**, **Chile**, **Paraguay** and **Venezuela**, foresees some form of *loss of state authorization and fiscal benefits*. Despite the similarities with this last sanction, the number of States varies once more with regard to the *prohibition of contracting with the Public Administration*, only foreseen by **Argentina**, **Brazil**, **Chile** and **Ecuador**.

Similarly, the *closure of business premises* is explicitly foreseen only by **Colombia**, **Ecuador**, **Peru** and **Venezuela**; even less are the States foreseeing the specific sanction of the *publication of the conviction judgment*, or even only an excerpt thereof: **Argentina**, **Chile** and **Venezuela**.

3.4 *Specific Solutions with an Impact on the Sanctioning System*

Finally, there are some specific features of South American sanctioning systems which seem noteworthy, especially on a comparative note.

First, the possibility to impose "social duties" of public utility upon the legal entity. This is present in both **Brazil** and **Ecuador**. In **Brazil**, additionally, in the specific and relevant field of environmental crimes, there is the specific measure of *"Recolhimento domiciliar."* This is a procedure aimed at re-educating the convicted legal entity. This is done through a check over the management and a duty upon its managers to attend courses on the ways to treat dangerous activities. Always in the field of environmental protection, **Venezuela** and **Ecuador** include the possibility of *compensation* and *restoration* of damages.

A limited role is played, to this date, by organizational models aimed at reducing the risk of crimes. In **Chile**, among the corrective measures are *compliance programs*; in **Argentina** *effective collaboration agreements* are possible as a form of restorative justice ("*La persona jurídica y el Ministerio Público Fiscal podrán* *celebrar un acuerdo de colaboración eficaz, por medio del cual aquella se obligue a cooperar a través de la revelación de información o datos precisos, útiles y comprobables para el esclarecimiento de los hechos, la identificación de sus autores o partícipes o el recupero del producto o las ganancias del delito, así como al cumplimiento de las condiciones que se establezcan en virtud de lo previsto en el artículo 18 de la presente ley*"—art. 16 *Ley* 27.401/2017).

4 The Types of Sanctions in Europe

The main features of the sanctioning system analysed thus far with regard to South America find significant counterparts in those European legal systems with some form of corporate liability for crimes. Firstly, monetary fines are foreseen by all fifteen countries analysed in the present work. However, there are divisions upon the qualification of the nature of liability as administrative or criminal: once again, these differences are influenced not only by elements of the corresponding subject matter but also by theoretical reflections linked to theoretical traditions of each country's scholarship. *E.g.*, it is well-known that, in Germany, there is still today a vast number of scholars who oppose the possibility of recourse to criminal sanctions for corporate liability cases; however, there are ongoing proposals, even for new legislation, albeit still blocked at the project phase.

In Europe too, confiscation of assets is not as widespread among the legal systems considered. Only half of them include it among specific sanctions for legal entities, and specifically: **Switzerland**, **Finland**, **France**, **Italy**, **Norway**, **Germany**, **Spain**. Besides, the forms of confiscation vary greatly, especially on the determination of the amount (depending either on the net utility gained by the crime or on the whole, gross sum).

Perhaps more uneven is the mapping of the third group of corporate sanctions, the interdictory ones: with respect to those, there are only some common choices, always between different States, together with some features characterizing only some countries.

In particular, the most widespread is the *publication of the conviction judgment* (possible in **Belgium**, **France, United Kingdom, Ireland, Italy**, **Norway, the Netherlands**, **Portugal** and **Spain**). Those same countries, except the **United Kingdom** and **Ireland,** also foresee the *prohibition to carry out an activity*. This is done in different forms: thus, **Belgium** excludes public service activities; the **Netherlands** think of it as a deprivation of a right; **Spain** as a suspension of activities.

The same group of systems, excluding Italy and Norway, also foresee a similar, different type of sanction: *closure of business premises*, thus a minority option. Even more of a minority is represented by countries adopting the possibility to *wind up or dismember* the legal entity, which are only four: **Belgium, France, Italy** (only if the profits gained thanks to the crime were high and there was a recidivism of illicit behaviours within a determined timeframe), **Spain**. The same number of countries (this time including **Portugal** and excluding **Belgium**) also foresee the *prohibition of contracting with the Public Administration*, as well as the *appointment of a judicially-chosen manager* for the legal entity.

Specific and often original solutions might be found in **Belgium** (*warning*); **France** (prohibition to keep animals and confiscation thereof); Italy (prohibition to advertise goods and services and, as an accessory sanction to interdiction, the suspension and/or repealing of authorizations, licenses, funding needed to carry out business).

The adoption, by the legal entity, of a compliance model on prevention of crimes indirectly has an impact on the sanctioning side, as it can exclude or limit sanctions. This is still a relatively young topic of great interest and is foreseen by Italy, the **United Kingdom,** and **Ireland.** At the same time, there is a renewed interest towards adopting such a mechanism (see e.g., scholarship on the issue in **Spain** or **Germany**).

Some systems diverge in the sanctioning treatment of legal entities as compared to the ordinary treatment of individuals: *e.g.*, when it comes to the determination of the amount of monetary fines, **Italy**, the **United Kingdom,** and **Ireland** all adopt peculiar methods.

Therefore, in Europe as well, and perhaps in Europe even more than in South America, the framework emerging from this analysis on sanctions appears fairly manifold. It is challenging to retrace which choices were made by each legal system in selecting some of the possible applicable sanctions, once they opted to introduce some form of corporate liability for crimes. It is thus arduous to highlight which is the sector where the need for harmonization is greater.

5 The Harmonization of Sanctions for Corporate Criminal Liability in International Sources

Confronting the emerging picture, one might think that the issue has until now been lying outside the scope of the general trend of harmonization among different legal systems, were (s)he an outsider unaware of the international debate in criminal law scholarship.

(S)he would then be astonished in reading that "corporate liability represents a key theme in criminal policies of the early twenty-first century. There is no international treaty or, in our regional context (author's note: the European Union), framework decision or directive which does not require sanctions for corporations."[13]

This, though, is only a seeming contradiction: when analysed more in depth, it emerges that international tools do require more and more often the introduction of forms of corporate liability for crimes, especially for serious criminality. However,

[13]Nieto Martin (2008), p. 37.

their wording focuses on the basic option of criminal policy and aims at overthrowing the traditional concept of *societas delinquere non potest,* which had been the mantra and theoretical dogma of several civil law legal systems at least until the second half of last century. To avoid endangering the achievement of this goal, however, international legislators left it to each legal system to choose between a criminal or administrative nature of corporate liability, as well as to determine its requirements and the criteria for the attribution of liability. As to the important role of sanctions, they confined themselves to general suggestions, amounting to a boilerplate clause in most international conventions.

An example of this is the UN Palermo Convention against Transnational Organized Crime, which represented a stimulus to reforms for the South American legal systems here considered. In particular, in its art. 10, it first states that State Parties shall establish a liability for legal persons—without prejudice to the criminal liability of the natural persons (para. 3)-, which participate in serious crimes. These are defined as offences punishable with a minimum sentence of four years in their maximum, involving an organized criminal group or offences established in accordance with articles 5, 6, 8 and 23 of this Convention. In the following, in para. 4, it requires that State Parties foresee "effective, proportionate and dissuasive (...) sanctions, including monetary sanctions," be they criminal or non-criminal sanctions. Thus, it reiterates what para. 2 stated on the indifference of the nature of liability, which may be "criminal, civil or administrative."

Almost identical is the wording of the 1999 UN Convention for the suppression of the financing of terrorism (art. 5) and in the 2003 UN Merida Convention against corruption (art. 26).

The breadth of such a wording as the recalled one is probably linked to a certain caution used to proceed in national legal systems on this matter. There was a will to avoid that the high variety of sanctions existing globally could be paired with the traditional belief that sanctions are a typical element left to the autonomous determination of each legal system. That might have endangered the implementation of an international instrument, had it included stricter indications on the list of sanctions, their severity and their determination.

However, it would be erroneous to derive from this a proof at the global level of a perceived failure of harmonization policies in criminal matters, as has been already noted for example in some sectors of the European Union's action in criminal matters.[14] That last consideration needs be carefully considered and downsized, already with regard to the original European context in which it had emerged. Besides, the impact of those international UN instruments upon the legal systems of South American States in the field of corporate liability for crimes is particularly clear.

Suffice it to underline that, before those treaties, only two out of the considered pool of countries included a provision on this issue: in **Brazil** there was a corporate

[14]See, in general, Satzger (2010), p. 123 ff.; Weyembergh (2006), p. 188; Pastor Muñoz (2010), p. 90. Specifically on the participation to a criminal organization, see Manacorda (2008), p. 267 ff.

criminal liability for environmental crimes, whose law (Lei 9.605/1998) was based upon a provision in the Federal Constitution (art. 225). **Paraguay** bestowed a sanctioning and regulatory (as such, administrative) power on the Central Bank towards individuals and corporations under its oversight for bank, credit, finance and exchange offences (art. 83 and 91 Ley N° 489/95 *Orgánica del Banco Central*).

After the UN Conventions on transnational organized crime and corruption started being implemented in national legal systems, the number of countries which have introduced corporate liability, of any kind (be it of an administrative or criminal nature), surged until reaching, as already highlighted, almost the entirety of those considered.

Thus, **Peru** ratified the Palermo Convention on 23.1.2002 and the Merida one on 16.11.2004. Then, in 2007 they amended the criminal code, in particular its art. 105 on sanctions applicable to legal persons in case of crimes committed within the business context (Legislative Decree N° 982, 22 July 2007).

At turn, **Chile** ratified the Palermo Convention on 29.11.2004 and the Merida one on 13.9.2006. Then, in 2009 adopted corporate criminal liability for crimes of terrorism, corruption and money laundering (Ley 20.393/2009).

Furthermore, **Colombia** adopted a law on corporate criminal liability for crimes against the public administration only after implementing those two UN Conventions (ley 1474/2011, with the ratification of the two conventions respectively on 4.8.2004 and 24.10.2006).

In a similar vein, **Venezuela** foresees such a liability in two different fields, with two separate pieces of legislation, strongly interrelated in terms of time and subject matter (*Ley Orgánica contra la Delincuencia Organizada y Financiamiento al Terrorismo-LOCDOFT*, G.O. N° 39.912, 30.4.2012; and *Ley Penal del Ambiente* G.O. N° 39.913, 2.5.2012): both these 2012 laws thus follow the national ratification of the UN Conventions mentioned above (respectively on 13.5.2002 and 2.2.2009).

In **Ecuador** too, the insertion of corporate liability in the *Codigo Penal Integrado* (arts. 49–50, Ley N. 180, 10.2.2014) comes after the ratification in that country both those two Conventions, on 17.9.2002 and 15.9.2005.

Lastly, **Argentina** introduced in 2017 corporate criminal liability for a series of crimes against the public administration (Ley 27.401 *de responsabilidad penal de las personas jurídicas por delitos de cohecho, concusión y otros delitos*); even in this case, the two UN Conventions had already been ratified by then: the one on organized crime on 19.11.2002; the second, on corruption, on 28.8.2006.

Bolivia represents a limited exception to the linearity of the time sequence highlighted in the previous paragraphs between the implementation of international norms and the adoption of internal norms. Indeed, one of the possible sources of liability for corporations, the 2003 tax code, precedes the ratification of the two UN conventions quoted above, which had occurred in 2005 (respectively on 10.10 and on 5.12). It should not be overlooked, though, that the additional two sources currently in force date back to a later time, thus confirming the highlighted trend for this country as well (2010 *Ley de Lucha contra la corrupción* and 2013 *Ley de Servicios Financieros*).

It cannot be denied or underestimated that the UN Conventions affected the criminal legal systems of the South American region by pushing for the introduction of forms of corporate liability. Even admitting that there have been local or different influences on the increased frequency of legislative initiatives on the matter, the existence of international obligations cannot be disregarded unless one sees as mere randomness the time sequence between the two normative levels reconstructed above.

Rather, a balanced picture of the two points needs to be painted: on the one side, the stimulus on the various South American systems towards introducing forms of corporate liability for crimes according to international obligations arising out of those UN Conventions; on the other side, the fragmented framework of sanctioning systems adopted in each national legal system. The balance could lie in acknowledging the harmonization completed thus far, while admitting it is a weak harmonization. In fact, even in geographical areas that are sufficiently homogenous, it worked as a patchwork. Some types of sanctions were left unknown in some countries; in some cases, there are differences in how the sanction is structured or how its measure is determined by the sentencing judge. Consequently, there are holes or at least differences in how effective the overall answer of systems of corporate liability for crimes is. The current stage of the path towards the acknowledgment of corporate criminal liability is, in any case, more advanced than it was before international harmonization tools were approved. This is a confirmation of their advancement function, at least if the advancement is seen as a principle—or a direction aiming at a progressive ever-improving situation—and not as a strict rule which can or cannot be adopted, without any chance of scaling its implementation.[15]

6 Ideas for a Summary Assessment

We have thus far gained an overall impression on the issue: that might not be able to trace in detail the specific national solutions in the two pools of legal systems; however, it seems sufficient to sketch some rapid synthesis evaluations. They are provided mainly as a starting point for future further and more detailed studies, which greatly overcome the boundaries of the present text.

First, the picture emerging from the current situation on the relevant issue neatly shows a choice in favour of corporate liability and the corresponding sanctions, now shared by most legal systems in South America and in Europe.

Such a choice remains totally independent from the nature of such a liability. This allows us to highlight a divergence between criminal policy and dogmatic theory: not only is there a resistance in countries, like **Germany**, deeply rooted in traditional dogmas on action, guilt and ability to undergo a punishment and its functions,

[15] We tried to develop such a concept of harmonization in criminal matters (specifically in the European Union context) in Militello (2014), p. 118 ff.

against national legislators adopting systems of corporate criminal liability; in countries—like **Argentina**—which have expressly labeled liability as criminal, as well, most scholars underline that it might be a "labelling scam". The driving force behind criminal policy needs in transforming the legal framework is proved, since the acknowledgment of such a form of liability is done by national legislators in relation to so-called serious crimes, attracting the interest of communities at the international and national level (*e.g.*, corruption, money-laundering, environmental crimes). At the same time, once corporate liability is introduced for some specific crimes, there seems to be a trend towards gradually expanding the number of types of crimes entailing corporate liability (examples can be, in Europe, **France** or **Italy**).

More specifically on sanctions for legal entities, national approaches significantly diverge, as seen above. The only proper similarity occurs in relation to the type of monetary fines, both within each of the two pool considered (with the exception of Peru in South America) and in a perspective of macro-comparison between South American and European countries. For all other forms of sanction, including confiscation and interdictory sanctions, the degree of implementation varies in relation to the type and actual content of each sanction.

Additionally, the sanctioning systems here considered differ not only because corporations are treated differently than individuals (*e.g.*, monetary fines in **Italy** have a fixed amount for individuals and daily rates for corporations) but also in how legal entities are subject to these sanctions in fifteen countries. Thus, the determination of the judgment may be done through a fine based upon illicit advantages (**Argentina** and **Venezuela**), or rather upon a legally predetermined, minimum, monthly salary (**Brazil**, **Colombia, Paraguay** and **Ecuador**) or in the form of a fiscal incentive (**Chile**). The degree of variety intensifies in the European context, where some of those forms of determination are unknown, while hovering between the two systems of the lump sum and of the daily rate.

We can thus define the harmonization of sanctions against legal entities as "weak" in the wake of supranational instruments on this matter. As to global initiatives, the preferred standard wording ("effective, proportioned and dissuasive sanctions") leaves actual possible interpretations open, on purpose. It should then not come as a surprise that legal systems in South America diversify their actual legislative solutions. Less understandable, though, are the analogous differences existing in the European context. There, we witness the existence of binding legislative tools, at least concerning the high number of criminality types covered by the provision of art. 83 TFEU.

It is worth noting that, even in the several cases where EU normative interventions foresee the specific kind of liability at issue, their indications on the corresponding sanctions are not too different between those sources of law which are less bound to achieve their harmonization goals (framework decisions),[16] and

[16]A significant example might be the provisions on the issue foreseen by Council Framework Decision, 2000/383/JHA of 29 May 2000 on using penal and other sanctions to increase protection against counterfeiting in connection with the introduction of the euro (GUCE n. L 140, 14/06/2000),

those which are more recent and more binding (as directives,[17] or, nowadays, regulations).[18]

Thus, detailing supranational norms on sanctioning of legal entities looks like a more arduous path than merely following the international and European trend towards the introduction of corporate liability, ever increasing the number of signing States. It is quite striking that, to this day, the most complete and detailed list of sanctions for legal entities in the European context dates back to the first supranational tool on this matter, amounting merely to a form of non-binding "soft law": The Council of Europe's recommendation R (88) 18.[19]

We should underline that both in South America and in Europe the process of spreading of corporate criminal liability represents a necessary requisite to build a common front of countering against corporate criminality; however, that alone is not enough to erase the different degree of sanctioning that a legal entity risks being subject to in different countries. That is highly significant in terms of impact upon the choices made by corporation transnationally, which might be influenced by systems less inclined to pursue specific offences.

---

which mandates corporate liability for those offences. As to sanctions, it uses the traditional wording of "effective, proportioned and dissuasive" sanctions, for offences committed by a person with leading position based on a power of representation of the legal person, or an authority to take decisions on behalf of the legal person, or an authority to exercise control within the legal person (*ex* art. 8 para. 1), not only paired with an explicit reference to monetary fines (leaving its criminal or administrative nature open) but also specifying a list of further possible sanctions: exclusion from entitlement to public benefits or aid; temporary or permanent disqualification from the practice of commercial activities; placing under judicial supervision; a judicial winding-up order.

In addition to that list: Council Framework Decision, 2004/757/JHA of 25 October 2004 laying down minimum provisions on the constituent elements of criminal acts and penalties in the field of illicit drug trafficking (GU L335 -11/11/2004), also referred to *temporary or permanent closure of establishments used for committing the offence* and *confiscation of substances, instrumentalities used or intended to be used for these offences and proceeds from these offences or the confiscation of property the value of which corresponds to that of such proceeds, substances or instrumentalities*.

[17]The wording is identical to the one included in the framework decisions mentioned in the previous footnote; in particular to the longer version in the decision on drug trafficking, albeit without its reference to confiscation of crime profits: *e.g.* Directive 2014/62/EU of the European Parliament and of the Council of 15 May 2014 on the protection of the euro and other currencies against counterfeiting by criminal law, and replacing Council Framework Decision 2000/383/JHA, art. 7; Directive 2011/36/EU of the European Parliament and of the Council of 5 April 2011 on preventing and combating trafficking in human beings and protecting its victims, and replacing Council Framework Decision 2002/629/JHA, art. 6; Directive (EU) 2017/541 of the European Parliament and of the Council of 15 March 2017 on combating terrorism, art. 18.

[18]In some EU regulations, the wording of the provisions on sanctions is even more general than what has been recalled in the two previous footnotes. They only require "effective, dissuasive and proportioned" sanctions, without any further specification: see Council Regulation (EC) No 2580/2001 on specific restrictive measures directed against certain persons and entities with a view to combating terrorism, art. 9; Council Regulation (EC) No 1338/2001 of 28 June 2001 laying down measures necessary for the protection of the euro against counterfeiting, art. 2.

[19]Council of Europe, Recommendation No. R (88) 18, Liability of enterprises for offences.

As to the observation that harmonization criteria are still totally vague as to what concerns sanctions for legal entities (referring to the hyper-general standard wording "effective, proportioned and dissuasive sanctions"), we deem it necessary to bring to the reader's attention some minimal needs that should be met as promptly as possible.

First, a supranational set of minimum sanctions should be identified: this should be sufficiently complete and distinguish at least between monetary fines, confiscation and interdictory sanctions. The actual usefulness of such a sketch does not rely upon their qualification as criminal, administrative or mixed/autonomous sanctions or upon their categorization as main or accessory sanctions. These are all issues strictly intertwined with choices that can continue being left to the national legal system and their traditional dogmatic scholarship.

Following this approach, it could be useful to identify, always at a supranational level, minimum and maximum thresholds for all monetary fines, interdictions and negative advertising. This would serve the need to avoid excessive distances, for better or worse, between the efficacy's degree of a single national legal system and the others.

Similarly, it would be desirable to widen the scope of research of a minimum shared value to rewarding effects of restorative behaviours and prevention of further offences. This would entail acknowledging the added value of tools like *compliance programs* and collaboration agreements. In a future perspective, we would advocate for the extension of known types of sanctions for legal entities, by adding forms of positive behaviour towards the communities hit by certain illicit acts of a determined corporation. E.g., for environmental crimes, one could fathom a form of restoration into the previous state of balance of a certain area ruined by the pollution produced by a single corporation.

Answering these needs will not be easy: scholarly reflections are tasked with the important duty to advance the debate on sanctions for legal entities. Let us remember the unforgettable *Klaus Tiedemann*, who considered the issue of legal entities' liability in recent years as "more of an issue of political will than of scientific analysis."[20] The usefulness of the present discussion seems to lie in reminding us all of the role still to be played by criminal law scholarship on these issues.

References

De Maglie, C. (2002). *L'etica e il mercato, La responsabilità penale della società* (p. 12 ff). Milano: Giuffrè Editore.

De Simone, G. (2012). *Persone giuridiche e responsabilità da reato*. Pisa: Edizioni ETS.

Eser, A. (2017). *Comparative criminal law* (p. 16). München: C. H. Beck.

[20]Tiedemann (2002), p. 17.

Gargani, A. (2006). La tendenza eccentrica della disciplina sanzionatoria di cui al d.lgs. n. 231/2001 tra 'ibridazioni' normative e nuovi sottosistemi. In P. Pisa (Ed.), *Verso una riforma del sistema sanzionatorio* (p. 79 ff). Torino: Giappichelli editore.

Gentile, G. (2009). *L'illecito colposo dell'ente collettivo. Riflessioni alla luce del Corporate Manslaughter*. Torino: Giappichelli.

Guerini, R. (2006). *La responsabilità da reato degli enti* (pp. 140–188). Siena: Sanzioni e loro natura.

Kremnitzer, M., & Ghanayin, K. (2001). Die Strafbarkeit von Unternehmen. *ZStW, 113*, 539.

Manacorda, S. (2008). La « parabole » de l'harmonisation pénale: à propos de dynamique d'integration normatives relatives à l'organisation criminelle. In M. Delmas-Marty, M. Pieth, & U. Sieber (Eds.), *Les chemins de l'harmonisation pénale* (p. 267 ff). Paris: Société de Législation comparée.

Militello, V. (2012). Il dialogo fra la dogmatica penale italiana e tedesca alla luce del contributo di Manfred Maiwald. *Rivista Italiana di Diritto e Procedura Penale*, 348 ff.

Militello, V. (2014). L'identità della scienza giuridica penale nell'ordinamento multilivello. *Rivista Italiana Di Diritto E Procedura Penale, LVII*(1), 118 ff.

Militello, V. (2015). *La rilevanza della nozione di organizzazione criminale nell'Unione europea: percorsi di armonizzazione*. Bruxelles: EU-Parliament Group Socialists & Democratics.

Mongillo, D. V. (2018). *La responsabilità penale fra individuo e ente collettivo*. Milano: Quaderni di diritto penale comparato, internazionale ed europeo.

Nieto Martin, A. (2008). *La responsabilidad penal de las personas juridicas: un modelo legislativo* (p. 37). Madrid: Iustel.

Pastor Muñoz, N. (2010). Europäisierung des Strafrechts und mitgliedstaatliche nationale Besonderheiten in der EU. *Goltdammer's Archiv für Strafrecht*, 86 ff.

Satzger, H. (2010). *Internationales und europäisches Strafrecht* (p. 123 ff). Baden-Baden: Nomos Verlagsgesellschaft.

Sieber, U. (2006). Strafrechtsvergleichung im Wandel. In U. Sieber & H. J. Albrecht (Eds.), *Strafrecht und Kriminologie unter einem Dach* (p. 94). Berlin: Duncker & Humblot.

Tiedemann, K. (2002). *Wirtschaftsstrafrecht in der Europäischen Union (Freiburg-Symposium)* (p. 17). Berlin, München: Köln.

Weyembergh, A. (2006). Le rapprochement des incriminations et des santiones pénales. *Rev Int Dr Pén, 77*, 188.

Proposal for Criminalization of Cyberbullying Among Children

Liat Franco and Khalid Ghanayim

July 2019 witnessed a ruling passed by the Tel Aviv District Court in a case involving two 13-year-old children who engaged in a FaceTime video call with their fellow 13-year-old female classmate. During this call, the parties also engaged in a game of Truth or Dare during which the female classmate engaged in certain activities of a sexualized nature after being asked to do so by the other two classmates. Among other things, the game required the female classmate to undress completely—at which point she was filmed by the other two classmates without her knowledge and consent. This nude video was later distributed by the classmates and caused their female classmate a great deal of suffering and humiliation. The court convicted the two male classmates of sexual harassment and sentenced them to 120 h of community service. The court was shocked by the defendants' young age: "reading [the materials involved in] this case caused us a great degree of sadness and pain; [our] eyes were repeatedly and instinctively drawn to the indictment header which relates the defendants' ages alongside the date in which the offense was committed, hoping that either of the two was mistaken. You cannot but enquire as to the source from which people of such a young age drew the ideas constituting the markedly ugly factual basis of this case." Nonetheless, the court decided to convict the defendants despite their young age: "the war against the demeaning video phenomenon must be total, and the courts must make their voices heard clearly and decisively. It is indeed unfortunate that the offenders' ages are becoming ever younger... if this is the "public" that commits these offenses, then the courts' words must be directed toward it and about it."[1]

[1] AAC (TA) 70841-03-19 The State of Israel v. M. (2019) in Hebrew.

L. Franco
Zefat Academic College, Safed, Israel

K. Ghanayim (✉)
Faculty of Law, University of Haifa, Haifa, Israel
e-mail: khalidg@law.haifa.ac.il

K. Ghanayim, Y. Shany (eds.), *The Quest for Core Values in the Application of Legal Norms*, https://doi.org/10.1007/978-3-030-78953-4_8

This article has been written against the background of a widespread phenomenon of social network violence among young adults and of the difficulties encountered by all strata of the legal system in identifying, indicting, and convicting minors of such behaviors.[2] With this in mind, the present article seeks to foreground harmful behavioral phenomena among male and female children which takes place on social networks and to present a rethinking of existing law.

The domain of social network violence among young adults contains other key players beside the perpetrators and the victims, such as the operators of the various websites and online services, the young adults' parents, teachers, and the education system. Nevertheless, the present article focuses on the definition of the harmful behavior itself and on the criminalization of the actual internet-based perpetrators without assuming that they are the only parties that should bear criminal liability.[3] An examination of the issue of criminal liability should consider the uniqueness of the digital medium, as well as the identity and age of both perpetrators and victims alongside the ramifications of long-term harms that have been recorded on social media.

Lest it be unclear, we wish to stress that the data presented hereunder as well as our suggested definition for cyberbullying as a phenomenon refers to children and young adults up to and including the age of 18 for a number of reasons. First, on account of the special place social networks occupy in their lives, which is, on the whole, more influential, more all-encompassing and more constitutive than in the lives of adults.[4] Second, on account of the criminal justice system's disparate treatment of minors as opposed to adults. Third, on account of the fact that there are legislators who define cyberbullying as a characteristic phenomenon associated with young adult behavior. Our suggested definition shall permit the victims and their environment (parents, teachers, and law enforcement authorities) to characterize criminal cyberbullying severe online behaviors that require legal interventions, as opposed to less offensive juvenile online behavior that is characteristic among children and young adults and requires handling within educational frameworks.

The law must not remain silent in the face of serious violence online despite the wide range of possible harms—from mere childish taunts to the encouragement of

[2]For an extensive discussion of this issue, see Franco L, Almog S, Ghanayim K (2021) A Social Network Childhood – A Lawless Domain, 2 *Researches in Regulations* 61–99 (2020) in Hebrew.

[3]It is possible that parents, teachers, and professionals who have been made aware of severe cases of cyberbullying may be made criminally liable (via duty of reporting).

[4]The children and young adults forming this generation are known as "digital natives," and are profoundly different when compared to their parents, who may be considered "digital immigrants." See Palfrey J (2008) Born Digital: Understanding the First Generation of Digital Natives. Basic Books, New York; Prensky M (2011) Digital Wisdom and Homo Sapiens Digital. In: Thomas M (ed) Deconstructing Digital Natives: Young People, Technology, and the New Literacies. Routledge, New York, p 15–29. As a population, children are considered technologically superior when compared to its surrounding adult population, and one in three internet users is currently estimated as being <18 years old. See Livingstone S, Carr J, and Byrne J (2016) One in Three: Internet Governance and Children's Rights. Innocent Discussion Paper No. 2016-01. UNICEF Office of Research, Florence.

suicide—and all the more so given its unique characteristics which include the ages of those involved: the bullies, the bystanders, and the victims themselves, as well as the extent of the harm in terms of its wide-ranging and persistent visibility; the damages of cyberbullying are not only long lasting due to the but also constant—the offensive content is posted over digital platforms 24 h a day with no place to hide.

A legislative reading of cyberbullying gives rise to a distinction between three types of laws: (1) laws created to provide the education system with tools for handling the phenomenon, such as mandatory reporting and educational measures to be implemented against perpetrators, as well as the provision of tools to victims which facilitate a proper handling of the harms of cyberbullying[5]; (2) laws that require content providers to remove harmful messages and which also make these providers criminally liable[6]; and (3) laws which imbue cyberbullies with criminal liability—the latter being the creators and distributors of harmful messages.[7] Our present discussion is concerned with the third type of liability, viz. the criminal liability of cyberbullies.

It is important to note that the present article does not argue that we are concerned with a new kind of epidemic with no cure and does not seek to give rise to a "moral panic," but rather to discuss the kind of bullying committed by children and young adults on social networks.[8]

---

[5]The US state of Wisconsin, for example, is threatening to pass a law that will require teachers to pay a fine if they do not respond to cyberbullying. See Associated Press, Wisconsin Educators Wary of Plan to Fine Teachers for Ignoring Bullying (2013) Milwaukee-Wisconsin Journal Sentinel (21.3.2013). http://archive.jsonline.com/news/education/wisconsin-educators-wary-of-plan-to-fine-teachers-for-ignoring-bullying-8j98iik-199374821.html/

[6]Consider, for example, the case of a 14-year-old girl from northern Italy, Carolina Picchio, who committed suicide after a series of cyberbullying incidents. On the day of her suicide, Picchio received more than 2600 harmful and denigratory messages via the WhatsApp mobile application. See Wedeman B (2013) Facebook May Face Prosecution over Bullied Teenager's Suicide in Italy. CNN Breaking News (July 31, 2013). http://edition.cnn.com/2013/07/31/world/europe/italy-facebook-suicide. This case, in turn, led the Italian government to pass a law which makes content providers liable for removing harmful content if they have been made aware of its existence.

[7]Consider, for example, Amendment No. 10 to Israel's Prevention of Sexual Harassment Law, 5758 – 1998. This amendment was passed in January 2014, and is also known as the "Video Law"—and was actually designed to specifically handle violent online behaviors which involve some aspect of sexuality. The amendment appears in §3(a)(5a) of the Prevention of Sexual Harassment Law and states that one of the acts construed as sexual harassment is: "the publication of a photograph, video, or recording of a person which focuses on that person's sexuality, under circumstances calculated to humiliate or demean said person, who did not consent to said publication..." Prevention of Sexual Harassment Law (Amendment No. 10) 5774 – 2014 S.H. 263 (hereafter referred to as the "Video Law").

[8]While we refrain from defining the phenomenon of cyberbullying as an epidemic, there are scholars of child and adolescent behavior, such as Amos Rolider, who refer to it as such. See Eli Ashkenazi: "'A widespread epidemic:' More than 50% of our children experience cyberbullying" (2015) Walla!News (13.5.2015). https://news.walla.co.il/item/2853874 (Hebrew). 'Moral Panic' is a term first coined in 1830, but one which became widely publicized when it was used by British sociologist Stanley Cohen in a 1972 study of adolescents and the media. See Cohen S (1972) Folk Devils and Moral Panics. MacGibbon & Kee, London. Within the range extending between

Furthermore, the phenomenon does not appear to be transitory given that young adults have adopted the Internet as an inseparable part of their lives. Moreover, and given the increasing accessibility of mobile devices and computers, we are safe in assuming increased exposure to cyberbullying at ever earlier ages.

The fact that young adults spend a long time in the online domain and the considerable increase in the commission of offenses associated offensive behaviors, namely cyberbullying, casts doubts on the suitability of existing legal regulation. If it is indeed no longer suitable, it is worth considering a new type of legal regulation, such as the purpose-made legislation of a dedicated "cyberbullying" offense, or the adaptation of existing legislation, and all the while taking the characteristics of the young adult population and the technology concerned into account.

In what follows, we seek to offer a new model for handling cyberbullying among young adults centered on the formulation of three "**aggravating categories**," that would facilitate the examination of violent online acts as acts justifying criminalization. These would be the harmful communication's **extent of sexuality, degree of intensity, and extent of violence**, with one of the three sufficing for the application of the criminal offense. The aggravating categories are meant for distinguishing between anti-social behaviors which should not be criminalized and which require extra-criminal, and even extra-legal handling, and anti-social behaviors that constitute severe and substantial violations of social values and thus necessitate criminal regulation.

1 The Increasing Use of Social Networks Among Young Adults

A discussion of cyberbullying committed by young adults on social networks that seeks to handle the phenomenon in a juridical manner is insufficient if it only examines the phenomenon by analyzing individual cases and treats the problem as a localized phenomenon. The problem must also be analyzed as a sociocultural and communal phenomenon, as well as an institutional problem, and the discussion must

defining the phenomenon as an epidemic and giving rise to a moral panic, we seek to argue that we are concerned with a significant phenomenon which is widespread and which exerts serious effects on children and young adults. For an extensive discussion of this, see Heiman T, Olenik Shemesh D, Eden S (2014) Violence and Harms on the Internet – Characteristics, Patterns, Risk Factors and Protective Factors among Children and Young Adults (Ministry of Education Research Report, 7 January 2014): https://ecat.education.gov.il/%D7%90%D7%9C%D7%99%D7%9E%D7%95%D7%AA-%D7%95%D7%A4%D7%92%D7%99%D7%A2%D7%95%D7%AA-%D7%91%D7%A8%D7%A9%D7%AA-%D7%94%D7%90%D7%99%D7%A0%D7%98%D7%A8%D7%A0%D7%98-2 (Hebrew). This study included 1094 elementary, junior high and high school students, and found that 27% of the respondents were harmed by cyberbullying. We have chosen to focus on Facebook and on WhatsApp as the baseline for our discussion, but this choice should not be seen as possessing any further significance, since most social networks are similar in character.

also, *inter alia*, rely on theories concerned with the interrelations of law and culture.[9] However, the present article does not presume to engage in such an in-depth cultural analysis, but rather discusses in general outlines the role of culture as a necessary background for discussing the need for a dedicated legal definition.

Technology is presently readily accessible to children, and a number of US studies have found that the extensive use of smartphones has further increased the extent of Internet use. In Israel, 81% of children begin using mobile devices when they are <12 years old,[10] and 83% of respondents aged 8–15 own a smartphone.[11] Data concerning Internet use patterns in Israel reveal that 91% of 12–17-year-olds use the Internet every day, with the average age of initial Internet access being 7.[12]

The lion's share of young adults' time online is spent using social networks—creating content, sending and receiving instant messages, and visiting profiles.[13] A significant percentage of Israeli and US young adults enjoys readily available Internet access and uses social networks[14] on a daily basis.[15] We are therefore confronted with a phenomenon involving considerable amount of time per day in which the Internet in general and social networks in particular provide a platform that constitutes a 'living environment' and a chief source of entertainment for most

---

[9]Our discussion in the present article treats children under the age of 18 as a uniform group and does not separate children and young adults, with the jurisprudentially relevant point of separation being the age of criminal responsibility (in Israeli law, this is established by §34(f) of the Penal Code 1977). The development of a solution incorporating the dedicated criminalization of cyberbullying offense among young adults might also gain from the consideration of such theories as the "developing skills," theory while taking a specific minor's age and degree of maturity into account, or—alternately—creating a hierarchy of ages that would be treated differentially.

[10]See Mann R, Lev-On A (2014) Annual Report: Israeli Media 2014: Agendas, Uses, and Trends, p 81 in Hebrew.

[11]Sarid Institute (2015) Results of a Survey of Smartphone Use among Children: https://www.isoc.org.il/wp-content/uploads/2015/02/sarid_institute_january_2015_kid_cellphone_survey.pdf (Hebrew).

[12]See Israel Internet Association (2012) Perceptions of and Standpoints on Online Dangers among Children and Young Adults. Database on the Israeli Internet: http://data.isoc.org.il/data/297 (Hebrew).

[13]Ibid. It is worth noting that data from elsewhere in the world are similar: 95% of American young adults use the Internet, and 74% of them do so via a mobile device. See Hinduja S, Patchin J W (2016) 2016 Cyberbullying Data. http://cyberbullying.org/2016-cyberbullying-data

[14]A 2015 study found that 76% of US young adults aged 12–17 use social networks, while more than 90% of Israeli 12–14-year-olds do the same.

[15]A survey conducted by the Teenk marketing company reveals that young adults spend an average of 3.8 h a day on using social networks. See Weissblai E (2011) Children on Online Social Networks. The Knesset Research and Information Center. (Hebrew). Page 5 of Weissblai's study cites the Teenk Marketing Company's survey entitled "Young Adults – Media, Lifestyle, and Consumer Behavior – Quantitative Survey Findings, January-May 2010". See also the Israeli National Council for the Child (2010) Children in Israel 2010 – Statistical Yearbook (Hebrew). The January 2014 Ministry of Education Study report, supra note 7, suggests that children use their mobile devices for about 2.8 h a day (and another survey states that about a quarter of young adults use their mobile devices for more than 5 h a day. See the Sarid Institute Survey, supra note 11.

of the world's young adults.[16] In addition, we should not assume a reduction in the number of social network users, since we are concerned with networks which are constantly developing and increasing their number of users, the variety of the activities they offer and the range and diversity of devices which may be used for accessing them.[17]

Scholars have recently identified a change in young adults' Internet usage patterns and have noticed a shift from the use of digital media for consumption to their use as means of communication.[18] Some have referred to the social network domain as children's primary life domain—to an even greater extent than the physical domain.[19] As noted above, young adults mostly use the Internet for social purposes and spend most of their Internet usage time on interpersonal communication—usually for maintaining existing connections.[20] Consequently, the online era has transformed children and young adults from content consumers into content creators. The definition of "content creation" is complex and includes creating an avatar (a character which represents the user on the social network), writing a blog, distributing content via content distribution software, etc.,[21] but for the purposes of the present discussion we shall construe it as forming part of any communication: sending a message to an individual, writing a message in a group, distributing an image, etc. Children and young adult are thus presently capable of creating content that other people would be exposed to.

However, and alongside the advantages associated with content creation, such as the freedom of expression, the encouragement of participation in democratic discourse, etc., the content created by young adults might also be harmful. A study conducted in England found that 19% of 11–16-year-olds had been exposed to

---

[16]See Aizenkot D (2017) WhatsApp Shaming Among Children and Young Adults in Israel: A Pioneering Study, XX 358 (Hebrew).

[17]The number of active Facebook users in 2013 increased by 23% compared to 2012. See Number of Active Users is Growing Over the Years (2013) Yahoo News (1.5.2013). https://news.yahoo.com/number-active-users-facebook-over-230449748.html. The Israeli Ministry of Education is also planning to digitize the curriculum through the use of a learning scheme known as BYOD (Bring Your Own Device) and the transformation of schools into digitized organizations with a particular emphasis on the development of digital literacy. See the official Ministry of Education website at https://sites.education.gov.il/cloud/home/tikshuv/Pages/tikshuv.aspx (Hebrew). In implementing this program, participating schools will require the students to come to school with end user devices—tablets or smartphones—and use them during classes. For more on this, see https://sites.education.gov.il/cloud/home/tikshuv/Pages/isum_degem.aspx (Hebrew).

[18]See Third A et al. (2014) Children's Rights in the Digital Age: A Download from Children Around the World. http://aeema.net/WordPress/wp-content/uploads/2014/10/Childrens-Rights-in-the-Digital-Age.pdf

[19]See Aizenkot, supra note 16.

[20]See Boniel-Nissim M, Dolev-Cohen M (2012) Children Writing… on Walls: Facebook Culture. Studies and Research in Teacher Training, XIII, p 207–209 (Hebrew).

[21]Livingstone S, Haddon L, Görzig A, Ólafsson K (2010) Risks and safety for children on the Internet: the UK Report. p 19.

http://eprints.lse.ac.uk/43731/1/Risks%20and%20safety%20for%20children%20on%20the%20internet(lsero).pdf harmful content created by their social network "friends," and this percentage increased to 32% among young adult girls aged 14–16.[22] It is thus the case that young adults are often harmed by content created by other young adults rather than by content created by an adult stranger.[23]

Such harmful content is diverse, and may include rumors, threats, taunts, harassments, intimidation, and even content of a sexual nature.[24] It has been reported that a significant percentage of young adults transmit sexual images of themselves, receive sexual images and even send them to others.[25] It is possible to assume that the exchange and even the very exposure to sexual images at a young age are harmful in and of themselves,[26] regardless of the consent (or lack thereof) involved in the creation of such content in the first place.[27]

---

[22]Ibid, p 9. Similar findings were reported in Germany—See Cornelius K (2014) Plädoyer für einen Cybermobbing-Straftatbestand. ZRP 2014, 164. And in Australia—see Dwyer A, Easteal P (2013), Cyberbullying in Australian Schools: The Question of Negligence and Liability. ALTERNATIVE L.J. 38:92.

[23]See Ringrose J, Gill R, Livingstone S, Harvey L (2012) A Qualitative Study of Children, Young People, and "Sexting:" A Report Prepared for the NSPCC. p 8.

[24]See Wright M (2015) Cyber Victimization and Perceived Stress: Linkages to Late Adolescents' Cyber Aggression and Psychological Functioning. Youth and Society 47(6):790–792.

[25]A 2010 survey conducted at the University of Utah in the US and involving more than 600 male and female young adults aged 14–18 found that 20% of them transmitted sexual images of themselves as text messages, and that 40% of respondents admitted to receiving sexual messages, with more than 25% of these admitting that they sent these messages to others. See Strassberg D S, McKinnon R K, Sustaíta M A, Rullo J (2013) Sexting by High School Students: An Exploratory and Descriptive Study. Arch. Sex. Behav., Springer, 42(1):15. A British study indicates much higher percentages: 40% of young adult respondents reported that they knew someone who sent nude images, and 27% claimed that this is a regular and normal phenomenon which takes place all the time. See Phippen A (2009) Sharing Personal Images and Videos Among Young People. South West Grid for Learning. http://childnetsic.s3.amazonaws.com/downloads/Research_Highlights/UKCCIS_RH_10_Sexting.pdf. A 2015 Israeli survey involving 739 young adults found that at least half of them received a nude image, about half took nude pictures of themselves, and among these 40% sent these nude videos or pictures to others. See Ha'Baron E, Ha'Baron S (2017) What and When in Sexual Education: Guiding Principles for the Formulation of Sexual Education Programs for Young Adults in Israel: https://www.hebpsy.net/articles.asp?id=3570 (Hebrew). A 16-year-old boy from Southern Israel, for example, stated that "every school in town has nude pictures of girls. Every year group has them. It's like card games, kids exchange them. I'll send some to you and you'll send some to me." These images are occasionally sent after the payment of a 5 NIS fee. See Ben Dror A (2014) Are you Awake? Wake Up!. You [At] Magazine 60 (Hebrew).

[26]See Karniel Y, Wismonsky H (2007) Freedom of Expression, Pornography, and Community on the Internet, Bar-Ilan Studies in Law, XXXIII 259, 301 (Hebrew).

[27]It is also possible to argue that no true consent exists among children and young adults who are pressurized toward sending pictures and revealing details about themselves in order to stay relevant and up to date in relation to their peer group.

2 The Extent of Cyberbullying Among Children and Young Adults

Many perceive cyberbullying as an epidemic.[28] As shall be detailed below, the distribution and frequency of the phenomenon serve to illustrate that existing laws do not provide a proper response to cyberbullying. A message may be harmful in a number of ways, and children use the technological means at their disposal in order to create harmful content via a wide range of means such as spreading rumors, making threats, taunting, harassing, and intimidating.[29] Studies concerned with the frequency of cyberbullying report percentages ranging between 10% and 40% with respect to children and young adults who have been victims this phenomenon, with the gap explained by the lack of uniformity in defining cyberbullying,[30] as well as by variances in the measurement methods involved.[31]

A 2015 Israeli survey conducted among 1295 3rd–9th graders found that 47% of respondents reported experiencing online taunts (as opposed to 69% who experienced taunting in their school's physical domain).[32] An additional study submitted to the Ministry of Education in January 2014 reveals that 27% of the participants, which included 1094 students from 18 schools throughout Israel, reported being the victims of cyberbullying (as opposed to 49% who reported being the victims of face-to-face violence). Furthermore, 46% of the study's participants witnessed violent online communication directed at another person.[33] Despite the difficulty associated with collecting data about other Israeli populations (Ultra-Orthodox Jewish

[28]Protocol of Meeting No. 43 of the Science and Technology Committee, the 19th Knesset, 20 (May 12, 2014) (hereafter: Science and Technology Committee Protocol 43). Also see Public Health Problem Injury Prevention and Control: Division of Violence Prevention: Electronic Aggression. http://www.cdc.gov/violenceprevention/youthviolence/electronicaggression

[29]See Wright, supra note 24, p 790; also see Aizenkot, supra note 16, p 360.

[30]See Kowalski R M, Giumetti G W, Scheroeder A N, Lattaner M R (2014) Bullying in the Digital Age: A Critical Review and Meta-Analysis of Cyberbullying Research Among Youth. Psychol. Bull. 2014 (140):1074, 1108.

[31]See Mitchell K J, Jones L M, Turner H A, Shattuck A, Wolak J (2016) The Role of Technology in Peer Harassment: Does it Amplify Harm for Youth?. Psychology of Violence 6(2):193.

[32]See The National Insurance Institute (2017) Young Adults Online - Dangerousness and Opportunity for Introducing Care, pp 3–4. https://www.btl.gov.il/Publications/Kranot/Documents/kranot_5.pdf (Hebrew). The types of bullying reported by the child and young adult respondents were classified as social exclusion and humiliation, verbal harm, and deception—40% reported being subjected to insults, 37% were the victims of mockery and ridicule, and 35% reported being called offensive names; 29% were excluded by a digital group, 22% were the subjects of a humiliating message, and a harmful virtual group was set up against 10%; 25% of the respondents were subjected to internet deception, 20% reported that they were subjected to threats, and 12% reported that they were the victims of imposture in online communications. Also see Ephraim O, Chai S, Zagrizak A, Rimmerman R (2017) Report: Suicide Attempts, More Poverty, and More Criminal Acts Among Young Adults, Ynet, January 16 2017. https://www.ynet.co.il/articles/0,7340,L-4907756,00.html (Hebrew).

[33]See the January 2014 Ministry of Education Report, supra note 8.

populations, Arab-Israeli populations, and various National-Religious Jewish populations), the figures appear to be similar for these populations too.[34] Another study, conducted in 2017 and including 1111 4th–12th graders, reveals that 30.7% of the respondents were victims of shaming (another term employed for describing cyberbullying) on their class's WhatsApp group.[35] In addition, there are studies indicating that 10–15 years of age is the age range at which children and young adults are most exposed to cyberbullying.[36] Moreover, we estimate that the percentage of children harmed by cyberbullying is much greater than the data presented above suggest on account of the reporting difficulties we discussed above and given that victims of cyberbullying are not limited to the direct victims themselves, but also include male and female children and young adults who are exposed to the violent and harmful communication as bystanders,[37] or even direct victims that fail to recognize they are victims of offensive behavior due to the commonality of offensive online communication. Exposure to violent material might also be harmful toward them and affect their attitudes toward themselves and toward their online domain, which they subsequently perceive as hostile and unsafe.[38]

---

[34]It is interesting to note that complaints about cyberbullying are even more widespread among the Arab-Israeli population. About 28% of the communications on this issue that reach the Israel Internet Association come from the Arab-Israeli population, a percentage that is comparatively higher than the relative size of their population compared to the size of the Israeli population as a whole. See Science and Technology Committee meeting (2018) Protocol no. 185 of the Knesset Science and Technology Committee meeting "Marking the [National] Fight against Violence and Crime in Arab-Israeli Society Day", 20th Knesset (July 10 2018) (Hebrew). There is a lack of data concerning Internet use patterns among Ultra Orthodox Jewish young adults, but it seems that the Internet is a great source of attraction to at-risk Ultra-Orthodox young adults and to Ultra-Orthodox young adult dropouts from Ultra-Orthodox Jewish educational frameworks, since it permits the expression of flexibility and liberation from conventions and rules even as it also increases the chances of exposure to such inappropriate content as cyberbullying. See Friedman C (2017) Cyberbullying. PsychoActual, p 17 (Hebrew). Also see the Henrietta Szold Institute - The National Institute for Research in the Behavioral Sciences (2016) Young Adults Online - Dangerousness and Opportunity for Introducing Care: Literature Review and Interviews with Key Personalities, p 14 (Hebrew).

[35]Shaming is defined as a deliberate aggressive action calculated to harm another person on the Internet via the use of technological means of communication. See Aizenkot, supra note 16, p 357 and at p 366.

[36]See Kowalski, supra note 30, p 1112.

[37]See Database on the Israeli Internet, (2014) Survey Concerning Internet [Use] Among Young Adults. http://data.isoc.org.il/data/563 (Hebrew).

[38]A study published by Almog and Franco reveals that the circle of victims of cyberbullying is far wider than the victims themselves. Male and Female children who know the victim her or himself find it difficult to go back to normal, and report feeling that the online domain is unsafe for them, and that they could be exposed to harm at any given moment. See Franco L, Almog S (2019) Precarious Childhood: Law and Its (Ir) Relevance in the Digital Lives of Children. Penn State Journal of Law and International Affairs 7(1):54.

Cyberbullying as a phenomenon among young adults is widespread and might give rise to such phenomena as diminished educational achievement,[39] depression, loneliness, low self-esteem, anxiety, eating disorders, psychiatric disorders, health implications,[40] and in extreme cases even suicide.[41] A survey conducted by the Israeli Child Welfare Institute [IBC] founds that 47% of respondents experienced suicidal thoughts as a result of online harassment, and 36% knew someone who tried to harm her or himself as result of shaming or cyberbullying.[42]

3 Characteristics of the Technology as Behavior Definers and Shapers

It should go without saying that we do not ascribe young adult violence to technology; young adult violence had existed and was commonplace long before the age of social networks and still exists besides them.[43] This notwithstanding, we still argue that the character and characteristics of Internet use, and especially social network use, facilitates the existence of harmful group discourse, both visual and textual, and even encourages it. The mutual relations between technology and society, in turn, have given rise to a wide ranging legal and social discourse incorporating several schools of thought.[44] However, it is clear that we are concerned with a wide-ranging social phenomenon that is fed by the technology itself and operates from within and based on its characteristics. In addition, the socio-technical combination is what, *inter alia*, facilitates the harmful reality that the present article wishes to define and for which it seeks to offer a mitigation policy.

---

[39]See Nansel T R, Craig W et al. (2004) Cross National Consistency in the Relationship between Bullying and Psychological Advancement. Arch. Pediatr. Adolesc. Med. 158(8):730.

[40]See Sansone R A, Bohinc R J, Widerman M W (2015) Childhood Bullying and Healthcare Adherence in Adulthood. International Journal of Social Psychiatry 1.

[41]See Bhat S C (2008) Cyber Bullying: Overview and Strategies for School Counsellors, Guidance Officers, and All School Personnel. Australian Journal of Guidance and Counselling 18(1):53, 56; Cyberbullying Statistics New Zealand (Apr. 15, 2015). https://m.recoveryonpurpose.com/upload/Cyberbullying%20Overview%20and%20Strategies%20Australia.pdf

[42]Henrietta Szold Institute, supra note 34, p 9.

[43]According to the January 2014 research report submitted to the Ministry of Education, supra note 8, p 36, where it is revealed that 49% of Israeli young adults have experienced physical violence.

[44]Such as the Social Construction of Technology (SCOT) approach, which points out the effects society and human agents exert on technology. See Dror Y (2011) Social Construction of Technology: On the Way in which Values, Laws, and Enforcement are Embedded in Technology, p 79, 80 (Hebrew). Another school of thought is known as the Social Shaping of Technology (SST) school. It argues that a tight relation exists between society and technology, meaning that both are intertwine and feed on each other to such an extent as to become a single entity a "socio-technical" system. See Bracha O (2011) Hale and Foucault in the Digital Domain: Power, Technology, and the Law in the Information Society, Reshet Mishpatit, p 117, 119.

The Internet as a technology and social networks as a technological platform can be identified as "defining technologies:" the digital domain, on account of its unique characteristics (distribution, replication, manipulation, etc.), affects behavior to such an extent so as to determine and define the unique behavioral characteristics that should be moderated.[45] In other words, the technological capacities manifested in social networks allow new behaviors to exist, and in fact re-define them. In this case, the expression "the medium is the message" becomes all the more relevant.[46] The technology's characteristics shape the behaviors that take place within it, affect them, and thus renders them an inseparable part of the message. When compared to behaviors in the physical domain, harmful behavior in the digital domain presents unique characteristics: we are concerned with a behavior that is entirely unlimited by time and space, that does not have an "expiry date," whose target population is unlimited and occasionally unknown, and in which distributed messages are open to unlimited modification and shaping. The convenient and immediate use of social networks therefore allows cyberbullies to give rise to persistent and wide-ranging harm that is intensified by technological characteristics.[47]

At times, the transition to a digital environment transforms the meaning of traditional physical domain jurisprudence in a dramatic fashion, and it might be the case that such a transition requires a new definition of proscribed Internet behaviors such as to necessitate the expansion of criminal law.[48] In fact, an examination of cyberbullying through the prism of unique technological characteristics reveals that we must acknowledge the fact that the medium itself, the Internet domain in general and social networks in particular, act as a separate component which contributes to the intensification of cyberbullying as a phenomenon.

---

[45]Almog, supra note 38, p 15.

[46]This is a concept that was coined by Marshall McLuhan, one of the founding fathers of media studies as an academic discipline. See McLuhan M, Fiore Q (1967) The Medium is the Message. New York, p 123.

[47]Passive participants can become part of the harming party by sharing the violence with more of their online friends or by clicking the 'Like' button. Data published in 2015 reveal that 43% of 12–17 year-old adolescents shared, 'Liked,' or distributed images containing harmful content within the online domain. See selection of data from Children in Israel – 2015, §407, p 36. https://web.archive.org/web/20160731204408/http://children.org.il/Files/File/SHNATON/Leket2015.pdf (Hebrew). Moreover, the online domain gives rise to an illusion of anonymity alongside invisibility and the distance between the discourse participants contribute toward the occurrence of a disinhibition phenomenon which manifests as less restrained behavior, openness, authentic sharing, and a heightened expression of emotions and needs that are often concealed, such as the expression of severe criticism or anger and hate. Meyran Boniel-Nissim, *Me'afyeney Ha'Tikshoret Ba'Internet* [*Characteristics of Internet Communication*], *SHEFINET* (2013), http://cms.education.gov.il/NR/rdonlyres/7618EA9F-94B8-4C9D-8F55-19FE6C818B0A/88036/mefyaneiTikshoretbeinternet.pdf

[48]Almog, supra note 38, p 15–18.

Despite the similarity between patterns of cyberbullying and online victimhood and bullying in the physical domain,[49] social network "friends"—both harming parties and victims—are affected by the characteristics of the technology involved despite knowing each other. These characteristics allow them to hide behind their computer screen and reach tens of thousands of children anywhere and at any time. As stated by the Israeli Supreme Court: "the immediate availability, the anonymity, and the ability to initiate contacts with many victims, as well as the slim chance of getting caught render sexual offenses in the Internet arena even more dangerous than in the real world."[50] We believe that the characteristics of the online domain as described hereunder render not just sexual offenses but any kind of harmful online behavior even more violent and dangerous than harmful behavior taking place in the physical domain. As noted above, the Internet domain does indeed constitute a "defining technology" that affects and shapes harmful behavior in such a manner as to necessitate a rethinking of existing legislation.

4 The Lack of Supervision and the Lack of Reporting as Aggravating Factors with Respect to Cyberbullying

The availability and accessibility of the technology at almost any time and almost anywhere, as well young adults' use of smartphones, only permits a limited degree of parental supervision. Indeed, parents are considered 'digital immigrants' while their children are referred to as 'digital natives.'[51] In other words, children are more familiar and more capable of orienting themselves in the digital domain, and on social networks, compared to their parents. In fact, parents are often absent from this domain altogether. This absence might also explain the scope of the cyberbullying. In this respect, Cohen and Felson's routine activity theory argues that the chances of harm increase in the presence of suitable victims and the lack of efficient supervision.[52] With such a lack of efficient supervision and the ability to engage in mass

[49]Studies show that adolescents who reported engaging in violent behavior toward others were 2.5 times more likely to engage in cyberbullying. This finding is also true with regard to victims. See Zhou Z, Tang H, Tian Y, Wei H, Zhang F, Morrison C M (2013) Cyberbullying and its risk factors among Chinese high school students. School Psychology International 34(6):630–647. Also see Hinduja S, Patchin J W (2008) Cyberbullying: An exploratory analysis of factors related to offending and victimization. Deviant Behavior 29(2):129–156.

[50]CA 707/14 Anonymous v. The State of Israel (2015), para 19 of Justice Mazuz's decision (2015).

[51]Palfrey J, Gasser U (2008) Born Digital: Understanding the first generation of digital natives. Basic Books, New York. Also see Prensky M (2011) Digital wisdom and homo sapiens digital. In: Thomas M (ed) Deconstructing digital natives: Young people, technology and the new literacies. Routledge, New York, pp 15–29.

[52]See Tsur I et al. (2016) Cyberbullying among Young Offenders Cared for by the Juvenile Probation Service, Society and Welfare XXXVI(1), 41 in Hebrew.

communication, harming parties are thus provided with an opportunity to harm many victims.[53]

The lack of supervision not only explains the phenomenon's existence, but also indicates its deficient handling. Indeed, parents are not a party involved with coping with online harm in most cases.[54] As things stand, parents are insufficiently involved, are not accountable for their children's online activity and are unaware of the latter group's online conduct.[55]

As a matter of fact, the environment's response—parents' and teachers'—contributes toward the continued existence of cyberbullying.[56] There is a great deal of confusion and uncertainty concerning the school's role insofar as incidents cyberbullying are concerned, and concerning the role of teachers and the limits of their authority with respect to what happens to their students while they are online.[57] In addition, cyberbullying does not leave visible external signs on its victims, and technological barriers limit the possibilities for effective supervision over the social network domain by teachers who are not members thereof.[58] The lack of reporting to teachers and parents can be explained by the child-victim's sense of embarrassment, by the fear that reporting to parents will lead to the revocation of the victims' Internet access,[59] and by the fear of parents of being unable to help the victims in the Internet domain. The victim may thus be led to cope with serious harm or threat of harm on her or his own.[60] These characteristics intensify the phenomenon's severity, the intensity of the harm inflicted, and the difficulty of acting against it. In more than one sense, cyberbullying is thus severer than traditional bullying, leading the Internet domain to become the scene of serious harm.[61]

Even when the environment is made aware of cases of cyberbullying, it often refrains from responding to these with due seriousness since they take place in the virtual rather than the physical world, and are thus perceived as being less invasive

---

[53]Ibid, p 42.

[54]See Rolider A, Boniel-Nissim M (2015) School and Virtual Domain Bullying among Children: A Report of our Findings. https://www.isoc.org.il/wp-content/uploads/2015/06/bullying_2015.pdf (Hebrew).

[55]Henrietta Szold Institute, supra note 34, p 14).

[56]Studies reveal that teachers refrain from responding to cases of cyberbullying or tend to respond in an unsuitable manner. Young adults translate this lack of response into agreement with this kind of violent conduct. See Anagnostopoulos D, Buchanan N T, Pereira C, Lichty L F (2009) School Staff Responses to Gender-Based Bullying as Moral Interpretation. An Exploratory Study [of] Educational Policy 23(4):541.

[57]Henrietta Szold Institute, supra note 34, p 18.

[58]Despite being extremely rare, see the following German case for an example of an arraignment pertaining to cyberbullying: Schönmüller L (2014) Vom Schulhof ins Internet – Eine Analys des Phänomens Cybermobbing und wie ein Computerspiel davor schützen könnte. Bachelorarbeit, Hochschule Mittweida, p 34–35.

[59]See Heiman T, Olenik D (2011) On the Net – the Victim of Violence has Nowhere to Run To, The Open University: Articles/Studies, p 54, 29–33 (Hebrew).

[60]Hinduja, Patchin, Cyberbullying, supra note 13, p 3.

[61]Knesset, Science and Technology Committee Protocol No. 43, supra note 28, p 9.

than cases of physical violence.[62] Despite many who perceive cyberbullying as a clear symptom of contemporary youth culture with destructive implications, some adults perceive it as "trivial" behavior, and as an inseparable part of the maturation process. This gap, which more often than not exists between the victim's personal experience and the perceptions of her or his environment, might explain both the difficulty of enforcing existing laws as well as the unwillingness or inability of legislators to formulate policies pertaining to the online environment.[63]

Insofar as reporting is concerned, studies on this issue have found that young adults prefer seeking Internet-based aid over other means. For example, a 2014 study suggests that 25% of Israeli young adults up to the age of 17 contacted a source of Internet-based aid as opposed to 2% who contacted a source of phone based aid.[64] The primary strategies employed by young adults when they experience online harm or taunting is seeking help from a family member (20%), contacting the harming party and asking them to stop (17%), distancing themselves from the harming party (15%), and finally, contacting members of staff at their school (12%).[65] In addition, data published in late 2016 by the Israel National Council for the Child,[66] indicate that a significant percentage of young adults harmed by cyberbullying chose not to report it: 40% of victims did not contact anyone for help and did not tell anyone about their experiences. 63% of victims who chose not to report their experiences noted that they refrained from reporting them because they did not perceive it as an issue of sufficient importance.[67] Furthermore, and as noted above, young adults rarely report cyberbullying incidents to their parents because they fear the revocation of their Internet access or because they believe that their parents cannot help them in such a case. A comparison between these action strategies and those employed by young adults when they are the victims of physical violence reveals that fewer coping strategies are available for online harm.[68] Generally speaking, it is apparent that young adult victims find it difficult to report cyberbullying, and various studies show that victims of cyberbullying are less likely to report the harms that had been

[62]See Terrance C, Logan A, Peters D (2004) Perceptions of Peer Sexual Harassment Among High School Students. Sex Roles 51(7–8):479.

[63]For the need for legislation, see Goldschmidt (2014) Cyberbullying Among Young Adults, The Knesset, Research and Information Center, pp 8–12 (Hebrew); Knesset, Science and Technology Committee Protocol No. 43, supra note 28, p 5–6; Protocol of Meeting no. 18 of the Knesset Science and Technology Committee entitled "Summary of the Issue of the Limits of Internet Discourse", 20th Knesset, 6–8 (October 13, 2015).

[64]Henrietta Szold Institute, supra note 34, p 13.

[65]It is important to compare these data with their physical bullying equivalents, where 43% of children harmed on school grounds contact their school for help. See Rolider, Boniel Nissim, supra note 54.

[66]See selection of data from the "Children in Israel – 2016" yearbook at http://fs.knesset.gov.il/20/Committees/20_cs_bg_367605.pdf (Hebrew).

[67]Ibid.

[68]See Rolider, Boniel Nissim, supra note 54.

inflicted on them.[69] The aforementioned underreporting, in turn, makes it difficult for educational staff and care providers to know about cases of cyberbullying and to handle them as is necessary.[70] We can conclude, therefore, that a lack of reporting is more characteristic of cyberbullying as opposed to physical violence, that this, in turn, makes it more difficult to handle cyberbullying properly, and consequently inflicts severe and ongoing harm on its victims.

5 Legal Aspects of Handling the Phenomenon of Violence Among Children and Young Adults

We believe the characteristics of the relevant technology as noted above might explain the intensity of its associated harms and the need for a rethinking of the phenomenon's definition and delimitation. This technology has led to a reduction in the costs of anti-social and destructive behavior, and to the infliction of harm at the touch of a button. Moreover, it has also led to the distribution of anti-social behavior to an extremely large number of people, that is, to the infliction of severe and intense harm on a victim with severer implications. Communication has thus become more vulgar, more visually aggressive, and more wide-ranging.[71] The touch of a button therefore allows the commission of serious violence with severe implications for both the victim and her or his surrounding environment. These changes in the 'cost-benefit' analysis might, in turn, indicate the need for novel legal responses unlike those that were formerly applied to this end to offline bullying.[72]

In February 2018, a meeting of the Knesset's Special Committee for the Rights of the Child was convened to discuss bullying among young adults. The cyberbullying phenomenon was defined as a severe phenomenon that needed to be handled and whose expansion must be addressed.[73] July 2018, in turn, saw the publication of a report of a committee issued by the Israeli Knesset which reviewed the authorities'

[69]See Heirman W, Walrave M (2008) Assessing concerns and issues about the mediation of technology cyberbullying. Cyberpsychology: Journal of Psychosocial Research on Cyberspace 2 (2). Also see Stewart D M, Fritsch E J (2011) School and Law Enforcement Efforts to Combat Cyberbullying. Preventing Sch. Failure 55:79, 84.

[70]See Rolider, Boniel Nissim, supra note 54.

[71]See Chaffin S M (2008) The New Playground Bullies of Cyberspace: Online Peer Sexual Harassment. Howard L.J. 51:773, 774; Franek M (2006) Foiling Cyberbullies in the New Wild West. Educ. Leadership 63:39–40.

[72]See Kumar Katyal N (2001) Criminal Law in Cyberspace. U. Penn. L. Rev. 149:1003, 1006.

[73]See Protocol of Meeting no. 204 of the Knesset Special Committee for the Rights of the Child entitled "Cyberbullying among Children and Young Adults," 20th Knesset (February 26, 2018).

handling of the offenses associated with publishing sexualized images, recordings, or videos without the subject's consent.[74]

Israeli law applies physical domain offenses, such as the offenses of intimidation and defamation, to violent behavior in the online domain. In addition, an amendment to the Prevention of Sexual Harassment Law known as the "video law" was passed in January 2014. This amendment states that "the publication of an image, video, or recording of a person which focuses on said person's sexuality" without the subject's knowledge constitutes sexual harassment punishable by a maximum of 5 years' imprisonment.[75] According to a statement provided by Adv. Gaël Azriel of the Ministry of Justice,[76] in the course of a meeting of the Knesset's State Control Committee, the video law was primarily meant for young adults.[77] The law was considered a global breakthrough, and was viewed with interest by other parliaments, such as the US Congress, the Italian Parliament, the British Parliament, the Swedish Riksdag and the UN Human Rights Committee.[78] February 2017 guidelines from the Israel State Attorney's Office stated that "there exists an actual public interest in enforcing the video law even where the offenders concerned are minors with no criminal record. This is due to the severe harms caused by the offense and its far-reaching implications on the offense's victims, and due to the need to embed the criminal proscription even among young adults."[79]

There is an upwards trend in the offense's enforcement,[80] and the State Attorney's Office has defined the phenomenon of cyberbullying as a "national epidemic."[81] However, others believe that the law has been under-enforced,[82] due, among other things, to an under-reporting of the offense—<2% of cases involving severe

---

[74]Knesset Research and Information Center (2018) The Authorities' Handling Offenses Associated with the Publication of Images, Recordings, or Videos of a Sexual Nature without the Subject's Consent, July 12, 2018 (Hebrew).

[75]Also see the explanatory portion of the Prevention of Sexual Harassment Bill, 5773 – 2013, B. 516.

[76]At the time, Adv. Azriel worked in the Ministry's Counseling and Legislation Department and served as the Coordinator of the Ministry of Justice's Public Committee for the Formulation of Means of Protecting the Public from Harmful Publications.

[77]the State Control Committee (2015) Protocol of Meeting No. 33 of the State Control Committee entitled "Request for the State Comptroller's Opinion on the Elimination of the Violent Discourse in the Virtual Domain as Part of the Special Day Marking this Issue in the Knesset, 20th Knesset, p 15 (October 13, 2015) (hereafter referred to as State Control Committee Protocol No. 33).

[78]Ben Dror, supra note 25, p 60.

[79]State Attorney (2017) Interrogation and Arraignment in Offenses Involving the Publication of Sexualized Images, Recordings, or Videos of a Person without That Person's Consent, State Attorney's Guidelines 2.29, 7 (5777): .file:///C:/Users/HIGH-NET/Downloads/02.29.pdf (Hebrew).

[80]Protocol of Meeting No. 33 of the State Control Committee, supra note 77, p 15.

[81]Israel State Attorney's Guidelines, supra note 79.

[82]Law, and Justice Committee (2015) Protocol of Meeting No. 45 of the Knesset Constitution "Distribution of Humiliating Content and Videos on the Internet", The 20th Knesset, p 4 (October 13, 2015) (Hebrew). Also see Protocol of Meeting No. 18 of the Knesset Science and Technology Committee, supra note 63, p 8.

incidents of cyberbullying are reported.[83] In the course of a Knesset Constitution, Law, and Justice Committee meeting, Police Superintendent Gilad Bennett, Assistant Chief Counsel at the Ministry of Public Security's Cyber Operations Unit stated that while there was a significant increase in the law's enforcement—when compared to 2014, which witnessed the opening of 209 investigation cases throughout the entire year, the first half of 2015 had already witnessed the opening of 162 investigation cases. However, during the same meeting, Dr. Wismonski, the Head of the State Attorney Office's Legislation Division, claimed that only ten indictments pertaining to violations of this law were submitted on the basis of the aforementioned 162 investigation cases.[84]

Over and above the video law, Israeli law provides additional offenses that are applied to the digital domain on account of violent and harmful online behavior, and it is often the case that the distribution of videos involves the commission of a number of offenses.[85] We shall now turn to an analysis of these offenses and shall examine their suitability to acts of cyberbullying.

1. **The Defamation Offense**: there is little doubt that the offenses of defamation and the violation of privacy also apply to publications in the online domain. The definition of the concept of "publication" is wide enough to also encompass Internet publications. Moreover, the characteristics of "perpetuity" and "wide distribution" increase the harm inflicted on a person's good reputation and privacy.[86] However, it should be noted that the enforcement of criminal **defamation** laws is very much lacking in spite of the fact that 27% of young adults are exposed to cyberbullying,[87] and only one criminal case for this offense involving young adults was opened in 2014.[88] This deficient enforcement also reflects Israel Police Force policy, as expressed in the statement made by Police Commander Chayun, then head of the Israel Police Force's Cyber Operations Unit and

[83] See Nagar G (2015) Survey on Online Criminality/Cyberbullying, Israel Ministry of Public Security Research Department (Hebrew).

[84] Protocol No. 45 of the Knesset Constitution, Law, and Justice Committee, supra note 82, p 8, 14.

[85] A report prepared for the Knesset's Research and Information Center noted that additional offenses, including intimidation, violation of privacy, sexual offenses, extortion, the publication of obscenities, assault, grievous bodily harm, and abduction, were also committed over and above the main offense in two thirds of the investigation cases opened by the Israel Police Force on account of the distribution of harmful videos satisfying the criteria of the video law. These additional offenses might affect the subsequent handling of these investigation cases. See Knesset Research and Information Center (2018) The Authorities' Handling of Offenses Involving the Publication of Sexualized Images, Recordings, or Videos Without the Subject's Consent ("Video Law" [offenses]), Hebrew.

[86] CC (Petah Tikvah) 33837-09-13, The State of Israel v. Yossef Yitzchak Cohen (2015) ¶16, ¶24 (2015).

[87] See January 2014 Ministry of Education Research Report, supra note 7, p 32.

[88] Based on data obtained on February 9, 2015 from Police Sergeant Major Gila Kalderon, Coordinator of the Israel Police Force's Freedom of Information Unit and Public Complaints Unit, as a result of a Freedom of Information request.

currently the Commanding Officer of the Israel Police Force's Anti-Violence and Online Criminality Apparatus during an October 2015 meeting of the Knesset Science and Technology Committee entitled "The Elimination of the Violent and Bullying Discourse in the Virtual Domain and on Social Networks."[89] According to Chayun, there is a great difficulty present in enforcing this law due, among other things, to the lack of reporting among young adults in the online domain.[90]

2. **The Violation of Privacy Offense**: Existing law provides a protection of **privacy** from harm in the online domain, and courts have recently begun recognizing the immense damage present in the commission of privacy violations and their distribution on social networks, damage that is even greater than privacy violations committed in "the old world."[91] Data obtained from the Israel Police Force reveal that 112 cases concerned with the Violation of Privacy offense among young adults had been opened in 2014 (72 of these for the publication of a humiliating image).[92] This datum is particularly interesting when we compare the data to 2011, when 30 cases were opened for the Violation of Privacy offense (7 of these for the publication of a humiliating image). The considerable increase in the number of cases opened for the Violation of Privacy offense indicates the law's enforcement, and it is thus possible to assume that it protects people from harms that might be inflicted on them in the online domain.
3. **The Threat/Intimidation Offense**: The Intimidation offense requires the commission of an act in any fashion with a view to causing a person to fear harm to her or his body, liberty, property, good reputation or her or his livelihood or that of another person. The offense is behavioral, so it stresses the actual commission of the act: intimidation and threat. There is little doubt that this offense is suitable

[89]Protocol of Meeting No. 18 of the Knesset Science and Technology Committee, supra note 63, p 17.

[90]Also see the Protocol of Meeting no. 145 of the Knesset Committee on the Status of Women and Gender Equality (2017) The Powerless Enforcement of the 'Video Law'. The 20th Knesset (February 7, 2017). On p. 5, Adv. Revital Swid MK explains: "the thing which surprised me was the fact that despite the existence of a law which explicitly prohibits the distribution of harmful sexual content–not via video and not via [still] image–and despite the fact that this is punishable by five years' imprisonment, that it is an actual criminal offense, schools and junior high schools were not always aware of these facts. The victim did not always know [. . .] that she was a victim, and the victimizers, who are often her friends, did not always know it is a criminal offense [. . .] but the second difficulty we encountered was in fact with respect to our enforcement capacity. Whether this was because of a lack of ability or a difficulty associated with the ability to remove harmful sexual content since it had already been distributed online, [. . .] and the second thing that encountered difficulties was also the fact that --- perhaps the word [I should use] is not difficulty, but the fact that there was a certain degree of mercifulness since we are mostly concerned with youths and young adults."

[91]See CC (Petah Tikva) 33837-09-13 (2015) The State of Israel v. Cohen (2015); CAA 1728/17 Anonymous Person v. The State of Israel (2017); CJA 8878-08-16, The State of Israel v. A Minor (2017).

[92]The data were obtained on February 9, 2015 from Police Sergeant Major Gila Kalderon, Coordinator of the Israel Police Force's Freedom of Information Unit and Public Complaints Unit, as a result of a Freedom of Information request.

for application to online intimidation and it has indeed been enforced properly in the online domain since 2010 (3204 Intimidation cases were opened in 2010 compared to 3576 in 2014, of which 47 were opened on account of threats and intimidations on a social network).[93]

When we contacted the Israel Police Force's Freedom of Information Unit a second time in order to obtain more up to date data pertaining to the offense's enforcement in 2018, we were told that the Israel Police Force's systems do not employ "social networks" as a key for indexing offenses committed by minors.[94] Since there is no direct indexing of bills of indictment filed against children for offenses committed on social networks, our analysis is limited and is only made possible by way of a general comparison of the number of cases opened against children for offenses committed in 2017 as opposed to 2010.[95] The two offenses that exhibit a significant increase are the offenses of Sexual Harassment—the publication of a sexualized image, video, or recording of a person (the "video law")— and the Violation of Privacy offense. In 2017, 87 cases were opened against children for a video law offense as opposed to a mere 16 cases in 2014. Insofar as the Violation of Privacy offense is concerned, a total of 101 cases were opened against children in 2017, as opposed to 53 cases in 2010.[96] It is possible to assume that the source of this significant increase lies in the use of social networks. As a whole, it appears that there is a certain increase in the opening of cases for particular offenses (video law and Violation of Privacy), but this increase is limited to these offenses alone and is still far from reflecting the harmful reality experienced by children in the digital domain.

Data obtained from other sources also indicate very low enforcement rates. The statistical yearbook published by the Israel National Council for the Child "Children in 2018" indicates a decrease in the overall number of cases (criminal and conditional handling cases) opened against children who are alleged to have committed offenses against other children between 2009 and 2017—from 5328 in 2009 to 3511 in 2017.[97] Since 2014, for example, and despite the fact that studies had indicated

[93]Based on data that were obtained on February 9, 2015 from Police Sergeant Major Gila Kalderon, Coordinator of the Israel Police Force's Freedom of Information Unit and Public Complaints Unit, as a result of a Freedom of Information request.

[94]Based on data obtained on March 20, 2018 from Police Chief Inspector Adv. Sagit Shalev, Public Complaints Officer at the Israel Police Force's Public Complaints Unit, as a result of a Freedom of Information request.

[95]Ibid. The Defamation and Intimidation offenses do not present a significant difference. In 2017, a total of two Defamation cases were opened against children as opposed to a single case in 2010. Insofar as the Intimidation offense is concerned, a total of 3263 cases were opened against children in 2017 as opposed to 3162 cases in 2010.

[96]Ibid.

[97]See Israel National Council for the Child (2018) Statistical Yearbook Children in 2018 [Yeladim/ot Bi'Shnat 2018]. Selected Data File No. 10 (Hebrew) https://www.children.org.il/wp-content/uploads/2019/01/1.7.19-לקט.pdf

that 27% of children had reported being the victims of cyberbullying,[98] witnessed the opening of a mere 64 cases pertaining to children's violent and harmful behavior on social networks.[99] Given the extent of the phenomenon, we are obviously concerned with a minuscule enforcement rate.

6 The Proposed Model: Aggravating Categories

The Internet is not an "anarchy" or a "no man's land," but part of social life where criminal proscriptions still apply.[100] Freedom of speech is still protected on the Internet, as are other important interests.[101] However, the applicability of physical domain criminal prescriptions to cyberbullying requires certain adaptations arising from the technology's unique characteristics. In this respect, it should be noted that it is not merely the character of the child population that shapes the form of online communication, but also the characteristics and nature of the Internet itself that permit the existence of the visual and verbal harmful group discourse, and even encourages it.

The technology itself must be taken into account and manifested in the legal, legislative, and enforcement arenas too. We believe that the use of physical domain definitions therefore arises from a basic premise suggesting that physical and virtual domain behaviors are similar or comparable, while ignoring the unique effect exerted by technology. As a result, the establishment of a focused examination of the components, nature and severity of cyberbullying requires a new viewpoint.

---

[98]See the Ministry of Education Research Report, supra note 7, p 32.

[99]Forty seven cases were opened for the Intimidation offense, five cases for the Sexual Harassment via the Publication of an Image or Recording offense, a single case for the Defamation offense, and 11 cases for the Violation of Privacy offense. Based on data obtained on February 9, 2015 from Police Sergeant Major Gila Kalderon, Coordinator of the Israel Police Force's Freedom of Information Unit and Public Complaints Unit, as a result of a Freedom of Information request. It is important to note that in 2019 the National Online Child Protection Center was established in Israel. This center receives inquiries regarding cyberbullying from the public and it offers an array of responses- from mere consolation, removing offensive contents from the digital platforms, through filing a criminal charge. See https://www.gov.il/he/departments/child_online_protection_bureau. It has been reported that during the Coronavirus pandemic cyberbullying incidents reports rise at 60% (about 1000 reports on average a month). Nava Cohen-Avigdor, spokesperson for the National Online Child Protection Center stated that 67% of the reports are handled with 'criminal means'. Itszik Saban, An Alarming Increase in Calls to the Online Child Protection Center, Israel Hayom, 27.10.2020 https://www.israelhayom.co.il/article/813965. Even though statistics are not available yet, and we don't know the scope of 'criminal means', it is clear that the enforcement in the area of cyberbullying among children and youth is becoming stricter and wider.

[100]For a position that suggests the Internet as a place for freedom see Perry Barlow J (1996) A Declaration of the Independence of Cyberspace. https://www.eff.org/cyberspace-independence

[101]See Reno v. ACLU (1997) 521 U.S. 844; Lessig L (1996) Reading the Constitution in Cyberspace. Emory L.J. 45:869; Etzioni A (2004) On Protecting Children from Speech. Chi. Kent L. Rev. 79:3.

At this point, we must stress the tension between the considerations of danger and dangerousness present in these acts and considerations of guilt: **On the one hand**, the phenomenon of social networks, despite existing since 2004,[102] is a relatively new one, and it continues growing and contributing to the intensification of violent behavior among young adults. As noted above, it is very easy to commit acts of cyberbullying by typing on a keyboard at home or anywhere else via a smartphone, which is why certain social values are very gravely endangered by the commission of such acts. **On the other hand**, the technology also permits the infliction of harms at low costs; the significant ease involved in the commission of the dangerous acts, and the fact that the perpetrator is by her or himself and is not faced with a flesh and blood victim testifies to reduced guilt; the commission of these acts does not require effort on the part of the perpetrator, nor does it require any special planning or investment, which is another cause for reduced guilt. It therefore follows that the characteristics of the technology give rise to a reality which on the one hand presents an extremely severe danger on account of the acts but on the other hand and at the same time gives rise to a greatly reduced degree of guilt on the perpetrator's part. An in-depth examination of the technology's characteristics is required for the prevention of perversions of justice as well as cases involving the over-criminalization of the perpetrator.[103]

The need for a re-mapping of the phenomenon of cyberbullying and its definition has also recently arisen among enforcement authorities. In this respect, it seems that handling of the phenomenon by legislatures, the police, prosecutors, courts, teachers and parents is characterized by a lack of policy, lack of consistency, and a sense of helplessness. During the course of a May 2014 Knesset Science and Technology Committee meeting, (then) Police Chief Superintendent Meir Chayun, the head of the Israel Police Force's Cyber Operations Unit, stated that the Israel Police Force finds it difficult to act when it is required to deal with cases of violence among young adults originating in Facebook. This is mainly because, he argued, that there is no criminal law that classifies this behavior as a criminal offense.[104] Over and above problems associated with enforcement authority in offenses that take place on social networks, the very lacuna inherent in the non-definition of cyberbullying as a criminal offense makes it difficult for the Israel Police Force to act. During the same meeting, (then) Israel National Council for the Child Executive Director Dr. Yitshak Kadman, called for a significant revision of legislation, since the existing legislation was not suited for our new reality.[105] This point of origin and the focus on

---

[102]We are referring to the establishment of Facebook, the most popular social network of them all. See 10-K Annual Report (2016) SEC Filings. Facebook. https://yahoo.brand.edgar-online.com/DisplayFiling.aspx?TabIndex=2&dcn=0001326801-16-000043&nav=1&src=Yahoo

[103]See Almog, supra note 38, p 15–18; also see Elkin-Koren N, Birnhack M (2011) Legal Network: The Law and Information Technologies, p 14 (Hebrew); Also see Birnhack M (2010) Private Space: The Right to Privacy, Between Law and Technology, p 50–55 (Hebrew).

[104]Protocol No. 43 of the Knesset, Science and Technology Committee, supra note 28.

[105]Ibid., p 10. Dr. Kadman argued that the law was behind the new reality since commercials that were banned from broadcast television were being broadcast on the Internet.

violent online behavior's harmful potential leads to the formulation of three "aggravating categories" that take the characteristics of the technology and the characteristics of child and young adult behavior into account: sexuality, violence, and intensiveness. Here we are concerned with characteristics that further aggravate cyberbullying's anti-social nature and its perpetrator's guilt, which is why we have an aggravating characteristic (aggravating category) which justifies the phenomenon's very criminalization.

- **The Degree of Sexuality**. It is necessary to ask whether we are concerned with violent communication involving a sexual dimension. Put differently, we are concerned with the extent of sexuality in the harmful and/or violent discourse under consideration.[106]
- **The Degree of Intensity**. It is necessary to examine the harmful communication's degree of intensity. It is necessary to examine the number of harmful messages under consideration, the number of participants involved in their distribution,[107] whether it was recurring,[108] and whether it was accessible to many people and for a long period of time.
- **The Extent of Violence**. It is necessary to examine whether we are concerned with an actual threat to the victim and to determine its extent and the nature of the violence entailed. The more detailed and the more violent the harmful communication, the more likely the tendency toward its criminalization, while a communication that only gives rise to a suspicion of harm—might not, or at least should not, be criminalized.[109]

Only violent behaviors that satisfy at least one of these factors is a severe wrongful act that might be suitably handled as a criminal phenomenon and defines by criminal law.[110] Each aggravating category is a standalone factor that may aggravate the harm being inflicted. A sexualized online communication or one

[106]The Israeli regulator had acknowledged the unique aspect of sexual offences in the digital realm-regulating the video law-see note 75 above. We can refer to this law and adopt its fdefinition regarding what is considered 'sexual' and offensive in a sexual manner.

[107]For the distinction between an active participant who created the violent online content, and the passive participant who sent the publication to others, see Knesset, Science and Technology Committee Protocol no. 18, supra note 63, p 14; State Attorney's Guidelines, supra note 79, p 4–6.

[108]This would have to be examined on a case-by-case basis. The intensiveness metric may at times be satisfied when the distribution of a harmful message would be carried out numerous times, and at others when the message is distributed once, but to a group with a large membership.

[109]Akin to the discussion of the offense of incitement to violence as a suspicion and risk offense. See Kremnitzer M, Ghanayim K (1996) Incitement, not Sedition, p 41 (Hebrew).

[110]We argue that we must have an enforceable criminal tool that would act as a deterrent to young adults with respect to the commission of cyberbullying despite the high rates of recidivism among convicted and imprisoned young adults in Israel (75%). see Avgar I (2016) Rehabilitation of Juvenile Prisoners, The Knesset Research and Information Center, p 3–5. This is primarily because the phenomenon of cyberbullying is so widespread, and because we believe that a proper education and a focus on the delimitation of proscribed behaviors would lead to a reduction in the phenomenon's prevalence on the one hand and to a reduction in recidivism on the other hand.

which recurs intensively or one which is detailed in its violence is a communication that may inflict a great deal of harm on the victim. The other violent online behaviors that are not suited to these categories are "soft violence" or "childhood crimes" that require addressing and handling outside criminal law, i.e. via extra-criminal means.[111]

The three aggravating categories mostly address the unique characteristics of the technology we presented in the first chapter, and they are concepts from which it is possible to derive the severity of the behavior and to determine whether they require legal interventions with all that they entail. In a digital world where harm is measured by the intensity of the damage inflicted by a violent and harmful message, we believe that our chosen categories will accurately suggest severe cases of cyberbullying that justify criminalization: the extent of the harmful message's exposure, its violent nature, or its sexual character shall indicate the severity and intensity of harm inflicted on the victim. We believe that these categories would prove useful to enforcement authorities and to the courts themselves in determining whether a given behavior justifies criminalization and criminal labelling, or whether it requires some form of extra-judicial handling.

7 Conclusion

Given the centrality of technology in social life, and especially in the social lives of young adults, it is necessary to engage in a search for suitable solutions to the increasingly more prevalent phenomenon of cyberbullying in both the legal sense and in other senses. Cyberbullying is a social-communal phenomenon; it should not be viewed as a phenomenon that solely concerns young adults, and its elimination requires the rallying of all relevant professional parties in the education system, the enforcement apparatus, and the legal system, and should address the prevention of as well as interventions meant to address the harms being inflicted. We believe that focusing on the characteristics of the phenomenon, the characteristics of the digital domain in general and social networks in particular shall lead to a raising of awareness and to the possibility of intervening in severe cases of cyberbullying in an efficient and uniform manner. Moreover, the definition and delimitation of the behavior while focusing on categories which reflect the potential damage inflicted by a harmful message in the digital domain shall lead to an increase in the reporting of severe cases of cyberbullying and thus contribute to efficient enforcement. Parents, the educational framework, and enforcement authorities would be able to join forces while employing a uniform definition and acting toward the phenomenon's elimination. There is a need to provide a holistic and uniform response to the

[111]For these concepts, their relation to cyberbullying among young adults and criminal law, also see Brenner S W, a Rehberg M (2009) 'Kiddie Crime?' The Utility of Criminal Law in Controlling Cyberbullying. First Amend. L. Rev. 8:1, 29, 78–80.

cyberbullying as a phenomenon committed toward and by children and young adults. The commencement of this uniform handling via the adoption of a uniform definition of the phenomenon and an unambiguous understanding of the phenomenon's characteristics shall lead it toward being construed as a criminal offense. There is also a need for creating partnerships between the various parties involved in this field.[112] Indeed, the formulation of policies and legislation for handling cyberbullying is a matter of crucial importance.[113]

[112]Some degree of partnership between the various parties already exists; for example, there is a ministerial and inter-ministerial committee established by the Ministry of Education. In addition, the Ministry of the Interior established the MAOR (Prevention of cyberbullying and Criminality, Center, a civilian police center for the prevention of cyberbullying among minors, which includes a dedicated police unit charged with handling the phenomenon as well as a citizen hotline call center (reached by dialing 105 from any phone in Israel). This apparatus was primarily established to assist children and young adults who are harmed by cyberbullying and criminality, which is why it shall unify the resources and powers at the disposal of various state bodies and including civilian parties and Internet industry parties who will join the apparatus in handling the phenomenon. See Israel Ministry of Public Security (2016) The MAOR Apparatus, Prevention of cyberbullying and Criminality: https://www.gov.il/he/departments/Units/105_call_center (Hebrew). We believe that the establishment of this apparatus is a welcome development, but one that nonetheless does not address the juridical need for the behavior's definition and delimitation. The opposite is in fact true, since the apparatus' establishment will only make it even more necessary to formulate a proper juridical definition that would facilitate the effective handling of the phenomenon of cyberbullying.

[113]Kids Online Network (2014) (EU).

The German Network Enforcement Act on the Test Bench

Eric Hilgendorf

1 Genesis and Rationale

Combating hate speech poses significant challenges to the legal systems of the Western world. Up to now, enforcement of the law, ie prosecuting those responsible for the posting of unlawful content, has been time-consuming and difficult. Admittedly, in 2015, social network providers committed themselves to introducing user-friendly mechanisms to facilitate the reporting of such content in order to make it possible to examine them in context.[1] Unfortunately, this first step was insufficient to meet the demands of today's digital development and networking environment. Using the mechanisms put into place, it was simply impossible to identify and delete a high enough percentage of postings containing illicit content.

This state of affairs led to the German Parliament's adoption of the Network Enforcement Act ("NetzDG"),[2] the goal of which is to make it possible to efficiently monitor and quickly remove objectively illicit content from social networks. Thus, hate messages, for example those triggered by the refugee debate which has been ongoing since 2015, as well as so-called fake news, are to be curbed.[3] NetzDG requires social networks to introduce compliance measures to help resolve the above-mentioned problems.

[1]Liesching M (2018) § 1 NetzDG, Rn. 4. In Spindler G, Schmitz p (eds). TMG Kommentar, 2nd edn, C.H.Beck, Munich.

[2]Act to Improve Enforcement of the Law in Social Networks (hereonafter: Network Enforcement Act) (2017) (Germany).

[3]OLG München (The Higher Regional Court of Munich), 29 U 1156/17, BeckRS 2018, 8539, Rn. 37.

E. Hilgendorf (✉)
Julius Maximilians Universität, Würzburg, Germany
e-mail: hilgendorf@jura.uni-wuerzburg.de

K. Ghanayim, Y. Shany (eds.), *The Quest for Core Values in the Application of Legal Norms*, https://doi.org/10.1007/978-3-030-78953-4_9

The act came into force on 1.10.2017. It mandates reporting and comprehensive complaint management duties for social networks covered by its provisions, subject to significant fines for non-compliance.[4] The advantages and disadvantages of NetzDG are discussed below.

2 Pros and Cons of NetzDG

2.1 NetzDG's Aim and Strengths

2.1.1 The Increasing Incidence of Hate Crime

Facebook, Twitter and the like are becoming increasingly important as means of communication in the age of digitization. All of these platforms were primarily designed to share news and information. Messages are written, images are sent and other texts, so-called posts, are published. The last one, in particular, conceals a risk which has been growing for some years and which needs to be stopped: the dissemination of so-called hate messages. For better or worse, the Internet has evolved from an information medium,[5] into a platform that can be used for spreading all sorts of propaganda, hatred, antisemitism and other forms of racism.[6]

The tone used in discussions and debates on the Internet, particularly on social networks, has changed massively. The trend is now towards aggressiveness, often involving insulting and illegal content.[7] Discriminatory statements referring to various personal characteristics such as religion, origin or sexuality have become everyday occurrences. In addition, social media is used to spread so-called fake news, ie the deliberate dissemination of disinformation which has the appearance of serious journalistic reporting.[8] It is generally accepted that this was a huge problem during the 2016 US presidential election campaign,[9] as well as in the run up to the Brexit referendum in Britain.[10] The German Parliament, by enacting NetzDG, set itself the goal of stemming the tide of disinformation and hate messaging. It remains to be seen whether NetzDG will be effective in stopping or at least reducing such

[4]Liesching M (2018) N. 25 NetzDG, Vorbemerkungen, Rn. 1. In: Erbs G, Kohlhaas M (eds), Strafrechtliche Nebengesetze, C.H.Beck, Munich.

[5]Paal B P, Hennemann M (2017) Meinungsvielfalt im Internet. ZRP 76, p 76.

[6]Heldt A P (2017) Terror-Propaganda online: Die Schranken der Meinungsfreiheit in Deutschland und den USA. NJOZ 1458, 1460.

[7]Network Enforcement Act, BT Drs. 18/12356, S. 1.

[8]Paal, Hennemann, supra note 5, p 77.

[9]Kollanyi B, Howard P N, Woolley S C (2016) Bots and Automation over Twitter during the U.S. Election. COMPROP Data Memo.

[10]Drexl, MPIIC Research Paper No. 16–16, S. 3 ff.

contents. Hate crimes pose serious dangers not only to personal honor and dignity,[11] but also to democracy itself, because they destroy the bonds that hold society together.

2.1.2 Efficient Monitoring and Deletion of Unlawful Content

A reading of § 3 NetzDG suggests that the provision will allow faster control and, if necessary, faster deletion of illegal content. §3(2)(1) NetzDG requires that the complaints handling procedure must ensure that content is examined and, if necessary, removed immediately after the complaint is noted by the provider. The word 'immediately' makes clear that the examination cannot simply be postponed for a long time after it has become known to the provider. In German law 'immediately' means without undue delay.[12] Therefore, analysis of the content should begin without unnecessary delay, so that illegal content can be removed as soon as possible. If the content is 'manifestly unlawful' it should be removed within 24 h. This ensures that as few users as possible can view the text. Under §3(2)(3) NetzDG offending content that is not 'manifestly unlawful' must be removed within 7 days. This also represents a relatively short time frame.

In this context, the obligations put in place for providers seem quite expedient. Under §3(1)(2) NetzDG the procedure should be "easily identifiable, directly accessible and permanently available" for the purpose of submitting complaints to the provider. Thus, potential victims or third parties can easily put forward complaints about violations of their rights for examination. This is a great improvement on the situation prior to NetzDG. Although social network providers were required to block or delete unlawful content immediately after becoming aware of it under §7 et seq Telemedia Act (TMG),[13] the previous legislation, users have now been given a simpler complaints procedure in order to spur providers to take action. In addition, under § 3(3)-(4) NetzDG there are documentation requirements, monthly inspections, and semi-annual training requirements for staff.

[11]The dignity-argument should be used with care, see Hilgendorf E (2018) The Abuse of Human Dignity – Difficulties in Using the Human Dignity Topos Taking the Bio-Ethical Debate as an Example. In: Hilgendorf E, Kremnitzer M (eds), Human Dignity and Criminal Law: Würzburg Conference on Human Dignity, Human Rights and Criminal Law in Israel and Germany, July 20–22, 2015. Duncker & Humblot, Berlin, p 39.

[12]Franzen I (2014) JurisPK-BGB. 7th edn, § 121, Rn. 11; Armbrüster (2015) MüKo-BGB. 7th edn, § 121, Rn. 7; Ellenberger S (2018) Palandt. 77th edn, § 121, Rn. 3, who argues that this definition holds good for civil law as a whole.

[13]Spindler G (2018) Rechtsdurchsetzung von Persönlichkeitsrechten. GRUR, pp 365, 366.

2.1.3 Comprehensive Reporting Obligation

§2(1) NetzDG created a new and detailed reporting obligation for social networks that receive more than 100 complaints about unlawful content per calendar year. Providers are required to publish the said reports semi-annually both in the German Federal Gazette as well as on their websites.

An extensive list of the data which must be included in the reports is contained in §2(2) NetzDG. The far-reaching scope of this reporting obligation is very positive. It contributes to clarity, comprehensibility, optimization, and better control. Information on preventive measures put in place by providers and mechanisms developed to improve their complaints procedures will lead to the continuous improvement in the handling of complaints as provider networks will be able to obtain ideas from other providers' reports, and then adapt those measures to optimise their own complaints handling procedures.

Furthermore, due to the high level of transparency created by the publication of reports on the Internet, which are always directly and instantly available, both users and authorities can easily and effortlessly maintain an overview of the situation on the ground.

2.1.4 The Establishment of Self-Regulation Organizations

Under the conditions set out in §3(6)-(8) NetzDG, self-regulation organizations are introduced. These organizations are established by the online-platforms (the law calls this "regulated self-regulation") and are specialized in decision-making on the existence of unlawful content. Such specialization is especially useful in cases where content is not manifestly unlawful.[14] If the social network transfers the decision on the illegality to such a body of "regulated self-regulation" and submits to its decision within 7 days of receipt of the complaint, it may exceed the seven-day deadline for removing the content.

Such organizations relieve providers of the burden of assessing complaints, which may at times be difficult and time-consuming,[15] where the factual constellations are complex. A teleological interpretation of §2(2)(4) NetzDG permits social networks to second staff for this purpose in order to guarantee the fulfilment of their duties.[16] These are of course statutory duties created by NetzDG. It therefore contributes to the proportionality of the statute for providers to be able to make use of such external organizations. This is also a way to at least partly achieve the goal of the uniform handling of complaints where the risk exists that decision-

---

[14]Beschlussempfehlung und Bericht des Ausschusses für Recht und Verbraucherschutz (2017). BT Drs. 18/13013, S. 21.

[15]BVerfG (Federal constitutional court) NJW 1999, 1322 at 1324.

[16]Liesching M, supra note 4, N. 25 NetzDG, § 2, Rn. 8.

making could at times be very subjective where it is only carried out by network providers.

2.1.5 Compliance and Regulatory Fines

The statute contains rules on compliance and a large section on regulatory fines. In general, compliance means that a firm respects the rules and laws it is subject to so that it does not incur criminal liability.[17] Creating a consistent approach to dealing with complaints ensures that they are followed up in an efficient manner. The penalty provisions in §4 NetzDG are comprehensive. §4(1) lists a wide range of offences by reference to the respective sections of StGB (German Criminal Code). Such offences can be committed either intentionally or negligently.

The list contributes immensely to making social networks aware of their duties and focusing their attention on compliance with those duties.[18] After all, it is the providers' platforms upon which unlawful content can be published. Accordingly, it should be the providers who remove such unlawful content. If they fail to comply with their reporting obligations or their duties to remove unlawful content, they risk very high fines. The fines can reach up € 5 m under §4(2)(1) NetzDG, and up to € 50 m under §4(2)(2) NetzDG read in conjunction with §30(2)(3) OWiG (German Act on Regulatory Offences). This is a significant incentive for providers to implement the compliance rules and meticulously monitor compliance. These immense sums are also intended to nullify any economic advantages providers might derive from turning a blind eye to illegal content, cf. §17(4) OWiG.[19]

Under §4(3) NetzDG, read in conjunction with §5 OWiG,[20] the territorial scope of application was extended by Parliament to include administrative offences that were not committed in Germany. This is particularly useful because most providers of social networks do not have their headquarters or their administrative offices in Germany.[21] Within Germany, however, there must under §5(1-2) be a person authorized to receive service, as well as a person authorized to receive requests for information.

All in all, the NetzDG can be seen as a powerful weapon in the fight against hate speech online.

[17]Beckmann E M (2018) Compliance – wenn man nicht alles selbst macht. CCZ, pp 137, 138.

[18]Network Enforcement Act (2017), BT Drs. 18/12356, p 24.

[19]Network Enforcement Act (2017), BT Drs. 18/12356, p 25.

[20]Liesching M, Spindler G, Schmitz p (eds), supra note 1, § 4 NetzDG, Rn. 1.

[21]Fischer T (2020) Strafgesetzbuch mit Nebengesetzen. C.H.Beck., Munich, 67th edn, Vor §§ 3–7, Rn. 3; Rogall (2018) Karlsruher Kommentar zum Gesetz über Ordnungswidrigkeiten. In: Wolfgang M (ed). 5th edn, C.H.Beck, Munich, § 5, Rn. 6 ff.

2.2 NetzDG's Weaknesses

2.2.1 Lack of Legislative Competence?

Some commentators argue that the German Federal Government does not possess the legislative powers to enact NetzDG; if this were be true, the act would be formally unconstitutional.[22]

According to the explanatory memorandum, which accompanied the bill, the statute aims at "the protection of minors from harmful media".[23] However, provisions which primarily pursue different objectives are not covered by this provision.[24] The provision would have to serve almost exclusively the protection of minors, which it does not do. It can be argued that this justification is just a pretence as adults are just as affected as children.[25] Accordingly, legislative competence cannot be based on Art. 74(1)(7) GG.

In the memorandum of explanation federal competence to enact this legislation was founded on German Federal Constitution (GG) Art. 74(1)(11) (economic matters) and Art. 74(1)(7) (public welfare).[26]

According to one viewpoint in the literature, *economic matters* under Art. 74(1)(11) GG are not relevant to this legislation.[27] This term is generally to be interpreted broadly; it covers all norms and laws governing economic life and economic activity.[28] In the majority of cases, it is also assumed that so-called tele-media with an economic focus are also covered.[29] If NetzDG were to impose duties on social networks in respect of their business activities, that would be covered. Whether a statute is constitutional depends on its object, not its point of reference.[30] In the instant case, the goal is to prevent hateful, illicit content from being published on social networks.[31] Parliament wanted to change the behaviour of social network users, rather than regulate social networks' economic activities.[32] But of course, in reply, it can be argued that the statute does regulate the way social networks conduct

[22]Kalscheuer F, Hornung C (2017) Das Netzwerkdurchsetzungsgesetz – Ein verfassungswidriger Schnellschuss. NVwZ, pp. 1721, 1724.

[23]Network Enforcement Act (2017), BT Drs. 18/12356, S. 12.

[24]Maunz T, Dürig G (2016) Grundgesetz Kommentar. 79. EL, 12/2016, Art. 74, Rn. 115 f.

[25]Liesching M (2018) Die Durchsetzung von Verfassungs- und Europarecht gegen das NetzDG. *MMR*, p 26, 26.

[26]Network Enforcement Act (2017), BT Drs. 18/12356, p 13.

[27]Kalscheuer F, Hornung C, supra note 22, pp. 1721, 1724.

[28]BVerfGE (The Federal Constitutional Court) 68, 319 at 330.

[29]Seiler C (2013). In: Epping V, Hillgruber C (eds) Grundgesetz Kommentar. C.H.Beck, Munich, 2nd edn Art. 74 Rn. 45.1; Degenhardt C (2014). In: Sachs M (ed) Grundgesetz Kommentar. C.H. Beck, Munich, 7th edn, Art. 74 Rn. 51.

[30]BVerfGE (The Federal Constitutional Court) 68, 319 (329).

[31]Network Enforcement Act (2017). BT Drs. 18/12356, S. 11.

[32]Kalscheuer F, Hornung C, supra note 22, pp 1721, 1725.

their business.[33]As a result, the arguments in favour of a legislative competence of the federal government are stronger.

2.2.2 Violation of the Freedom of Expression?

Some commentators argue that NetzDG violates freedom of expression as set forth in Art. 5(1) GG.[34]

First of all, § 3(2) NetzDG stipulates assessment times of only 1 week or 24 h for content for which a complaint has been received. Such time frames are too short to guarantee adequate protection of freedom of expression. It is argued that the balancing of legal interests such as freedom of expression, protection of honor (or *due respect*) and the public peace, requires a case-by-case analysis, which is hardly possible in such short periods of time.[35] On the other hand, there is a lot of jurisprudence on the issue. Moreover, AI might help to identify clear cases—and increasingly so in the future. Last but not least, the self-regulating institutes mentioned above can help to reduce time pressure.

Some people argue that combating 'poisoning people's minds' is not a legitimate reason for infringing on freedom of expression.[36] Social networks are 'essential for public debate' and can influence 'the mood in the country'.[37] It is argued that it seems unclear to what extent freedom of expression should be restricted for this reason. The importance of statements spread on social media should not be underestimated. One can compare this position to arguments in support of freedom of the press under Art. 5 (1)(2) GG. Print media contribute significantly to public debate. This supports the German Supreme Court's reasoning in the *Wunsiedel Judgment*. The court stated that "an understanding of public peace aimed at protecting citizens from subjective uneasiness through confrontation with provocative opinions and ideologies or at safeguarding social or ethical views regarded as fundamental" is not sufficient justification for encroaching on freedom of expression.[38]

In addition, some commentators fear there is no guarantee that the weighing of interests can be done consistently, from a procedural perspective. This is because the NetzDG does not contain any procedural provisions stipulating precisely how complaints should be dealt with.

Fourthly, it follows from § 4(1)(2) NetzDG that only the failure to fulfil the obligation to remove or block illegal content is a regulatory offence that can lead to a

[33]Schiff A (2018) Meinungsfreiheit in mediatisierten digitalen Räumen. MMR, pp. 366, 366.
[34]Kalscheuer F, Hornung C, supra note 22, pp 1721, 1723 f.
[35]Kalscheuer F, Hornung C, supra note 22, pp 1723.
[36]Kalscheuer F, Hornung C, supra note 22, pp 1721, 1724.
[37]Network Enforcement Act (2017). BT Drs. 18/12356, p 20.
[38]BVerfGE (The Federal Constitutional Court) 124, 300 (334).

fine. The illegal removal of lawful content is not an offence.[39] This could lead to social networks to 'overblocking', ie removing content, in cases of doubt, simply in order to avoid possible fines.[40] The consequence would be blatant interference in freedom of expression, especially since social networks would not weigh up the conflicting interests on a case-by-case basis; more weight would likely be given to legal interests that clash with freedom of expression.[41]

Additional criticism has been raised on the ground that decisions on the legality of content are being shifted from the state to the private sector. This, too, could constitute a violation of freedom of expression.[42] Art. 20(2–3) GG make it unmistakably clear that decisions on compliance with the law are a matter for the courts. The NetzDG, some people argue, could deprive the persons concerned of the possibility of direct legal protection against measures which interfere with their rights. On the contrary, only court action at the civil law level against the social network will remain available, whereby the fundamental right of freedom of expression is only indirectly enforceable against third parties. This leads to a shift in state duties to the private sector. Frequently high court costs could lead to the restriction of freedom of expression, because the affected population does not want to defend its rights before the courts.[43]

On the other hand, it is hard to overlook the fact that hatred on the net is leading to more sensitive people being deterred from expressing themselves at all, let alone participating in a process of exchanging opinions. Those who are afraid to express their opinions freely will refrain from doing so.[44] One could speak of the *paradox of freedom of expression*: too much freedom of expression leads to its disappearance. Rational argumentation depends on the observance of a certain framework of rules. It is the task of the law to ensure and defend such a framework.

[39]Ladeur K H, Gostomzyk T (2017) Gutachten zur Verfassungsmäßigkeit des Entwurfs eines Gesetzes zur Verbesserung der Rechtsdurchsetzung in sozialen Netzwerken. Netzwerkdurchsetzungsgesetz – NetzDG, BT-Drs. 18/12356. https://www.bitkom.org/noindex/Publikationen/2017/Sonstiges/NetzDG-Gutachten-Gostomzyk-Ladeur.pdf

[40]Papier H J (2017) Rechtsstaatlichkeit und Grundrechtsschutz in der digitalen Gesellschaft. NJW, pp 3025, 3030.

[41]Entwurf eines Netzwerkdurchsetzungsgesetzes Vereinbarkeit mit der Meinungsfreiheit (2017). https://www.bundestag.de/blob/510514/eefb7cf92dee88ec74ce8e796e9bc25c/wd-10-037-17-pdf-data.pdf

[42]Guggenberger N (2017) Das Netzwerkdurchsetzungsgesetz – schön gedacht, schlecht gemacht. ZRP, p 98; Spindler G (2017) Der Regierungsentwurf zum Netzwerkdurchsetzungsgesetz – europarechtswidrig?. ZUM, p 96 (100); a different position is held by Martin E (2017) Rechenschaftspflichten für soziale Netzwerke und Suchmaschinen. NJW, pp 1450,1451.

[43]Guggenberger N, supra note 42, pp 96,100.

[44]See also Canadian Supreme Court in https://scc-csc.lexum.com/scc-csc/scc-csc/en/item/12876/index.do

2.2.3 Infringement of the Principle that Law Must Be Precise and Clear

The principle that laws must be precise and clear requires legislation to be worded so clearly and so concretely that in principle, the meaning and scope of the law can be determined by looking at the literal meaning of the words.[45]

Illegal Contents

The expression 'unlawful content', in § 1(3) NetzDG is decisive and runs through the entire NetzDG. On the basis of the black letter text, contents are covered which fulfil the actus reus of specific offences contained in the German Criminal Code (StGB) as explicitly referred to in this section, but for which no legal justification (ie defence) exists. This approach is untypical for German criminal law doctrine. Strictly speaking, only 'actions', as such, can be unlawful or justified in the German criminal law.[46] The memorandum of information, which accompanied the original bill put forward in Parliament, adds to the confusion rather than reducing it.[47] It is neither clear from the wording of the statute, nor from the memorandum of information, whether network operators need only determine whether the objective elements of particular offences are present (as 'contents'), or whether, in addition to that, the perpetrator acted with the necessary level of intent,.[48] Thus, there exist concerns about the clarity and preciseness of this section. However, in view of the sense and purpose of the Network Enforcement Act, it seems obvious to interpret the law in such a way that only the objective side of the act (actus reus) has to be given.

Manifestly Unlawful Contents

In this context, concerns have also been raised about the 'manifestness' of the unlawful contents, as is required under § 3(2)(2) NetzDG.[49] What exactly does 'manifestly' mean, in particular how quickly must the unlawful nature of content become apparent to an observer? This is not defined anywhere in the statute. It is the task of the practice to develop the necessary legal certainty here.

---

[45]BVerfGE (The Federal Constitutional Court) 92, 1 (12); BVerfGE (The Federal Constitutional Court) 126, 170 (196).

[46]Liesching M, supra note 25, p 26.

[47]Heinrich B (2016) Strafrecht Allgemeiner Teil. Verlag W. Kohlhammer, 5th edn, Rn. 309.

[48]Liesching M, supra note 25, p 26 f.

[49]Ladeur K H, Gostomzyk T (2017) Das Netzwerkdurchsetzungsgesetz und die Logik der Meinungsfreiheit. K&R, pp 390, 391.

Provisions on Regulatory Fines

Following the discussion above about the vagueness of the expression 'unlawful content', this vagueness continues in the provisions on regulatory fines under § 4 NetzDG. The result is that, according to some authors, it is unclear to network service operators what elements of the StGB (Criminal Code) offences listed in the statute can be the subject of the complaint proceedings, and when such content must be deleted.[50]

Ambiguity is fuelled by the memorandum of explanation's discussion of § 4(1)(2) NetzDG. It states: "An offence is usually not made out by a one-time violation of the duty to delete or block manifestly unlawful content. In the case of a one-off infringement, it cannot generally be assumed that no effective procedure for dealing with complaints about unlawful content is being provided."[51] This commentary on the statute contains a number of vague expressions which, as a result, contribute to an overall lack of clarity of the regulatory fines provision. Thus, at least at first sight it seems possible that the instant section on regulatory fines does not fulfil the requirements on textual preciseness and clarity contained in Article 103(2) GG or § 3 Act on Regulatory Offences (OWiG). Here too, however, the practice of applying the Network Enforcement Act should bring about the necessary legal certainty.

2.2.4 Breach of the Requirement of Equal Treatment

The Media in General

NetzDG only covers social networks (cf. § 1(1)(1)). That includes, for example, Facebook and Twitter. Thus, print media as well as radio and television do not fall within the scope of the new law. This ignores the fact that radio and television, in particular, also have considerable influence on the population, which is either equivalent to that of social networks, or possibly still exceeds it. For that reason, it is arguable that unequal treatment within the meaning of Article 3 I GG exists in respect of social networks vis-à-vis other media.[52] However, this can be countered by the fact that classical media law also recognises claims for injunctive relief and correction of false statements. In addition, in traditional media, editors exercise a kind of pre-control and decide what can be printed and what cannot.

[50]Wimmers J, Heymann B (2017) Zum Referentenentwurf eines Netzwerkdurchsetzungsgesetzes (NetzDG) – eine kritische Stellungnahme. AfP, pp 93,101.

[51]Network Enforcement Act (2017). BT Drs. 18/12356, p 24.

[52]Ladeur K H, Gostomzyk T, supra note 49, pp. 390, 394; Nolte G (2017) Hate-Speech, Fake-News, das »Netzwerkdurchsetzungsgesetz« und Vielfaltsicherung durch Suchmaschinen. ZUM, pp 552, 560.

Unequal Treatment between Social Media

Another point of criticism is the less than two million user exemption under § 1 (2) NetzDG. This means that there are networks in which posts or news can be published without prior registration being necessary. These networks therefore per se fall outside the scope of application of NetzDG, as, due to the lack of controllability of the users, the de minimis exemption in § 1(2) applies.[53]

One could ask why networks with less than two million users should not need to meet the requirements of the NetzDG. In this context, the explanatory memorandum states that "smaller social networks should be exempted from costly testing obligations."[54] The validity of this argument has been questioned by Liesching, who argues that the number of registered users alone was not an indicator of a network's resources and capacities.[55] This may be so, but on the other hand it stands to reason that under normal circumstances, a network will be the more powerful—and dangerous—the more users it has.

2.2.5 Breach of EU Law

Much has been written expressing doubts about whether NetzDG is consistent with EU law.[56] Under § 3(2)(2-3) NetzDG the time limits for deleting unlawful content varies between 24 h and 7 days. These fixed time limits could be inconsistent with Art. 14 of the E-Commerce Directive (2000/31/EC).[57] Art. 14(I)(b) of the E-Commerce Directive stipulates network providers will act 'expeditiously', ie 'without delay' to block access or remove unlawful content which they have become aware of.[58]

In this context, it is necessary to consider different time limits for removing or blocking unlawful content. Whereas Art. 14(1)(b) of the E-Commerce Directive stipulates that action must be taken as soon as the provider becomes aware of unlawful content, under Art. 3 (2)(2-3) NetzDG the clock for taking action only starts when a complaint is received, although provider may have knowledge of the existence of the content long before the complaint is received. Thus, the two norms

---

[53]Liesching M, Spindler G, Schmitz p (eds), supra note 1, § 1 NetzDG, Rn. 72; Spindler G (2017) The Network Enforcement Act. K&R, pp 533, 534.

[54]Network Enforcement Act (2017). BT Drs. 18/12356, p 19.

[55]See: Liesching M, supra note 25, p 28.

[56]Guggenberger N, supra note 42, p 98; Spindler G (2017) Der Regierungsentwurf zum Netzwerkdurchsetzungsgesetz – europarechtswidrig?. ZUM, p 473; Liesching M, supra note 25, p 26; Liesching M, supra note 4, N. 25 NetzDG, Vorbemerkungen, Rn. 5.

[57]Guggenberger N, supra note 42, pp 98, 99.

[58]Härting N (2017) Kurzer Prozess für die Meinungsfreiheit: Entwurf eines "Netzwerkdurchsetzungsgesetzes". CR Blog, 14 March 2017. http://www.cr-online.de/blog/2017/03/14/kurzer-prozess-fuer-die-meinungsfreiheit-entwurf-eines-netzwerkdurchsetzungsgesetzes

have indeed different time limits. But this does not necessarily mean that the NetzDG is inconsistent with EU law.[59]

Knowledge under the directive means both knowledge of the existence of the content, as well as knowledge that it is unlawful.[60] In order to determine whether content is unlawful, a detailed analysis may be necessary. It is true that this can hardly be done within 7 days.[61] But again, technical means and experience might help.[62]

Furthermore, it is argued that it is not completely clear what NetzDG means by 'complaint'. The term is not defined in the statute. Is a formal report detailing all the content complained about required, or will a simple statement that there is probably unlawful content on the network suffice? The directive requires detailed information on the unlawful content.[63] Under the circumstances, further clarification of the meaning of the term in the statute is needed for NetzDG to be consistent with EU law on this point.[64]

In the literature, many hold the view that NetzDG violates the country of origin principle in Art. 3 of the E-Commerce Directive and is therefore contrary to EU law.[65] Art. 3(2) of the directive stipulates that member states may not restrict the freedom to provide information society services from other Member States. Thus, providers may not be subjected to the (stricter) law, or respectively enforcement measures, of countries of destination to which their services are provided.[66] Art. 3 (4-5) contains the exception to that rule, but this is only for individual cases.[67] Thus, as much as NetzDG tries to apply (and enforce) German law upon all providers,[68] regardless of where they are located, it may indeed violate EU law. The best solution to this problem would be a pan-European approach.

[59]A different stance is held by Spindler G, supra note 56, pp 473, 480.

[60]Eck S, Ruess P (2003) Haftungsprivilegierung der Provider nach der E-Commerce-Richtlinie. MMR, pp 363, 365; Helle J (2002) Persönlichkeitsrechtsverletzungen im Internet. JZ, pp 593, 597.

[61]Spindler G, supra note 56, pp 473, 481.

[62]See Sect. 2.2.2 (at the beginning).

[63]BGH (Federal Court of Justice) (2004) ZUM, p 67, 67; Moritz, CR 1998, 505 (507).

[64]Spindler G, supra note 56, pp 473, 482.

[65]Feldmann T (2017) Zum Referentenentwurf eines NetzDG: Eine kritische Betrachtung. K&R, pp. 292, 296; Wimmers J, Heymann B, supra note 50, pp 93, 96 f.; Spindler G, supra note 53, pp 533, 535; Liesching M, supra note 4, N. 25 NetzDG, Vorbemerkungen, Rn. 5.

[66]Wimmers J, Heymann B, supra note 50, pp 93, 96.

[67]Spindler G, supra note 56, pp 474, 476 f.; Feldmann T, supra note 65, pp 292, 296; Wimmers J, Heymann B, supra note 50, pp 93, 96.

[68]Feldmann T, supra note 65, pp 292, 296; Spindler G, supra note 56, pp 474, 477.

2.2.6 Compatibility with the Right Against Compelled Self-Incrimination

The explanatory memorandum does not even mention the possible violation of the right against compulsory self-incrimination under Art. 2 GG. The situation and procedures prescribed by NetzDG lead to this right being endangered. According to the memorandum of explanation, the owners of provider firms may be held legally responsible as natural persons for infractions by the firm.[69] That means that owners first fulfil their reporting obligation under § 2(3) NetzDG, and can then be fined on the basis of the information provided. This could represent a violation of the right against compulsory self-incrimination.[70]

2.2.7 Violation of the Principle of Ex-Officio Investigation

The official investigation of crimes and regulatory offences is a fundamental principle of criminal law procedure under § 244(2) German Code of Criminal Procedure (StPO), and, *mutatis mutandis* under § 46(1) OWiG. In contrast, the memorandum of explanation assumes that decisions on regulatory fines under § 4(5) NetzDG will be made on the basis of investigations carried out by administrative authorities.[71] Making decisions on such a basis could be considered inconsistent with the procedural requirements set out above.

2.2.8 Latest Developments

At the beginning of 2020, a draft bill of the Federal Ministry of Justice and Consumer Protection was announced, which provides for a tightening of the Network Enforcement Act. A deficit of the previous law was considered to be the fact that the prosecution authorities often did not obtain knowledge of the criminal contents deleted on the basis of the NetzDG, the posting of such content therefore remained without criminal consequences and the Internet was thus likely to develop further towards a legal vacuum. Therefore, the providers subject to the NetzDG should be obliged to report certain severe forms of criminal content to the Federal Criminal Police Office (Bundeskriminalamt). As a result, criminal prosecution could then be initiated by the responsible authorities. However, this procedure might give rise to concerns about data protection. In addition, substantive criminal law is to be tightened in order to be able to take more effective action against hate crime; for example, insulting statements on the Internet might be covered by a qualifying offence under § 185 German Criminal Code in the future. The definition of a threat

[69]Network Enforcement Act (2017). BT Drs. 18/12356, p 12.

[70]Wimmers J, Heymann B, supra note 50, pp 93, 101 f.

[71]Network Enforcement Act (2017). BT Drs. 18/12356, p 26.

(§ 241 German Criminal Code) is also to be tightened in order to be able to cover threats with acts against physical integrity or a thing of significant value in the future. These changes came into effect in March 2021.

This further development of the NetzDG appears to be consistent; it adapts it to the reality of hate crimes on the Internet. But of course, here too, there are again opposing voices warning with strong arguments against taking too strict a measure and, above all, bringing constitutional reasons into play.[72]

3 Summary

NetzDG has supporters and detractors. Some voices in the academic literature consider it unconstitutional, as it is said that the German Federal Government did not have legislative competence to enact it, and because the statute violates the freedom of expression under Art. 5(1) GG and the principle of equal treatment under Art. 3(1) GG. On the other hand, the law is well designed to efficiently fight hate messaging and certain types of fake news. This is a legitimate and important goal. Not only freedom of speech, but democracy itself is endangered by the sheer amount of hatred and racist propaganda on the internet. The tools the law employs have enacted detailed rules on complaints handling and reporting in a statute with extraterritorial scope. It remains to be seen to what extent, considering all reservations and criticisms, but also the praise, the statute will achieve its objectives. If the law proves successful, it may serve as a blueprint for combating hate crime across Europe and perhaps even beyond.

4 Outlook: Criminal Liability of Internet Providers

Without the cooperation of internet providers, the effective enforcement of the criminal law on the internet would be extremely difficult. The particular way that the internet functions means that even for simple communications a number of computer servers and stations operating in different places are always involved. Take the hypothetical situation where A wants to disseminate information from a website. First, he needs a network provider, who makes available to A the necessary software for uploading the data. Then A needs a host provider, who leases to him the required storage capacity. The network and host providers can be identical but need not be such. If internet user B, located anywhere around the world, wants to read the information on the website, he needs the services of an access provider, who gives

[72]Liesching M (2020) Karneval der Jakobiner "Zum Schutz der Freiheit – Schafft sie ab!". 6 Jan 2020. https://community.beck.de/2020/01/06/karneval-der-jakobiner-zum-schutze-der-freiheit-schafft-sie-ab

him access to the internet. Thus, in this hypothetical case, which seems simple at first glance, there are five different parties participating in the operation—the sender, the receiver and three providers. If publication of the information transgressed some criminal prohibition—for example child pornography—all five parties could in principle be prosecuted.

Directive 2000/31/EC of the European Parliament and Council of 8 June 2000 on Electronic Commerce[73] regulates providers' liability in the following way: full criminal liability may attach to those persons who place their own content online ('content providers'). The provider of storage space ('host provider') is only liable if he positively knows that the contents he is 'hosting' are illegal (Art. 14). Access providers, who simply provide access to the internet, do not incur criminal liability for illegal contents on the Internet, unless they initiate the transmission, select the receiver of the transmission or select or modify the information during transmission (Art. 12). Providers are under no general obligation to monitor the information which they transmit or store (Art. 15).

On the other hand, Art. 12(3) of the Directive stipulates that an access provider is nevertheless obliged to remove or block access to contents which is otherwise proscribed by law even where the access provider is not responsible for the contents, if he is ordered to do so by a court or an administrative authority. This means, for example, that an access provider could incur criminal liability, where he did not block a user placing illegal contents onto the internet, if he positively knew that the contents were illegal and was ordered by a court or an administrative authority to terminate or prevent the infringement. Of course, full criminal liability would only apply if all the other elements of criminal liability were present as well. The counter-position, which has been argued vigorously, is that an access provider cannot be held criminally liable, even if he intentionally allows a criminal to continue to use the internet despite being ordered to block that person's access by a court or an administrative authority. This position, however, can hardly be reconciled with the text of the Directive.[74]

The issue of provider liability will play an increasingly important role in the future. It is to be hoped that the European legislator will also address this issue in the planned EU Digital Service Act.[75] In order to make the internet a better place, we need both: A regulation like the Network Enforcement Act *and* a clear position on provider liability.

[73]https://eur-lex.europa.eu/legal-content/EN/ALL/?uri=celex%3A32000L0031

[74]Hilgendorf E, Valerius B (2012) Computer- und Internetstrafrecht. 2nd edn, Springer, p 66.

[75]https://eur-lex.europa.eu/legal-content/en/TXT/?uri=COM:2020:825:FIN

How to Balance Fundamental Rights on the One Hand with the Duty of the State to Protect the Fundamental Rights of Its Citizens on the Other

Kurt Graulich

Democratic societies committed to the rule of law find it hard to fight terrorism with legal means, since restrictions—intended to prevent severe crimes from being planned or committed by unlawful offenders—are often suspected as a ploy to exercise control over the normal life of peaceful citizens. In such a situation, discussions typically do not end in parliament, but are continued through complaints before the highest court, which in Germany is the Constitutional Court (Bundesverfassungsgericht—BVerfG). The 9/11 attack on the Twin Towers in New York caused the enactment of many state measures to combat international terrorism, not only in the USA, but also in other allied nations. In 2006 a new authorisation was created, Art. 73 sec. 1 no. 9a of the Basic Law (Grundgesetz—GG),[1] which enabled the lawmaker to repel threats of international terrorism through law enforcement action by the Federal Criminal Police (Bundeskriminalamt—BKA).

1 The Matter of Dispute

On the basis of Art. 73 sec. 1 no. 9a GG, the federal legislature assigned the BKA tasks extending beyond its previous law enforcement duties, reaching into the domain of protection against threats from international terrorism, a task hitherto reserved solely for the Laender (federal states).[2] As can be expected, from 2008 onwards, constitutional complaints were directed against these provisions of the

[1]BGBl I, p. 2034.

[2]BVerfGE 141, 220-378 mn. 1.

K. Graulich (✉)
Humboldt-Universität zu Berlin, Berlin, Germany

K. Ghanayim, Y. Shany (eds.), *The Quest for Core Values in the Application of Legal Norms*, https://doi.org/10.1007/978-3-030-78953-4_10

Federal Criminal Police Office Act (Bundeskriminalamtgesetz—BKAG).[3] An additional subject-matter of the constitutional complaints was a provision in the Federal Criminal Police Office Act on the transfer of data to third countries, the scope of which has been extended by the newly attributed powers.[4]

Consequently, two aspects of the constitutional complaints could be distinguished. The first was directed against the granting of various investigative powers to the BKA. The challenged powers include the authorisation to question persons pursuant to § 20c BKAG (§ 20g BKAG [Interrogation and duty of disclosure]), as well as the use of special means of data collection outside of private homes pursuant to § 20g secs. 1 to 3 BKAG (§ 20 sec. 1 [special means of data collection outside of private homes]), including, in particular, the covert monitoring and recording of non-public speech, image recording, the application of tracking devices, and the use of police informants and undercover investigators. The constitutional complaints also challenged the power to carry out visual and acoustic surveillance of private homes pursuant to § 20h BKAG (§ 20h BKAG [Special assignments on application of technical means]), to conduct electronic profile searching pursuant to § 20j BKAG (§ 20j BKAG [Conducting electronic profile searching]), to access information technology systems pursuant to § 20k BKAG (§ 20k BKAG [Covert access to information technology systems]), to monitor ongoing telecommunications pursuant to § 20l BKAG (§ 20l BKAG [Monitoring ongoing telecommunications]) as well as to collect telecommunications traffic data pursuant to § 20m secs. 1 and 3 BKAG (§ 20m BKAG [Collecting telecommunications traffic data]). In addition, the challenges also encompass § 20u BKAG, which deals with the protection of persons having the right to refuse to give evidence, as well as § 20w BKAG which sets out the duty to inform affected persons at the conclusion of the surveillance measure.[5]

The second bundle of constitutional complaints was directed against provisions on the use of data. This affected, firstly, the provision on the use of data collected in accordance with Sub-Title 3a of the Act pursuant to § 20v sec. 4 sentence 2 BKAG by the Federal Criminal Police Office itself. The power pursuant to § 20v sec. 5 BKAG—with the exception of sentence 3 no. 2—to transfer this data to other domestic public authorities was also challenged. Finally, § 14 sec. 1 sentence 1 nos. 1 and 3 and sentence 2, sec. 7 BKAG, which generally permitted the transfer of data to authorities in third countries, was also challenged. § 14a BKAG, which further established a separate power to transfer personal data to Member States of the European Union, was not at issue in these proceedings.[6]

It is worth regarding the verdict of the Bundesverfassungsgericht not primary for its result, which—like in the present case was sophisticated, but for its way of reasoning. The main topics of the Bundesverfassungsgericht's BKAG-Judgement

[3]Inserted as Sub-Title 3a by the Act on Prevention by the Federal Criminal Police Office of Threats from International Terrorism of 25 December 2008, effective 1 January 2009.

[4]BVerfGE 141, 220-378 mn. 1.

[5]BVerfGE 141, 220-378 mn. 2.

[6]BVerfGE 141, 220-378 mn. 3.

were first the principle of proportionality as applied from different aspects (see below Sect. 2), and second, the principles of purpose limitation and change in purpose when the state is using and transferring—before by it has having been collected—data (see below Sect. 3).

2 Fundamental Rights and Constitutional Principles to Be Regarded in the Case of Collecting Data

Following the usual guideline of reasoning in a judgement, the Bundesverfassungsgericht developed its holdings in three steps. Firstly, it addressed how the challenged surveillance and investigative powers authorise interferences with fundamental rights, depending on which fundamental right had been affected (see below Sect. 2.1). Secondly, the varying weight of the interference had individually to be measured against the principle of proportionality and the principle of legal clarity and specificity (see below Sect. 2.2). And thirdly, what the powers had in common was that the potential interferences they authorised were intended for the most part very serious, yet since their objective were to protect against the threat of international terrorism, they had a legitimate aim and were, to that end, suitable and necessary (see below Sect. 2.3).[7]

2.1 Fundamental Rights Being Affected by Surveillance and Investigative Powers

The constitutional complaints were directed mainly against authorisations for surveillance and investigation by the Federal Police Office. The challenged powers authorised the Federal Criminal Police Office to covertly collect personal data in the context of protection against threats and the prevention of criminal offences. This allowed for—depending on the power in question—interferences with the fundamental rights of Art. 13 sec. 1 GG (Article 13 [Inviolability of the home]), Art. 10 sec. 1 GG (Article 10 [Privacy of correspondence, posts and telecommunications]) and Art. 2 sec. 1 (Article 2 [Personal freedoms]) in conjunction with Art. 1 sec. 1 GG (Article 1 sec 1 [Human dignity]), the latter both in its manifestation as the right to the guarantee of the confidentiality and integrity of information technology systems as well as the right to informational self-determination.[8]

These authorisations enabled severe interferences since they should be executed in a clandestine way. All these powers provided the legal bases for investigative and surveillance measures which were usually carried out covertly without the

[7]BVerfGE 141, 220-378 mn. 90.

[8]BVerfGE 141, 220-378 mn. 91.

knowledge of the parties concerned and could produce a serious interference with the right to privacy. Even if legitimate expectations of confidentiality were affected in differing degrees and the powers' weight of interference varied significantly, all of these powers generally implied a level of interference which weighed heavily. Only the individual measures pursuant to § 20g secs. 1 and 2 BKAG (§ 20g BKAG [Special means of data gathering]) constituted an exception to this conclusion.[9]

2.2 *The Weight of the Interference, Must Be Measured Against the Principle of Proportionality and the Principle of Legal Clarity and Specificity*

Judicial control by the Bundesverfassungsgericht follows a certain scheme which is laid out by the grounds for the verdict: The constitutionality of the powers depends on the limits arising from each of the affected fundamental rights and the proportionality requirements which must be determined for each of the powers. According to the principle of proportionality, the granting of these powers must always pursue a legitimate aim and must be suitable, necessary and, in the strict sense,[10] proportionate to achieving its aim.[11] Last but not least, police law typically contains blanket clauses to facilitate efficient procedures. But this legislative practice must be moderated by notions such as the principle of legal clarity and specificity, which aim to increase the predictability of interferences for citizens, constitutes an effective limit on administrative powers and enables effective judicial review.[12] With regard to the powers in question that pertain to the covert collection and processing of data that have the potential to produce serious interferences with privacy, the principle of proportionality sets up particularly strict requirements. Since affected persons can for the most part neither notice nor challenge the use of these powers, their content—in contrast to, for example, administrative law terms that are open to interpretation and are executed by means of an administrative act—can only be rendered more specific to a very limited extent within the interplay between actual application and judicial review. Still, the requirements differ in distinct cases, depending on the weight of the interference,[13] and the relevant respective substantive requirements of proportionality.[14]

---

[9]BVerfGE 141, 220-378 mn. 92.

[10]Cf BVerfGE 67, 157 (173); BVerfGE 70, 278 (286); BVerfGE 104, 337 (347 et seq.); BVerfGE 120, 274 (318 and 319); BVerfGE 125, 260 (316); established case-law.

[11]BVerfGE 141, 220-378 mn. 93.

[12]Cf BVerfGE 113, 348 (375 et seq.); BVerfGE 120, 378 (407 and 408); BVerfGE 133, 277 (336 para 140); established case-law.

[13]Cf BVerfGE 110, 33 (55); BVerfGE 113, 348 (376).

[14]BVerfGE 141, 220-378 mn. 94.

2.3 The Protection Against the Threat of International Terrorism as a Legitimate Aim of the Powers

There was a broad consensus in German politics and the relevant parts of the society that profound measures had to be initiated after the 9/11 attacks and the threat of religiously motivated terrorism. Consequently, the Bundesverfassungsgericht underlined that the challenged provisions pursued a legitimate aim and were suitable and necessary to that end.[15]

The Bundesverfassungsgericht stated that the powers pursued a legitimate aim in that they provide the Federal Criminal Police Office with means of gathering information which can be used in fulfilling its new task of protecting against threats from international terrorism. The term "international terrorism" as set out in the description of tasks in § 4a sec. 1 BKAG (§ 4a BKAG [Protection against the threat of international terrorism]) and its reference to § 129a secs. 1 and 2 of the Criminal Code (Strafgesetzbuch—StGB) (Section 129a StGB [Forming terrorist organisations]), is in line with the EU Framework Decision of 13 June 2002 and international terminology,[16] and was in conformity with the notions of the constitution amending legislature upon the creation of Art. 73 sec. 1 no. 9a GG,[17] which was limited to specifically characterised criminal offences of particular weight. Criminal offences characterised as terrorism in this sense aim to destabilise society and comprise reckless abuse of other people and attacks on the life and limb of random third parties. At a deeper level, they are directed against the basic pillars of the constitutional order and of society as a whole.[18] The provision of effective means of gathering information for protecting against terrorism constitutes a legitimate aim and is of great significance for a democratic and free basic order.[19]

The Constitutional Court judged that the granting of the surveillance and investigative powers in question was suitable for achieving this aim. They provide the Federal Criminal Police Office with the means for gathering information that can play a role in countering the threat of international terrorism. The different powers are, at least in principle, necessary for this. Each power allows specific measures that cannot always be replaced by others. Less intrusive measures that provide equally effective and broad possibilities for gathering information for protecting against international terrorism are not apparent. Evidently, this does not affect the fact that in

[15]BVerfGE 141, 220-378 mn. 95.

[16]OJ L 164, p. 3; Draft Comprehensive Convention on International Terrorism. In: Measures to eliminate international terrorism, Report of the Working Group of 3 November 2010, UN Doc. A/C.6/65/L.10.

[17]Cf Bundestag document, Bundestagsdrucksache—BTDrucks 16/813, p. 12.

[18]BVerfGE 141, 220-378 mn. 96.

[19]Cf BVerfGE 115, 320 (357 and 358); BVerfGE 120, 274 (319); BVerfGE 133, 277 (333 and 334 para 133).

each individual case, the exercise of these powers, too, must be undertaken in accordance with the concepts of suitability and necessity.[20]

One important limitation the court underscored is as follows: with the use of modern and, in particular, covert investigative methods, security authorities must, with respect to the potential for harm inherent in the "additive" interference with fundamental rights, coordinate their activities with one another to ensure that the overall extent of surveillance remains limited.[21]

As a jurisdictional creation of the court—still another restriction flows from the principle of proportionality: Specific requirements for transparency,[22] the judicial protection of individuals, and supervisory control. The requirements applicable in this respect are derived from the fundamental right in question in conjunction with Art. 19 sec. 4 GG.[23]

3 Principles to Be Regarded in the Case of Further Use and Transfer of Data: Purpose Limitation and Change in Purpose

Police and other security agencies depend on "use", "further use" and "transfer of data". Authorisations for these practices follow the principles of "purpose limitation" and "change in purpose". On the base of the above-mentioned requirements, the Constitutional Court found that certain provisions of the BKAG were unconstitutional. This conclusion resulted from a complex review of the requirements for the use and transfer of data having been collected by the state.

The constitutional restrictions on an exchange of data between authorities arising from the principle of purpose limitation (Zweckbindung), remain unaffected by this.[24] The scope of a purpose limitation depends on the specific legal basis for the data collection: the data collection initially takes its purpose from the respective investigation procedure.[25] The legislature may allow a use of the data beyond the specific procedure of the data collection in the context of the original purposes of the

[20]BVerfGE 141, 220-378 mn. 97.

[21]Cf BVerfGE 112, 304 (319 and 320).

[22]BVerfGE 133, 277 (365 para 204); see also BVerfGE 65, 1 (44 et seq.); BVerfGE 100, 313 (361, 364); BVerfGE 109, 279 (363 and 364); BVerfGE 125, 260 (334 et seq.); established case-law; cf. similarly the Proposal for a Directive of the European Parliament and of the Council on the protection of individuals with regard to the processing of personal data by competent authorities for the purposes of prevention, investigation, detection or prosecution of criminal offences or the execution of criminal penalties, and the free movement of such data of 25 January 2012, COM/2012/010 final—as of the conclusion of the trilogue, 16 December 2015: 15174/15; as of 28 January 2016: 5463/16, annex.

[23]Cf BVerfGE 125, 260 (335); BVerfGE 133, 277 (366 para. 206).

[24]BVerfGE 141, 220-378 mn. 130.

[25]BVerfGE 141, 220-378 mn. 279.

data (further use). This implies that the use of collected data is limited to the same authority acting in the same function and for the protection of the same legal interests. For data derived from surveillance of private homes or from access to information technology systems, each further use must additionally also fulfil the relevant risk situation requirements applicable to the data collection.[26]

Above all, the legislator may also allow the further use of data having been collected by the state for other purposes than those determining the original data collection (change in purpose). The Bundesverfassungsgericht newly stated that proportional requirements for such a change must conform to the principle of a hypothetical recollection of data. According to this, the further use of the data must serve the protection of legal interests or aim to investigate criminal offences of such weight that would, by constitutional standards, justify collecting them again with comparably weighty means. A specific risk situation, as required for the initial data collection, is generally not required a second time; it is necessary but generally also sufficient that there be a specific evidentiary basis for further investigations.[27] With regard to data derived from the surveillance of private homes and from remote searches of information technology systems, a change in purpose is only permitted if the relevant risk situation requirements applicable to the collection of the data are again fulfilled.[28]

[26]BVerfGE 141, 220-378 mn. 281.

[27]BVerfGE 141, 220-378 mn. 284.

[28]BVerfGE 141, 220-378 mn. 283.

About Putative Self-Defence

Francisco Muñoz Conde

1. Systems of Criminal law in the Western countries are inspired or influenced by two different systems: The Common law and the Continental law. Both systems have virtues and defects.

The Common law system, applied in the countries formerly or still associated with the British crown, is virtually unknown in the jurisprudential world of the European Continental or Civil law. This is due, no doubt, to the particularities of the Common law system and the distinguishing features of the Continental European legal culture, and also to the Common law method of thinking.

There is no doubt that knowledge of the Common law system is progressively becoming more important. The influence of this system, particularly as developed in the United States, is felt widely in the fields of Procedure, Commercial and Constitutional law. The same influence will eventually reach the field of Criminal law as well. Yet it is obvious, at least in the past, that the Common law system in the field of criminal law is little inclined to theoretical speculation. Its primary focus is on the solution of particular cases (*case law*). But rather than seeing this attribute as a defect, we should consider it, for certain purposes, as an advantage. Once decided, the cases live on in the thinking and in the opinions of judges, thus establishing themselves as "precedents." A system of this sort is not likely to be formulated in abstract principles; but paradoxically, it has enormous influence on judicial thinking and on students who learn the law by studying these precedents.

At the same time, the structural conceptual categories in the way they have been elaborated on by the German doctrinal system of Criminal Law (*Strafrechtsdogmatik*)—an abstract set of categories that lends itself to application to any system of criminal law regardless of its legislative foundations—are more refined and sophisticated than the concepts used in the Common law. Anyway, a

F. Muñoz Conde (✉)
Universidad Pablo de Olavide, Sevilla, Spain
e-mail: fmuncon@upo.es

K. Ghanayim, Y. Shany (eds.), *The Quest for Core Values in the Application of Legal Norms*, https://doi.org/10.1007/978-3-030-78953-4_11

minimum of systematic elaboration is necessary in any modern legal system, as well in the system of the Common law, in order to reduce the complexity and to facilitate its mastery. This task could be rendered possible only by identifying some basic concepts of criminal law that would enable the development of a universally applicable system of thinking.[1]

The merit of the doctrinal system developed in Germany and applied in other countries, is that it in fact exhibits a set of categories that might apply to any legal system. This system is very simple in its principles and shows a tripartite sequential structure of the elements of the crime:[2]

1. The first step is the *Definition* of the crime according to the Law (in German *Tatbestandsmässigkeit;* in Spanish *Tipicidad*);
2. The second one is the *Wrongfulness* (in German *Rechtswidrigkeit;* in Spanish *Antijuricidad*) of the act defined as crime by the Law, and its negative side *Justification* (*Rechtfertigung, Justificación*) for the case the act despite is defined by the Law as a crime in certain cases could be legally correct or even done as a duty (self-defence, necessity, enforcement of law);
3. The third element is the *Culpability* or individual subjective *Responsibility* (in German *Schuld-Verantwortung;* in English, *Culpability/Responsibility;* in Spanish, *Culpabilidad/Responsabilidad*) of the actor for the concrete act defined by the Law as a crime and not justified, and its negative side *Excuse* (in German *Entschuldigung;* in Spanish, *Exculpación*) for the case the actor is not to blame because he or she at the time of the commission of the crime is not yet an adult person, is mental ill or acts by mistake of fact or of law.

The first step coincides with the differentiation in the Criminal law system of the Common law between *Actus Reus* and *Mens Rea*, that is, between the objective, materiel side, and the subjective, mental side of the criminal act, as it is defined by the Law. The principal gap between the German system of Criminal law and the system of Criminal Law in the Common law is in the field of the *Defences*. Most criminal lawyers of the Common law system, as mentioned above at least in the near past, do not admit the differences between *Justification* and *Excuse;* nowadays, the distinction between *Justification* and *Excuse* is well-known, but there are differences deprived these distinction, for instance in relationship with the called putative

---

[1]See Fletcher (1998). Spanish edition Muñoz Conde F (1997) Conceptos básicos de Derecho penal. He develops a structure of basic distinctions and concepts that would accommodate the tensions felt in all democratic legal systems. A tentative list of these distinctions would include those between substantive law and procedural norms, between punishment and treatment, between human causes and fortuitous events, between act and actor, between offenses and defences, between intention and negligence, between relevant and irrelevant mistakes, between attempts and consummated offenses, and between perpetration and complicity. These distinctions represent a set of polar contrasts. Attraction and repulsion between these poles is arguably common to all legal systems that engage in debate about the basic questions of criminal responsibility. See as well Fletcher (2020).

[2]Roxin (2005a), pp. 195–198.

self-defence, but as well in the field of necessity in relationship with the difference between justified necessity and excused necessity or duress.

Nevertheless, the structured distinction between *Justification* and *Excuse* is not particularly difficult to understand and can illustrate the nature of defenses that generate exemptions from penal responsibility better than a unitary, flat consideration of the defenses under the same name.

Claims of justification concern the rightness of an act that nominally violates the law. Examples of justifications include self-defence, necessity, consent, and the use of force in law enforcement. No one is entitled to defend himself from a justified act, and third parties are permitted to assist the justified actor.

Excuses, such as insanity, involuntary intoxication, duress, or mistake of law, imply that the actor is not personally to blame for the unlawful act.[3]

2. This purely systematic approach to the *General Theory of the Crime* (in German, *Allgemeine Verbrechenslehre*; in Spanish, *Teoría General del Delito*), that the German Dogmatic of Criminal law (*Strafrechtsdogmatik)* cultivates the best and to whose theoretical elaboration has devoted its principal efforts from the beginning of the twentieth century until today,[4] is not enough to explain and to solve all the problems that present the borderline cases between *Justification* and *Excuse*. This systematic approach has to be related as well to another question of immediate practical importance. And this question is: To what extent must universal categories and principles accommodate the local details of legislation and case law?

A theoretical System of Criminal law at the age of Globalization can't then just a purely systematic approach, but as well must be contextualized in our present situation—one which emphasizes internationalization and globalization of legal thinking.

---

[3]About this distinction, see generally Eser and Fletcher (eds) (1987); Roxin (2005b), pp. 1–13. In Anglo-American Criminal law, this distinction was introduced and reworked for the first time by Fletcher (1978), pp. 759–870; and then in other books and articles, see e.g. Fletcher (1985), p. 949. Spanish translation: Busato p, Muñoz Conde F (2006) Lo justo y lo razonable; Fletcher (1998), pp. 73–92. The most important of Fletcher's essays in relationship to this distinction have been again published in Fletcher (2013), pp. 121–228. For a comparative study between Common Law and Civil Law related to the works of Fletcher, see Stile et al. (2018). Some British criminal law scholars are sceptic about this distinction. For instance, Lacey N, Wells C (1988) Reconstructing Criminal Law: Critical Perspectives on Crime and the Criminal Process. "the neat conceptual frame may be useful as a model, but on close inspection we find that its elements shade into one another in a way that ultimately defies the analytical clarity to which doctrine aspires". In general, British scholars are against this distinction; see, e.g. Smith (1989) (also in Smith J C & Brian Hogan B (1992), Criminal Law. 7th edn, 187–188. (7th ed. 1992)) and Jefferson (2003), p. 260 (6th ed. 2003) ("the division is a toll of analysis"); and in the USA, Dressler (2006), pp. 221–232 (4th ed., 2006); and Dressler's reply, in Fletcher's Essays, 225–230. Nonetheless, Fletcher and George P. Fletcher and Albin Eser (1 Justification and Excuse: Comparative Perspectives), and I agree with them, have emphasized the utility of this distinction as a basis for a general theory of criminal law that is applicable, in principle, in all legal cultures; see for instance as well US Model Penal Code, distinguishing between "General principles of Justification (Article 3) and General Principles of liability (Article 2) which includes excuses.

[4]See the evolution of the German system in Roxin (2005a), pp. 198–231.

In a book published in 1970, *Kriminalpolitik und Strafrechtsystem (Criminal policy and System of the Criminal law)*, Claus Roxin stated that "[the realm] of wrongdoing is the place where solutions to social conflicts are afforded, the domain in which collisions between conflicting individual interests or between social exigencies and personal necessities occur ... [In sum, this dominion] is always about the socially fair regulation of contradictory interests."[5] Moreover, when Roxin discusses this realm, he is above all making a reference, as is logical, to justification defenses—the negative component of wrongdoing that brings to light the true battleground in which the interests of individuals are pitted against each other or against societal interests on a daily basis.

Looking for a solution to these conflicts that would not derive solely from an automatic application of doctrinal concepts, and always seeking that such a solution be adequate from the standpoint of the aims of the criminal law, in the above-mentioned book Roxin proposed the elaboration of "a limited number of guiding substantive principles that, upon different combinations, would determine the scope of justification defenses and whose application in concrete cases would fix determinations about the utility or social harm of a given conduct, and about the justification or wrongfulness [of the act]."[6]

But it is in the domain of self-defence, a topic to which Roxin later dedicated other articles,[7] where there exists a unique necessity to revise the conclusions that follow from the automatic application of doctrinal concepts that have been elaborated without taking into account criminal policy considerations, which in this context have a strong social connotation. The right to self-defence is evidently a fundamental right of the individual, as elemental and old as the human condition and the instinct of self-preservation. However, in modern states that abide by the rule of law, recourse to self-defence should be the exception rather than the rule, and, in any case, the boundaries of the defence should be demarcated with as much precision as possible. In this, as in many other topics, the works of Claus Roxin in Germany and of George P. Fletcher,[8] in the US have been influential and masterful. They have always seen self-defence as one of those areas in which one can immediately grasp the apparent contradiction between the solutions that follow from standard criminal law systems and those that derive from an examination of normative considerations. The gap between these two solutions is more inexcusable in this context than in any other.

Why must one appeal, asked Roxin in 1970, to the principle of "defense of the legal order against unlawful aggression" in cases involving attacks carried out by

---

[5]Roxin (1970), p. 15. Spanish translation: Muñoz Conde F (1972) Política criminal y Sistema del Derecho penal. 40.

[6]Roxin (1970), p. 26.

[7]See Roxin (1963), p. 541; Roxin (1975), p. 106; Roxin (1981), p. 68. See a general view of his position in Roxin (2005a), pp. 650–719.

[8]See Fletcher (2013), pp. 121–230, 274–275. About self-defence in the Law of War, see Fletcher and Ohlin (2008); Fletcher (2020), pp. 212–214.

children or the mentally ill in order to justify the application of self-defence in circumstances in which the defensive response would have been prevented merely by avoiding the initial confrontation with the aggressor?[9] The state, not the individual, is the only one called to "defend the legal order against unlawful aggression."[10] Furthermore, the legal order doesn't need to be defended against people who cannot be motivated by the norms they have infringed upon, particularly when it is because of this very reason that their acts are not punishable.[11] These considerations led Roxin to limit self-defence only by appealing to the principle of self-protection. Thus, he declared the use of force by individuals to be taboo unless it is employed exclusively for one's own protection and, even then, he placed limits on the right of self-defence in light of "ethical and social considerations."[12]

In fundamental agreement with these premises, Mordechai Kremnitzer and Khalid Ghanayim objected to the notion that someone who kills a nonculpable (psychotic) aggressor acts in self-defence.[13] For them, such a case falls within the purview of justifiable necessity rather than self-defence.

3. In the following I will examine the applicable defense in the context of cases of *putative self-defence.*

The Spanish Penal Code of 1995 contains no legislated solution for the problem. Some systems, such as the French and Anglo-American systems, which have shown little concern about elaborating the distinction between justification and excuses and exploring its implications, treat putative justification as a justification in itself. In this sense, the Model Penal Code has taken the position that putative self-defence should be treated just like actual self-defence: if the actor believes that she is being attacked or that the use of force is immediately necessary to repel the attack, then the use of force is justified.[14] The German courts and theorists support the position that putative justification negates intent and, by analogy, apply the rule for mistakes of fact to mistakes about the factual elements of a justification, and if the mistake is avoidable apply the punishment because of negligence.[15] Fletcher thinks that the correct view in cases of putative justification is to treat it as an excuse, if the mistake is reasonable.[16]

In my opinion, the standard of "a reasonable person in the defendant's situation" belongs to the concept of wrongdoing, and thus can be applied to solve problems of

---

[9]Roxin (1970), p. 28.

[10]Roxin (1981).

[11]Ibid.

[12]Ibid.

[13]See Kremnitzer and Ghanayim (2004), pp. 887–888: "The necessity defense is a residual framework that is appropriate for treating situations that are not entirely appropriate to self-defence."

[14]See Fletcher (1998), pp. 88, 161–162.

[15]Same opinion Ghanayim (2007). ouclf.iuscomp.org who from the point of view of a "reasonable person" considers that reasonable mistaken justification negates the "mens rea", and unreasonable has to be considered and eventually punished as negligence. For discussion, see below note 41.

[16]See Fletcher (1998), pp. 90–91.

putative justification (putative self-defence, putative necessity, putative law enforcement and consent).[17] When someone has reason to believe that he is going to be attacked, and perhaps killed, and employs force against a person who is not really an aggressor, the defensive force employed to repel the imaginary aggression that is objectively inexistent can as well constitute a case of self-defence. The problem, however, does not lie in the fact that he or she may be relieved of liability, but in determining whether their exemption from responsibility has the same basis and hierarchical importance as the real self-defence, that is, if their act can be considered as a case of justification and not as a simple excuse.

In my opinion that in a such situation it is possible to admit a claim of justification, is not objectionable as long as the "rational and well-grounded" nature of the belief is used as an objective criterion with which to judge the defensive reaction that took place and not as a subjective standard that allows the actor to make up facts that have nothing to do with what really transpired.

In the most cases of self-defence, a total congruence between objective reality and subjective perception is practically impossible. There are always circumstances that are incorrectly or incompletely perceived and facts that the individual misinterprets.

It would be absurd to require a person who needs to act quickly in light of the imminence of what objectively looks like an aggression, that he or she calmly and coolly corroborates all of the objective criteria that support his beliefs before proceeding to defend himself. One cannot require everyone to exhibit the coolness of character and serenity that are needed to effectuate such corroboration. Furthermore, if one wastes too much time trying to corroborate the facts, the defensive response might lose efficacy because it could come too late. Instead, only the imminence of such an attack is required, coupled with a showing of the seriousness of the threatened aggression and of the rational and well-grounded belief in the existence of the threat.

As in many cases in which one tries to establish an objective standard with which to compare a person's conduct, recourse is made to the objectifiable criteria of the "rational," or more properly, as the Anglo-Americans typically say, to the "reasonable," that is, to what an average person would have done if she had faced the same circumstances. This standard is frequently employed in other contexts, such as when one examines the "*reasonable* foreseeability" of harm as a way of analyzing whether the actor's conduct was the proximate cause of a result. It is also employed when determining whether the actor's conduct was negligent or reckless because she did

[17]See, e.g., Muñoz Conde (2004), pp. 951–953; Muñoz Conde and García Arán (2019), pp. 308–309; Muñoz Conde (1995), pp. 213–227. Spanish version: Muñoz Conde F (1995) ¿"Legítima" defensa putativa?: Un caso limite entre justificación y exculpación, in Fundamentos de un sistema europeo del derecho penal. In: Libro Homenaje a Claus Roxin 183–204; and Muñoz Conde (2008) (as well in Californian Criminal Law Review, 2009).

not exhibit due diligence,[18] and when distinguishing between non-punishable "impossible" attempts and punishable "impossible" attempts.[19]

An appeal to reasonableness is also central to law enforcement defenses. The use of deadly force by police officers is justified if they reasonably believed it was necessary to use such force in order to prevent the commission of a crime that threatened the life or limb of third parties. Thus, as the U.S. Supreme Court stated in the *Garner* case, the use of deadly force by an officer is lawful if he "has probable cause to believe that the suspect poses a significant threat of death or serious physical injury to the officer or others, and such force is necessary to make the arrest or prevent escape."[20]

In this vein, New York's Penal Code requires to justify use of physical force in defense of a person (§ 35.15), or in defense of premises, or in defense of a person in the course of burglary (§ 35.20), that the actor "reasonably believes" that he or she is about to be the victim of a robbery or homicide in order for a claim of self-defence to be successful. Notice that in both cases the conduct is deemed justified as long as it falls within the scope of reasonably available alternatives. A perfect (i.e., non-mistaken) appreciation of the circumstances leading to the use of force is not required.

As well the Self-Defence provisions of the Canadian Penal Code, § .34, 2, b and 35 (a) ii, use the expressions "he believes, on reasonable ground."[21]

4. Notions of reasonableness also inform the "communicative concept of action."[22] This theory holds that human conduct is a form of expression or relevant communication between human beings. Judgments of reasonableness under this

---

[18]In context of "recklessness," the Model Penal Code Section 2.02 uses the expression "law-abiding person": "Disregard involves a gross deviation from the standard of conduct that a *law-abiding person* would observe in the actor's situation."

[19]See Muñoz Conde (2004), p. 946: "An attempt can only exist if the 'ordinary reasonable man in the defendant's situation' could have believed that the facts were as the defendant believed them to be."

[20]See Tennessee v. Garner (1985) 471 U.S. 1. That was the issue in the "Rodney King case"; see Fletcher (1995), p. 57. Spanish translation: Medina Ariza J J, Muñoz Aunión A (1997) Las víctimas ante el Jurado. Valencia. See as well N.Y. Penal Code § 35.30: "may use physical force when and to the extent he or she (a police officer or a peace officer) reasonably believes such to be necessary to effect the arrest, or to prevent the scape from custody, or in self-defence or to defend a third person from what he or she reasonably believes to be the use or imminent use of physical force; except that deadly physical force may be used for such purposes only when he or she reasonably believes that."

[21]See Valls Prieto and Renke (2010), pp. 813–835.

[22]This is compatible with the analytical philosophy of Wittgenstein. Fletcher (2007), pp. 281–283. Spanish translation: Muñoz Conde F (2008) Gramática del Derecho penal. And the Spanish criminal law scholar Vives Antón T (1996) Fundamentos del sistema penal, have developed this "communicative" concept of action. For an exploration of this concept and its consequences for the theory of criminal law, see Muñoz Conde and Chiesa (2007), p. 2461. Kyron Huigens criticizes this theory in his, Huigens (2007), p. 2408; but Dan-Cohen (2007), p. 2425, agrees with the "communicative theory of action" by Fletcher: "in interpreting an action … we must eventually reach a unitary judgment in which semantic as well as pragmatic and contextual factors are combined." See as well, Muñoz Conde and García Arán (2019), pp. 201–205.

theory are contextual. Think, for example, about whether we would recognize as reasonable a belief that someone is acting in self-defence when the alleged aggressor put his hand in his pockets and at the same time said: "I am going to kill you." The reasonableness of the belief seems to depend on the context surrounding the act and the knowledge that the threatened person has regarding the reputation and personality of the alleged aggressor. Maybe the threatened person knows that the aggressor is a killer for hire who always has a gun in his pocket, or maybe he knows that the supposed aggressor is mentally ill and that he threatens people with killing them all the time without meaning any real harm.

There is nothing to object to in this standard, as long as one is conscious that it establishes an objective test that is not intended to substitute real facts with the subjective beliefs of the actor, even if it allows for the consideration of the circumstances surrounding the actor's conduct. This objectification of subjective perception is perfectly proper and remains within the boundaries of objectivity that are needed in order to evaluate the presence of factual elements of claims of justification in a concrete case. However, to the degree that the standard allows for a certain amount of discretion when evaluating the reasonableness of the subjective perceptions of the actor, it introduces a possibility of arbitrariness that is difficult for the trier of fact to control.

From a juridical point of view, to act reasonably can be considered as to act correctly. American jurists, strongly influenced by notions of the "reasonable" introduced by Coke and Blackstone, believe that there can be more than one reasonable response to a legal problem. For Americans, as George Fletcher has asserted, the voice of reason has transformed itself into the spirit of tolerance, since "others might be mistaken, but their reasons might still be within the scope of reasonable alternatives."[23]

5. Nevertheless, recently, Fletcher argues against my opinion, that, as he says, it is "sided with the common law view" and denies that putative self-defence can be as well considered as a claim of justification in cases of reasonable mistakes. He says, I "misunderstand(s) the idea of a reasonable mistake and equate(s) it with a mistake that any sensible person might make. In these cases, where there is no way to find out the truth of the matter about, say, the timing of a hurricane, the defendant may treat the best available scientific as equivalent to reality."[24]

In fact, Fletcher's critique poses another different question: whose reason should we appeal in order to apply a "reasonableness" standard?

My position does not mean that the only requirement for justification is the good-faith subjective beliefs of the defendant, but rather that the subjective beliefs and reactions of the defendant must be tested against the objective community standard of reasonableness. This standard is then a "'two-pronged' or 'hybrid' test."[25] In its

[23]Fletcher (1985), p. 40.

[24]Fletcher (2013), p. 313.

[25]See Fletcher (1988), p. 42 (Spanish translation by Francisco Muñoz Conde and Fernando Rodríguez Marín, Valencia 1992).

first prong, the test requires that the defendant actually believes that the factual elements of justification exist (an aggression in case of self-defence, a risk to life or physical integrity of the woman in cases of legal therapeutic abortion, the consent of the woman in case of rape, legal authority to arrest and detain a suspect in a case of kidnapping). The second prong is that this belief must correspond with what a reasonable person would believe under the circumstances. Only if the test passes both prongs, the subjective and the objective standards, could the action be justified. The right of the victim to defend her- or himself, which Fletcher considers incompatible with this position,[26] can be admitted as a claim of justification that is different in nature than the claim of justification that the putative actor can invoke. When Fletcher says "[o]thers may be wrong, but their wrong path might still be on the map of reasonable alternatives,"[27] why not on the map of justified alternatives too? The question that then raises is to choose between self-defence for the putative defender and necessity for the victim of the reasonable mistake of the mistake, or to admit that both, putative defender and innocent victim, act in self-defence, but any way justified.

My position preserves the distinction between *Justification and Excuse* as basic elements of a structured analysis of criminal liability. One should not forget that deciding whether a person is justified is not a purely theoretical question that can (or should) be answered by appealing to perfect standards of conduct that are unattainable. It is true, as Greenawalt states, that "the criminal law does not demand ideal behaviour from people."[28] Consequently, as Joshua Dressler has correctly asserted, "all that the law can fairly expect of a person is that she (or he) make(s) a conscientious effort to determine the true state of affairs before acting. If she (he) does this, ... her (his) conduct is justifiable, although the result of her conduct may prove be tragic."[29] Joshua Dressler has described the difficulties that arise when applying the "reasonable person standard" in self-defence cases in the following way:

> The law of self-defense represents a compromise. The right of self-defense is not based on objective reality (whether the person about to be killed represents a real threat to the life of the actor) but neither is it based solely on the actor's subjective impressions: A person may only defend himself if he subjectively believes that deadly force is required and a reasonable person would also believe that it is appropriate under the circumstances. The crux of the issue, at least as courts see the matter, is: Who is the "reasonable person" to whom the defendant is compared? Or, put slightly differently, to what extent should courts permit juries, as factfinders, to incorporate the defendant's own characteristics or life experiences in the "reasonable person" standard?[30]

---

[26]See generally Fletcher (1998), pp. 89–91.

[27]Fletcher (1988), p. 40.

[28]Greenawalt (1984), p. 1905.

[29]Dressler (2006), p. 232; see as well, Dressler's reply to Fletcher in Fletcher's essays, supra note 3, pp. 225–230.

[30]Dressler (2006), p. 253.

A subjective approach would lead to considering that any belief of the actor, as long as it is an honest belief, should be deemed reasonable. This approach subjectifies the concept so much that it conditions the assessment of reasonableness on whether the conduct seemed reasonable *to the actor*. Such a high level of subjectivity would perforate the objective efficacy of legal norms, reducing them to a dead letter. Furthermore, it would lead to intolerable results because it would grant a license to kill to anyone who honestly believed that he was about to be attacked, regardless of the rationality of the belief.

Therefore, it seems preferable to adopt an objective approach to reasonableness that would justify conduct only when it is compatible with the hypothetical conduct that a normal and reasonable person would have observed in the circumstances of the actor. However, this objective approach cannot be taken to the extreme of not allowing for the consideration of any of the subjective beliefs and representations held by the actor. This would entail substituting the "normal person" for a "hypothetical and standardized person" that has never existed. It is difficult not to take into account the knowledge that the putative defender had about past acts of violence of the supposed aggressor or of his violent nature when objectively evaluating whether the actor's defensive response was reasonable.

The prosecutor in the *Goetz* case adopted a similar approach when building his case against the famous "subway avenger." He believed that the resolution of the case required two levels of analysis: (1) an assessment of whether the actor honestly believed the use of force was necessary in order to repel an attack, and, if so, (2) an examination of whether his belief is compatible with what a reasonable person would have believed in the circumstances of the actor.[31] This analysis is proper as long as the assessment of the actor's subjective beliefs is used as a vehicle for establishing the objective reasonableness of the conduct, not as a factor that bars engaging in an objective evaluation of the act.

So conceived, I do not object to considering that cases of putative self-defence where there is a "rational and well-grounded belief" in the existence of a wrongful attack should be considered full-blown claims of justification, even if it turns out that no aggression took place. The actor's subjective belief in the existence of an aggression is objectified by the judicial process in a way that transforms it into a legal fact. We should thus consider these cases to constitute authentic instances of justification, with all of the consequences that this entails. To talk about "putative self-defence" here is pointless. Thus, from this standpoint, a joke or an attack with a toy gun could be considered wrongful aggressions as long as they are capable of generating in the putative defender an objective, rational, and well-grounded belief that he is about to be attacked.

There are several reasons underlying this approach. On the one hand, there are evidentiary reasons that require courts to focus their attention on those facts or criteria that can objectify and add credibility to the allegations made by defendants with regard to their motivations and their beliefs. Subjective elements are

[31] Quoted by Fletcher (1988), p. 42.

notoriously difficult to prove during the criminal process, since the fact finder can only infer them, not directly observe them. This inference should be based on facts or criteria (*indicators*) that can be empirically corroborated and that can reveal in the most trustworthy manner the subjective element that is sought to be proven.[32]

6. But if the actor's conduct does not satisfy the objective standard discussed in the previous section, he or she cannot remain in the domain of justification. In this case the actor's subjective belief that he is going to be attacked, understandable as it may be, cannot exclude the objective wrongfulness of the act if it is not deemed to be "rational and well-grounded." The timorous or paranoid actor who interprets a verbal threat, an insult, or a slight physical contact as an imminent aggression to his bodily integrity can, from his own subjective point of view, be acting in self-defence. However, this conclusion is difficult to defend if one assesses the situation from an objective standpoint. In these cases, we have fully entered the realm of putative self-defence, for the reality of the aggression only exists in the mind of the actor who believes to be defending himself, since an impartial observer in the circumstances of the actor would not harbor such a belief. Thus, these instances represent authentic cases of mistakes involving discrepancies between reality and subjective perceptions that cannot be resolved by way of an objective evaluation of the circumstances. These types of mistakes can be unavoidable from the perspective of the actor, and thus excusable, but they cannot negate the objective wrongfulness of the act.

In such cases, equating putative self-defence with true claims of justification would lead to subjectifying assessments of wrongfulness in a way that is incompatible with the objective nature of the concept. This is the case because in order to determine whether an act is wrongful, one needs to engage in an impartial evaluation about whether the conduct conforms to legally appropriate standards of conduct. Not engaging in this type of objective and impartial evaluation of the conduct could lead to an infelicitous conflation of the concepts of wrongfulness and culpability, and of their respectively negative sides, justification and excuse.

Cases in which battered women kill their partners in non-confrontational situations in order to avoid being subjected to further abuse, raise important questions with regard to how to determine the reasonableness of such courses of action. It seems difficult to justify homicides in such non-confrontational situations when there is not an imminent threat to the life and bodily integrity of the battered woman. This is particularly the case when she had other alternatives available, such as abandoning and denouncing her partner, seeking help from institutions devoted to helping battered women, etc. Of course, if the mental state of the woman at the moment she kills her partner is abnormal, because of, for instance, the so-called "battered woman syndrome," it is possible to provide her with a full or partial excuse on the grounds of insanity, necessity, or diminished capacity.

[32]See Hassemer W (1980) Einführung in die Grundlagen des Strafrechts. 170 (Spanish translation: Muñoz Conde F, Zapatero L A (1984) Fundamentos del Derecho penal. 277). About the difficulties to consider premeditation, an specific mental subjective element, as an element of the definition of murder, see Kremnitzer (1998), pp. 626–660, who despite the critique on premeditation as an element of murder (645–650), concludes "that it is too soon to bury (it)."

Furthermore, as a result of the difference between being justified and excused, if the sleeping partner were to unexpectedly awaken, he would be justified if he uses force to avoid the excused attack of the woman.[33]

One must recognize, however, that it is very difficult to differentiate "rational and well-grounded beliefs" from "purely personal beliefs." Nonetheless, the differentiation can and should be made in much the same manner as one can and should always try to distinguish intention, recklessness and negligence. In the cases involving judgments of justification, we should compare the act performed with objective standards of reasonableness and consider the conduct wrongful, if it falls short of the standard. In the cases involving judgments of culpability, we should delve more deeply into the subjectivity of the individual in an attempt to determine whether, notwithstanding his failure to meet objective standards of reasonableness, his personal circumstances, character, or psychological makeup warrant a full or partial *excuse*, an exemption or mitigation of punishment.

Furthermore, in cases where the aggression is inexistent *ex post,* but one can rationally, reasonably, and objectively presume its *ex ante* existence,[34] we should conclude that the actor's defensive response falls within the range of legally acceptable courses of action. Thus, such conduct should not be considered wrongful and should not generate penal liability in the case of the actor who defends himself and in the cases of third parties who come to his aid.

This "*ex ante*" evaluation is accepted by most German scholars. For instance, Claus Roxin admits a full right to self-defence (*volles Notwehrrecht*) when someone kills another who is threatening him with a toy gun, and he does not know that the gun is a toy. Nevertheless, Roxin,[35] does not admit self-defence, but necessity, when someone after having carefully examined the situation (*ohne objektive Sorgfaltspflichtverletzung*) believes that he is in danger of an imminent attack that really does not exist. In this case Roxin shifts from the risk that the actor took to the invasion of the victim's interest; for him, only the innocent victim and not the "putative" defender has the right to self-defence. By doing so, he avoids the contradictory conclusion that both parties are acting in self-defence, but he does not negate that both parties of the conflict are justified: necessity in case of the putative defender and self-defence in case of the innocent victim.[36] The problem is that the "innocent" victim is not always so innocent, because he can have provoked the mistake of the "putative" defender, for instance, by joking around. In this case I do not see why his right has a priority over the right of the "putative" defender.

---

[33]See Dressler (2006), pp. 263–265; State v. Norman (1989) 378 S.E. 2d 8, 21 (Judith Norman Case) and commentary by Fletcher (1995), p. 132; Chiesa (2007) (Spain).

[34]Roxin (2005a), p. 659.

[35]Ibid., p. 662.

[36]Ibid., p. 662: "the correct and the most flexible solution" *(die richtige und flexibleste Lösung).* Against my opinion see also Schünemann B (1995) Die Funktion der Abgrenzung von Unrecht und Schuld für das Strafrechtssystem. In: Coimbra-Symposium für Claus Roxin, supra note 17, p. 173; and Conceicao S Valdagua M (1995) Notwehr und Putativnotwehr, Bemerkungen zum Referat von Muñoz Conde. In: Coimbra-Symposium für Claus Roxin, supra note 17, p. 229.

For Vera Bergelson, in case of a conflict between two incompatible justifications, as self-defence und necessity, "the lowest priority belongs to the defence of necessity, which, by design, may involve violation of right of innocent, unoffending individuals."[37]

For different reasons, Mordechai Kremnitzer and Khalid Ghanayim object that someone who kills a nonculpable (psychotic) aggressor acts in self-defence. For them, such a case falls within the purview of justifiable necessity rather than self-defence. But anyway, as a claim of justification and not as a simple excuse.[38]

In any case, the relationship between necessity and self-defence has always been troublesome. As Fletcher[39] has stated:

> The future boundary between self-defence and necessity will depend in large part on how important the distinct rationales of the two defences remain in our legal consciousness. The collective, utilitarian argument for balancing competing interests is well grounded in modern legal thought, and therefore we can assume that the defence of necessity will remain a powerful argument. Whether self-defence flourishes as a theoretically distinct defence depends largely on the political future of libertarian thinking.[40]

However, in cases where one cannot *ex ante* reasonably presume the existence of an aggression, we should conclude that the actor's defensive response does not constitute a legally permissible course of action. Consequently, even if the actor could end up being *totally or partially excused* in light of his personal circumstances, his act remains wrongful.[41]

---

[37]Bergelson (2007), p. 2503; see as well Chistopher (1998), pp. 537–574.

[38]Kremnitzer and Ghanayim (2004), pp. 887–888: "The necessity defense is a residual framework that is appropriate for treating situations that are not entirely appropriate to self-defence."

[39]Fletcher (1998), p. 145.

[40]About the different approaches to "political theory" and their influence on the theory of criminal law, see as well Fletcher (2007), pp. 13–15 (Spanish translation by Francisco Muñoz Conde, Buenos Aires, 2008).

[41]That is the position of the so-called German dogmatic "culpability theory," but this theory considers that "reasonable" mistakes are excuses and not justifications. This is also Fletcher's position, in Fletcher (1998), p. 162. The Model Penal Code § 3.09(2), provides that in such cases the defendant should be convicted of a reckless or negligent offense if the defendant's mistake was due to recklessness or negligence. This is the position of the "negative elements of the offense theory." see Ghanayim (2007). Dressler (2006), p. 273, also agrees with this outcome. In my opinion, this solution confuses mistake of facts with mistakes about a factual element of a claim of justification. Art. 14 of the Spanish Penal Code distinguishes between (i) mistake about the fact constitutive of the crime, and (ii) mistake about the wrongfulness of the conduct. This distinction corresponds to the distinction between "Tatbestands-und Verbotsirrtum" in sections 16 and 17 of the German Penal Code, § 16, 17 StGB (Germany). The first kind of mistake (mistake of fact)—whether reasonable or unreasonable, avoidable or unavoidable—negates the required intent for the offense, and if the charged offense cannot be construed as having been committed negligently, it categorically bars the possibility of a conviction. The second kind of mistake (mistake of law) only negates culpability if it is reasonable (i.e., unavoidable), but if it is avoidable it leads to conviction for the offense charged with a mandatory mitigation of punishment (in the German Penal Code the mitigation is discretional). In my opinion, the latter solution (treating mistakes about factual elements of justification as *excusable* mistakes of law) is the best way to deal with unreasonable mistakes

References

Bergelson, V. (2007). Rights, wrongs and comparative justifications. *Cardozo Law Review, 28*, 2503.

Chiesa, L. E. (2007). Mujeres maltratadas y legítima defensa, 20 Revista Penal 50.

Chistopher, R. (1998). Self-defence and objectivity, a reply to Judis Jarvis Thomson. *Buffalo Criminal Law Review*, 537–574.

Dan-Cohen, M. (2007). Thinking criminal law. *Cardozo Law Review, 28*, 2425.

Dressler, J. (2006). *Understanding criminal law* (4th ed., pp. 221–232).

Eser, A., & Fletcher, G. P. (Eds.). (1987). *Justification and excuse: Comparative perspectives*. New York: Dobbs Ferry.

Fletcher, G. P. (1978). *Rethinking criminal law* (pp. 759–870).

Fletcher, G. P. (1985). The right and the reasonable. *Harvard Law Review, 98*, 949.

Fletcher, G. P. (1988). *A crime of self-defence: Bernhard Goetz and the law on trial* (p. 42). New York: Free Press.

Fletcher, G. P. (1995). *With justice for some* (p. 57). Boston: Addison Wesley.

Fletcher, G. P. (1998). *Basic concepts of criminal law*. New York: Oxford University Press.

Fletcher, G. P. (2007). *The grammar of criminal law, American, comparative, and international: Volume one: Foundations*. New York: Oxford University Press.

Fletcher, G. P. (2013). *Essays on criminal law* (pp. 121–228). New York: Oxford University Press.

Fletcher, G. P. (2020). *The grammar of criminal law, volume two: International criminal law*. New York: Oxford University Press.

Fletcher, G. P., & Ohlin, J. D. (2008). *Defending humanity: When force is justified and why*. Oxford: Oxford University Press.

Ghanayim, K. (2007). The role of reasonable and unreasonable mistake in justified defences a comparative and analytical study. *Oxford University Comparative Law Forum*, 3.

Greenawalt, K. (1984). The perplexing borders of justification and excuse. *Columbia Law Review, 84*, 1905.

Huigens, K. (2007). Introduction. *Cardozo Law Review, 28*, 2408.

Jefferson, M. (2003). *Criminal law* (6th ed., p. 260).

Kremnitzer, M. (1998). On premeditation. *Buffalo Criminal Law Review, 1*(2), 626–660.

Kremnitzer, M., & Ghanayim, K. (2004). Proportionality and the aggressor's culpability in self-defence. *Tulsa Law Review, 39*(4), 887–888.

Muñoz Conde, F. (1995). Putativ Notwehr, in Bausteine des europäischen Strafrechts. In *Coimbra-Symposium für Claus Roxin* (pp. 213–227).

Muñoz Conde, F. (2004). Universalizing criminal law. *Tulsa Law Review, 39*, 951–953.

Muñoz Conde, F. (2008). Putative self-defence: A borderline case between justification and excuse. *New Criminal Law Review: An International and Interdisciplinary Journal, 11*(4).

Muñoz Conde, F., & Chiesa, L. E. (2007). The act requirement as a basic concept of criminal law. *Cardozo Law Review, 28*, 2461.

Muñoz Conde, F., & García Arán, M. (2019). *Derecho penal, Parte General* (10th ed., pp. 308–309).

Roxin, C. (1963). Die provozierte Notwehrlage. *Zeitschrift für die gesamte Strafrechtswissenschaft, 75*, 541.

Roxin, C. (1970). *Kriminalpolitik und Strafrechtssystem* (2nd ed., p. 15). Berlin: De Gruyter.

Roxin, C. (1975). Über den Notwehrexzess. Festschrift für Friedrich Schaffstein zum 70. Geburtstag 106.

about factual elements of claims of justification that are the product of duress or of an extreme emotional disturbance provoked by fear or terror. see Muñoz Conde and García Arán (2019), pp. 370–372.

Roxin, C. (1981). Die "sozial-ethischen" Einschränkungen des Notwehrrechts. *Zeitschrift für die gesamte Strafrechtswissenschaft, 93*, 68.
Roxin, C. (2005a). *Strafrecht, Allgemeiner Teil* (Vol. 1, pp. 195–198). München: C. H. Beck.
Roxin, C. (2005b). *Strafrecht, Allgemeiner Teil* (Vol. 1, pp. 1–13). München: Verlag C H Beck, Introduction.
Smith, J. C. (1989). Justification and excuse in the criminal law.
Stile, A. M., Manacorda, S., & Mongillo, V. (2018). *Civil Law e Common Law: Quale «grammatica» per il diritto penale? a cura di Alfonso Maria Stile Stefano Manacorda Vincenzo Mongillo*. Napoli: Edizioni Scientifiche Italiane.
Valls Prieto, J., & Renke, W. N. (2010). A comparison of the Spanish and Canadian law of self-defence. *Alberta Law Review, 47*, 4.

Life Imprisonment and Other Long-Term Sentences in the Finnish Criminal Justice System: Fluctuations in Penal Policy

Raimo Lahti

1 Introduction

1. The changes in the system of criminal sanctions normally reflect well the more general transition of criminal or penal ideologies and policies. In an earlier article,[1] I have illustrated this contention by making a survey which covers the development of the Finnish system of criminal sanctions from the latter part of the nineteenth century up to 1977, the year when the report of the Penal Law Committee was published. The committee had the task of preparing a report on the ideological foundations of the overall reform of the Penal Code (PC) of 1889.

The Finnish Penal Code of 1889 was originally permeated by the spirit and principles of the classical school of penal law wherein punishment was primarily regarded as retribution for the offence, and thereby the penal system was tolerably in harmony with the demands of general deterrence. More weight was given to individual prevention at the beginning of Code drafting. Later the influence of the sociological penal-law school—focusing on the offender and in individualized criminal sanctions—led to partial reforms of the penal system: for example, the introduction of Conditional Sentences Act in 1918, Dangerous Recidivists Act in 1932 and Young Offenders Act in 1940.

The system of criminal sanctions and the theory of criminal liability are the two main areas of the general doctrines of criminal law. The establishment of the Penal Law Committee in 1972 launched the process of the overall reform of criminal law in Finland which lasted until 2003. The preparatory work was done mostly by a task force named "Criminal Code Project" within the Ministry of Justice (1980–1999).

---

[1] Lahti (1977), pp. 119–157.

R. Lahti (✉)
University of Helsinki, Helsinki, Finland
e-mail: raimo.lahti@helsinki.fi

K. Ghanayim, Y. Shany (eds.), *The Quest for Core Values in the Application of Legal Norms*, https://doi.org/10.1007/978-3-030-78953-4_12

The major enactment of the final stage—the reform of the general doctrines—was adopted in 2003 and entered into force at the beginning of 2004.[2]

The main focus of the overall reform was on the special part of the Penal Code, i.e. the reassessment of punishable acts on the basis of criminalization principles ("what acts should be punishable and how severely should they be punished?"). The system of criminal sanctions had undergone numerous partial reforms ever since the early 1970s, but no larger enactments in this area had been produced in the context of the overall reform before the final stage in 2003. The 2003 reform (Act 515/2003) contained an important systematic change: it conceptualized criminal sanctions, i.e. the provisions on sentencing and the choice of the type of punishment were unified and collected into one chapter of the Penal Code (Chapter 6 of the PC).

In more recent articles I have provided overviews of the reform trends in the system of criminal sanctions and its individual amendments from the 1980s to the 2010s as well as an assessment of their impact. I have also put forward certain critical viewpoints which could be useful in the revision of criminal policy and in the development of the criminal justice systems in countries comparable to Finland, primarily in the Member States of the European Union (EU).[3] There are comprehensive accounts of the Finnish and Scandinavian criminal justice systems.[4]

2. Finland adheres to the so-called civil law countries, as do the other Nordic (Scandinavian) countries. These countries (Denmark, Finland, Iceland, Norway and Sweden), which have together a population of 27 million (with 5,5 million inhabitants in Finland), have many common features. They are highly advanced, industrialized welfare states. Economic, social and cultural development has been very much the same throughout Scandinavia. There has long been an intensive co-operation in legal and political matters between the Nordic countries.[5]

A more detailed examination of the facts would of course reveal differences, a part of which is understandable in the light of divergent historical developments of the countries. An example may be clarifying. It is true that relatively strict legalism is typical to all the Scandinavian criminal justice systems: legal predictability is based on written law (as in other civil law countries), and the balance of power between the legislator and the criminal justice agencies gives to the agencies in Scandinavia less power than in many other countries. Finland has been particularly cautious in extending the discretionary powers of criminal justice agencies.

Thus, for a long time, the principles of legal security (as the main manifestation of the rule of law) and the consistency of judicial praxis (more generally, the equality of citizens) have been strongly emphasized in Finland. These values were very clearly

---

[2]As to the comprehensive reform of Finnish criminal law, see generally Lahti and Nuotio (eds) (1992); Lahti (1993), pp. 100–117; Lahti (2019).—An unofficial translation of the Finnish Penal Code, as amended up to Act 766/2015, is available from the website of the Ministry of Justice: https://www.finlex.fi/fi/laki/kaannokset/1889/en18890039_20150766.pdf.

[3]See, in particular, the recent article Lahti (2017). As well as other reviews of the present author: Lahti (2000), pp. 141–155; Lahti (2020).

[4]See, in particular, Tonry and Lappi-Seppälä (eds) (2011); Bondeson (ed) (2005).

[5]See, e.g., Nordic Council (1984); Husa et al. (eds) (2007).

reflected in the Finnish Penal Code in its original form from 1889. This code was thoroughly permeated by the spirit and principles of the so-called classical school of penal law: punishment was primarily regarded as retribution for the offence committed. Any thought of reformation was subordinated to this.

3. The development in the laws of the Nordic countries over the 1960s and 1970s was marked by an increasing similarity in approaches to crime control policy and, through a series of legislative amendments, by a consequent harmonization of penal legislation. Scandinavian co-operation in legal and criminal policy became more diversified and active since the 1960s. The 1962 co-operation agreement includes a special article on criminal policy in accordance with which the parties agree to strive to bring into harmony their legal provisions on offences and on penal sanctions. In 1960, a permanent body of civil servants, the Scandinavian Criminal Law Committee, was established. To the committee was given tasks for drafting proposals designed to further the harmonization of criminal legislation by the respective Ministries of Justice. This committee outlined a common approach, among other things, as for provisions on parole, alternatives to imprisonment, meting out of punishment and sanctioning legal persons.

The harmonization of approaches in criminal policy was reflected most clearly in the work on reforming the systems of penal sanctions. In most of the Nordic countries, such major reforms were prepared in the 1970s. The official reports which appeared at the end of the 1970s reflected similar ideologies on the development of criminal sanctions.[6] In Finland and Norway preparations for the total reforms of their Penal Codes were started and enforced several decades later. Following ideological trends can be discerned in Finnish and Scandinavian criminal policy: criticism of treatment ideology (c. the 1960s) and revival of "neo-classicism" in criminal law (c. the end of the 1970s and the beginning of the 1980s). After that (in the 1980s and 1990s) an intensive pragmatic reform work took place for the recodification of Finnish criminal law.

These movements and the reasoning behind them are very relevant for understanding the current sentencing legislation in Finland, and therefore I will explain them in more detail (Sect. 2). After that the current legislation on life imprisonment and other long-term sentences will be analysed (Sect. 3). As for last-mentioned category, I will deal only with the legislation on prisoners serving their entire sentence in prison due to their dangerousness to the life or health of others (a regulation which replaced the earlier provisions on the incarceration of dangerous recidivists). Act on the Procedure for Release of Long-Term Prisoners (781/2005) concerns these two types of long-term sentences only.

---

[6] Rikosoikeuskomitean mietintö [Report of the Penal Law Committee] (1977) Komiteanmietintö [Committee report]. 1976:72; Alternativer til frihedsstraf – et debatoplaeg [Alternatives to imprisonment – a contribution to the debate] (1977) Betaenkning nr. 806; The National Swedish Council for Crime Prevention (1978) Report No. 5. A New Penal System – Ideas and Proposals (English summary); Om kriminalpolitikken [On criminal policy] (1978) Stortingsmelding nr. 104.

2 Criticism of Treatment Ideology (in the 1960s), Revival of "Neo-classicism" (in the 1970s) and the Principles Governing the Total Reform of Finnish Penal Code (in the 1980s–1990s)

1. Coercive treatment of the individual, regardless of whether its goals involved criminal justice, social welfare or health care, became the subject of critical attention in the Nordic countries from the 1960s. Among the questions taken up in this Scandinavian discussion were the notions of offence and illness, the reality of alcoholism treatment and the actual effects of various forms of deprivation of liberty. In that critical discussion it was argued, among other things:[7]

- coercive treatment in an institution did not cause the individual less suffering when this sanction was called treatment than it was termed punishment (still in the former case, less attention was paid to the legal safeguards of the individual than when it was a question of punishment);
- the fact that the length of treatment was not set in advance (but imposed for an indeterminate period and was based on the "needs" of the person) was in itself in conflict with such basic legal principles as culpability and proportionality or, on a more general level, the principles of fairness and predictability;
- even though increasing research had been carried out on the special preventive effects of different methods of treatment, no methods had been found which would generally have a clear and positive effect on the rate of recidivism for an individual.

Among the most important results of the criticism during the 1970s were legislative reforms in Scandinavia which either abolished the special sanctions which were imposed for an indeterminate period or at least clearly limited their scope of application. Such kinds of sanctions were in the Nordic countries, as everywhere in the Western countries, introduced in the spirit of the dominant treatment or incapacitation ideology of the first half of the twentieth century.

The model for the individualization of the sanctions was primarily applied to special categories of offenders (as to dangerous offenders and/or mentally disordered offenders). It should be noted that in the Nordic countries the most common penal sanction imposed by the courts has traditionally been the fine (both Finland and Sweden make extensive use of the day-fine system). Furthermore, the sentences of imprisonment imposed in these countries are, by international standards, short: for common crime such sentences are usually at most a few months in length.

It should also be noticed that the influence of the treatment or incapacitation ideology differed from one Scandinavian country to another. This influence was traditionally profound in Denmark and Sweden but relatively weak in Finland. For

[7] One of the most notable critical papers was an article of the Finnish Professor Inkeri Anttila; see Anttila (1971), pp. 9–21; reprinted in Anttila (2001), pp. 33–47.

example, Finland never followed the Scandinavian model in the matter of establishing a special treatment institution for psychopathic offenders; such a Danish institution under the leadership of the psychiatrist Georg K. Stürup was internationally known.

The most obvious and immediate effects of the described criticism against coercive treatment on legislative reforms in Finland consisted of the abolition of compulsory castration (in 1970) and an essential narrowing down of the conditions for the indeterminate incarceration of dangerous recidivists (in 1971).

During the first years after the enforcement of the act on compulsory castration in 1950, several dozen men—who had in criminal procedure been found guilty of sexual offences—were by administrative authorities each year ordered to be castrated against their will (in the 1960s, people were no longer castrated, not even on grounds of a voluntary request).

As a result of the law reform in 1971,[8] the possibility of indeterminate incarceration of dangerous recidivists was retained within very strict limits. The sanction could then be applied only to such recidivists who were regarded as dangerous, in a legally specified manner, to other people's life or health. While in the 1960s there were 200–400 offenders incarcerated into this "preventive detention" at the same time (i.e., 6% of the total number of prison population at most), the law reform dropped the number below ten persons (under one percent of the whole prison population).

2. In international discussion, the Scandinavian movement in criminal law since the end of the 1970s has often been characterized as a "neo-classicism". When doing this, references has been made especially to the official documents mentioned above,[9] saying that these put a relatively strong emphasis on the aim of general prevention and on the principle of justice and are correspondingly critical against the treatment ideology.

As for the legislative reforms in Finland supposed to reflect a neo-classical revival, two legal acts from the year 1976 are normally mentioned. First, a new Conditional Sentences Act was given. Certain provisions of it were obviously influenced by the idea of general prevention, while the earlier act aimed at the individualization of these sanctions.

The new provisions on the meting out of punishment (Chapter 6 in the Penal Code) were more interesting. These provisions, which replaced the earlier complicated regulation on recidivism, seek—according to travaux préparatoires—to guide the courts in the meting out of punishments in order to distribute severe and lenient punishments more equitably and more consistently, and so that they would be more instrumental in preventing criminality.

[8] More about this reform, see Anttila (1975); reprinted in Anttila (2001), pp. 91–103.

[9] See Rikosoikeuskomitean mietintö (1977) Valtioneuvosto, Finland; Alternativer til frihedsstraf (1989) Aarhus universitetsforlag, Denmark; The National Swedish Council for Crime Prevention (1978) Report No. 5. A New Penal System – Ideas and Proposals (English summary); Om kriminalpolitikken [On criminal policy] (1978) Stortingsmelding nr. 104.

These provisions have obviously increased consistence and uniformity in sentencing practice. This effect has been partly caused by the fact that there is increasingly available statistical information about the so-called normal punishment zones. The Supreme Court has also given precedents about meting out punishment. Another effect concerns the weight of recidivism as an aggravating ground. It is now more seldom an aggravating factor than earlier, but it is still affecting too strongly, especially when choosing the type of penal sanction.

Many debaters have regarded the characterization of neo-classicism as misleading—and I belong to those people. For instance, the Finnish scholars Inkeri Anttila and Patrik Törnudd, who were the key persons in creating the new crime control policy, emphasize that the new thinking is future oriented and should not be mixed up in a "just deserts" philosophy. The emphasis on justice is associated with the traditional legal safeguards and with attempts to create a more just crime control system (e.g., by modernizing definitions of crime). They also say that the incapacitation ideology was at its strongest in those days when the decision-makers could hope that an extended period of incarceration would also serve to rehabilitation of the offender. However, imprisonment has not proved to rehabilitate, and it is also extremely expensive both for the offender and for society. Crime control policies should be cost-conscious, defining social cost in as wide a sense as possible.[10]

The proponents of the new crime control policy did not see any inconsistency in attempting to reduce the use of long prison sentences while at the same time asserting that punishments are and should be punitive. "The temptation to shroud the punitive intent in euphemism is not only dishonest but may even be dangerous when we admit the punitive intent we also admit the necessity of fairness and strict standards of humanity and justice."[11]

3. An important effect of the new crime control policy can be seen in the reduced use of custodial sentences in Finland. Since the mid-1970s, the relative number of offenders sentenced to unconditional imprisonment was on the decrease until 1999: from 118 persons in 1976 to 65 in 1999 per 100,000 inhabitants which was the imprisonment level of the other Nordic countries. At the same time, the number of reported crimes followed the same trends in all Nordic countries. Therefore, the dramatic cut in the prisoner rate in Finland did not result in a proportional increase in crime rates compared with other Nordic countries where the prisoner rates remained the same. In 2000–2005, the number of incarcerated people increased to 90 in 2005, but in the most recent years, the level seems to be normalized to 60–70—in the 2010s even under 60—per 100,000 inhabitants.[12]

This effect should be assessed against the background of the general objectives and values of the criminal policy which was adopted in Finland. Cost-benefit thinking in policy-making, as it was originally formulated in the late 1960s,[13]

[10]See Anttila and Törnudd (1980), pp. 48–51; reprinted in Anttila (2001), pp. 121–124.

[11]Anttila and Törnudd (1980), p. 50.

[12]In more detail, see Lappi-Seppälä (2012), pp. 85–111, ch IV.5; Niemi (ed) (2018), p. 131.

[13]See Törnudd (1971), pp. 23–33.

suggests that we should aim at the reduction and distribution of the suffering and other social costs caused by crime and of the control of crime. In addition to crime prevention, a strong emphasis should be put on justice and humaneness. For instance, the argument of justice requires a just allocation of the social costs of crime and crime control among different parties, such as the society, offenders and victims, and the argument of humaneness speaks in favour of parsimony and leniency of penal sanctions and the respect of humanity in crime control.

The reduced prisoner rate should be assessed in relation to the preventive effects of the system of criminal sanctions. The above-described Nordic experience, in addition to other criminological data, is an argument against the fear that a cut in the number of inmates will result in a proportional increase in the incidence of crime. Accordingly, the variations in the prisoner rate should not be looked at as a phenomenon separate from other events, nor should the criminal policy changes since the late 1960s be seen merely as a result of some ideological agenda pursued by a group of penal experts.

The Finnish scholar Tapio Lappi-Seppälä has extensively studied the relationship between penal policy and prisoner rate. His conclusions include the following assertions: the penal severity is closely associated with the extent of welfare provision, differences in income equality, trust and political and legal cultures. So, the Nordic penal model has its roots in consensual and corporatist political culture, high level of social trust and political legitimacy as well as a strong welfare state. These different factors have both indirect and direct influences on the contents of penal policy.[14]

4. The total reform of Finnish Penal Code was prepared and mainly implemented in the 1980s and 1990s. To my mind the principles governing this overall reform can be described in the following way: towards a more rational criminal justice system: efficient, just and humane criminal justice.[15]

The existence of the criminal justice system is justified on utilitarian grounds. The structure and operation of the penal system cannot, however, be determined solely on the basis of its utility. The criteria of justice and humaneness must also be applied. The penal system must be both goal-rational (utility) and value-rational (justice, humaneness). The following exemplary arguments clarify the content of these various criteria.

Utility (efficiency, expediency):

- A criminal justice system shall be used for the prevention of unacceptable behaviour only to the extent that proves necessary in a cost-efficiency comparison of criminal policy measures.
- The expediency of a criminal justice is measured first and foremost through its general preventive effects.

[14]See, among many articles, Lappi-Seppälä (2012), pp. 85–111, IV.5.

[15]See, originally, Lahti (1985), pp. 884–885; reprinted in Lahti (2019), pp. 43–64. See also Lahti (1993), pp. 101–103.

- The contents of a penal justice system are defined so that the system causes as little suffering and other social costs as possible without allowing any essential reduction of general prevention.
- Although the efficiency of a criminal justice system is evaluated primarily on the basis of general prevention, other utilitarian grounds are also important when individual penal sanctions are imposed and sentences executed. These goals include rehabilitation and incapacitation.

Justice:

- A penal justice system shall be used only to the extent that is reasonable when a just distribution of the harmful effects caused by crime and its control is realized.
- The justice of a penal system is evaluated first and foremost by asking whether or not it furthers the principles of equality, fairness and predictability.
- The definitions of criminal acts and penal sanctions are legally bound (the legality principle in criminal law: nulla poena sine lege).
- The threats of punishment as well as actual penal sanctions are, in accordance with the principles of guilt and proportionality, i.e. reasonable relationship to the harmfulness and blameworthiness of the acts.
- A criminal justice system shall fulfil the requirements of legal safeguards (especially: fair trial, due process).
- The criminal procedure shall be organized so that the interests of the victim are taken into consideration to a reasonable extent.

Humaneness (including postulates in the border area between the principles of justice and humaneness):

- The contents of the criminal justice system are determined so that it is harmony with the principles of human dignity, integrity, freedom of the individual and other human rights.
- When imposing a penal sanction and executing a sentence, the principles of equity and mercy shall be taken into consideration.

It is possible largely to apply the main criteria for rationality in the criminal justice system—utility, justice and humaneness—without leading to conflict over the development of the system.[16] In order for it to be possible to regard these criteria as parallel, inter-complementary, they must be defined in a particular way. Thus, in respect of the mechanisms through which the general preventive (i.e. utilitarian) effects can be achieved, the emphasis must be on features other than the deterrent effect of the punishment itself. In Scandinavia, another mechanism has long been in the foreground: the punishment shall demonstrate socio-ethical reproach and so influence one's sense of morals and justice: therefore, the legitimacy of the penal system is of special importance. Similarly, the criteria of justice cannot only refer to formal legal safeguards (for example, predictability) but must also encompass justice

[16]Cf., e.g., the discussion on the connection between culpability and human dignity in Germany and Israel: Kremnitzer and Hörnle (2011), pp. 116–117.

and legal safeguards that are determined on the basis of material criteria (for example, reasonableness in casu).

5. The foregoing description has shown that in Finland and elsewhere in Scandinavia there was since the late 1960s a negative attitude towards indeterminate sanctions based on an individual's need tor treatment or his dangerousness. Legislative reforms since the 1970s have either abolished these sanctions or at least clearly limited their scope of application.

However, it should also be noted that these reforms have normally led to the adoption of stricter conditions of application, i.e. the adoption of upper limits for sanctioning. It has been the intention to ensure that the offender would not be a subject to coercive treatment in an institution or to incapacitation tor a period longer than can be considered just and reasonable in regard to the seriousness of his offence. But within these limits, the sanctions should satisfy the requirement to provide voluntary treatment for the individual.

The scope of the law on the incarceration of dangerous offenders was crucially restricted in 1971. According to the Penal Law Committee (1976), this sanction should be fully abolished. The use of this sanction in 1971–1986 was evaluated in an empirical study by the Finnish scholar Heikki Pihlajamäki.[17] Following conclusions could be made on the basis of its results and meta-analysis:

- In the selection of dangerous recidivists, special preventive criteria had been decisive. However, the decision on release on parole had become a more automatic one, where the dangerousness of the offender was not reconsidered. Indeterminate incarceration had become an additional punishment for certain types of violent crime.
- There was an apparent risk of false predictions of dangerousness, and there were no guarantees that the really violent offenders could be identified through the present methods. The selection system, which operated through a number of stages, contributed to the same result: the ambiguity of the legal criteria and the difficulty of prediction left the discretion to the prosecutor, the court and the national prison board with considerable scope for value judgements.
- Being labelled dangerous recidivist could be fateful, in particular when only a small group of recidivists was labelled as dangerous at the end of a rigid process of selection.
- There had been relatively few efforts in Finland to develop methods for predicting dangerousness. The assessments laid throughout on an intuitive level, although the national prison board also relied on clinical data. On the other hand, studies done abroad made suspicious as to the possibilities that sufficiently reliable prediction methods could be developed in near future. In this situation there was a risk that the variables which were in fact used would socially discriminate certain groups of offenders.

[17]Pihlajamäki (1987).

During the preparation of the overall reform of criminal law it proved obvious that the reassessment of the incarceration of dangerous offenders would be connected with the future of life imprisonment or, more generally, with the future of sentencing for particularly serious crimes. Life imprisonment has traditionally imposed in practice for murders only, although it is provided as an alternative punishment also for certain other serious crimes by the Penal Code (such as genocide, PC 11:1, or homicide with terrorist intent, PC 34a:1). In murder cases life imprisonment has been a compulsory sanction, if the offender was not young (under 18 years when the crime was committed) and not regarded as being in the state of diminished responsibility (when the crime was committed). Those who had been sentenced to life imprisonment could be released on parole after pardoning by the President of the Republic only, in practice at the earliest when the offender had served his prison sentence for over ten years.

It should be noted that life imprisonment has been the harshest punishment, because capital punishment was in 1972 finally abolished from the system of sanctions in Finland. Even though that abolition was important in principle, its practical significance was slight, as a statute passed over 20 years before forbade the use of capital punishment in time of peace, and capital punishment had been out of use under normal conditions for more than a century and a half.[18]

3 Current Legislation on Life Imprisonment and Other Long-Term Sentences After the Reforms in the 2000s and 2010s and Its Critical Evaluation

1. When the Criminal Code Project for the overall reform of Finnish criminal law finished its work in March 1999, it left behind many unfinished draft proposals for partial reform of the system of sanctions. In the last meeting of the Steering Committee of the Project, the topic of discussion concerned the policies and principles governing the overall reform of the system of criminal sanctions. In a memorandum drafted for that meeting, the present author noted that, as the neo-classicism in criminal law thinking—as formulated originally in the 1970s—had already been modified with the introduction of individualized sanctions such as community service and juvenile punishment, it would be advisable to consider the broader implications which that modification have on the principled assessment of the relations between the various types of sanctions and on the drafting of the substantive provisions within their respective scope of application. My memorandum did not receive any support.[19]

The further preparation of the partial reforms concerned custodial sentences of imprisonment and their enforcement as well as the conditional release of prisoners

[18]See, in more detail, Anttila (2001), pp. 166–174.

[19]See Lahti (2017), ch. 6.

on parole. These revision tasks were assigned to specific law drafting bodies of the Ministry of Justice. The reform work led to the new Prison Act (767/2005), which adjusted the prison law to fulfil the requirements of the new Finnish Constitution (731/1999) and human rights obligations as well as with the strengthened legal safeguards and transparency of prison administration. This reform also included the enactment of new provisions on the release of prisoners on parole (780/2005), and as a novelty, a regular release of prisoners serving a life sentence on parole by the decision of Helsinki Court of Appeals (781/2005).[20]

The legislation on incarceration concerning dangerous offenders (preventive detention) was repealed and replaced by new provisions on prisoners serving their entire sentence in prison due to their dangerousness to the life or health of others as manifested in their criminal activity (780/2005). The application of these provisions presupposes multidisciplinary risk assessments of the offender, and it is a manifestation of the aim of incapacitation.

Both of these regulations on the long-term sentences have been crucially amended in the 2010s: on the life imprisonment in 2010 (1099/2010) and 2013 (628/2013) and on the prisoners serving their entire sentence in 2017 (800/2017), when the last-mentioned sanction was also renamed as a combination punishment.

2. These reforms concerning prison sentences and their enforcement reflect a change in the sanctioning policy in relation to the criminal law thinking describe above in chapter 2, because they stress the aim of incapacitation either by being indeterminate (life sentence) or by being based on the risk assessment of the offender's dangerousness to others (prisoners serving their entire sentence).

These reforms are examples of the fluctuations in penal policy. As Tapio Lappi-Seppälä points out, there have been some indication of a return of risk-based, predictive sentencing, which was ruled out by the 1970s sanction reforms. However, the overall use of these risk-based measures has remained low in the Nordic countries.[21]

One reason for the change in Finland was a moral panic, which was caused by a shooting in the city Porvoo in 2010, when it claimed three lives and engendered considerable discussion on offender risk assessment and the need for it, especially in the case of conditional release of life prisoners. A special working group was set up by the Ministry of Justice for examining means to decrease serious violence. This working group proposed in its report among other things that the risk of recidivism of those prisoners who had been sentenced for violent or sexual crimes should be assessed before releasing them on parole.[22] In the strategic programme of the former Government of Prime Minister Juha Sipilä (2015–2019) it was stated that the use of risk assessments will be increased for prisoners when deciding on their parole. In the similar programme of the present Government under Prime Minister Sanna Marin

[20]In more detail, see Lappi-Seppälä (2010), pp. 135–168.

[21]Lappi-Seppälä (2016), p. 500.

[22]See Vakavan väkivallan vähentäminen [Reduction of serious violence] (2012) Reports and Statements of the Ministry of Justice No. 37.

(dated on 10 December 2019) it is stated more generally that the preconditions of parole regarding the most dangerous prisoners will be evaluated carefully.

The harshness of life imprisonment is illustrated by the fact that, according to the general provision (PC 2c:2), the fixed period of imprisonment shall be at most 12 years or, when imposing a joint sentence, 15 years, and such a prisoner shall be conditionally released when he or she has served two thirds or, in first offender's case, a half of the sentence (PC 2c:5). Taking an example from the special part of the Penal Code, the penal scale for the basic form of homicide, i.e. manslaughter (PC 21:1), is imprisonment for a fixed period of at least 8 years (up to 12 years), when in the aggravated case of homicide, i.e. murder (PC 21:2),[23] the penal scale provides life imprisonment only.

In the reform of the prison legislation in 2005 human rights aspects were emphasized in line with the case-law of Article 3 in the European Convention on Human Rights (ECHR), which requires a mechanism or possibility for review of a whole life sentence.[24] A regular release of prisoners serving a life sentence on parole was introduced and the Helsinki Court of Appeals was tasked with the decision-making in accordance with the Procedure for the Release of Long-Term Prisoners Act (781/2005). In addition, the power of the President of the Republic to pardon was retained.

Doris Schartmueller has found in her comparative study crucial similarities in the processes of release for life-imprisonment offenders between Denmark, Finland and Sweden (in Norway life imprisonment is not in use); according to her findings, the new release process exemplifies the traditionally strong role that judges have played in penal decision-making in Scandinavia, and the amount of discretion of the court seemed to be strongest in Finland.[25]

A person sentenced to life imprisonment may normally be conditionally released at the earliest when he or she has served twelve years in prison. After the amendments at the beginning of 2010s, there shall be made an overall risk assessment in order to determine whether the sentenced person is dangerous to others. So in considering conditional release attention shall be paid to (a) the nature of the offence or offences that had led to the sentence of life imprisonment, (b) other punishments incorporated in the sentence of life imprisonment or that have been served during the period of imprisonment, (c) the other possible subsequent criminality of the convicted person, and (d) an assessment based on the conduct of or threats made by the prisoner whether there is an evident danger that on release he or she would

---

[23]Penal Code 21:2: "If the manslaughter is (1) premeditated, (2) committed in a particularly brutal or cruel manner, (3) committed by causing serious danger to the public, or (4) committed by killing a public official on duty maintaining public order or public security, or because of an official action, and the offence is aggravated also when assessed as a whole, the offender shall be sentenced for murder to life imprisonment."

[24]For a list of ECHR cases, see European Court of Human Rights (ECtHR) (2017) Factsheet of the European Court of Human Rights. http://www.echr.coe.int/Documents/FS_Life_sentences_ENG.pdf; Schartmueller (2018); De La Cuesta (2011), pp. 457–476.

[25]Schartmueller (2018).

commit an aggravated offence against life, health or liberty. Attention shall also be paid (e) to the implementation of the plan for the term of sentence and to the person's conduct while in prison. Attention may also be paid to (f) the undertaking of the prisoner to comply with the conditions of the medical treatment and other related treatment and support. Before a person sentenced to life imprisonment is conditionally released, he or she may be placed in probationary liberty under supervision (See PC 2c:9–10).

In a recent precedent of the Finnish Supreme Court (KKO 2019:89), the preconditions of the release on parole regarding a life-imprisoned offender were examined. The offender had been serving over 14 years in the closed prison. Helsinki Court of Appeals would have granted the release, although the Criminal Sanctions Agency was in its statement resisting it, after a pros and cons arguing. According to Helsinki Appeal Court, the pros (over 14 years' serving in the prison, the person's such a conduct in prison and such supportive networks in freedom which would further his rehabilitation) weighed more than the cons (murder and attempted murder as serious offences that had led to the sentence of life imprisonment, the person's joining the United Brotherhood organization of criminals and problems with intoxicants while serving his sentence).

The Supreme Court balanced the cons and pros otherwise and rejected the application for release. The main differences in the reasoning were following: According to Supreme Court, the serious nature of offences in question, murder and attempted murder, as well as other punishments incorporated in the sentence – in addition to the defects in the implementation of the plan for the term of sentence (membership in the UB organization and problems with intoxicants) supported a longer period in the closed prison than what the person had already served. Therefore, the release on parole should be postponed.

The reasoning of the Supreme Court is open to critique, because the arguments are to my mind not enough connected with the normative preconditions as defined in the provisions of PC 2c:9–10. As far as I can see, the most important criterion for the postponement of the release should be the assessment that there is an acute, evident danger that on release the person would commit an aggravated offence against life, health or liberty. However, the reasoning does not foresee such a prospect.

There was a substantial increase in the number of life imprisonments for murder at the beginning of the 2000s, although the amount of homicide crime was at the same time decreasing (and the judgements for murders stayed quite steady). For instance in 2015, the number of life sentenced prisoners was 193, which was 9 percent from the prisoners on a certain day; the corresponding number in Sweden was 142 und 4 percent. In average, life imprisonment means in Finland serving 14–15 years in the closed prison (the longest one 26 years). The increase of life imprisonments in Finland can to great extent be explained by the amendment of the provisions of Penal Code (PC 3:4.3; 6:8) in 2003, according to which the diminished responsibility does not affect the applicable maximum punishment (such as life imprisonment), and by the tightened interpretation of the psychic-normative criteria of criminal irresponsibility since the 1990s (PC 3:4.2). The enclosed Fig. 1 illustrates this development from 1990 to 2011.[26] After that period, at the beginning of 2018, there were 195 life sentenced, i.e., their number increased in 2012–2018 up to near

[26]Cf. a similar observation as for the court practice in Israel: Kremnitzer and Hörnle (2011), p. 117.

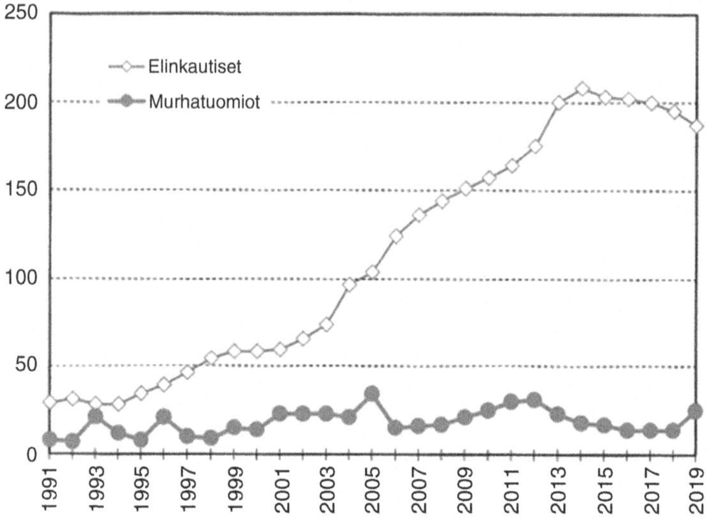

Fig. 1 Life sentenced and murder judgments in 1991–2019. Elinkautiset = Life sentenced; Murhatuomiot = Murder judgements. Source: Kuusisto Mäkelä F E (ed) (2021) Seuraamusjärjestelmä 2019 (The system of criminal sanctions in 2019). Review of the Institute of Criminology and Legal Policy, University of Helsinki, p. 141

200 persons; meanwhile the annual number of murder judgements has remained between 10 and 30.[27]

3. Already before the reform of the legislation on dangerous offenders in 2005 it had been applied so that those prisoners served their entire sentence in prison but not in practice for an indeterminate period, as the original contents of that legislation from the year 1953 allowed. However, a consequence of the attempt to prevent dangerous offenders from reoffending, based on a positive future dangerousness evaluation, was that these offenders were banned from getting on regular conditional parole to serve the rest of his or her sentence in freedom. Therefore, the time to be served in prison was longer than in the case of a normal sentence, which shall be determined so that is in just proportion to the harmfulness and dangerousness of the offence and the culpability of the offender manifest in the offence (PC 6:4). By using a metaphor of Inkeri Anttila, the offender who was assessed to be dangerous was punished in part for crimes which he or she had not committed (see also above Sect. 2, Item 5).[28]

The prerequisites for this sanction, which was in 2017 renamed as a combination punishment, are defined quite strictly so that (a) the offender in question must have committed one or more of serious violent crimes which are specifically listed in the Act, (b) he or she is not a first-time offender, and (c) the offender is to be deemed

[27]See Niemi (ed) (2018), p. 129.

[28]Anttila (1975).

particularly dangerous to the life, health or freedom of another. The combination punishment means that in addition to serving the entire sentence in prison the offender shall be in probationary liberty under supervision for one year (See PC 2c:11).

In a critical evaluation of the described reforms on the long-term sentences, various values and interests of criminal policy as well as basic and human rights considerations must be balanced. In her recent doctoral thesis on the subject (2017) Annakaisa Pohjola summarizes that "evaluating the dangerousness of offenders is complicated, as it is necessary to weigh against each other the concrete elements of dangerousness, formal and substantive justice along the overall legal safeguards of the judicial system". According to Pohjola, in order to decrease false positive assessments, there is a need for exact and comprehensive legislation which would define the requirements for conducting valid forensic psychiatric evaluations of the future dangerousness of offenders. She also criticized the too strong reliance of the judges on the statements provided by forensic psychiatry experts, and she calls them to consider all the evidence and to make the decision on the dangerousness of the offender independently on normative grounds.[29]

It is noteworthy that the European Convention on Human Rights implies also positive obligations, for instance its Article 2 an obligation on the authorities to take preventive operational measures to protect an individual whose life is at risk from the criminal acts of another individual. However, this obligation has limits, and it will arise where the authorities knew or ought to have known of the existence of a real and immediate risk to the life of an identified individual or individuals and failed to take measures within the scope of their powers which, judges reasonably, might have been expected to avoid that risk.[30] So to the jurisprudence of the Strasbourg Court should be referred only cautiously as a justification of the legislation in question.

When the scope of preventive justice is expanding in many ways in the name of public protection and security, we scholars should be prepared to critically assess the foundations for this development.[31] Michael Tonry summarizes the most recent research results by saying that "[p]redictive sentencing can thus be justified neither empirically nor morally", although "prevention concerns and prevailing emotionalism may make the elimination of preventive sentencing unachievable".[32]

[29]Pohjola (2017), passim, esp. 409–411 (Abstract).

[30]See esp. ECtHR Giuliani and Gaggio v. Italy, Judgment 24 March 2011, Grand Chamber, paras 244–246 with references to earlier case-law.

[31]See, in particular, Ashworth and Zedner (2014).

[32]Tonry (2019), pp. 290–291.

References

Anttila, I. (1971). Conservative and radical criminal policy in the Nordic countries. *Scandinavian Studies in Criminology, 3*, 9–21.

Anttila, I. (1975). *Incarceration for crimes never committed.* The Publications of the National Research Institute of Legal Policy No. 9.

Anttila, I. (2001). *Ad ius criminale humanius. Essays in criminology, criminal justice and criminal policy.* Helsinki: Finnish Lawyers' Association.

Anttila, I., & Törnudd, P. (1980). Reasons for punishment. In N. Bishop (Ed.), *Crime and crime control in Scandinavia.* Scandinavian Research Council for Criminology.

Ashworth, A., & Zedner, L. (2014). *Preventive justice.* Oxford: Oxford University Press.

Bondeson, U. (Ed.). (2005). *Crime and justice in Scandinavia.* Copenhagen: Forlaget Thomson.

De La Cuesta, J. L. (2011). The principle of humanity in penal law. *Revue Internationale de Droit Pénal, 82*, 457–476.

Husa, J., Nuotio, K., & Pihlajamäki, H. (Eds.). (2007). *Nordic law – Between tradition and dynamism.* Intersentia: Antwerp.

Kremnitzer, M., & Hörnle, T. (2011). Human dignity and the principle of culpability. *Israel Law Review, 44*, 115–141.

Lahti, R. (1977). Criminal sanctions in Finland: A system in transition. *Scandinavian Studies in Law, 21*, 119–157.

Lahti, R. (1985). Zur Entwicklung der Kriminalpolitik in Finnland. In *Festschrift für Hans-Heinrich Jescheck* (pp. 871–892). Berlin: Duncker & Humblot.

Lahti, R. (1993). Recodifying the Finnish Criminal Code of 1889: Towards a more efficient, just and humane criminal law. *Israel Law Review, 27.*

Lahti, R. (2000). Towards a rational and humane criminal policy – Trends in Scandinavian penal thinking. *Journal of Scandinavian Studies in Criminology and Crime Prevention, 1*, 141–155. https://doi.org/10.1080/140438500300076135.

Lahti, R. (2017). Towards a more efficient, fair and humane criminal justice system: Developments of criminal policy and criminal sanctions during the last 50 years in Finland. Law, criminology and criminal justice. *Cogent Social Sciences, 3*, 1303910. https://doi.org/10.1080/23311886.2017.1303910.

Lahti, R. (2019). *Zur Kriminal- und Strafrechtspolitik des 21. Jahrhunderts. Der Blickwinkel eines nordischen Wohlfahrtsstaates und dessen Strafgesetzreformen: Finnland.* Berlin: De Gruyter. https://doi.org/10.1515/9783110647990.

Lahti, R. (2020). Multilayered criminal policy: The Finnish experience regarding the development of Europeanized criminal justice. *New Journal of European Criminal Law.* https://doi.org/10.1177/2032284419898527.

Lahti, R., & Nuotio, K. (Eds.). (1992). *Strafrechtstheorie im Umbruch.* Helsinki: Finnish Lawyers' Publishing Company. English edition: Lahti, R., & Nuotio, K. (Eds.), *Criminal law theory in transition.* Helsinki: Finnish Lawyers' Publishing Company.

Lappi-Seppälä, T. (2010). Finland. In N. Padfield, D. van Zyl Smit, & F. Dünkel (Eds.), *Release from prison. European policy and practice* (pp. 135–168). Cullompton: Willan Publishing.

Lappi-Seppälä, T. (2012). Penal policies in the Nordic countries. *Journal of Scandinavian Studies in Criminology and Crime Prevention, 13*(1), 85–111. https://doi.org/10.1080/14043858.2012.740858.

Lappi-Seppälä, T. (2016). Life imprisonment and related institutions in the Nordic countries. In D. van Zyl Smit & C. Appleton (Eds.), *Life imprisonment and human rights* (pp. 461–505). Oxford: Hart Publishing.

Niemi, H. (Ed.). (2018). *Seuraamusjärjestelmä [Criminal sanctions system].* Institute of Criminology and Legal Policy, University of Helsinki.

Nordic Council. (1984). *Level of living and inequality in the Nordic countries: Denmark, Finland.* Sweden: NORD.

Pihlajamäki, H. (1987). *Indeterminate incarceration of dangerous recidivists, 1971–1986 (Summary)*. The Publications of National Research Institute of Legal Policy No. 85.
Pohjola, A. (2017). *Vaarallinen rikoksentekijä? [Dangerous offender?] (A study on offender risk assessment within the Finnish penal system)*. Helsinki: Finnish Lawyers' Association.
Schartmueller, D. (2018). How long is life? Comparing the process of release for life-imprisoned offenders in Denmark, Finland and Sweden. *European Journal on Criminal Policy and Research. Introduction*. https://doi.org/10.1007/s10610-018-9388-z.
Tonry, M. (2019). Sentencing and prediction. Old wine in old bottles. In J. W. de Keijser, J. V. Roberts, & J. Ryberg (Eds.), *Predictive sentencing. Normative and empirical perspectives* (pp. 269–298). Oxford: Hart Publishing.
Tonry, M., & Lappi-Seppälä, T. (Eds.). (2011). *Crime and justice in Scandinavia. Crime and justice 40*. Chicago: The University of Chicago Press.
Törnudd, P. (1971). The futility of searching for causes of crime. *Scandinavian Studies in Criminology, 3*, 23–33.

A Probe into the Soul of Israeli Criminal Law

George P. Fletcher and Shachar Eldar

The following are excerpts from a dialogue conducted face to face and by correspondence during 2019 between George P. Fletcher (GPF) and Shachar Eldar (SE) about the evolution of Israeli criminal law, with emphasis on its distinctive history and idiosyncratic terminology.

GPF There is a vital question that intrigues many scholars of law and of cultural studies, which is whether law is primarily an analytical tool consisting of sets of rules, abstract ideas, and pure reasoning, or a creation of language, of history, and of culture. I would like us to explore the latter of these possibilities with regard to Israeli criminal law.

SE All the dynamic tensions that shape a legal structure are apparent in Israeli criminal law. Where would you like to start?

GPF Let's take on the historical context first. What was the state of Israeli criminal law in the mandatory period?

SE It is tempting to say that because mandatory Palestine was under British rule, the applicable law was English common law. This is not bad for a short answer, but it overlooks some important distinctions. First is the issue of codification: whereas the laws in England at the time were for the most part judge-made, the Colonial Office in London succeeded in imposing comprehensive criminal legislation on many of the territories of the Empire, including Palestine. Therefore, accounts of mandatory criminal law often begin and end with the provisions of the Criminal Code

G. P. Fletcher
Columbia University, New York, NY, USA

S. Eldar (✉)
Ono Academic College, Kiryat Ono, Israel
e-mail: eldar@ono.ac.il

K. Ghanayim, Y. Shany (eds.), *The Quest for Core Values in the Application of Legal Norms*, https://doi.org/10.1007/978-3-030-78953-4_13

Ordinance enacted by the British High Commissioner in 1936.[1] When you first encountered Israeli criminal law, in the early 1970s, this ordinance was still in force. Can you recall how it struck you at the time, compared with your prior experience with US and German criminal law?

GPF In 1972, I came to Jerusalem to teach at the Hebrew University. Parenthetically, since you ask for my recollections, you may find it interesting that Miri Gur Arye attended my class on the law of theft, and Mota Kremnitzer came in IDF uniform to one of my other classes, I think on comparative criminal law. Frankly, I did not realize until many years later that the soldier who had shown up in uniform was Mota. These were interesting times for criminal law studies at the Hebrew University, particularly as Zalman Feller was Dean of Law. Feller had a colourful background, as did many in that generation of Jewish immigrants to Israel, and it seemed to me that he was pushing a French variation of criminal jurisprudence, which was based on his experience in Romania. The law in force was, as you say, the mandatory Criminal Code Ordinance 1936. As I recall, I did not pay much attention to this Ordinance, and accordingly, there are no references to Israeli law in my Rethinking Criminal Law.[2] I now wish to rectify this oversight and learn more about the criminal law in the mandatory period. You gave the short answer. What is the long answer?

SE The Criminal Code Ordinance 1936 does not provide a complete portrait of mandatory criminal law. One difficulty is that the criminal law of Israel does not fit into neat temporal boundaries. Britain had obtained the mandate over Palestine from the League of Nations in 1922, after 5 years of de facto rule following its conquest. To facilitate the transition from Ottoman rule, Britain declared the continued authority of existing law,[3] which meant that the French-inspired Ottoman criminal code of 1859 remained in effect until it was replaced by the Criminal Code Ordinance, in 1936. In the interim, the High Commissioner amended the criminal law in the spirit of the common law. A comprehensive amendment, in 1927,[4] formulated the principles of attempt liability and the liability of parties to an offense and introduced or redefined the offenses of incitement, conspiracy, banknote and coin forgery, blasphemy,[5] obscene publications, offenses against public order, perjury, rape, and keeping a brothel. Later, when Israel gained its independence, in 1948, smooth

[1]For the sources of the code, see Shachar (1979), p. 75 (Hebrew).

[2]Fletcher (1978).

[3]The British Order-in-Council (1922) Article 46.

[4]See the Criminal Law Amendment Ordinance (1927), comprised of 106 sections.

[5]Ibid., article 21: "Any person who, in a public place and in the hearing of another person, utters any word or sound calculated or intended to outrage the religious feelings or belief of such other person is guilty of an offense and is liable to imprisonment for one year." In the Criminal Code Ordinance 1936, a similar offense definition (even broader in scope, as it replaces the emotive "intended to outrage" with the factual "tending to outrage") is found in section 149, under the new title of "outrage to religious feelings." The definition of the Criminal Code Ordinance was translated as section 173 of the Penal Code 1977.

transition once again required a continued effect clause, this time for mandatory law.[6] Consequently, although the mandatory period ended in 1948, the Criminal Code Ordinance continued its reign for three more decades, which explains why it was in force when you came to teach at the Hebrew University. The Ordinance was finally replaced by the Penal Code 1977, but not entirely repealed, as Penal Code 1977 is really a consolidated version of the criminal legislation that was in effect at the time, and most of its provisions consist of a Hebrew translation of the Ordinance. Thus, there are no obvious watersheds to demarcate mandatory criminal law proper. Naturally, Israel is not the only country into which a foreign legal system was transplanted more or less integrally.

GPF Transplantations of legal systems create various problems. The critical question, in my view, is language. For example, some common law concepts do not translate readily into European languages. Take the word "fairness." In virtually all European languages, the word is translated as "justice." There is, of course, an enormous difference between the two. Victims want justice ("no justice, no peace" has become a slogan in racial conflicts in the US). Defendants, who might well be guilty, do not want justice: they properly want a fair trial. Curiously, Hebrew has a word for fairness (hognut) but I don't know whether it appears in Hebrew translations of international documents. But let's stick to our discussion of mandatory criminal law. I am interested in the way in which English law was transplanted in mandatory Palestine. Surely, this process was not airtight.

SE It was not, and the fact that the transplantation of legal systems cannot be entirely comprehensive is the source of another difficulty with a "short answer" that equates mandatory criminal law with the Criminal Code Ordinance 1936, a difficulty concerning scope. The Ordinance was never meant to be exhaustive, and it left clear openings through which the evolving rules and notions of the common law could infiltrate. By enacting a comprehensive criminal code, the mandatory legislator may have wanted to create the appearance of forsaking the flexibility of the unruly common law for a more systematic apparatus, where every punishment must rely on a specific enacted source. Yet, the flexibility with which its articles were drafted made the Code particularly receptive to conceptions and rulings imported from England. Article 4 of the Ordinance stated that the Code "shall be interpreted in accordance with the principles of legal interpretation obtaining in England, and expressions used in it shall be presumed, so far as is consistent with their context and except as may be otherwise expressly provided, to be used with the meaning attaching to them in English law and shall be construed in accordance therewith." The flexibility of the Code is at its most extreme in article 105, which defined misdemeanour as "any act which may cause or tend to a public mischief." The wide and indeterminate net cast by this provision enabled mandatory courts to fill any gaps found in the Code by importing common law offenses or by devising local judge-made prohibitions. The former technique was already sanctioned by article

[6] The Law and Administration Ordinance (1948) Article 11.

46 of the Order-in-Council, which stipulated that the mandatory courts will seal any lacuna in the law with the substance of the common law and the doctrines of equity in force in England, "so far only as the circumstances of Palestine and its inhabitants [...] permit and subject to such qualification as local circumstances render necessary."

GPF I am particularly fascinated with periods of transition between divergent legal systems. Doesn't the interaction between British law and Ottoman law become rather complicated during the first stages of the mandatory period? And could you please clarify the language issue, that is, was the governing language English, Hebrew, or perhaps Turkish?

SE The state of the law in the early stages of the Mandate was as messy as one would expect in a prolonged period of transition in a multicultural territory. The British Order-in-Council provided that Ottoman law remained in effect, but Mandate authorities gradually replaced it with common law-influenced ordinances. Areas of the law not covered by Ottoman legislation were to be regulated by common law doctrines, but only as far as these doctrines accorded with the circumstances of the land and its people. The Mandate judiciary was controlled by the British, but the majority of the magistrate judges were local inhabitants, both Jewish and Arab, most of whom received their legal training in Turkey or in Jerusalem.[7] You can see why legal historians of the period express frustration over their inability to derive valid conclusions about the everyday workings of the law in these bewildering conditions. The entanglement of various doctrines was amplified by a Tower of Babel effect. The Criminal Code Ordinance 1936 was published in English, and a Hebrew translation soon appeared in the Official Gazette. But the official language of the Ottoman Penal Law, which was in effect during the first 19 years of British rule, was Turkish, and no authoritative translation was ever produced. Uncertified private translations were available in French and English. By the time Meir Laniado published his Hebrew translation, in 1933, the Ottoman Penal Law was already on its way to becoming obsolete. Courtroom proceedings were supposedly conducted in English. I say "supposedly" because whereas district courts heard cases in panels presided over by British judges,[8] cases in the magistrates' courts were heard before a single local judge, either Jewish or Arab, and it stands to reason, especially where the judge and all litigants shared a common language, that proceedings in some lower courts were conducted in Arabic or in Hebrew. The historians' frustration is also due to the dearth of court-generated documents of the period. Official publication of court rulings in the Palestine Law Reports commenced only in 1934 and included only a select number of Supreme Court decisions. Another publication, from 1935 to 1938, was a multi-volume unofficial collection of mainly district court decisions

[7] Brun (2014), pp. 534–541 (Hebrew). The forum for legal studies in Jerusalem during the mandatory period is discussed later in this dialogue.

[8] Brun (2008), p. 151 (Hebrew).

from 1918 to 1936,[9] and a third publication was the unofficial Annotated Law Reports, which ran from 1943 to 1947. The decisions reported in all three publications were terse, and the editors betrayed a preference for reporting private law appeal and Court of Justice decisions over criminal cases. Industrious legal historians can gain access to unreported district court files through state archives,[10] but the decisions of magistrates' courts, save for a few available protocols, can be discovered only through second-hand reports in the local newspapers of the time. Legal theorists are not inclined to read lower court rulings, but of course for legal historians they serve as a significant source for understanding the workings of the legal system.

GPF That's right. From an American point of view, the dearth of reports of lower court rulings persists to this day. The rulings of trial courts in the US are very laconic, particularly where the case is concluded in a plea bargain or where a jury is involved. Appellate court scrutiny is curtailed by the fact that victims have no standing and prosecutors cannot appeal verdicts of not guilty. The US Supreme Court hears only appeals on constitutional matters. Interestingly, US Supreme Court justices know little about criminal justice. The reason is that they come from elite law schools, which emphasize tax and corporate law. There are exceptions: Alan Dershowitz had a brilliant career at Harvard, and I am still teaching classes about the "jurisprudence of crime" at Columbia. Admittedly, my classes are advanced and based on voluntary enrolment, and virtually all the students come from civil law jurisdictions. It is true that criminal law is a required first-year course in all law schools, but teaching these classes at elite law schools is not enjoyable. The students would rather be doing something more germane to their career plans. Furthermore, our curriculum does not distinguish clearly between criminal law and criminal procedure, and procedural issues, most notably constitutional issues such as Fourth Amendment search and seizure, take the fore. The interest in the Constitution dictates a focus on Supreme Court decisions, which indeed do not portray the everyday workings of the US criminal justice system.

SE As you know, the Israeli Supreme Court hears criminal appeals both on questions of constitutional and doctrinal importance, as well as on more mundane matters, such as the procedure used, and the evidence heard in a particular case. Most serving justices, today and in the past, have prior experience in the operations of the criminal justice system, having served either as state prosecutors or judges of the first instance in criminal trials. Past affiliations do not necessarily dictate present inclinations, but academic critique of Supreme Court decisions in criminal cases generally calls for leniency in doctrine and in punishment. Naturally, it is possible that

[9]This is The Collection of Judgements of the court of Palestine (1937). L.M. Rotenberg Law Publishers, Tel Aviv.

[10]A notable example is Alyagon Darr (2018). Alyagon Darr reports 147 cases of trials for sexual offenses in Mandate Palestine, mainly from the Haifa District Court.

certain sociological factors incline the legal academia disproportionally to the side of the defense.

GPF When I was teaching at UCLA, the local district attorney concluded that academics were biased in favour of the defense. As a result, several of us took on summer jobs prosecuting in the Los Angeles County Courthouse in Santa Monica. Of course, we had to be members of the California Bar. Now, California has an unusual legal system. It is one of the few states that have not been influenced by the Model Penal Code, drafted in the 1950s. The judges use standardized jury instructions called CALJIC. I recall a rape trial in which the complaining witness admitted on the stand that she had prior sexual experience. The instruction read to the effect: she has admitted that she is not "chaste," and therefore you may infer that she consented on the present occasion. This all seems a bit quaint now. But in fact, it was not easy to get the instruction changed. It required a nationwide effort and several famous books, like Susan Brownmiller's Against Our Will. But these memories lead us far astray from the topic of the publication of court rulings in Mandate Palestine.

SE To get us back on track, I want to mention a research currently being conducted by a group of Israeli legal historians[11] who endeavour to uncover the events leading to the publication of the Palestine Law Reports. One of their intermediate findings is that lawyers in Mandate Palestine generally advocated for the official publication of the case law. According to the researchers, a possible reason for this support is that Mandate era lawyers assumed that amassing volumes of legal decisions would enhance their professional status and discourage lay people from conducting their legal affairs without qualified help. Call this a prosaic, narrow, and self-interested explanation. Another, more romantic possibility, is that some lawyers idealized English law, whereas others, either because they genuinely opposed the Mandate or because they desired to eschew allegations of being disloyal to their community by helping to operate the legal system imposed by a foreign power, hoped that the publication of local precedents would facilitate the creation—real or perceived—of a local law distinct from common law. Surely, you have found similar dilemmas in your encounters with jurists working under communist regimes.

GPF Communist regimes did not leave much space for romanticism, except an infatuation with the strand of communism du jour. In the USSR, the most common charge used against dissenters and against those who wanted to leave was treason (betrayal of the motherland). A particular problem with being a lawyer in the USSR was that you needed a security clearance (called a dopusk) to appear in a politically charged case. One memorable case in this regard was that of Anatoly Shcharansky (Natan Sharansky), in 1977. As you know, he was a famous refusenik who later became a prominent figure in Israeli politics. Sharansky chose to defend himself before the Soviet court. He may have done this because he did not trust the type of lawyers who were eligible for a dopusk. In any event, we, observers in the West,

[11]Consisting of Eyal Katvan, Yair Sagy, and Yoram Shachar.

knew that the Soviet court would not impose the death penalty on someone who defended himself. This was an incidental benefit of the inquisitorial system. The thing to remember about Soviet criminal justice is that it was impossible to rule the courts from Moscow. Therefore, the Party did not attempt to control the judges (although calls from Party officials to the judges were not unheard of) but rather administered the proceedings through the all-powerful "procuracy"—the state agency responsible for administering criminal justice. I have written in the New York Review of Books[12] about my personal observations as a visitor to the Soviet Union in the glasnost era, as a member of a Helsinki Watch mission investigating the state of human rights there, and particularly about my visits to local courts, to examine how ordinary criminals are tried. Returning to mandatory Palestine, there too, jurists coming from different backgrounds must have been astonished at each other's legal cultures.

SE Indeed, the clash of laws and languages coincided with a clash of cultures. The British design to import English law into Palestine met with local resistance. A popular sentiment was reflected in Paltiel Dikshtein's nationalist wrath:

> This code, the typical product of British genius, gifted with all its inordinate virtues, but also afflicted with all its failings, which are not at all slight, exudes to the last of its letters the spirit of the nation that has brought it forth, tethered as it is by a thread to this nation's exceptional history and to its inimitable measures, both good and bad, is not suited, not in the smallest degree, to the needs of this land, a land that is anything but tabula rasa, a clean slate for that moderate nation, bearer of culture, to scribble on at will, as it did in the African colonies where it has installed similar codification. In constructing this new Ordinance, Britain gave at most the minutest consideration to the unique character of this land, and the three great religions that make up its people. [...] The criminal systems governing local criminal law are the product of the unique conditions that shaped this special land and the particular characteristics of its inhabitants; penetrating its core requires a wide perspective of the universal developments that shaped the penal practices of nations, for this land is a crossroad for the spiritual influences of a few dozen generations and a few dozen nations.[13]

Dikshtein was an advocate, lecturer on criminal law and procedure, and one of the founders of the School of Law and Economics in Tel Aviv, in 1935. Two years after the enactment of the Criminal Code Ordinance 1936, he authored the first comprehensive Hebrew text on criminal law in the Land of Israel.

The protest during the stages preceding the enactment of the Ordinance, such as it was, was not entirely ineffective. Dikshtein's primary practical grievance was against the intention to replace the relatively lenient Ottoman code, a relic of the French Criminal Code of 1810, with the harsh laws of England. He found the former to be better suited to the Mediterranean psyche, and he was not alone to hold this opinion. For example, in a memorandum to the Chief Justice of the Palestine Supreme Court, from 1929, the Attorney General wrote: "It would, in my opinion, do unnecessary violence to public opinion to introduce the English conception which

[12]Fletcher (1989).

[13]Dikshtein (1938), pp. 19, V (Hebrew) (paragraph translated by SE).

treats wilful homicide as a capital offence in every case unless the accused person can establish it was manslaughter."[14] The Criminal Code Ordinance of 1936 alleviated some of the severity of the common law, most notably in the curtailment of the death penalty and corporal punishment (flogging) by comparison to English law, and in the drafting of unique and relatively lenient homicide provisions, famously described by Justice Moshe Zilberg[15] as a mosaic of half-baked ideas plucked in parts from English, French, and Ottoman sources.

A further cause of cultural clash was the profusion of local traditions. The Mandatory Supreme Court demonstrated a variety of judicial attitudes vis-à-vis local traditions: sympathy for distinctive customs; colonial snobbism toward the local "tribes," which were deemed too primitive to benefit from certain aspects of the English common law; and a commitment to the project of civilizing the local inhabitants. Likhovski reported a case in which the court favourably considered varying the "reasonableness" test in provocation to accommodate the possibility that each of the races inhabiting Palestine has its own image of a "reasonable Person," together with several other cases in which the Court was unwilling to accept a defense for murder based on the local Muslim custom of killing to preserve family honor. In one such case, from the 1940s, Chief Justice FitzGerald declared the unwillingness of the Court to recognize local customs that were repugnant to "natural justice as conceived by British standards."[16] The merit of honor killing is incomprehensible to Western thought. But it would be fair to say that at least in some areas, the practice of enforcing cultural change through criminal law by banning existing customs and traditions takes the modernization ideal one step too far. Surely, shunting aside deviating cultures is not limited to colonial rule, but it is also a feature in the law of autonomous states, examplified by the unwillingness to recognize certain religious exceptions.

GPF American constitutional law has absolutist tendencies, as compared, say, with Canadian law. The First Amendment reads: "Congress shall make no law respecting an establishment of religion, or prohibiting the free exercise thereof..." The issue not discussed is whether there is an implicit Christian bias in the Constitution. I am afraid there is. Native American religions, Islam, and Judaism are not treated with the same degree of deference. Christmas is a national holiday, Hanukkah is not. It is important to add that the Catholic Church is ridiculed in the popular culture of the US. The dominant religion is that of the collective Protestant sects. We have had one Catholic president (JFK), and never a Jewish or a Muslim one. Things are changing, however. There are many women running in 2020, as well as one openly gay candidate, and at least one Jew. I was under the impression that in the area of family law, Israeli law was very tolerant (and still is) of Muslim autonomy concerning polygamy and divorce, and the rabbinical courts have jurisdiction over Jewish

---

[14]Reported in Abrams (1972), p. 27.

[15]In Jacobovitz v. Attorney General (1950) C.A. 125/50, P.D. 6, 514.

[16]Likhovski (2014), pp. 78–79.

family law. As I recall, Chief Justice Aharon Barak wrote a decision pushing back religious authority over inheritance and replacing it with Israeli civil law.

SE Israeli law leaves the regulation of marriage to the authority of religious law, a reality that sends many couples who wish to unite in a civil marriage, and particularly those who are barred from marriage under religious law (gay couples, a cohen and a divorcée), to wed outside the state. But the prohibition against polygamy is regulated by state law (Penal Code 1977, section 176) and is enforced—although not always with great zeal—on the Muslim community. By contrast, the Mandate authorities did not enforce the prohibition on Muslims. Criminal Code Ordinance 1936, article 181(c) stated that it is a good defense for a charge of polygamy "that the law governing the personal status of the husband both at the date of the first and at the date of the subsequent marriage allowed him to have more than one wife." Whether this defense is the expression of cultural tolerance or a submission to discriminatory norms is up for debate. The Israeli legislator decided that it was the latter when it repealed the religious defense for polygamy in the Equality of Female Rights Law 1951, section 8. Whenever the prosecution pursued cases of polygamy, the courts enforced the prohibition, and in some cases, imposed prison sentences on polygamous Muslim men, expressing the expectation that they would adjust their customs to the law of the land.[17] Recently, the Ministry of Justice appointed a committee aimed at reducing polygamy in the Bedouin communities.[18]

GPF Do you mean to say "law" or "laws" of the land? I ask this question because it has always seemed odd to me that law faculties in Israel are called Faculties of Laws (mishpatim). This differs from the practice in other countries, for example, in the US and in Europe.

SE Now that you point it out, it does seem odd that all the faculties in Israel devoted to legal studies, without exception, employ the plural, mishpatim. Add to the conundrum the fact that the Hebrew term for the Israeli Ministry of Justice translates literally to the Ministry of Laws, whereas courts in Israel are named courts of law (beit mishpat). The term mishpatim appears in 35 verses of the Bible, but of course there it does not denote a faculty or a ministry.

GPF This brings to light another oddity, about the title of the legal department. It is never the faculty of justice (though in the US we have a Department of Justice). It is typically the faculty of law (in the singular). Israel is curious in this regard.

SE The first faculty to employ the plural form was the faculty of mishpatim at the Hebrew University in Jerusalem, which was inaugurated in 1949. The two Mandate-era law schools that preceded the Jerusalem faculty used the singular form. In 1920, the Mandatory authorities created in Jerusalem a night school for training local advocates, called "Law Classes," which was translated into Hebrew as shiurim

---

[17]For example, Ahmed Goda v The State of Israel (1952) C.A. 185/52, P.D. 37(1) 85, 88–89.

[18]See Report of the Intra-Office Team on Coping with the Negative Effects of Polygamy (2018) (Hebrew).

le'mishpat, and in 1935, a small group of emigrant jurists and economists, mainly of Russian and continental descent, opened in Tel Aviv a semi-private institute called originally in Hebrew beit ha'sefer le'mishpat ve'calcala, which translates as The School of Law and Economics. (The latter was one of the institutes that in the 1950s joined together to create Tel Aviv University, changing its name to the plural form, "faculty of mishpatim"). It is possible that the use of the singular served an ideological purpose. The Mandatory school was intended to instil in the local jurists-to-be a unified system of colonial law. It also needed to portray law as a uniform and neutral phenomenon that can be imported from England to the colonies regardless of sociological and cultural differences.[19] The School of Law and Economics was an explicit response to colonial law: its founders regarded law to be a local phenomenon and sought to generate a unique law, tailored to suit—and to fashion—the emerging Israeli nationality.[20] By contrast to both schools, the faculty in Jerusalem was originally oriented toward the integration of Jewish identity and academic universalism, as part of the general vision of the Hebrew University. These pluralistic aspirations perhaps explain why Chaim Weizmann used the plural form in his initial draft plan for the Hebrew University (1913). Weizmann envisioned among the first faculties to make up the university, alongside medicine and the humanities, a faculty of mishpatim.[21]

In 1949, the Jerusalem faculty was established through a merger of three distinct areas of legal studies that were already conducted at the time in different departments of the Hebrew University: the Jewish law course, taught in the Department of Talmudic Studies, initially by Professor Asher Gulak; the international law classes given by the former Attorney General in Mandatory Palestine, Norman Bentwich, and later by Nathan Feinberg, both acting as chairs of foreign relations studies; and the course in general law conducted by the research fellow, Guido (Gad) Tedeschi. The three courses were integrated into one faculty of "laws."[22]

It is possible that the faculties of mishpatim that were created thereafter adopted the ideology of the Jerusalem faculty, but more probably they simply copied the name. Whatever the historical reasons for the morphological peculiarity in the name of Israeli legal faculties, they have by now been muddled up and forgotten. I see no plausible explanation for the fact that currently the two Israeli academic institutions that refer in their name to legal studies use the singular form "law"—The Academic Center for Law and Science (shearei mada u'mishpat) and The College for Law and Business (ha'merkaz ha'acedemi le'misphat u'leasakim)—although both have faculties of "laws;" nor do I see why the faculties of "laws" publish "law" reviews: of the

[19]Likhovski (2001), pp. 306–309 (Hebrew).

[20]Cohen (2009), p. 187 (Hebrew).

[21]The plural term continued to appear in correspondence relating to the establishment of the Hebrew University (see citations in Reinharz (1988), p. 127 (Hebrew)), and later to the formation of the faculty of law[s] (see citations in Feinberg (1975), pp. 234–240 (Hebrew)).

[22]Feinberg, ibid, p. 233.

legal reviews published in Hebrew, 11 have in their title the singular mishpat, and only two (both are reviews of the Jerusalem faculty) use the plural mishpatim/hukim.

GPF I have always been interested in the terminology used to talk about legal studies. In virtually all Western languages, there are words to denote two conceptions of law—one abstract and binding as a matter of principle (Recht, droit, derecho, pravo), and another referring to law enacted by the legislative branch and binding only because it is backed by the threat of force (Gesetz, loi, ley, zakon). The interesting question is how Israeli law fits into this dichotomy. I see two problems. One is that English is one of the few languages that does not have the distinction. Therefore, when we speak about the "rule of law" in English, we are not sure what we mean. Typically, in Europe, the faculty of law is denominated by the word for law as principle. Another is that we have a mystery in Israeli law with the use of the word mishpatim. And thus the question: how does the typical Israeli lawyer or law student understand "the rule of law" when expressed in Hebrew?

SE The Hebrew term for the rule of law does not use the plural mishpatim, and adds to the mystery by not using the singular mishpat either. Instead, the term used is shilton ha'hok, which literally translates back to "rule of (or perhaps, by) the enacted law." More inclusively, this could refer to the enacted law as interpreted by the courts, and by further stretching the simple usage of hok, it could incorporate law in principle.[23] The sway of the term underlies one of the endless (and perhaps now growing) battles in the political trenches over the shape of Israeli democracy. But in my experience, the issue plays a minor role in the law school curriculum, and is hardly mentioned in the criminal law class. Israeli criminal law textbooks refer instead to the more technical principle of legality (nullum crimen sine lege) and its derivatives, i.e., that criminal prohibitions should be clear, public, and prospective. In general, Israeli textbooks are analytical rather than critical. Unlike most American and British textbooks, they rarely discuss, let alone critically, specific offenses, but are devoted exclusively to an exploration of the doctrines of the general part. I bear in mind that the most apparent, and to me also the deepest and most novel feature of your Rethinking Criminal Law, is that the discussion of offenses precedes that of the principles of the general part.

GPF My 1978 book, Rethinking Criminal Law, was designed to be contrarian. I treat the specific part first, beginning with the complexities of the law of theft. I recall that my German friends, namely Winfried Hassemer, were surprised by this inversion. Hassemer said at one point that I was creating a "middle part" of the criminal law. If we look at the timeline, it seems apparent that my stay in Israel influenced this structure. As I mentioned earlier, I was then giving a course on the law of theft. While teaching this course, I began to develop my ideas about the general lessons that can be learned by closely examining the development of specific offenses. Also,

---

[23]To support this understanding of shilton ha'hok, Leon Shelef proposed the alternative term marut ha'mishpat, which translates into English as "the authority of the law." See Shelef (1996), Tel Aviv (Hebrew).

my main interest while teaching at the Hebrew University was the tension between French (as embodied in Feller) and German influences (my own education). This has been a persistent theme in my writing.

SE Apart from your interest in the law of theft, another area of criminality that has attracted your attention over the years is that of disloyalty offenses, to which you have devoted large parts of your book Loyalty: An Essay on the Morality of Relationships.[24] Since the focus of our discussion is the singularity of Hebrew legal terminology, it is of interest that Hebrew dictionaries treat "trust" (emun) and "loyalty" (ne'emanut) as synonym, and that scholarly legal writings follow suit by not being meticulous in the use of these terms, as evidenced by the common use of a term that I find idiomatic, "duties of trust" (hovot emun). At least in the legal context, we should be more accurate in using our terms. People, institutions, and societies may be expected to be loyal to others (or, more generally, trustworthy), but a duty to be trustful of others, that is to give emun in someone or something, is senseless. Trust expresses the value inherent in the ability of persons, institutions, or societies to rely on each other; the protection of this value is realized by imposing certain duties of loyalty or allegiance. I suggest that we limit our discussion to offenses in which language alludes to the duty of loyalty—predominantly treason—and examine whether they are indeed concerned with trust, and not with different values altogether. As a forerunner of this discussion, I want to draw attention to a central strand in legal thinking, common to some contractarians and communitarians, that emphasizes the value of trust as the fundamental rationale for having a criminal law, and identifies civil loyalty as the basis for the obligation to comply with criminal directives. For this strand of thinking, the value of trust underpins all legal prohibitions, and even where the corresponding duty of loyalty does not appear explicitly in the definition of the offense, as in the case of treason, this duty is implicit. The thief and the murderer violate the social expectation of maintaining loyalty by adhering to accepted rules of behaviour. I believe that the trust-loyalty accounts of criminal law cannot do all the work in explaining criminalization, because it is still necessary to answer what breaches of loyalty deserve the protection of criminal law, and whether there are any further constraints on criminalization (for example the harm principle). But as sketches of a broad political theory of criminal law (broad enough to appeal to both contractarians and communitarians), these accounts do have persuasive force, particularly when complemented with the element of reciprocity. For trust and loyalty to form the basis of a theory of legitimate authority, they need to acknowledge at least two kinds of mutual obligations, in citizen-to-citizen and citizen-to-polity relations. The former is self-explanatory. In the latter, reciprocity means that it is not sufficient for a legitimate criminal law to require civil loyalty, but it must answer the expectations of citizens that the polity will dispense justice in accordance with the rule of law. Any deviation from legality, as for example, retroactive incrimination for conduct that was not prohibited when it

[24] Fletcher (1995).

was carried out, is a breach of the guarantees that a legitimate society affords its citizens, i.e., a breach of the loyalty owed by the polity to its citizens. A society that systematically violates its commitment to the rule of law undermines the duty of its citizens to show loyalty to its institutions.

A particular problem with a duty of loyalty is that loyalty is an emotion, a sentiment, or perhaps a character trait, neither of which form a sound basis for criminalization under the action theory of criminal law. In practice, therefore, criminalization is an option only for concrete manifestations of disloyalty. In principle, a liberal regime should show restraint when deciding which revelations of disloyalty are criminally prohibited. The choices made by legislators indicate the level of tolerance the regime displays toward its citizens. The Penal Code 1977 does not prohibit the internal feeling of disloyalty to the state—and its broader parallel, the lack of loyalty to the state. Nor does it require participation in modern incarnations of "imperial cult" rituals, or demand declarations of loyalty and salutes to the flag. Penal laws enforce conscription,[25] which requires great sacrifices on the part of Israeli citizens, at times the ultimate sacrifice, but soldiers are not required to exhibit loyal sentiments, and may serve only for fear of sanction. It stands to reason that conscription is a matter of national security more than it is an enforcement of loyalty. Less obviously, this is also the case for treason. The Penal Code 1977 specifies grave penalties for offenses that fall under the heading of treason, including capital punishment. The latter may be imposed (although it has never been) when the country is involved in armed conflict, on "anyone who has committed, with the intention of harming the sovereignty of the State, an act which may impair its sovereignty;"[26] "anyone who has committed, on the intention that any territory will be excised from the sovereignty of the State or come under the sovereignty of a foreign State, an act which can bring about this effect;"[27] "anyone who has committed, with the intention of bringing about military action against Israel, an act that can bring about this effect," if he did so with the aim of assisting the enemy;[28] and "anyone who has committed, with the intention of assisting the enemy in its war against Israel, an act that has the potential of providing such assistance."[29] Offenses of treason seem by definition to punish betrayals of loyalty. Because loyalty can be betrayed only by someone who owes loyalty in the first place, we expect the offenses of treason to target certain actors, i.e., those who owe allegiance to the State of Israel through some definition of citizenship or domicile. But of the nine offenses grouped under the heading of treason, only one is contingent upon a specific agent of this kind. The other eight offenses are applicable also to foreign citizens, including those whose loyalties are owed to enemy states or entities.

[25]Israel, Military Service Act [consolidated version] 1986, section 46.

[26]Israel, Penal Code 1977, section 97(a).

[27]Israel, Penal Code 1977, section 97(b).

[28]Israel, Penal Code 1977, section 98.

[29]Israel, Penal Code 1977, section 99(a).

Examining the content of these offenses solves the puzzle. Acts against the sovereignty or integrity of the state, resulting in war, and assisting those who wage war against Israel are harmful to the state regardless of the identity of the perpetrators. Therefore, the prohibition against what the law calls treason protects an interest of the state that is quite apart from the abstract idea of loyalty to it. The rhetoric of treason is revealed to be empty: the heading befitting these offenses is "harm to the state and the security of its borders."

The sole offense in the section of the Penal Code 1977 devoted to treason that is contingent upon the offender being "an Israeli citizen and any other person who owes allegiance to the State of Israel, whether because he has a legal duty of military service… or because he served in the civil service of the state" criminalizes service in enemy armed forces.[30] Specific mention of the actors who owe allegiance to the state should not be attributed to an idiosyncratic motivation on the part of the legislation to emphasize the loyalty motif, but rather to a sensible choice to limit the liability of foreign citizens who served in the armies of their states of origin. The heart of the prohibitions that use language that seems to require loyalty to the state is the harm to the material interests of the state which may stem from certain manifestations of disloyalty, and not the value of trust or the idea of loyalty. Would you say that this analysis holds generally?

GPF This is a difficult question. In the universe of common law, treason is a crime of the heart—disloyalty to the state is likened to adultery. Sedition addresses the problem of tangible harm to national security. I will add that loyalty is a parochial as opposed to a universal value. I remember a conversation with David Hartman, in Jerusalem, in which he responded to my interest in Kant's philosophy of law by asking me whether Kant knew anything about the Covenant.

SE I think that the parochial dimension of loyalty reflects not only the law but also prevailing personal sentiments. One could conceptualize the offenses against humanity as reflecting a duty of loyalty, but stretching the concept of loyalty to the whole of mankind goes beyond the intuitive meaning of the term. I believe that only very few people are unflinching Kantians, who feel themselves in any real sense trustees of humanity as a whole. From the legal aspect, offenses against humanity, such as the Israeli Prevention and Punishment of Genocide Law 1950, can be explained in ways that do not include the individual's loyalty to humanity, for example, through the loyalty of the state to other nations.

GPF This takes us back to the relationship between law and religion—a subject on which our particular traditions influence our outlook in matters of community and loyalty.

SE Of course, the spheres of loyalty in our lives exceed those that are covered by law, and extend to our communities and religions, to family members and friends, to peers, and to people we idealize. Furthermore, the law does not cover loyalty to

---

[30]Israel, Penal Code 1977, section 101.

abstract values, such as truth (fraud offenses do not protect truth as such, but are limited to obtaining gains that would not be received but for the fraud, as a variation on the offense of theft). Turning away from state values in the name of personal commitments and ideals still requires a known degree of courage, as in the well-known line by E. M. Forster, "if I had to choose between betraying my country and betraying my friends I hope I should have the guts to betray my country."[31] But let us move on to other subjects pertaining to the language of Israeli criminal law. The ball is in your court.

GPF The use of that metaphor "in your court" in itself raises new questions, namely the sporting theory of justice. English is full of metaphors that come from the world of games and sports, for example hitting below the belt, levelling the playing field, hitting a home run, knocking it out of the ballpark. I have a hunch that Israel is different because these metaphors seem to come from sports common in the US and Britain. Assuming that soccer is the most common sport in Israel, I am not sure how this plays out (note the additional metaphor: plays out).

SE Let me confine my answer to the rare usage of sporting metaphors by Israeli judges. I have a feeling that you will find my speculation in this regard amusing, because it is premised on a terminological peculiarity of the Hebrew language. The reason for the scarcity of sporting metaphors in judicial rulings may be the result not of the indifference of Israeli judges to sports (or to metaphors), but rather of the meaning of the term "judge" in Hebrew, which denotes both courtroom judges and sports referees. By "not playing ball," the judges whose job it is to write legal opinions distinguish themselves, perhaps subconsciously, from the "judges" on the soccer field. Israeli courtroom judges resort to allegories of more refined games, exemplified in Chief Justice Moshe Smoira's proclamation in deciding the first criminal appeal to come before the Israel Supreme Court,[32] that "the criminal process should not be fashioned as a game of chess, in which one false move determines the final outcome." But I think that in our dialogue we allowed ourselves to spar more freely, wouldn't you say?

GPF Indeed, we did, Shachar. This has been a wonderful dialogue. I hope it will be interesting to Mota and to others.

References

Abrams, N. (1972). Interpreting the criminal code ordinance, 1936—The untapped well. *Israel Law Review, 7*, 25.

Alyagon Darr, A. (2018). *Plausible crime stories: The legal history of sexual offenses in mandate Palestine*. Cambridge: Cambridge University Press.

[31]Forster (1951), p. 67, 68.

[32]Silvester v. Attorney General (1948) C.A. 1/48, P.D. 1, 5.

Brun, N. (2008). *Judges and lawyers in Eretz Israel*. Jerusalem: Magnes Press.
Brun, N. (2014). *Law, passions and politics: Judges and lawyers between the British mandate and the State of Israel*. Tel Aviv: Steimatzky Press.
Cohen, U. (2009). The pursuit of academic legitimacy: The School of law and economics in Tel Aviv 1935-1948. *Bar Ilan University Studies in Law, 25*, 179.
Dikshtein, P. (1938). *Criminal law*. Tel Aviv: School of Law and Economics Publishing.
Feinberg, N. (1975). On the twenty-fifth anniversary of the faculty of laws. *Hebrew University Law Review, 6*, 231.
Fletcher, G. P. (1978). *Rethinking criminal law*. Boston: Little, Brown & Co.
Fletcher, G. P. (1989, May 18). *In Gorbachev's courts*. The New York Review of Books.
Fletcher, G. P. (1995). *Loyalty: An essay on the morality of relationships*. Oxford: Oxford University Press.
Forster, E. M. (1951). What I believe. In *Two cheers for democracy 67*. London: Edward Arnold.
Likhovski, A. (2001). Legal education in mandatory land of Israel. *Tel Aviv University Law Review, 25*, 291.
Likhovski, A. (2014). *Law and identity in mandate Palestine*. Chapel Hill: University of North Carolina Press.
Reinharz, J. (1988). A Foundation for the Hebrew University in Jerusalem, the role of Haim Weismann 1913–1914. *Cathedra, 46*, 123.
Shachar, Y. (1979). The origins of the criminal code ordinance 1936. *Tel Aviv University Law Review, 7*, 75.
Shelef, L. (1996). *The rule of law and the nature of politics*. Papirus/Tel Aviv University Press.

Part III
Core Values in International Law

Collateral Killings of Civilians: Reflecting Recent German Judgments on Co-responsibility for Foreign Drone Attacks

Albin Eser

1 Preliminary Remarks

Among other legal fields, so-called "preventive killing" is one that also has attracted the interest of *Mordechai Kremnitzer*,[1] to whom this contribution is dedicated for his 70th birthday. This is done with gratitude for memories of a long-standing friendship and cooperation that began with his participation in a German-Anglo-American workshop entitled "Basic Problems in Criminal Theory" in Freiburg,[2] continued with the co-organization of a bi-national Israeli-German colloquium entitled "The Reform of Criminal Law" in Jerusalem,[3] and was enriched by many other academic encounters, in particular due to his membership in the Scientific Advisory Board of the Max Planck Institute for Foreign and International Criminal Law (as the Institute was then known). It was on one of these occasions that he expressed his deep concern about the taking of excessive actions against supposed terrorists in situations that, framed as they were in terms of war, seemed to confer an unconditional license to kill.[4]

As this widely shared supposition is still far from being debunked, *Kremnitzer*—like others engaged in this field—may be interested to learn of the recent judgment of

[1] Kremnitzer (2004), pp. 201–222.

[2] See Durham (1988), pp 1492–1554, with comments of Kremnitzer on pp 1493, 1500, 1512, 1520, 1533.

[3] See Kremnitzer (1996), p. 1 (special issue on "Reform of Criminal Law"). See also Kremnitzer and Ghanayim (2005), pp. 514, 513-533.

[4] Our discussion ran along lines that were made widely known in a public commentary: Kremnitzer (2015) Thou shalt not kill? The right to self-defense against illegal attacks is by no means an unconditional license to kill. In: The Jerusalem Report, November 30, p 6 s.

A. Eser (✉)
Max Planck Institute for the Study of Crime, Security and Law, Freiburg, Germany
e-mail: a.eser@csl.mpg.de

K. Ghanayim, Y. Shany (eds.), *The Quest for Core Values in the Application of Legal Norms*, https://doi.org/10.1007/978-3-030-78953-4_14

a higher German court, the Oberverwaltungsgericht für das Land Nordrhein-Westfalen (OVG NRW), in the so-called Yemen case, in which the Federal Republic of Germany was found co-responsible for American drone attacks that had been supported by a satellite relay station operated by the United States on German territory.[5] This decision, which is the focus of this paper, was not, however, the first case in which German courts addressed the harmful results of drone attacks.[6] But while other judicial authorities have chosen to shy away from holding actors involved in drone attacks responsible—be it by shielding military actions from traditional scrutiny,[7] or be it by declaring the lethal attacks compatible with the international law of war[8]—the OVG NRW, as far as I am aware, seems to have been the first judicial body that has dared to declare the collateral killing of innocent civilians by US drone attacks to be violations of international law and to hold the Federal Republic of Germany co-responsible.[9]

My reflections on these judicial findings will be approached in the following steps: after a brief description of the facts of the Yemen case at issue here, as well as some procedural peculiarities (Sect. 2), the compatibility of fatal airstrikes supported from German territory with constitutional law and international humanitarian law will be examined (Sect. 3). Since the Court casts doubt on this compatibility, the question of judicial authority to adjudicate violations of law by military operations arises (Sect. 4). This question, having been answered in the affirmative, implicates Germany's responsibility, as a state, to protect life (Sect. 5). As also touched upon in

[5]Yemen case OVG NRW, Upper Administrative Court of North Rhine-Westphalia, 4 A 1361/15 of 19 March 2019. https://www.justiz.nrw.de/nrwe/ovgs/ovg_nrw/j2019/4_A_1361_15_Urteil_20190319.html.

[6]This applies, in particular, to the Somalia case OVG NRW, 4 A 1072/16 of 19 March 2019. https://www.justiz.nrw.de/nrwe/ovgs/ovg_nrw/j2019/4_A_1072_16_Urteil_20190319.html; regarding differences between this case and the aforementioned Yemen case, cf infra Sect. 2. 2nd paragraph and Sect. 6.

[7]As, though with some caveats, assumed by the administrative court of first instance in the Yemen case: Verwaltungsgericht (VG) Köln, 3 K 5625/14 of 27 May 2015. https://www.justiz.nrw.de/nrwe/ovgs/vg_koeln/j2015/3_K_5625_14_Urteil_20150527.html, margin numbers 57 ss.; let alone the "political question doctrine" by which a suit of the victim against the United States was blocked by the District Court for the District of Columbia, in: Ali Jaber v. United States (2016) 155 F. Supp. 3d 70, 77-81 (D.D.C.), pp 77 ss, affirmed—with a critical, though finally concurring opinion by Circuit Judge Brown—in (2016) 861 F.3d 241 (D.C. Cir. 2016), and certiorari denied in (2017) 138 S. Ct. 480 US S. Ct.). For further discussion of this issue cf Sect. 4.

[8]As in the highly debated Kunduz case in which the Attorney General at the (German) Federal Supreme Court terminated the investigation of the commander of a German military unit in Afghanistan who had advised the International Security Assistance Force (ISAF), performed by US fighter pilots, to bomb an apparent Taliban unit, while the victims killed had in fact been innocent civilians; see, Einstellungsverfügung des Generalbundesanwalts im Ermittlungsverfahren gegen Oberst Klein 3 BJs 6/10-4. In: Neue Zeitschrift für Wehrrecht (2010), pp. 172–174. As to further law suits and decisions in this case cf Sect. 6 note 63.

[9]As may already be noted, however, by a recent decision of the Bundesverwaltungsgericht (Federal Administrative Court), promulgated after the submission of this manuscript, the decision of the OVG NRW was partly overturned; cf. Sect. 5 to fn. 56.

the Somalia case, in addition to the public obligation to prevent unlawful fatal airstrikes, civil liability for damages must also be considered (Sect. 6). The same applies to the criminal responsibility of individuals involved in unlawful airstrikes (Sect. 7). Finally, a principled discussion challenging the mainstream assumption that lethal military actions are lawful as long as they are not forbidden will follow (Sect. 8).

2 Facts and Procedure

In the Yemen case, the plaintiffs requested the Federal Republic of Germany to inhibit the use of the German air base facilities in Ramstein for the performance of drone attacks by US forces in Yemen. This request, in short, was based on the fact that the "global war on terror" proclaimed by US President George W. Bush in response to the Al Qaeda atrocities in 2001 began to escalate in 2009. "Targeted killings" and "signature strikes" in which persons were made targets of an attack due simply to certain behavioral patterns or external circumstances—with the potential consequence of collateral or erroneous killing of innocent civilians—became more and more common. As innocent relatives of the plaintiffs were indeed killed and as the plaintiffs themselves felt permanently threatened by such attacks, they first sought relief in US courts, where they hoped the drone strikes would be declared violations of humanitarian and customary international law and, as such, stopped. After the holding of the US Court that it lacked subject matter jurisdiction due to the "political question doctrine", the plaintiffs turned to the German judiciary for help, since drone strikes in Yemen are also assisted by German facilities (data streams that guide the drones are transmitted via fiber optic cables from the United States to the air base in Ramstein and from there are radioed to the drone by way of a satellite relay station). Since, due to the earth's curvature, the piloting of a drone directly from the United States to Yemen is not possible without the satellite relay station in Ramstein, it appeared promising to the plaintiffs to request the Federal Republic of Germany to block the use of this relay station for US drone strikes in Yemen, or—alternatively—to obtain a declaration that the failure of the German government to adopt appropriate blocking measures was unlawful.[10]

Regarding the procedure for seeking satisfaction for damage already suffered or protection from future threats, it is interesting to note that in the Yemen case the plaintiffs did not ask for compensation for the loss of their relatives—which would have to be pursued in a civil court—nor for criminal prosecution of the collateral killings as murder or manslaughter; rather, they chose the route of administrative courts. This choice has both advantages and disadvantages. On the one hand, it is

[10]For details of the facts and claims see the Yemen case judgments of the VG Köln, supra note 7, and the OVG NRW, supra note 5; for details to the to find satisfaction in US courts see Ali Jaber v. United States, supra note 7.

certainly an ambitious approach: instead of merely seeking civil compensation or criminal retribution (both addressed to specific persons and thus focused on the individual level), it raises the issue of collateral killings through drone strikes to a public level (it seeks not only to force the German government to take action, but also for the action to extend beyond the plaintiffs' personal satisfaction and to inure to the benefit of the endangered population as a whole). On the other hand, administrative court procedures in Germany are not easy to handle because they entail special formalities. The formalities depend on the type of litigation chosen: If the plaintiff applies merely for a declaratory judgment ("Feststellungsklage"), he may fail because he should have chosen an action for affirmative relief ("Leistungsklage").

This procedural difference was one of the reasons why, on one and the same day, the OVG NRW handed down two such disparate holdings in the Somalia and the Yemen cases, despite their substantive similarities. Since the plaintiff in the Somalia case had asked merely for a declaratory judgment regarding Germany's failure to block the use by the United States of the Ramstein Air Base for drone attacks in Somalia (the plaintiff's father was killed by such a drone strike while he was herding cattle), his claim was already rejected as inadmissible both because of the absence of a concrete legal relationship between the plaintiff and the Federal Republic of Germany as a defendant, and because of the subsidiarity of the sought after declaratory judgment vis-à-vis a potential action for affirmative relief.[11] By contrast, in the Yemen case, the plaintiffs' primary cause of action was for affirmative relief and, in the alternative, an action for declaratory judgment:[12] while the primary cause of action was found admissible,[13] the alternative cause of action was, as in the Somalia case, rejected.[14]

At any rate, to the extent the claim was admitted, its substantive merits had to be adjudicated. Among the manifold issues to be considered in the context of the request for the Federal Republic of Germany to block the use of the satellite relay station at the Ramstein Air Base for US drone attacks in Yemen, two questions played a decisive role: first, whether and to what extent the collateral killing of innocent civilians is reconcilable with German constitutional law and international humanitarian law (infra Sect. 3); and second, whether Germany can be held co-responsible and, if so, whether it can be obliged to take countermeasures (infra

---

[11]For details see the first-instance Somalia judgment (2016) VG Köln, 4 K 5467/15 0f 27 April 2016. https://www.justiz.nrw.de/nrwe/ovgs/vg_koeln/j2016/4_K_5467_15_Urteil_20160427.html, margin numbers 1 ss, 26 ss, and the appellate judgment of OVG NRW, Somalia case, supra note 6, 1 ss, 44 ss. As to substantive questions dealt with by the Courts, see Sect. 6 and 7 1st paragraph.

[12]As described in the preceding paragraph.

[13]Both by the first-instance judgment of VG Köln, Yemen case, supra note 7, margin numbers 20 ss and the appellate judgment of OVG NRW, supra note 5, margin numbers 70, 73–135.

[14]But expressly so only in the appellate judgment of OVG NRW, Yemen case, supra note 5, margin numbers 70, 585.

Sect. 5). While both issues are dealt with by the OVG NRW at considerable length,[15] only the main arguments can be outlined here.

3 Lack of Compatibility with German Constitutional Law and International Humanitarian Law

Whereas the basic question of the legitimacy of killing in war as a matter of principle may be left open at this point, it appears likely that the OVG NRW started from the traditional assumption that killing in war is lawful as long and insofar as it is not forbidden (by any law).[16] Along this line of argument, when regarding the involvement of Germany in airstrikes performed by another state with collateral killings of civilians in a foreign country, three essential questions had to be answered: Was the causing of the death of innocent civilians prohibited under any national or international law and if so, on what level? To the extent that there exists a prohibition, did the US drone attacks keep within the non-prohibited range? If not, for what reason may this also be a matter of German concern?

Although the last question will be dealt with in more detail later (infra Sect. 4), at this point it is important to note that the argumentation of the OVG NRW is based on the right of every human being to life—irrespective of citizenship or abode—as guaranteed by both international law (e.g., in article 6 (1) International Covenant on Civil and Political Rights—ICCPR) and German constitutional law (article 2 (2) Basic Law) and the corresponding public duty to protect this right.[17] The degree to which this responsibility to protect can be reduced in time of war (or a comparable armed conflict) is determined in accordance with international humanitarian law.[18]

Since life is guaranteed only against "arbitrary" deprivation (article 6 (1) sentence 3 of the ICCPR) and since fatalities caused by military operations are not considered arbitrary as long as they are not prohibited by international humanitarian law,[19] the Court did not outlaw the use of drones in general.[20] Therefore, the US airstrikes could be deemed unlawful only if they failed to satisfy the requirements as prescribed for the protection of the civilian population in article 51 Additional Protocol I of 1977 to the Geneva Convention of 1949.[21] Three of the requirements included in

[15] OVG NRW, Yemen case, supra note 5, Sect. 3, running from margin numbers 135-583, not to mention the substantive aspects already addressed in the procedural admission part, supra note 13.

[16] For a criticism of this position as a matter of principle see Sect. 8.

[17] OVG NRW, Yemen case supra note 5, margin numbers 185 ss.

[18] Ibid., margin numbers 185 ss.

[19] Cf Ibid., margin numbers 291, 372, 392, 418 s, 425.

[20] Ibid., margin number 372 s.

[21] Protocol Additional to the Geneva Conventions of 12 August 1949, relating to the Protection of Victims of International Armed Conflicts, of 8 June 1977 (Protocol I).

this rather lengthy article are relevant here: the existence of an armed conflict; the distinction between combatants and civilians; and the proportionality between the military advantage anticipated and the potential loss of human life.[22]

Thus far, regarding the legal requirements for lawful airstrikes, the OVG NRW has remained within traditional boundaries; as to the question of whether these requirements were satisfied in the fatal drone attacks at issue, however, the Court has dared to deviate from longstanding practices. As far as the requirement of distinguishing between civilians and combatants is concerned, the Court expressed considerable doubt as to whether this demand is met by the general airstrike practice of the United States.[23] This was expressly questioned because the United States, in a practically limitless and potentially global war against international terrorism, follows an understanding of armed conflict that is so broad as to be irreconcilable with international humanitarian law.[24] These doubts are intensified by the fact that the United States claims a right of "preemptive" use of force that, according to the Court, is not granted by international law.[25]

If the question arises as to why the OVG NRW did not explicitly declare the fatal US drone attacks in Yemen to be in violation of international humanitarian law but rather contented itself with casting significant doubt on their legality, this can be explained by the fact that full information on the relevant circumstances was lacking. And, since this lack was found to be due to the German Government's failure to ensure the compatibility of the US drone strikes in Yemen and the use of the German air base with constitutional and international law,[26] the question of German co-responsibility came into play.

4 German Co-responsibility for Fatal US Airstrikes: Judicial Access

Prior to considering German co-responsibility, however, the question of whether military operations are ever subject to judicial assessment and adjudication had to be clarified. In this respect, too, the OVG NRW opened a door that hitherto had been almost completely closed.

This is particularly true with regard to the US justice system, as experienced in *Ali Jaber v. United States*,[27] in which the plaintiffs first sought satisfaction before a US court. Their suit was found inadmissible because it presented "non-justiciable

[22]For details concerning these requirements see OVG NRW, Yemen case supra note 5, margin number 343 ss.

[23]Ibid., margin number 459.

[24]Ibid., Leitsatz 7, and margin numbers 460 ss.

[25]Ibid., Leitsatz 5, and margin numbers 328 ss, 504 ss.

[26]Ibid 5, margin number 459. For details see margin numbers 229 ss, 460 ss.

[27]The Ali Jaber case, supra note 7.

political questions." This finding was based on the so-called political question doctrine, according to which courts are prevented from passing judgment on policy choices and value determinations that are "by their nature committed to the political branches to the exclusion of the judiciary."[28]

Though not with the same degree of judicial self-restraint, similar reservations were also raised against the plaintiffs in the Yemen case by the German court of first instance.[29] Although the VG Köln did not go so far as to exempt the political decisions of the executive branch from judicial review as a matter of principle, it recognized the broad discretion ("Gestaltungsspielraum") accorded to the relevant competent state power—here the executive branch. Accordingly, this Court opined that the judiciary should not be permitted to replace the discretionary decisions of the competent authority with its own assessments; otherwise the review of legality granted the courts by the constitution would amount to a "last decision control by the judiciary" that would be incompatible with the principle of the separation of powers.[30] Since such a final power could not be granted (especially in external affairs), "national courts should be barred from unlimited international-legal assessments of the external power."[31]

This self-disempowerment of the judiciary was countered by the OVG NRW with the lapidary statement that "the prohibition of arbitrary killings according to article 6 (1) (sentence 3) ICCPR would be practically ineffective if there was no procedure for examining the lawfulness of the application of deadly force;"[32] therefore, in light of the fact that both executive and judiciary are bound by law and justice according to article 20 (III) (German) Basic Law and in light of the guarantee of effective legal protection according to article 19 (IV) (1) Basic Law, the executive has, in principle, "no non-justiciable area of discretion."[33] Furthermore, as apparent from the Court's reasoning regarding the required legal interest in bringing proceedings, this right of the plaintiffs could not be denied on the basis of a greater subject-matter proximity of legal protection in the United States (as the starting point of the drone strikes at issue);[34] similarly, potential tensions in German-American relations could not be raised as an argument against the examination of the lawfulness of deadly drone attacks.[35]

The significance of this bold ruling, taken despite the German Government's stated aversion to being presented to other sovereign states as a "world public

---

[28]Schneider v. Kissinger (2005) 412 F.3d 190, 193 (D.C. Cir.), referred to by the US District Court for the District of Columbia in Ali Jaber v. United States, supra note 7, p 77 with further references to this doctrine.

[29]VG Köln, Yemen case supra note 7.

[30]Ibid., margin numbers 57 ss.

[31]Ibid., margin number 80; cf also margin numbers 70 ss.

[32]OVG NRW, Yemen case, supra note 5, margin number 425.

[33]Ibid., Leitsatz 4, and margin numbers 553 ss, 564.

[34]OVG NRW, Yemen case, supra note 5, margin numbers 122 ss.

[35]Ibid., margin numbers 568 ss; cf also margin numbers 209, 218, 572, 574.

prosecutor's office,"[36] cannot be overestimated as this was the only way to open the gates to the judicial examination of foreign military actions involving German territory.

5 Germany's Responsibility to Protect

Once the jurisdiction of German courts to adjudicate German involvement in possibly unlawful foreign airstrikes was accepted, three aspects of the potential public liability[37] of the Federal Republic of Germany with regard to the substantive merits of the Yemen case had to be considered: a duty to clarify and investigate the lawfulness or unlawfulness of the airstrikes at issue; a duty to ensure the compliance of the military actions performed by the acting state with international-law obligations; and, if necessary, a duty to block unlawful military actions of other states by appropriate means.

As it is not possible to address the reasoning of the Court in detail here, the following points may be highlighted as essential for the co-responsibility of a state for foreign military actions.

As regards the substance of the decision, the determination—or denial—of the unlawfulness of the challenged military actions, including the individual concern of the plaintiff, was of crucial importance. In the Yemen case, the claim as to the unlawfulness of the American drone attacks was based mainly on "serious doubts as to whether the general airstrike practice of the United States take due account of the requirement of distinguishing [between combatants and civilians],"[38] while the plaintiffs' personal concern is seen in their being exposed by the US practice to a constitutionally relevant danger to life and limb.[39]

Regarding territoriality, for military actions that are not initiated from German soil, co-liability of the Federal Republic requires a sufficiently close link to Germany.[40] In the Yemen case, the existence of such a connection had been challenged by the Federal Government, which claimed that, given the fact that German authorities had no means of control, the use of the relay station in Ramstein in the performance of American drone attacks constituted an "independent public action of a foreign state without constitutional relevance in relation to German state power."[41] The OVG NRW had already objected to this contention, however, in its

[36]As to such objections cf VG Köln, Yemen case, supra note 7, p 6; OVG NRW, Yemen case, supra note 5, margin number 18.

[37]As the claims may be understood: cf OVG NRW, Yemen case, supra note 5, margin numbers 2, 11 ss, 72, Leitsätze 12 s.

[38]Ibid., margin number 459; for details see margin numbers 229 ss, 460 ss.

[39]Ibid., margin numbers 532 ss.

[40]Ibid., Leitsatz 1, margin numbers 116 ss, 218.

[41]Cited by OVG NRW, Ibid., margin number 18.

reasoning regarding the admissibility of the case, stating that the German state has a constitutional duty to protect its citizens against foreign powers and that a corresponding individual entitlement—since everyone's human rights to life and physical integrity are guaranteed—can be claimed by non-German as well as by German citizens.[42] The Court also concluded that a close link to the German state is to be assumed when "the other state performs its interfering acts—its 'encroachment upon fundamental rights'—in essential respects from German territory and thus from the original area of competence and responsibility of the German state power."[43] Thus, a sufficiently close link to Germany, one that establishes its co-responsibility, may result merely from its having permitted the foreign state to operate from domestic territory and its having failed to ensure the compliance of that foreign state's actions with constitutional law and international law.

The type and basis of a duty constituting German co-responsibility in connection with the actions of a foreign state can be both a claim to the prevention of infringements of fundamental rights committed by the claimant's own state organs ("Abwehranspruch") and a claim to protection against infringement of fundamental rights committed by another state or comparable military unit ("Schutzanspruch"). As far as the Yemen case is concerned, the first type of claim was denied since the Court saw neither direct nor indirect proof of infringements of basic rights attributable to German authorities.[44] Whereas this appears correct as far as direct responsibility is concerned (after all, there were no hints that German officials had been actively involved in the employment of the American drones),[45] the denial of even indirect German (co-)responsibility is less convincing. This is not so much due to the fact that the Federal Government, after having been informed by US forces about their airstrikes, did not raise any objections:[46] presumably, the Federal Government did not raise objections because it relied on its expectation that the use by the United States of the air base, as agreed upon, would comply with the German legal order,[47] and because it assumed that if the German authorities had any influence at all on the events at issue, this influence would not be decisive.[48] Viewed critically, however, could not this lack of German influence simply be the result of the failure of the Federal Government to engage in the very measures to which it was ultimately ordered by the Court?[49] At any rate, in terms of the "Schutzanspruch" mentioned above and as stated in a thorough reasoning by the Court, the Federal Republic of

[42]Ibid., margin numbers 90 ss, 103 ss. Within the admission part of the judgment, with further elaboration regarding the substantive merits in margin numbers 185 ss, 213 ff.

[43]Ibid., margin number 218.

[44]Ibid., margin numbers 137 s.

[45]Ibid., margin numbers 139.

[46]For more details see Ibid., numbers 159 ss.

[47]Cf Ibid., margin number 157.

[48]Cf Ibid., margin numbers 170 ss.

[49]Cf Ibid., margin numbers 535 ss.

Germany had a duty to protect both Germans and non-Germans from US drone strikes that factually or potentially contravened international humanitarian law.[50]

Regarding the legal consequences to be drawn from a judicially determined duty of protection, as a rule, everything that would be necessary and appropriate for an efficient fulfillment of the duty enters into consideration. With regard to the Court's competence to specify the adequate means, however, the border between the judicial examination of lawfulness ("Rechtmässigkeitsprüfung")—which the OVG NRW was not willing to give up—on the one hand,[51] and the administrative discretion of expediency ("Zweckmäßigkeitsermessen")—to which the executive is entitled—on the other, had to be respected. The more competent the administrative authorities appear to be in choosing and performing the appropriate measures—as in particular in external and military affairs—the greater is their leeway for design and assessment of possible measures.[52] In the eyes of the Court in the Yemen case, however, this administrative discretion was not free of error because the measures taken by the Federal Government to reach the constitutional goal—namely, the protection of the plaintiffs from dangers to life or limb posed by unlawful US drone attacks using the air base in Ramstein—was completely inadequate.[53]

Consequently, due to its co-responsibility for ensuring that the use of the Ramstein Air Base complied with international law, the Federal Republic of Germany, based on its above established duty to protect (in terms of a "Schutzanspruch") was rightly ordered to take investigative measures and, where necessary, to work towards ensuring compliance with international law—whereby the kind of the concrete protective measures to be taken was left to the executive discretion of the Federal Government.[54]

To the extent that the plaintiffs wanted the use of the Ramstein Air Base for drone attacks to be barred entirely, they did not succeed because the airstrikes could not be considered in contravention of international law *ab initio*.[55] This lack of success in the Yemen case cannot, however, be interpreted to exclude the possibility of blocking the use of the satellite relay station of an air base in cases of verifiably unlawful airstrikes—especially if the airstrikes are continued despite multiple diplomatic efforts calling for their discontinuation.

As already indicated, however, the OVG NRW's courageous decision requiring the Federal Government to exercise more control over the compliance of the United States with international law when employing lethal drone attacks via Germany was recently overturned on appeal by the Bundesverwaltungsgericht (the court of last

[50]For details see Ibid., margin numbers 136, 185 ss; as to the violation of constitutional and international law assumed by the Court, cf margin numbers 343 ss.

[51]Cf supra Sect. 4.

[52]OVG NRW, Yemen case, supra note 5, margin numbers 535 ss.

[53]Ibid., margin numbers 568 ss.

[54]Ibid., Leitsatz 13 and margin number 574.

[55]Ibid., margin numbers 136, 573 ss.

instance).[56] While the full written judgment is not yet available, its decision—as far as can be concluded from the Court's press release—appears to be ambiguous. On the surface, looking solely at what the Federal Government can be required to do to control US drone attacks via Germany, the OVG NRW, in the BVerwG's view, went too far. Thus, the Court held that—first—a duty to protect will be recognized only when there is a concrete expectation that actions irreconcilable with international law will also occur in the future, that—second—the administration has greater leeway to design and assess than conceded by the lower court, and—third—that the required link with German territory must be more than the mere technical use of a domestic air base as a relay station from one foreign country to another. Since, in the estimation of the BVerwG, the Federal Government did what it was supposed to do within this framework, its discharge by the BVerwG appears consistent. As a matter of principle, however, as far as the judicial control of governmental duties to protect against unlawful foreign actions is concerned, it is important to note that the BVerwG, rather than denying external obligations, confirmed that the basic duty of the German state to protect also applies to foreigners living abroad if their basic rights are infringed by a foreign state—as may be the case if, in violation of humanitarian international law, civilians are exposed to disproportionate collateral damages as a result of foreign actions whose link to domestic territory is not merely technical in nature but rather involves some sort of decision-making element. Although this standard for holding Germany co-responsible for possibly unlawful foreign airstrikes is higher than that required by the OVG NRW, the annulment by the BVerwG of the lower court's judgment cannot simply be understood as granting the United States free usage of the German relay station as has been claimed, rather superficially, in the German press.[57] For not only does the BVerwG depart from less strict judicial reviewability of administrative actions and stronger requirements for territorial co-responsibility (both merely questions of variable degree and factual provability), with regard to the principal question of lawfulness or unlawfulness of deadly drone attacks, however, the BVerwG leaves no doubt about the necessity of measuring this question according to national and international law—with potential consequences for the responsibility of the state to take appropriate protective measures.

[56]BVerwG (2020) 6 C 7.19 of 25 November 2020—Pressemitteilung Nr. 68/2020 of 25 November 2020. https://www.bverwg.de/pm/2020/68.

[57]Ibid., e.g., in Frankfurter Allgemeine Zeitung of November 27, 2020.

6 Civil Remedies: Damages—Compensation—Rehabilitation

While in the Yemen case protection from future airstrikes with potential fatalities among civilians was at stake, in the Somalia case, decided by the OVG NRW on the same day,[58] the target of litigation was not that clear. Formally, the plaintiff seemed only to be requesting the Court to declare that the Federal Republic of Germany, in disregard of its duty, had neglected to work towards blocking military operations with unmanned aircraft,[59] and that this omission resulted in the death of the plaintiff's father. As it appears from the explanatory memorandum of the interest in bringing proceedings, however, the plaintiff was apparently pursuing a twofold aim: first, rehabilitation and satisfaction for the killing of his father; and second, the prevention of drone attacks that might endanger him in the future.[60] Had he not already failed for procedural reasons with his action for a declaratory judgment (this being subsidiary to a potential suit for affirmative action),[61] he might have been successful had he taken the same procedural approach as the plaintiffs in the Yemen case, namely, if he had asked the Federal Government for protective measures.[62] Alternatively (or additionally), the plaintiff could have brought a civil claim for damages (for the loss of his father and any harmful side effects).

Under German law, an action for damages against the Federal Republic for the killing or injuring of an innocent civilian by American drone attacks in a foreign country that were supported from German territory could be based on public liability ("Amtshaftung"), that is liability of the state for the unlawful acts of its officials.[63]

---

[58]Cf supra note 6 and Sect. 2, 2nd paragraph.

[59]OVG NRW, Somalia case, supra note 6, margin numbers 2, 15.

[60]Ibid., margin numbers 8 ss; on the objections of the Federal Republic of Germany as defendant, cf margin numbers 18 ss.

[61]Ibid., margin numbers 44 ss; for partly different reasons, the Somalia plaintiff's declaratory claim had already been dismissed in the first instance: VG Köln, Somalia case, supra note 11, margin numbers 26 ss.

[62]Cf supra Sect. 5 text accompanying note 54.

[63]According to Article 34 (1) Basic Law in connection with § 839 Civil Code; for details regarding Germany's potential civil liability for the employment of deadly force of arms abroad, cf Neubert (2016), p. 325 with further references. To be sure, however, it must be noted that, as litigated in the Kunduz case (cf supra note 8), the availability of compensation for extraterritorial killings, in which German military personnel is involved, by way of a "Amtshaftung"-claim is still in dispute. While this had been denied by the civil courts, from the first instance up to the Federal Supreme Court, both as a matter of principle and *in casu* due to the lack of a culpable violation of a legal duty (Bundesgerichtshof - III ZR 140/15 of 6 October 2016. In: (2017) Entscheidungen des Bundesgerichtshofs in Zivilsachen [BGHZ] vol. 212, pp 173 ss, para 14 ss and 40 ss, respectively), the Federal Constitutional Court, though not admitting the plaintiffs' constitutional complaint for procedural reasons, by way of an *obiter dictum* questioned the Federal Supreme Court's principal denial of "Amtshaftung" as falling short of the non-territorially limited binding force of the basic rights and the obligation of compensation in case of their violation (Bundesverfassungsgericht -2 BvR 477/17 of 18 November 2020. In: (2020) BeckRS 35088, para 32 s). The Kunduz plaintiffs'

Civil damages and rehabilitation, although ultimately not granted in the Somalia case, would not have been precluded *ab initio* since for the Courts the problem was not a lack of law but rather a lack of factual proof.[64] From a procedural perspective, it is noteworthy that the issue of admissibility—a high hurdle in the Yemen case,[65] was not even raised in the Somalia civil suit.

As far as the requirements for civil suits against the Federal Government are concerned, the following two are particularly relevant. With regard to territoriality, the requirement is the same as in a public suit for protection:[66] civil claims also require a close link to Germany. Obviously, this requirement is most clearly fulfilled when German personnel are directly involved in military operations in a foreign country. Such a link, however, can also arise indirectly if, for example, Germany makes its domestic territory or other facilities available to foreign forces to be used in extraterritorial operations.[67]

With regard to the substantive basis of civil liability, the violation of a public duty is required. Such a violation can be presumed if fatal drone attacks such as those undertaken by the United States, which can be characterized as deadly interventions into the right to life, lack constitutionally-based authorization ("Eingriffsermächtigung").[68] If this is the case—as there is reason to suspect with regard to the current US airstrike practice via the Ramstein satellite relay station—the Federal Republic must be prepared to incur liability in cases involving broad civil claims for collateral damages in a foreign country.

But even if a general "Eingriffsermächtigung" has been granted, a breach of duty supporting a claim of civil liability can result from the concrete disregard of humanitarian prohibitions of certain military actions (e.g., article 51 Additional Protocol I to the Geneva Conventions).[69] As the OVG NRW seems to assume given its reference to the termination of the Kunduz case,[70] however, the disregard of humanitarian prohibitions would constitute an unlawful breach of duty only if it were to be qualified as an international crime as defined in the German International

further attempt to find relief by a complaint to the European Court of Human Rights, alleging that Germany had not conducted an effective investigation and prosecution, as required by the procedural obligation to protect the right of life according to Article 3 of the European Convention on Human Rights, also failed since the Court, after a lengthy reasoning on the admissibility of the suit, found the German authorities to have complied with the requirements of an effective investigation (ECtHR Application no. 4871/16 of 17 February 2021, para 154 ss on the merits), thus not having to deal with possible consequences regarding civil compensation.

[64]Cf the first instance judgment of VG Köln, Somalia case, supra note 11, margin numbers 118 ss, and the appellate judgment of OVG NRW, Somalia case, supra note 58, margin number 98.

[65]Cf supra Sect. 4.

[66]Cf supra Sect. 5 4th paragraph.

[67]In the same way as reasoned by OVG NRW in the Yemen case, supra note 5, margin numbers 218 ss.

[68]Cf Neubert, supra note 63, p. 325.

[69]Cf supra Sect. 3 text accompanying note 11.

[70]Cf supra note 8.

Criminal Code ("Völkerstrafgesetzbuch"—VStGB) of 2002.[71] This, however, fails to consider the fact that humanitarian prohibitions of certain military actions are not completely congruent with either the German VStGB or with the international Rome Statute since only the most grievous violations of humanitarian law are penalized as international crimes.[72] Moreover, humanitarian prohibitions would be deprived of any intrinsic importance if their violation were to lead to no consequences whatsoever, not even to civil liability for the violation of a humanitarian duty. In this sense I agree with Reinhard Merkel, who declared the ordering of the deadly airstrike by the commander in the Kunduz case, though not punishable, to be "not lawful", thus opening the door to asking the Federal Government to compensate the victims.[73]

7 Criminal Sanctions: Individual Responsibility

While in previous sections protective duties and civil liability of the state were at the center of discussion, in turning to criminal responsibility, the focus is on the individual perpetrator. Though the Yemen and Somalia cases were brought in administrative courts (which have no jurisdiction over issues of criminal law), criminal prosecution of the individuals involved in potentially unlawful deadly drone attacks would not be out of the question since in his action for a declaratory judgment, the plaintiff in the Somalia case also referred to the killing of his father as a possible instance of jointly committed murder.[74]

Two aspects of criminal prosecution deserve particular attention: the potential crimes and the punishable individuals. First, in order for a criminal investigation of military operations to be instigated and, ultimately, for a verdict of guilty to be reached, the military operations in question must be criminalized by a special legal prohibition. This is unquestionably the case if collateral killings of military operations are outlawed as international crimes. If this is provided for on the supranational level (as by article 8 (II) (b) Rome Statute), the jurisdiction to prosecute lies with the International Criminal Court in The Hague. If war crimes are also prohibited by national law (as by §§ 8-12 German VStGB), criminal jurisdiction rests with the respective domestic court.

Less clear is the punishability of military operations that, although not penalized as international war crimes, violate international humanitarian law. With regard to "civilian fighters" who do not enjoy special "combatant" status pursuant to

[71] Cf OVG NRW, Somalia case, supra note 6, margin number 98.

[72] Cf Ambos (2009).

[73] Merkel (2010).

[74] See the plaintiff's statement of claim in VG Köln, Somalia case, supra note 11, margin number 12; although it was ultimately terminated by the Federal Attorney General who determined it compatible with international law, the Kunduz case, supra note 8, can also serve an example of criminal prosecution of deadly airstrikes.

international humanitarian law (article 43 Additional Protocol I to the Geneva Conventions),[75] there is no reason why they should not be subjected to the prohibitions of the general criminal law, such as murder or bodily injury, according to the "criminal law paradigm."[76] In contrast, the treatment of "combatants" depends to a great extent on the scope of the traditional assumption derived from the so-called "war paradigm" that perpetrators are relieved from responsibility in terms of the general criminal law due to the special status of combatants under international humanitarian law. The question, however, is whether this privilege should go so far as to leave violations of humanitarian rules of conduct in war committed by combatants unpunished so long as they do not cross the threshold of an international war crime. That is not convincing, though, despite the longstanding position that in war everything not specifically forbidden is permitted. The time has come for this tradition to be overcome; moreover, if one does not want to see general criminal law suspended wholesale due to a state of war, a justification or excuse is required if the killing of a human being that fulfils the statutory elements of a homicide offense is to remain unpunished. Such a defense, however, cannot be recognized simply by arguing that the combatant violated a (mere) humanitarian prohibition but did not commit a war crime as defined by international criminal law. Thus, as far as German co-responsibility for US drone attacks in a foreign country is concerned, if it turns out that these attacks are not reconcilable with international humanitarian law, the Federal Government may not take the easy way out and simply provide administrative protective measures; rather it must acknowledge its obligation to instigate criminal investigations.[77]

Second, regarding personal liability, if collateral killings by drone attacks prove to be punishable, the question is which individuals can be held responsible in terms of criminal law. The answer very much depends on the rules of perpetration and participation, which differ both between countries and between domestic and international criminal law. Concerning German citizens, their interaction with extraterritorial US airstrikes probably constitutes mere aiding and abetting (§ 27 German Penal Code), unless the personal commitment and self-interest in the potentially fatal and knowingly unlawful airstrikes is high enough to cross the threshold of co-perpetration (§ 25 (II) German Penal Code), as was in fact suggested by the plaintiff in the Somalia case.[78]

[75]For details on this distinction, cf Ambos (2014), p. 152 ss. and, with particular attention to the classification of "terrorists", cf Kremnitzer, supra note 1, pp 207 ss.

[76]For more arguments in favor of this "law enforcement paradigm", also known as "rubric of criminal law", in contrast to "rubric of war", see Eser (2018), pp. 309–326.

[77]With particular regard to the Somalia case, the persuasiveness of the reasoning with which the disproportionateness of the collateral damages and discriminating effect was denied by the Courts may be left open here: cf VG Köln, Somalia case, supra note 61, margin numbers 23, 123, OVG NRW, Somalia case, supra note 6, margin number 98.

[78]Cf VG Köln, Somalia case, supra note 61, margin number 12.

Whatever the mode of complicity,[79] from a territorial perspective, airstrikes co-steered on German territory—even if started abroad—that resulted in collateral killings in a third country would be considered a domestic act (§ 3 German Penal Code) or domestic participation (§ 9 (II) German Penal Code) and as such subject to German criminal law.

Regarding foreign perpetrators or German participants employed abroad, the application of German law could be considered (§ 7 (II) No. 2 or No. 1 German Penal Code, respectively), provided, however, that the drone attack entailing collateral damage is a criminal offense at the locus of commission.[80] If the victims are civilians, punishability at the locus of commission may be questioned only if the drone attack is not classified as an international crime and if at the territorial state the mere violations of international humanitarian law are considered exempt from general criminal law.

8 Questionable Legitimacy of Killing in War

As much as the OVG NRW is deserving of praise—on the one hand—for opening the door to the judicial examination of military operations regarding their compatibility with constitutional and international guarantees of human rights and—on the other hand—for daring to declare the Federal Government co-responsible for foreign fatal airstrikes, it is regrettable that the Court did not go far enough in scrutinizing the legitimacy of killing in war, in general, and collateral fatalities among innocent civilians, in particular. Instead, obviously proceeding from the traditional view that, in war, killing is permitted as long as it is not forbidden, the Court merely looked for limitations on the permissibility of collateral fatalities (assuming them permissible as a matter of principle),[81] and thus sidestepped the primary question, namely, what is the basis, in the first place, for the legitimacy of such a license to kill: the mere fact of being at war or the simple conversion of a non-prohibition into a permission?

Be that as it may, perceptions of this kind are commonly accepted,[82] even, if I am not mistaken, by *Mordechai Kremnitzer*, to whom this contribution is dedicated.

[79]As to the range of persons who can come into consideration in autonomous weapons systems, cf. Wagner (2016), pp. 355–368.

[80]For details as to what is required for the application of German criminal law to crimes committed outside Germany's borders, see Eser and Weißer (2019).

[81]Cf supra Sect. 3 text accompanying note 20.

[82]See, e.g., the Israeli High Court of Justice HCJ 769/02 of 13.12.2006, para 23 (though distancing itself from Cicero's statement "silent enim leges inter arma", para 61). Remarkably, in the decision of the Federal Supreme Court, the Federal Constitutional Court and the European Court of Human Rights (dealt with supra note 63), the fundamental question of the legitimacy of killing in war, if not overlooked, was not even addressed. For further references to comparable positions, cf Eser, infra note 90, Schöch-Festschrift, p. 464 ss, Wahl-Festschrift, p, 678 s, CrimLaw&Phil (2018), pp. 311, 320 ss.

Even though he strongly argues that in the fight against illegal attacks of terrorists with possible fatalities among innocent bystanders the right to self-defense is "by no means an unconditional license to kill,"[83] he is in fact merely insisting on (secondary) limitations while apparently presuming a (primary) right to kill that does not require an explicit justification. Or when rightly warning against the use of excessive force as one of the far-reaching consequences entailed by the transition from a law enforcement paradigm to a war paradigm,[84] again he merely advocates restrictions rather than challenging the war paradigm-based right to kill as a matter of principle. The same approach is apparent already in *Kremnitzer's* article on preventive killing. Therein, he also forcefully strived both for a resolute and legally appropriate treatment of terrorist attacks by, on the one hand, denying terrorists the privileged status of combatants with their license to kill according to the war paradigm and, on the other hand, subjecting terrorists to the criminal law enforcement paradigm.[85] However, even when demanding that preventive killing remain a "clear exceptional case" due to the right to life,[86] and even when respecting the judicial guarantee of an ordinary proceeding substantively guided by the general elements of self-defense,[87] apparently he is merely looking for limitations on preventive killing while, in principle, considering killing in war "not forbidden", unless insidiousness is at play.[88]

Although it is regrettable that the criticism of airstrikes, drone attacks, targeting terrorists, or of any other form of preventive killings with collateral fatalities among civilians remains focused on limitations, it is important to note, in order to avoid misunderstandings, that this does not mean that such restrictive endeavors do not deserve the greatest recognition. They are at least a step towards—hopefully—increasing the containment and humanization of preemptive operations, not to mention a step toward a cessation of retributive executions (in the form of extra-judicial capital punishment). This criticism does not, however, go far enough because it is based on the assumption that killing in war, as a matter of course, does not require justification but merely needs appropriate limits. When instead challenging the general license to kill in war as a matter of principle, this does not mean that deadly force in armed conflicts is never justifiable. On the contrary, in the same way as a private citizen has the right to resort to—if necessary, even deadly—self-defense against an unlawful attacker, a country under attack—including the military personnel employed for its defense—must have the same right. Nevertheless, licenses to kill must be positively authorized and must be circumscribed in their requirements and limits.

---

[83] Kremnitzer, supra note 4, p 6.

[84] Ibid.

[85] Kremnitzer, Präventives Töten, supra note 1, p. 204 ss, 208 ss, 215, 221.

[86] Ibid., p. 201.

[87] Ibid., p. 201 s, 217 ss.

[88] Cf ibid., pp. 205, 215.

This demand is drawn from an inquiry into both the legal bases and ideological background of killings in war that has led to worrying findings: Whereas a "normal" homicide, unless individually justified, is undoubtedly unlawful, killing in war is, in principle, considered lawful without any further justification. This virtually unquestioned license to kill is all the more astonishing in that no legal norm—neither in domestic criminal law nor in international law—can be found that positively and explicitly declares killing in war to be lawful. The attempt to overcome this lack of legitimacy simply by referring to the status of being at war, according to the pre-constitutional assumption that "all laws are silent in the time of war,"[89] can hardly be reconciled with the constitutional and international guarantees of the right to life. The same applies to the widespread reverse conclusion from not forbidden to lawful: as the protection of the right to life is encompassed by the general prohibition of homicide, exceptions therefrom require justification that cannot simply be derived from the absence of a general prohibition of lethal military action.[90]

Therefore, instead of giving killing in war free rein as a matter of principle and merely restricting it by means of sporadic prohibitions and/or by criminalizing only selected military operations, the requirements and limits of lawful killing in war or comparable armed conflicts must be determined in a positive way. This would be of particular significance in the following respects:

First, if every human being has a right to life that is fundamentally protected against homicide, killing requires justification. As this justification cannot be derived from war as such, killing in war must be legitimized for other reasons. This requires that the goals and interests be determined for which human life may be sacrificed by going to war: be they losses of life on the enemy's side (combatants and civilians), or be they losses of one's own citizens (combatants and civilians). If such an identification and evaluation of the interests at stake were to be performed responsibly, then—apart from clear cases of defensive force used against an aggressive war waged in violation of the international prohibition of force—the lack of legitimacy of many conflicts undertaken for economic goals or ethnic purposes would be revealed. Of course, a requirement of greater precision with respect to the reasons for going to war could lead to renewed discussion as to what, exactly, a "just war" is.[91] This, however, is inevitable the more the use of force is withdrawn from the arsenal of autocratic state sovereignty and put at the service of humanitarian aims.[92]

---

[89] As Cicero's "fond saying", supra note 82, was phrased by Hobbes (1998), Chapter V para 2.

[90] These findings with further details and references have been presented in these three publications: first in search of justifications of killing in war with particular attention to criminal law, Eser (2010), pp. 461–480. www.freidok.uni-freiburg.de/data/9710; continued with inquiries into constitutional and international law, Eser (2011), pp. 665–687. www.freidok.uni-freiburg.de/data/9714; and combined in an updated English version, Eser A, Killing in War, supra note 76, pp. 309–326.

[91] Cf, in particular, the divergent approaches of Walzer (2006), pp. 24–25 and McMahan (2009), respectively, as well as the extensive historical review of Schockenhoff (2018), p. 104.

[92] Hereby the doctrine of "just war" may ultimately lead to a doctrine of "just peace": cf. Eser (2021).

Second, if a certain legitimizing ground must be given, it will be much easier to determine and describe the requirements and limits of lawful killing. When the permission to kill enemy combatants—and to sacrifice one's own—can no longer simply be derived from state sovereignty, other justifying arguments will be needed. Obviously, paradigms of self-defense and defense of others, as well as of necessity and lesser evils, are the first candidates to be considered.[93] Without ignoring the fact that these justifying concepts have developed primarily with individual conflicts in mind, they nevertheless contain criteria relevant to defense in inter-state or group conflicts and potential for the weighing up of the pros and cons of specific military actions, thereby making them useful for determining the requirements and limits of justifiable killing in war. This applies, in particular, to the killing of innocent civilians, the justification of which still awaits a satisfying solution.[94]

Third, if legitimized in a positive way, formal prerequisites of the rule of international and constitutional law could be better satisfied. Since, according to the modern prohibition of the use of force, military operations require international authorization,[95] going to war is no longer within the free will of individual states. The more clearly its conditions are formulated, the easier it is to evaluate such an authorization. And, insofar as constitutional law provides that infringements to the right to life that are attributable to the state presuppose statutory permission,[96] a license to kill cannot be derived in a merely negative way from the prohibition of selective modes of killing. Instead, killing as such requires legitimation in the form of a positive and at least quasi-statutory authorization.

That is all the more necessary the more the notion of "war" becomes blurred and extended to "armed conflicts" that are difficult to define. At first glance, extending the framework of war to these situations appears well-intentioned because it brings non-state combatants under the umbrella of modern humanitarian law. Yet this again loses much of its value if, according to traditional practice, the prohibition of killing in such contexts is, without more, simply suspended. Should this also apply beyond international wars to non-international armed conflicts, then "easy" killing does not remain limited to "external" enemies but will increasingly be extended to "internal" adversaries as well. It takes little effort to imagine where this development might lead if the traditional license to kill is applied to all of what nowadays is lightly called "war"—such as the "war on terror"—or expanded to "targeted killing," "machine wars" with remotely controlled drones, or even to the so-called "enemy criminal

---

[93]Maybe in a similar manner as demonstrated by Kremnitzer, supra notes 1, p. 85 for limiting the excessive use of force in reaction to terrorist attacks.

[94]For more details as to what is required for legitimizing the loss of life regarding the four main groups of possible victims of fatal armed conflicts (combatants and civilians on the adversary's side and combatants and civilians on the actor's side), cf Eser, supra note 76, pp. 312 ss, 317 ss.

[95]Cf Article 2(4), 40, and 51 United Nations Charter.

[96]With regard to Germany (but perhaps relevant for other constitutional systems as well), cf Eser, supra note 76, pp 316 ss.

law" as is hotly debated in Germany, Spain, and Latin America.[97] These undesirable developments, too, can best be countered by giving the justification of killing in war contours in a positive legal sense.

9 Concluding Remarks

Returning to the judgments that inspired these reflections, it would have been a welcome development if the respective courts had not ended their inquiry after merely examining whether the collateral killings of civilians by drone attacks transgressed international humanitarian prohibitions, but had taken a further step and scrutinized the underlying traditional assumption of a general license to kill in war, as it was criticized in the previous section. Nevertheless, the *OVG NRW* deserves recognition, particularly in three respects: first, for opening access to the judicial examination of military operations by rejecting the "political question doctrine;"[98] second, for finding US drone attacks on foreign territory potentially unlawful;[99] and third, for declaring the Federal Republic of Germany co-responsible because it allowed the use of its domestic facilities.[100]

By the same token, *Mordechai Kremnitzer* deserves credit for his strong commitment to the fight against the excessive use of force in armed conflicts, in particular with regard to preventive killing. Hopefully, these reflections, which are dedicated to him with my best wishes for continued enlightening writings, will encourage him to go a step further in challenging killing in armed conflict as an apparent "matter of course", seemingly requiring nothing more than calling it a war. It is peace, not violence and war, humankind is longing for. In the search for peace, Mota and I share a common purpose.

References

Ambos, K. (2009). Art. 8 VStGB [Völkerstrafgesetzbuch]. In *Münchener Kommentar Strafgesetzbuch* (Vol. 6/2). München, Germany: Vorbemerkungen zu Art.

Ambos, K. (2014). *Treatise on international criminal law, volume II: The crimes and sentencing* (p. 152). Oxford, UK: Oxford University Press.

Durham, W. C. (1988). Reminiscence of dialogue. beyond the papers of the Freiburg conference. In A. Eser & G. P. Fletcher (Eds.), *Rechtfertigung und entschuldigung/justification and excuse. Comparative perspectives* (pp. 1492–1554). Freiburg, Germany: Max Plank Institute.

[97]See, e.g., Gomez-Jara Díez (2008), pp. 529–562. For my own criticism, see Eser et al. (2000), p. 444.

[98]Cf supra Sect. 4.

[99]Cf supra Sect. 3.

[100]Cf supra Sect. 5.

Eser, A. (2010). Tötung im Krieg: zur Fragwürdigkeit eines Tabus. In D. Dölling, B. Götting, et al. (Eds.), *Verbrechen - Strafe - Resozialisierung* (pp. 461–480). Berlin, Germany: Festschrift für Heinz Schöch.

Eser, A. (2011). Tötung im Krieg: Rückfragen an das Staats- und Völkerrecht. In I. Appel, G. Hermes, et al. (Eds.), *Öffentliches Recht im offenen Staat* (pp. 665–687). Berlin, Germany: Festschrift für Rainer Wahl.

Eser, A. (2018). Killing in war: Unasked questions - Ill-founded legitimization. *Criminal Law and Philosophy, 12*, 309–326.

Eser, A. (2021). Töten im Krieg: aus der Sicht einer Theorie des gerechten Friedens. In C. Hillgruber et al. (Eds.), *Zum Fest der Freiheit*. Berlin, Germany: Gedächtnisschrift für Eberhard Schockenhoff.

Eser, A., Hassemer, W., & Burkhardt, B. (Eds.). (2000). *Die deutsche Strafrechtswissenschaft vor der Jahrtausendwende* (p. 444). München, Germany: Beck.

Eser, A., & Weißer, B. (2019). The explanations prior and to §§ 3, 7 and 9 German Penal Code. In A. Schönke & H. Schröder (Eds.), *StGB-Kommentar* (30th ed.). München, Germany: C.H. Beck.

Gomez-Jara Díez, C. (2008). Enemy combatants versus enemy criminal law: An introduction to the european debate regarding enemy criminal law and its relevance to the Anglo-American discussion on the legal status of unlawful enemy combatants. *New Criminal Law Review, 11* (4), 529–562.

Hobbes, T. (1998). *On the citizen*. Cambridge, UK: Cambridge University Press.

Kremnitzer, M. (1996). Preface. *Israel Law Review, 30*(1-2), 1.

Kremnitzer, M. (2004). Präventives Töten. In D. Fleck (Ed.), *Rechtsfragen der Terrorismusbekämpfung der Streitkräfte* (pp. 201–222). Baden-Baden, Germany: Nomos.

Kremnitzer, M. (2015). *Thou shalt not kill? The right to self-defense against illegal attacks is by no means an unconditional license to kill*. In: The Jerusalem Report (p. 6).

Kremnitzer, M., & Ghanayim, K. (2005). New humanistic trends in Israeli criminal law. In J. Arnold, B. Burkhardt, et al. (Eds.), *Menschengereches Strafrecht. Festschrift für Albin Eser zum* (Vol. 70, p. 514). München, Germany: Geburtstag.

McMahan, J. (2009). *Killing in war*. Oxford, UK: Oxford University Press.

Merkel, R. (2010). Die Schuld des Oberst. In: DIE ZEIT, Nr. 4 of 21 January 2020.

Neubert, C. (2016). *Der Einsatz tödlicher Waffengewalt durch die deutsche auswärtige Gewalt* (p. 325). Berlin, Germany: Duncker & Humblot.

Schockenhoff, E. (2018). *Kein Ende der Gewalt?* (p. 104). Freiburg, Germany: Friedensethik für eine globalisierte Welt.

Wagner, M. (2016). Völker(straf)rechtliche Überlegungen zu autonomen Waffensystemen. In W. Gropp, B. Hecker, et al. (Eds.), *Strafrecht als ultima ratio* (pp. 355–368). Tübingen, Germany: Gießener Gedächtnisschrift für Günter Heine.

Walzer, M. (2006). *Just and unjust wars. A moral argument with historical illustrations* (4th ed., pp. 24–25). New York, NY: Basic Books.

Command Responsibility and the Colombian Peace Process

Kai Ambos and Susann Aboueldahab

Mordechai Kremnitzer, being a citizen of a State with a long-lasting (armed) conflict, was always interested in International Humanitarian Law and the responsibility of (Israeli) commanders.[1] Against this background, we are confident that this paper, most warmly dedicated to Mordechai, will find his interest even if it concerns a region of the world not so close to his heart.

1 The Colombian Peace Process and the Special Jurisdiction for Peace

On 24 August 2016, the Colombian Government and the Revolutionary Armed Forces of Colombia—People's Army (*Fuerzas Armadas Revolucionarias de Colombia—Ejército del Pueblo,* FARC-EP) concluded a Peace Agreement, which marks the official end of more than 50 years of a non-international armed conflict between this group and the Colombian State, causing the death of more than 200.000 persons and leaving behind more than 25.000 disappeared as well as five million forcibly

The authors would like to thank Marieke Buchholz for her valuable assistance in the preparation of this article.

[1]See generally along these lines Kremnitzer and Cohen (2005), pp. 317–409; Kremnitzer (2004), pp. 201–222.

K. Ambos (✉) · S. Aboueldahab
Georg-August-Universität, Göttingen, Germany
e-mail: kambos@gwdg.de; susann.aboueldahab@jura.uni-goettingen.de

K. Ghanayim, Y. Shany (eds.), *The Quest for Core Values in the Application of Legal Norms*, https://doi.org/10.1007/978-3-030-78953-4_15

displaced persons.[2] The original Peace Agreement was voted down in a referendum on 2 October 2016 by a slim majority of 50.2%. Following this setback, the Colombian Government and the FARC-EP introduced several changes and signed a revised Peace Agreement on 24 November 2016. This version was subsequently adopted by the Colombian Congress and thus constitutes the Final Peace Agreement.[3] Its general aim is not only to end the conflict but also to build a lasting peace. The so-called Comprehensive System of Truth, Justice, Reparation and Non-Repetition (*Sistema Integral de Verdad, Justicia, Reparación y No Repetición*) lies at the heart of the Final Peace Agreement. It is designed as a "holistic" system whose different components are connected and mutually reinforcing. These mechanisms are apart from the JEP (which we discuss below): a Truth Commission (*Comisión para el Esclarecimiento de la Verdad, la Convivencia y la No Repetición*), a Search Unit for the Disappeared (*Unidad de Búsqueda para Personas dadas por Desaparecidas*), and comprehensive reparation measures for peacebuilding and guarantees of non-repetition (*medidas de reparación integral para la construcción de paz y garantías de no repetición*). The purpose of this comprehensive system is to establish a transitional institutional setting that satisfies and redresses the rights of the victims of the armed conflict and contributes to national reconciliation.

The JEP, officially set up in March 2018, is the system's exclusive judicial component. It consists of an Investigation and Prosecution Unit (*Unidad de Investigación y Acusación*), a Registry (*Secretaría Ejecutiva*) and a two-tiered court system, composed of the (higher) Tribunal for Peace (*Tribunal para la Paz*, TP) and the (lower) Justice Chambers (*Salas de Justicia*). The somewhat complex structure is shown in more detail in the following diagram.

[2]Centro Nacional de Memoria Histórica, 'Estadísticas del conflicto armado en Colombia' (covering the period between 1958 and 2012). Retrieved January 27, 2021, from http://www.centrodememoriahistorica.gov.co/micrositios/informeGeneral/estadisticas.html.

[3]Acuerdo Final para la Terminación del Conflicto y la Construcción de una Paz Estable y Duradera (Final Peace Agreement). Retrieved November 24, 2016, from https://www.unidadvictimas.gov.co/sites/default/files/documentosbiblioteca/nuevoacuerdofinal.pdf. The English version to the agreement: Final Agreement to End the Armed Conflict and Build a Stable and Lasting Peace, 24 November 2016. Retrieved January 27, 2021, from http://especiales.presidencia.gov.co/Documents/20170620-dejacion-armas/acuerdos/acuerdo-final-ingles.pdf.

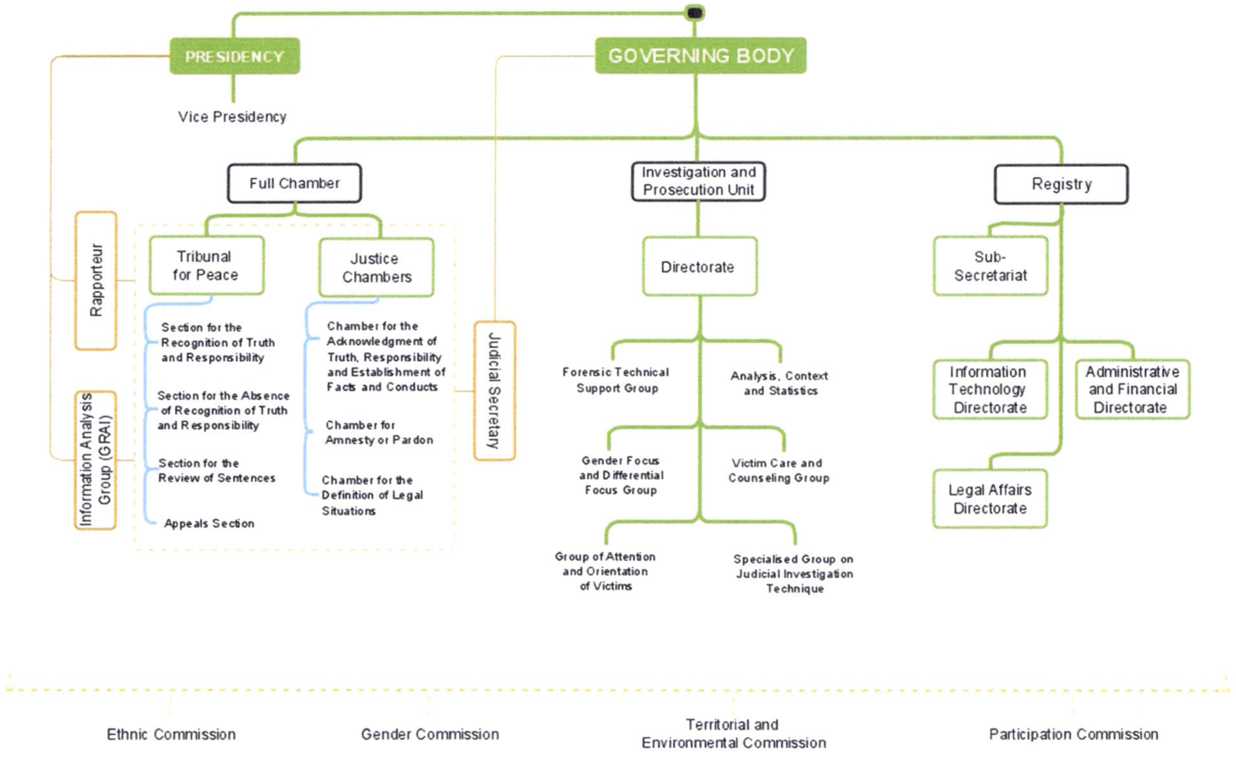

Diagram elaborated (simplified) by the authors based on the Spanish original by the JEP. https://www.jep.gov.co/Paginas/Transparencia/Talento/Organigrama.aspx. Accessed 29 January 2021

The JEP's objectives are to bring to justice those who participated directly or indirectly in the armed conflict[4] and to protect the rights of the victims—especially with regard to acts that constitute serious breaches of International Humanitarian Law (IHL) and serious violations of Human Rights.[5] Its jurisdiction *ratione materiae* covers crimes against humanity, genocide, serious war crimes—that is, any violation of IHL committed systematically or as part of a plan or policy—hostage-taking or another severe deprivation of physical liberty, torture, extrajudicial executions, forced disappearance, rape and other forms of sexual violence, child abduction, forced displacement, and the recruitment of minors.[6] The JEP's jurisdiction *ratione personae* covers demobilized members of the FARC-EP and Colombian Security Forces (armed forces and police). Furthermore, it extends to third parties who participated directly or indirectly in the armed conflict[7] but only, in line with a Constitutional Court judgment,[8] if they voluntarily submit themselves to the JEP. The JEP's jurisdiction *ratione temporis* encompasses crimes committed since the beginning of the armed conflict until 1 December 2016 (the date of the ratification of the Final Peace Agreement).[9]

---

[4]Final Peace Agreement (n 3) 145, 152, 164.

[5]Ibid., pp. 145, 149, 152, 164.

[6]Ibid. No. 40; Constitutional Court of Colombia, *Demanda de inconstitucionalidad contra el artículo 1° del Acto Legislativo 01 de 2012*, Judgment, C-579, 28 August 2013.

[7]Final Peace Agreement (n 3) Nos. 32, 63.

[8]*Reforma a la Estructura orgánica del Estado en el marco del Proceso para la Terminación del Conflicto Armado en Colombia*, Judgment C-674 of 2017, 14 November 2017. Retrieved January 27, 2021, from http://www.corteconstitucional.gov.co/relatoria/2017/C-674-17.htm. The Court argued that third parties' *voluntary* submission to the JEP does not violate their right to a natural judge (para. 5.5.2.2.) since this submission "results precisely from their willingness to submit themselves to a jurisdictional authority that is distinct from the ordinary authorities of the State and that offers them sufficient guarantees" ["el sometimiento de los alzados en armas a la JEP no comporta una sustitución el principio del juez natural, puesto que dicho sometimiento resulta, precisamente, de su voluntad de sujetarse a una autoridad jurisdiccional diferenciada de las ordinarias del Estado y que les ofrezca suficientes garantías"], adding that the JEP's "framework [...] offers symmetrical and equivalent guarantees" that do not diminish "procedural and substantive guarantees" ["el traslado competencial se realiza en el marco de un diseño que ofrece garantías simétricas y equivalentes a las que se contemplan para los grupos alzados en armas, sin que se advierta el propósito de disminuir las garantías orgánicas, procesales y sustantivas o de hacer más gravosa la situación de quienes se someten al sistema institucional de transición"], cf. para. 5.5.2.3. (last sub-paragraph). See generally with regard to the content and scope of the guarantee of the natural judge paras. 5.2.5.2. et seq. of the judgment.

[9]Crimes that were committed after that date fall under Colombia's ordinary jurisdiction with two exceptions: First, this timeframe is extended to cover crimes committed by FARC-EP ex-combatants that are closely related to the disarmament process. In these cases, the jurisdiction *ratione temporis* is expanded (beyond 1 December 2016) until this process is completed. Second, the SJP's jurisdiction also covers crimes that were committed before 1 December 2016 but have a continuing effect beyond that date (*crímenes continuos*). See, Transitional Article 5 of Legislative Act No. 01 (4 April 2017). Retrieved January 27, 2021 http://es.presidencia.gov.co/normativa/normativa/ACTO%20LEGISLATIVO%20N°%2001%20DE%204%20DE%20ABRIL%20DE%202017.pdf.

Given that the JEP's mandate is limited to 15–20 years,[10] it will not be possible to fully investigate all serious offences committed during the armed conflict—particularly in view of the conflict's long duration and magnitude. The Final Peace Agreement does not define which cases shall be prioritized; thus, it is upon the JEP to establish the relevant prioritization and selection criteria.[11] On June 28, 2018, the JEP's chamber for the acknowledgment of truth, responsibility and establishment of facts and conducts (*Sala de Reconocimiento de Verdad, de Responsabilidad y de Determinación de los Hechos y Conductas*) published criteria and methodology for prioritizing cases and situations[12] but these are not binding on other Chambers and in particular not on the—hierarchically higher—TP.

At any rate, the criteria and methodology document makes some important proposals and triggered an overdue (internal) debate on how to select and prioritize cases. The Chamber suggests giving primacy to emblematic cases and persons holding key positions within the structure of criminal organizations—depending on the impact of the case and the availability of information.[13] Within this framework, the Chamber particularly stresses the gravity and representativeness of the offences and the decisive participation ("*participación determinante*") of the alleged responsible (which is not necessarily restricted to the armed structure's leadership but derives from an overall assessment of the facts) as well as the scale of the victimization caused by the respective offences (especially the number of victims as well as the extent and concentration of the victimizing events in a particular territory).[14] Consequently, the JEP shall focus on paradigmatic crime patterns in the context of macro criminality committed during the armed conflict. This has been confirmed by the Constitutional Court.[15] This strategy confirms previous prioritization criteria adopted by the Attorney General's Office (*Fiscalía General de la*

[10]The JEP will be functioning 10 years as of 15 January 2018, with an optional subsequent period of 5 years and a maximum period of 20 years in total to complete its judicial activities. Jurisdicción Especial para la Paz, Resolution 001 of 15 January 2018, passed by the President of the SJP. Retrieved January 27, 2021, from https://www.jep.gov.co/Marco%20Normativo/Resolución%20001%20de%202018%20Apertura%20al%20Público.pdf. Additionally, see, Art. 34 of the JEP Statutory Law.

[11]However, the Peace Agreement contains certain references in Nos. 48, 51 and 60.

[12]Jurisdicción Especial para la Paz, *Criteria and methodology for prioritizing cases and situations by the Chamber for the Acknowledgment of Truth, Responsibility and Establishment of Facts and Conducts* (28 June 2018). Retrieved January 27, 2021, from https://relatoria.jep.gov.co/documentos/providencias/1/10/Guia_Criterios%20y%20metodolog%C3%ADa%20de%20priorización%20de%20casos%20de%2028%20de%20junio%20de%202018.pdf.

[13]Ibid., p. 36 et seq.

[14]Ibid., p. 36 et seq.

[15]See in this regard, Constitutional Court of Colombia, *Control automático de constitucionalidad del Proyecto de Ley Estatutaria número 08 de 2017*, Judgment, C-080, 15 August 2018, [4.1.5.3.(viii)]. Retrieved January 27, 2021, from https://www.corteconstitucional.gov.co/relatoria/2018/c-080-18.htm.

Nación).[16] According to this earlier position, the gravity of the crimes depends on the extent to which fundamental rights are being affected and on how exactly the conduct has been executed. The representativeness of the crimes on the other hand is correlated to the gravity of the acts and should illustrate the complex range of facts and behaviours that account for the dynamics of the crimes committed.[17] This encompasses not only offences that are established in the ICC Statute, but also several serious individual crimes, such as extrajudicial executions or child abduction.[18]

Based on these criteria, the JEP has opened seven macro cases (which concern whole crime situations) focusing on

- particular crimes (e.g. abduction (case no. 001) as well as the phenomenon of extrajudicial killings (case no. 003) and the recruitment of minors (case no. 007));
- the accumulation of several crimes committed against a certain population group (e.g. the persecution of members of the left-wing political party *Unión Patriótica*[19] (case no. 006)); and
- certain regions that were affected disproportionately by the armed conflict (e.g. the departments *Nariño* (case no. 002) and *Norte del Cauca* (case no. 005), or the subregion *Urabá* (case no. 004)).[20]

---

[16]Attorney General's Office, *Directive No. 1* (4 October 2012). Retrieved January 27, 2021, from https://www.fiscalia.gov.co/colombia/wp-content/uploads/Directiva-N°-0001-del-4-de-octubre-de-2012.pdf.

[17]Ibid., p. 30.

[18]Final Peace Agreement (n 3) No. 40.

[19]The *Unión Patriótica* is a political party that was founded by the FARC-EP in 1985 as a result of peace negotiations with the Colombian government of then president Belisario Betancur. In the subsequent years, the party was subject to political violence that led eventually to its extermination.

[20]For an overview of all seven cases, see: Retrieved January 27, 2021, from https://relatoria.jep.gov.co/salareconocasos; https://www.jep.gov.co/Sala-de-Prensa/Paginas/JEP-abre-caso-007-sobre-reclutamiento-y-utilizacion-de-niñas-y-niños-en-el-conflicto-armado.aspx. For additional information, particularly regarding the number of persons that have been brought/submitted themselves to the JEP (12,168 in total) and the number of decisions passed (16,500 in total), see 'La JEP ha tomado 16,500 decisiones y tiene a 12,168 personas sometidas', El Tiempo, 12 December 2019. Retrieved January 27, 2021 from https://www.eltiempo.com/justicia/jep-colombia/rendicion-de-cuentas-de-la-jep-desde-neiva-este-jueves-442862. Regarding the activities of the SJP within its first year of functioning: 'Estos son los casos que ha asumido la JEP en su primer año', Ámbito Jurídico, 16 January 2019. Retrieved January 27, 2021 from https://www.ambitojuridico.com/noticias/penal/constitucional-y-derechos-humanos/estos-son-los-casos-que-ha-asumido-la-jep-en-su.

2 Command Responsibility in the Colombian Context

Command responsibility came to the fore in the Colombian context as part of a controversial debate on how to hold senior military officers accountable for the so-called "false positive" killings (*falsos positivos*).[21] In these cases, Colombian Security Forces, especially the army, extrajudicially killed civilians who belonged to vulnerable population groups (e.g. LGBTIQ people, drug addicts, homeless people)[22] and presented them subsequently as members of guerrilla groups killed in combat in order to increase the Security Forces' body count.[23] Between 2002 and 2008, Security Forces allegedly killed more than 3000 civilians in this way.[24] The scandal first became known in 2008,[25] followed by investigations at the international[26] and national level.[27] Likewise, the ICC's Office of the Prosecutor (OTP) has

[21]See in this regard Juan Pappier, 'The 'Command Responsibility' Controversy in Colombia' (*EJIL: Talk!*, 15 March 2017). Retrieved January 27, 2021 from https://www.ejiltalk.org/the-command-responsibility-controversy-in-colombia/.

[22]Previously, many of them had been lured to remote parts of the country with work offers. See, Aylish O'Driscoll, 'Colombian soldiers paid $500 for victims to boost kill counts: Testimony', Colombia Reports, 5 December 2011. Retrieved January 27, 2021 from https://colombiareports.com/false-positives-recruiter-received-500-per-victim/.

[23]The increase of the "body count" often served the ultimate aim of ascension within the ranks of the Colombian Security Forces. See, Pappier (n 21) and Olasolo and Cantor (2019), p. 106.

[24]Pappier (n 21). According to *El Espectador*, 29 high-ranking officials of the Colombian Military alone are allegedly responsible for (at least) 1228 cases of 'false positives': '29 generales y coroneles, en la mira de la CPI por ejecuciones extrajudiciales', El Espectador, 9 July 2017. Retrieved January 27, 2021 from https://www.elespectador.com/colombia2020/justicia/jep/29-generales-y-coroneles-en-la-mira-de-la-cpi-por-ejecuciones-extrajudiciales-articulo-855577/.

[25]'Condenan a 21 militares por 'falsos positivos' de Soacha. Los uniformados son responsables de presentar a jóvenes como muertos en combate en el año 2008', El Espectador, 17 November 2016. Retrieved January 27, 2021 from https://www.eltiempo.com/justicia/cortes/condenas-por-falsos-positivos-de-soacha-31876.

[26]Statement by Philip Alston, UN Special Rapporteur on extrajudicial executions - Mission to Colombia 8–18 June 2009. Retrieved January 27, 2021 from https://newsarchive.ohchr.org/EN/NewsEvents/Pages/DisplayNews.aspx?NewsID=9219&LangID=E. See also, International Federation for Human Rights, 'Colombia. The war is measured in liters of blood' (21 June 2012). Retrieved January 27, 2021 from https://www.fidh.org/IMG/pdf/rapp_colombie__juin_2012_anglais_def.pdf; Human Rights Watch (HRW), 'On Their Watch: Evidence of Senior Army Officers' Responsibility for False Positive Killings in Colombia' (24 June 2015). Retrieved January 27, 2021 from https://www.hrw.org/report/2015/06/24/their-watch/evidence-senior-army-officers-responsibility-false-positive-killings.

[27]In 2011, eight soldiers from the battalion *Rafael Reyes de Cimitarra* were convicted for crimes against humanity due to their involvement in 'false positive' cases. In 2017, 21 soldiers were convicted for their involvement in the 'false positive' cases, amongst them former head of operations of the 15th Brigade in the department of *Norte de Santander* (Coronel *Gabriel de Jesús Rincón*) who was held responsible for forced disappearance, aggravated homicide as well as conspiracy to commit a crime. See, 'Falsos positivos de Soacha: condenan a 21 militares a penas entre 37 y 52 años de prisión', Semana, 3 April 2017. Retrieved January 27, 2021 from https://www.semana.com/nacion/articulo/falso-positivo-de-soacha-condenas-de-hasta-52-anos/520904.

continuously requested information regarding the status of national proceedings relating to these cases.[28] The JEP dedicated one of its first macro cases to these particular types of extrajudicial killings (case no. 003).[29] The outcome will depend greatly on the definition of command responsibility applied by the respective chamber. Indeed, given that the JEP will only investigate and prosecute those most responsible, the question of the correct definition of command responsibility to be applied has far-reaching consequences, well beyond the emblematic macro case 003.

2.1 Command Responsibility in the Final Peace Agreement

The Final Peace Agreement distinguishes, as to command responsibility, between superiors within the Colombian Security Forces on the one hand[30] and those in the FARC-EP on the other.[31] The common ground of these two provisions is that the

---

[28]ICC, Office of the Prosecutor, *Report on Preliminary Examination Activities 2019*, paras. 93, 129 (5 December 2019). Retrieved January 27, 2021 from https://www.icc-cpi.int/itemsDocuments/191205-rep-otp-PE.pdf. ICC, Office of the Prosecutor, *Report on Preliminary Examination Activities (2020) - Colombia*, paras. 135–145 (14 December 2020). Retrieved January 27, 2021 from https://www.icc-cpi.int/Pages/item.aspx?name=2020-otp-rep-PE-COL. See also ICC, Office of the Prosecutor, *Statement of the Prosecutor of the International Criminal Court, Fatou Bensouda, on the conclusion of her visit to Colombia (10–13 September 2017)* (13 September 2017). Retrieved January 27, 2021 from https://www.icc-cpi.int/Pages/item.aspx?name=170913-otp-stat-colombia; ICC, Office of the Prosecutor, *Office of the Prosecutor concludes mission to Colombia* (23 January 2020). Retrieved January 27, 2021 from https://www.icc-cpi.int/Pages/item.aspx?name=pr1510.

[29]Jurisdicción Especial para la Paz, *Sala de Reconocimiento de Verdad, de Responsabilidad y de Determinación de los Hechos y Conductas, Decision No. 005 of 2018* (17 July 2018). Retrieved January 27, 2021 https://www.jep.gov.co/Sala-de-Prensa/Documents/Auto%20005%20-%20Apertura%20Caso%20003%20Muertes%20ileg%C3%ADtimamente%20presentadas%20como%20baja%20en%20combate%20SRVR%20(1).pdf. See in this regard also Olga Patricia Rendón M., 'JEP priorizó investigación sobre falsos positivos', El Colombiano, 24 July 2018. Retrieved January 27, 2021 https://www.elcolombiano.com/colombia/jep-priorizo-investigacion-sobre-falsos-positivos-CX9044545.

[30]Final Peace Agreement (n 3), p. 44 stating:

"In accordance with the above, a special, simultaneous, balanced and fair treatment will be established for state agents, based on international humanitarian law. This differentiated treatment will take into account the provisions of operational law governing the Colombian Security Forces (which include both the Military Forces and the Police) in relation to IHL. In no case may command responsibility be based exclusively on rank, hierarchy or scope of jurisdiction. The responsibility of members of the Colombian Security Forces for conducts committed by their subordinates have to be based on the (1) effective control of the respective conduct, the (2) knowledge based on the information at their disposal before, during and after the respective conduct, as well as the (3) means at their reach to prevent it and, if it has occurred, to promote the appropriate investigations." (this and all following translations from Spanish by Susann Aboueldahab, emphasis added).

[31]Ibid., p. 59 stating:

(1) "Regarding the responsibility of members of the FARC-EP, international humanitarian law, international human rights law and international criminal law shall be taken into account as legal

responsibility of commanders shall not be based exclusively on rank, hierarchy or jurisdiction, but rather on: (1) the effective control of the respective conduct of the subordinates, (2) the knowledge based on the information at the commanders' disposal before, during or after the respective conduct, and (3) the means at their reach to prevent it, and, if the conduct has already occurred, to take appropriate steps.[32] While these aspects of the definition of command responsibility apply to both commanders of Colombian Security Forces and the FARC-EP, the Final Peace Agreement adds an important distinction regarding FARC-EP superiors:

> Effective control of the respective conduct shall be understood as the material ability that the superior had of exercising appropriate control over his or her [the FARC-EP commander's] subordinates in relation to the criminal behaviour occurring, *as established by international law.*[33]

Accordingly, the definition of command responsibility regarding FARC-EP superiors contains an explicit reference to international law, whereas no such reference can be found regarding the Colombian Security Forces' commanders.[34] This discrepancy can be explained by the complex negotiation process between the two parties subsequent to the rejection of the (First) Peace Agreement in the referendum of 2 October 2016.[35] This original version of the Peace Agreement did not include the cited paragraph and instead established one common definition of command responsibility applicable to both superiors of the FARC-EP and the Security Forces.[36] Following criticism regarding the definition's vagueness, an important modification was made in the revised Peace Agreement, including a paragraph applicable to both commanders of the FARC-EP and of the Security Forces.[37] Therein, Art. 28 ICC Statute was taken as the point of reference for the Peace Agreement, thus dispelling the previous doubts about the Colombian definition's scope and interpretation. As an immediate response, active and retired army

---

reference. [. . .] The command responsibility of FARC-EP officers for their subordinates' conducts shall be based on the (1) effective control of the respective conduct, the (2) knowledge based on the information at their disposal before, during and after the respective conduct, as well as the (3) means at their reach to prevent it and, if it has occurred, to take the corresponding decisions. Command responsibility cannot be based exclusively on rank or hierarchy.

(2) Effective control of the respective conduct shall be understood as the material ability that the superior had of exercising appropriate control over his or her subordinates in relation to the criminal behaviour occurring, as established by international law." (emphasis added).

[32]Final Peace Agreement (n 3), p. 44, 59.

[33]Ibid. p. 59.

[34]Ibid., p. 44.

[35]See, Sect. 1.

[36]Final Peace Agreement (n 3), p. 44, 59. Retrieved January 27, 2021 https://www.acore.org.co/wp-content/uploads/2016/08/24_08_2016acuerdofinalfinalfinal-1472094587.pdf, note that already in this version the wording of the definitions was not identical. None of the previous drafts of the Agreement contained the additional paragraph in question, see for example: Joint Draft of the Peace Agreement as of 15 December 2015. Retrieved January 27, 2021 http://wp.presidencia.gov.co/sitios/especiales/Documents/20150921-declaracion-proceso-paz/docs/Punto5-Victimas.pdf.

[37]See in this regard, Pappier (n 21).

officials protested against these changes, arguing in a public letter addressed to then President Juan Manuel Santos that the reference to the "controversial" Art. 28 ICC Statute in the added paragraph was unnecessary, caused "profound damage," and if not reversed would seriously affect the combatants' "moral and will to fight."[38] The government relented and decided to delete the just inserted paragraph—but *only* with regard to the Security Forces. In contrast, the amendment to the definition regarding FARC-EP commanders was maintained and only slightly modified, replacing the wording "as established in Art. 28 of the Rome Statute" with the above cited "as established by international law."[39]

This last change to the Final Peace Agreement was only announced on November 23, 2016, one day before its signing. Subsequently, the delegation of the FARC-EP indicated the "undoubtedly negative consequences" that would follow from the last modifications introduced by the government. The FARC-EP clarified that they only accepted the changes given the particular circumstances and the lack of time, leaving no doubt of the modifications' "unilateral" character.[40] Interestingly, the delegation further announced that they "did not permit" the government to undertake the same changes regarding their commanders.[41] The delegation based its position on the argument, that the newly modified definition of command responsibility applicable to Colombian Security Forces differed from the precisely regulated provisions in International Criminal Law (ICL) and particularly in the ICC Statute.[42] The rationale behind this reaction is that the ICC could act as a court of last resort—in line with the Statute's principle of complementarity (Art. 17)[43]—in case Colombia does not comply with its obligations under the ICC Statute. These last minute amendments to the Peace Agreement, which ultimately led to an asymmetric treatment of commanders of the FARC-EP on the one hand and those of the Colombian Security Forces on the other, have been highly criticized as a backtrack to accountability of commanders.[44] In sum, it is fair to say that the unbalanced definition was the result of external pressure by the military aimed at evading the responsibility of army

---

[38]Open Letter to Juan Manuel Santos signed by the president of the Colombian Association of Retired Officers (*Asociación Colombiana de Oficiales Retirados, ACORE*) (22 November 2016). Retrieved January 27, 2021 https://www.wradio.com.co/noticias/actualidad/la-carta-con-la-que-militares-en-retiro-cuestionan-justicia-transicional/20161122/nota/3311095.aspx.

[39]The Joint Communiqué No. 7 of the delegations of the Government of then President Santos and the FARC-EP (24 November 2016). Retrieved January 27, 2021 https://www.cancilleria.gov.co/sites/default/files/Fotos2016/comunicado_conjunto_7_fe_de_erratas_24_de_noviembre_de_2016_0.pdf.

[40]The communication by the delegation of the *FARC-EP*, 'Constancia de las FARC respecto a las definiciones y responsabilidades de los Agentes del Estado en la JEP' (26 November 2016) Retrieved January 27, 2021 https://partidofarc.com.co/farc/2016/11/26/constancia-de-las-farc-respecto-a-las-definiciones-y-responsabilidades-de-los-agentes-del-estado-en-la-jep/.

[41]Ibid.

[42]Ibid.

[43]Thereto in more detail Ambos (2016), p. 266.

[44]José Miguel Vivanco, 'Letter by José Miguel Vivanco on "Command Responsibility" in the Implementing Legislation of the Peace Agreement', Human Rights Watch, 25 January 2017.

commanders for crimes committed by their subordinates, thus ultimately ensuring their impunity.[45] The tensions surrounding the negotiations of a command responsibility definition are quite paradigmatic for the general political atmosphere of the peace talks. At any rate, despite criticism, the Final Peace Agreement's (final) provisions on command responsibility have been incorporated into domestic law.

2.2 Command Responsibility Under Colombian Law

Prior to the Final Peace Agreement, Colombian law did not provide for criminal liability of negligent superiors' omissions of their duties to prevent or repress their subordinates' commission of international crimes or to submit the matter to the competent authorities.[46] Neither the Colombian Penal Code nor the Military Penal Code contained relevant provisions.[47] Military superiors' omissions merely led to disciplinary consequences, when carried out with (gross) negligence.[48] Thus, the implementation of the command responsibility provisions of the Final Peace Agreement into Colombian domestic law was a novelty. The innovation was twofold: Provisions concerning the responsibility of Security Forces were included in the Colombian Constitution by Legislative Act 01/2017[49] while the provisions relating to FARC-EP superiors were incorporated into the JEP Statutory Law.[50]

Retrieved January 27, 2021 https://www.hrw.org/news/2017/01/25/letter-command-responsibility-implementing-legislation-peace-agreement.

[45]Ibid.

[46]As stipulated in Art. 28(a)(ii) to the Rome Statute of the International Criminal Court, in force 1 July 2002, 2187 U.N.T.S. 90 (ICC Statute). See in this regard Olasolo and Canosa Cantor (n 23) 66 et seq., 77-9.

[47]Also, civilian superiors were not held accountable under Colombian law prior to the Peace Agreement. See, Olasolo and Canosa Cantor (n 23) 94.

[48]A definition of command responsibility was only provided for by the Colombian Armed Forces Operational Law. See, The 2009 Road Map and the *MFE 6-27* Land Operations Manual of 2016, Detailed in this regard in Olasolo and Canosa Cantor (n 23) 94.

[49]Legislative Act 01/2017, *Acto Legislativo 01/2017. Por medio del cual se crea un título de disposiciones transitorias de la Constitución para la terminación del conflicto armado y la construcción de una paz estable y duradera y se dictan otras disposiciones*, 4 April 2017. Retrieved January 27, 2021 http://es.presidencia.gov.co/normativa/normativa/ACTO%20LEGISLATIVO%20N°%2001%20DE%204%20DE%20ABRIL%20DE%202017.pdf.

[50]Law No. 1957, *Estatutaria de la Administración de Justicia en la Jurisdicción Especial para la Paz* (SJP Statutory Law), 6 June 2019. Retrieved January 27, 2021 https://www.jep.gov.co/Marco%20Normativo/LEY%201957%20DEL%2006%20DE%20JUNIO%20DE%202019.pdf.

2.2.1 Regarding Colombian Security Forces (Legislative Act 01/2017)

Legislative Act 01/2017 was introduced in Congress shortly after the signing of the Final Peace Agreement. It passed as a constitutional amendment containing the command responsibility definition regarding Security Forces in March 2017.[51] The definition is set out in Transitory Article 24 of Legislative Act 01/2017 (hereinafter: Trans. Art. 24). The provision's first part reproduces almost verbatim the respective provision of the Final Peace Agreement,[52] calling for the existence of a superior-subordinate relationship and stipulating that the 'effective command and control' by the respective commander requires his/ her effective control over the subordinates' unlawful conduct.[53] Additionally, the *chapeau* of Trans. Art. 24 establishes that the sources of interpretation of command responsibility are: (1) the Colombian Penal Code; (2) IHL as *lex specialis*; and (3) the Colombian Army Forces Operational Law.[54] More interestingly, however, is the second part of Trans. Art. 24 deviating significantly from the Peace Agreement:

> The effective control and command of the military or police superior over the acts of his or her subordinate shall be understood to exist, when the following cumulative conditions can be demonstrated:
>
> a. That the criminal conduct(s) were committed within the area of responsibility assigned to the unit under his or her command and according to the respective level, and are related to the activities under his responsibility;
> b. That the superior had the legal and material ability to give orders, to modify or enforce them;
> c. That the superior had the effective capacity to develop and execute operations within the area where the criminal acts were committed, according to his or her specific level of command; and

---

[51] A Legislative Act is a type of law that is issued by the Congress by means of a special procedure and directed at modifying provisions in the Colombian Constitution. See, Arts. 374 and 375 of the Colombian Constitution (*Constitución Política de Colombia* of 1991). Retrieved January 27, 2021 http://www.secretariasenado.gov.co/index.php/constitucion-politica.

[52] Final Peace Agreement (n 3), p. 44.

[53] The first part of the provision reads as follows: Transitory Article 24. Command responsibility. For the determination of command responsibility, the Special Jurisdiction for Peace will apply, in the case of members of the Armed Forces, the Colombian Penal Code, International Humanitarian Law as lex specialis, and the operational rules of the Armed Forces in relation to IHL [...].

The determination of command responsibility shall not be based exclusively on rank, hierarchy or scope of jurisdiction. The responsibility of a member of the Armed Forces for acts committed by his or her subordinates must be based on the (1) effective control of the respective conduct, the (2) knowledge based on the information at his or her disposal before, during or after the commission of the respective conduct, as well as the (3) means at his or her reach to prevent the commission or continuation of punishable conduct, provided that factual conditions permit it, and, if the conduct has occurred, to promote appropriate investigations. (emphasis added).

[54] As long as it is not contrary to the Colombian legislation. While, as stated above, the Colombian Penal Code does not contain provisions on superior responsibility, the Operational Law in the MFE 6-27 Land Operational Manual defines superior responsibility. This definition, however, is more restrictive than international standards, thus creating a conflict, see in this regard Olasolo and Canosa Cantor (n 23) 97-8.

d. That the superior had the material and direct ability to take the adequate measures to prevent or suppress the punishable conduct(s) of his or her subordinates, provided that (s)he had actual or updatable knowledge of the conduct(s) commission.[55]

This supplement to the command responsibility definition is remarkable in various regards: First of all, it leads to a much more precise definition than the one agreed upon in the Final Peace Agreement and fills the gap left with regard to the effective control requirement. In fact, then President Santos had made clear that such a definition is to be made in the respective domestic act.[56] However, Santos also declared that the corresponding clarification would be similar to the one that applies to FARC-EP commanders,[57] which is obviously not the case: the above-quoted supplement lacks any reference to international law and at the same time limits command responsibility by introducing four cumulative requirements to establish "effective control and command". We will analyse below (*infra* Sect. 3) if this is compatible with Art. 28 ICC Statute.

2.2.2 Regarding FARC-EP (JEP Statutory Law)

More than 2 years after Legislative Act 01/2017 was adopted, the JEP Statutory Law entered into force on June 6, 2019. While this Law establishes a wide range of provisions that apply to all parties possibly involved in the JEP's proceedings, it only contains rules on command responsibility of FARC-EP superiors—somewhat surprisingly given the predominantly organizational nature of statutory laws. Art. 67 of the Statutory Law, which is the central provision, is—unsurprisingly—an exact quote of the Final Peace Agreement.[58] The said provision contained reference to international law and is strengthened by Art. 66 which is comparable to the chapeau of Trans. Art. 24 LA 1/17,[59] however extending the (international) legal reference applicable to the FARC-EP commanders, including ICL.[60] Art. 68, on the other hand, leaves no doubt that these references are not applicable to the Security Forces;

[55]Emphasis added.

[56]President Santos, 'Palabras del Presidente Juan Manuel Santos en la ceremonia de clausura curso de Altos Estudios Militares y curso Integral de Defensa Nacional' (28 November 2016). Retrieved January 27, 2021 http://es.presidencia.gov.co/discursos/161128-Palabras-del-Presidente-Juan-Manuel-Santos-en-la-ceremonia-de-clausura-curso-de-Altos-Estudios-Militares-y-curso-Integral-de-Defensa-Nacional.

[57]Ibid.

[58]Art. 67 SJP Statutory Law; Final Peace Agreement (n 3), p. 59.

[59]See, text (n 53).

[60]Art. 66 SJP Statutory Law reads as follows: With respect to the responsibility of the members of the FARC-EP, International Humanitarian Law, International Human Rights Law and International Criminal Law and the Colombian Criminal Code will be taken into account as a legal reference, always applying the most favourable norm.

their conduct is exclusively governed by the above-mentioned provisions of Legislative Act 01/2017.[61] As a result, the reference to international (criminal) law regarding command responsibility in the JEP Statutory Law is only applicable to FARC-EP superiors, but not to the Security Forces.[62]

In sum, it is fair to say that the asymmetrical treatment of command responsibility for members of the FARC-EP on the one hand and the Colombian Security Forces on the other was not in any way alleviated but aggravated by the implementing legislation.[63] In fact, the imbalance between the FARC-EP and the Security Forces was increased by providing for additional requirements for the latter, thereby restricting the scope of command responsibility, while maintaining the same ample definition for FARC-EP commanders, as contained in the Final Peace Agreement, including references to international (criminal) law.

3 The Colombian Approach in Light of the ICC Statute

Art. 28 ICC Statute is of particular interest in Colombia given that the Court has jurisdiction with respect to genocide and crimes against humanity committed in Colombia since 1 November 2002 and with respect to war crimes since 1 November 2009.[64] The Colombian situation is under preliminary examination since June

[61] Art. 68 SJP Statutory Law, titled 'Command responsibility of the members of the Security Forces', merely contains this clarification.

[62] See in this regard, Olasolo and Canosa Cantor (n 23), pp. 95–96.

[63] In November 2017 the Colombian Constitutional Court (CC) declared that Trans. Art. 24 LA 1/17 (n 53) is in line with the Constitution, Judgment C-674/17 (n 8) [4.7.3.8]. The Court argued that even though this provision does not adopt the ICC Statute's wording regarding command responsibility as enshrined in Art. 28, Colombia's duty to investigate, prosecute and punish international crimes is not hampered given the existence of alternative modes of liability in domestic law, paras. 5.5.1.9.-11 of the Judgment. In August 2018, the CC also upheld the constitutionality of the JEP Statutory Law. See, Colombian Constitutional Court, *Communiqué No. 32* (15 August 2018). Retrieved January 27, 2021 http://www.corteconstitucional.gov.co/comunicados/No.%2032%20comunicado%2015%20de%20agosto%20de%202018.pdf. Contrary to the CC's ruling, the Penal Chamber of the Colombian Supreme Court took a different approach in the case *Rodrigo Alberto Zapata Sierra and others* in its ruling of 5 December 2018 (rad. 50236), relying directly on Art. 28 ICC Statute to establish the defendant's responsibility, para. 2.2.3.6.1. (last sub-paragraph). Given this important judgment, it is fair to say that the current case law tends to a more inclusive view with regard to international law and fully embraces command responsibility pursuant to Art. 28 ICC Statute. For a critical analysis of this judgment see: Gustavo Cote, 'La responsabilidad por el mando en el Acuerdo de Paz firmado por el Gobierno Colombiano y las FARC-EP: un análisis sobre la base del caso Bemba de la Corte Penal Internacional' (2019) 15(92) *Nuevo Foro Penal*, 153, 174.

[64] Colombia deposited its instrument of ratification on 5 August 2002 so that the Statute entered, pursuant to Art. 126(2) ICC Statute, on 1 November 2002. For the domestic level see: Law 742/2002, *Por medio del cual se aprueba el Estatuto de Roma de la Corte Penal Internacional*, 7 June 2002. Retrieved January 27, 2021 http://www.suin-juriscol.gov.co/viewDocument.asp?

2004.[65] Ever since, Colombia's efforts to prosecute perpetrators have been under close observation.[66] In the course of its preliminary examination, the OTP has particularly expressed concerns regarding the definition of command responsibility in the Final Peace Agreement applicable to commanders of the Security Forces: In her November 2016 report, the ICC chief prosecutor decided to keep the definition of command responsibility under analysis in order to identify possible gaps which could impede the JEP from investigating and prosecuting potential ICC cases.[67] Shortly after the JEP Statutory Law was introduced into Congress, the ICC prosecutor presented her concerns to the Colombian public in a newspaper article, stating that the definition of command responsibility used in the Final Peace Agreement "could be 'interpreted' as limiting the definition of command responsibility in the Rome Statute."[68] One year later, on 18 October 2017, the ICC Prosecutor sent an *amicus curiae* brief to the Constitutional Court, noting with concern the elimination of all references to Art. 28 ICC Statute in the text of the Final Peace Agreement.[69]

Tensions between Art. 28 ICC Statute and the Colombian approach arise in three areas—effective control, causation and commander's knowledge—which will be analysed in turn. Although the reference to Art. 28 ICC Statute was deleted in both the JEP Statutory Law (regarding FARC-EP commanders) and Legislative Act 01/2017 (regarding Security Forces), the following analysis will only focus on the latter since this definition omits any reference to international (criminal) law and is much more restrictive than the definition in the Statutory Law.

ruta=Leyes/1667619. Colombia made a declaration under Art. 124 ICC Statute with respect to war crimes, so that the ICC's jurisdiction has been delayed until 1 November 2009.

[65]ICC, Situations and cases under preliminary examination. Retrieved January 27, 2021 https://www.icc-cpi.int/colombia.

[66]See, for example, ICC, Office of the Prosecutor, *Interim Report on the Situation in Colombia* (14 November 2012). Retrieved January 27, 2021 https://www.icc-cpi.int//Pages/item.aspx?name=Situation-in-Colombia-Interim-Report. See also the reports on the preliminary examination of the Colombian situation issued by the Office of the Prosecutor of the ICC on 25 November 2013, 2 December 2014, 12 November 2015, 14 November 2016, 4 December 2017 and 5 December 2019. Retrieved January 27, 2021 https://www.icc-cpi.int/colombia.

[67]ICC OTP report (n 28) 257, 263.

[68]Fatou Bensouda, 'El acuerdo de paz de Colombia demanda respeto, pero también responsabilidad', Semana, 21 January 2017. Retrieved January 27, 2021 https://www.semana.com/nacion/articulo/deseo-corte-penal-internacional-justicia-transicional-en-colombia/512820.

[69]ICC, Office of the Prosecutor, *Escrito de Amicus Curiae de la Fiscal de la Corte Penal International sobre la Jurisdicción Especial para la Paz Ante la Corte Constitucional de la República de Colombia* (18 October 2017). Retrieved January 27, 2021 http://cr00.epimg.net/descargables/2017/10/21/17135b6061c7a5066ea86fe7e37ce26a.pdf?int=masinfo, was sent to the CC as part of the review of Legislative Act 01/2017. In its most recent ICC OTP reports (n 28), the OTP is, somewhat surprisingly, silent on the matter.

3.1 *Effective Control* (Actus reus)

According to the interpretation of Art. 28 ICC Statute in the *Bemba* case, the only one so far dealing with responsibility of military commanders before the ICC, the commander needs to have effective authority and control over the subordinates that commit international crimes.[70] This view is largely shared by the doctrine.[71] However, the Colombian is more restrictive on several grounds.

3.1.1 Control Over Respective Conduct and Limitation to Immediate Subordinates

From the outset, the Colombian approach is more restrictive in requiring the commander to have effective control over the subordinate's respective *conduct*.[72] In addition, Trans. Art. 24 LA 1/17 imposes, as seen above,[73] further cumulative requirements, three of which directly relate to the existence of 'effective command and control.'[74] First, the unlawful conduct that was committed by the subordinates must fall within the area of responsibility assigned to the unit under the superior's command. This is difficult to reconcile with the ICC's approach to military commanders since this requirement is only provided for with regard to civilian superiors in Art. 28(b) ICC Statute. While these can only be required to have control over their subordinates' in work-related matters, the effective control of military commanders covers the subordinates' entire military life.[75] The decisive factor for a military commander's effective control is his/her material (*de facto*) ability to prevent or suppress the subordinates' international crimes, regardless of the normative scope of

[70]ICC, *Prosecutor v. Jean-Pierre Bemba Gombo*, Judgment on the appeal, ICC-01/05-01/08 A, Appeals Chamber, 8 June 2018 ('*Bemba* Appeals Judgment'), pp. 167–170; ICC, *Prosecutor v. Jean-Pierre Bemba Gombo*, Judgment pursuant to Article 74 of the Statute, ICC-01/05-01/08, Trial Chamber III, 21 March 2016 ('*Bemba* Trial Judgment'), p. 170; ICC, *Prosecutor v. Jean-Pierre Bemba Gombo*, Decision pursuant to Art. 61(7)(a) and (b) of the Rome Statute on the Charges of the Prosecutor Against Jean-Pierre Bemba Gombo, ICC-01/05-01/08, Pre-Trial Chamber, 15 June 2009 ('*Bemba* Confirmation Decision'), p. 407.

[71]Cryer (2019), p. 370; Arnold and Jackson (2021), marginal numbers, pp. 25–28; Schabas (2016), pp. 613–614; O'Keefe (2015), pp. 5, 105; Ambos (2013), pp. 210–211; Cassese (2013), p. 188.

[72]Trans. Art. 24 LA 1/17 (n 53).

[73]See, the provision cited in Sect. 2.2.1).

[74]The fourth (cumulative) requirement (sub-para. (d)), cited in Sect. 2.2.1, does not restrict the scope of effective control but is only relevant with respect to the knowledge (*mens rea*) requirement, to be discussed *infra* Sect. 3.2.

[75]Schabas (n 71) 613; Arnold and Jackson (n 71), mn. p. 28, 31; Werle and Jeßberger (n 71) 665-6; O'Keefe (n 71), p. 5, 106; Ambos, Treatise on ICL (n 71) 209.

his/her legal (*de jure*) power.[76] The majority of doctrinal writing on the topic shares this view.[77]

3.1.2 Legal and Material Ability to Give Orders

Secondly, Trans. Art. 24(b) establishes that Colombian Security Forces superiors must have the legal *and* material ability to give, amend or enforce orders.[78] This requirement thus excludes *de facto* commanders and disregards that commanders may have—even though not legally ascribed—effective control, just as Art. 28 ICC Statute explicitly stipulates ("effectively acting as").[79] While the *Bemba* Defense Appeals Brief argued that, in principle, a geographically far removed commander cannot be held liable for his lack of control,[80] the Appeals Judges took a different, more nuanced approach.

The Appeals Chamber's majority held that Mr. Bemba was a "remote commander" with "non-linear command"[81] and hence faced limitations in controlling his subordinates.[82] Judge Eboe-Osuji argued in his Concurring Separate Opinion that he "would not subscribe to any interpretation of the Majority Opinion as suggesting that the geographical remoteness of a commander is a factor all of its own, which would necessarily insulate him [Mr. Bemba] from criminal responsibility"[83] and leaves no doubt that evidence of effective material control is needed rather

[76]Bemba Appeals Judgment (n 70), p. 5, 167 ("The scope of the duty to take 'all necessary and reasonable measures' is intrinsically connected to the extent of a commander's material ability [...] a commander cannot be blamed for not having done something he or she had no power to do."); Bemba Trial Judgment (n 70), pp. 183–184; Bemba Confirmation Decision (n 70), p. 407.

[77]Cryer and others (n 71) pp. 370-1; Arnold and Jackson (n 71), mn. p. 25, 28, 75; Schabas (n 71) 612-613; Werle and Jeßberger (n 71) 663; O'Keefe (n 71), p. 5, 105; Ambos, Treatise on ICL (n 71) 209; Cassese and others (n 71) 188.

[78]Provided that they know about their subordinates' international crimes or have enough information at their disposal to put them on notice about such crimes, see (n 53).

[79]As well as Art. 7(3) ICTY Statute and Art. 6(3) ICTR Statute, see in this regard also Olasolo and Canosa Cantor (n 23) 99.

[80]ICC, *Prosecutor v. Jean Pierre Bemba Gombo*, Defense for Mr. Jean Pierre Bemba Gombo, *Public Redacted Version of Appellant's document in support of the appeal*, ICC-01/05-01/08-3434-Red 28-09-2016 1/196 EO A, 28 September 2016 ('*Bemba* Defense Appeals Brief'), pp. 175–185. The first author of this paper was part of the Appeals Defence team.

[81]Bemba Appeals Judgment (n 70), p. 171.

[82]See also ibid., p. 191 ("limitations that [he] would have faced in investigating and prosecuting crimes as a remote commander sending troops to a foreign country.") Critical in this regard: Leila Sadat, 'Fiddling While Rome Burns? The Appeals Chamber's Curious Decision in Prosecutor v. Jean-Pierre Bemba Gombo' (*EJIL: Talk!*, 12 June 2018). Retrieved January 27, 2021 https://www.ejiltalk.org/fiddling-while-rome-burns-the-appeals-chambers-curious-decision-in-prosecutor-v-jean-pierre-bemba-gombo/.

[83]ICC, *Prosecutor v. Jean Pierre Bemba Gombo*, Concurring Separate Opinion of Judge Eboe-Osuji to the Bemba Appeals Judgment, ICC-01/05-01/08-3636-Anx3, 14 June 2018, p. 258.

than *de jure* powers.[84] Judges Monageng and Hofmanski took a similar approach in their Dissenting Opinion, arguing that "[t]he specificities of the particular case, such as [...] the remoteness of the commander are part of the factual considerations that the Trial Chamber must assess in order to determine whether the accused had the material ability to prevent, repress or report the commission of crimes. However, this does not prevent the Trial Chamber from considering various relevant indicators of effective control"[85] The two Judges conclude that "effective control requires that the commander ha[s] the material ability to prevent or repress the commission of the crimes [...]"[86] and that Mr. Bemba, while admittedly facing "logistical difficulties,"[87] would have been able to overcome them. Although the Appeals Judges came to different findings in this particular case, they did not depart from the general interpretation of the "material ability" requirement pursuant to Art. 28 ICC Statute. Consequently, none of the Appeals Judges' approaches are as narrow as Trans. Art. 24(b)—namely requiring commanders' material *and* legal ability.

This is also consistent with the Trial Chamber's (TC) Approach, according to which "the question is simply whether or not the commander had effective control over the relevant forces,"[88] implying "a *de jure* or *de facto*" superior-subordinate relationship.[89] Thus, the gist of effective control is the material, not formal (legal) ability to control the subordinates. Accordingly, command responsibility arises for all commanders in the respective chain of command, also for those far removed from the crime scene, provided that they retain their material ability to prevent, suppress or submit their subordinates' crimes to the competent authorities.[90] Of course, the existence of legal responsibility on the part of a commander can be a criterion to determine his/her material ability.[91]

[84]Ibid. p. 262.

[85]ICC, *Prosecutor v. Jean Pierre Bemba Gombo,* Dissenting Opinion of Judges Monageng and Hofmanski to the Bemba Appeals Judgment, ICC-01/05-01/08-3636-Anx1-Red, 8 June 2018, p. 127.

[86]Ibid., p. 128.

[87]Ibid., p. 57. See in this regard also Alexander Heinze, 'Some reflections on the Bemba Appeals Chamber Judgment' (OpinioJuris, 18 June 2018). Retrieved January 27, 2021 http://opiniojuris.org/2018/06/18/some-reflections-on-the-bemba-appeals-chamber-judgment/.

[88]Bemba Trial Judgment (n 70), p. 184.

[89]Ibid. In the same vein Bemba Confirmation Decision (n 70), p. 410.

[90]Critical regarding the drawing of a legal distinction between remote and non-remote commanders Miles Jackson, 'Geographical Remoteness in Bemba' (*EJIL: Talk!*, 30 July 2018). Retrieved January 27, 2021 https://www.ejiltalk.org/geographical-remoteness-in-bemba/.

[91]Arnold and Jackson (n 71), mn, p. 28; Schabas (n 71) 614; Werle and Jeßberger (n 71) 663; Ambos, Treatise on ICL (n 71) 211–212.

3.1.3 Ability to Carry Out Military Operations Within a Limited Geographical Area

Thirdly, Trans. Art. 24 (c) requires that the superior must have the effective/direct ability to develop and carry out military operations within the geographical area in which his/her subordinates' crimes have been committed, according to his/her specific level of command.[92] This requirement takes out constellations in which military commanders retain effective control over their subordinates although they travel to/are present in areas outside of his/her actual (geographical) area of responsibility.[93] This aspect of the effective control requirement was a central issue in the *Bemba* appeals proceedings. The bone of contention there was whether the remoteness of a military superior always has an impact on his/her level of actual effective control over the crimes committed by his/her subordinates.[94]

Three of the five judges of the ICC Appeals Chamber did not consider that to be the case, but instead found that geographical remoteness is but one factor to be considered among others which does not necessarily have an impact on the level of effective control over subordinates.[95] The other two judges took the opposite view holding that a commander's remoteness is always a factor that impacts his/her actual effective control.[96] The majority judgment concluded that although Mr. *Bemba* did not have control over the geographical area where the military operations took place, he retained the ability to take several measures to prevent, impede and submit his

[92]The provision cited at Sect. 2.2.1.

[93]Olasolo and Canosa Cantor (n 23) 99.

[94]See Jackson (n 90); Sadat (n 82); In more detail Cote (n 63) 153-199; Olasolo and Canosa Cantor (n 23) 77 et seq. with further references. See also, 'Remoteness in itself cannot serve as a defence to command responsibility' (*Amnesty International*, 10 October 2018). Retrieved January 27, 2021 https://hrij.amnesty.nl/remoteness-command-responsibility-icc/.

[95]Bemba Concurring Separate Opinion of Judge Eboe-Osuji, (n 83), p. 3, 258 ("Geographic remoteness is only a factor to be considered among other circumstances or peculiarities of a given case."); Dissenting Opinion of Judges Monageng and Hofmanski to the Bemba Appeals Judgment (n 85), p. 127 ("The specificities of the particular case, such as [. . .] the remoteness of the commander are part of the factual considerations [. . .] in order to determine whether the accused had the material ability to prevent, repress or report the commission of crimes. However, this does not prevent the Trial Chamber from considering various relevant indicators of effective control [. . .])."

[96]ICC, *Prosecutor v. Jean Pierre Bemba Gombo*, Separate Opinion of Judge van den Wyngaert and Judge Morrison to the Bemba Appeals Judgment, ICC-01/05-01/08-3636-Anx2, 8 June 2018, p. 33 ("[. . .] what is required of a commander, both in terms of how closely they should monitor the troops and in terms of what measures they are expected to take to prevent criminal behaviour, depends on how proximate they are to the physical perpetrators in the chain of command."), p. 34 ("It is not the task of the higher-level commander to micro-manage all lower-level commanders [. . .]"), p. 36 ("[. . .] the Court should abide by the principle that command responsibility is not strict liability and that we do not ask the impossible of the military commander").

subordinates' crimes to the competent authorities—and thus ultimately exercised effective control.[97] The decisive factor for the existence of effective control is thus whether the commander had, in the particular case, the material ability to give, modify and enforce orders. While this is an ongoing debate, it is clear that neither the majority nor the minority positions in Bemba are as restrictive as the third requirement of Trans. Art. 24(c).

3.1.4 The ICC Prosecutor's Position

The ICC Prosecutor voiced her criticism regarding the Colombian approach in the above-mentioned[98] *amicus curiae* brief of October 2017. The Prosecutor took issue with all three requirements of Trans. Art. 24(a)-(c), arguing that ICL did neither limit the responsibility of commanders to crimes that were committed within their area of responsibility assigned to the unit under their command; nor require the commanders' legal ability to give, modify and enforce orders or the effective/direct ability to act on the crimes committed by their troops.[99] The Prosecutor made clear that even though ICL refers to these criteria when it comes to commanders' effective control, these are merely possible *indicia*, amongst several others, that may prove effective control; by no means do they constitute requirements to be proven cumulatively.[100] This position is also reflected by the *Bemba* Appeals Judgment, clarifying that the existence or absence of effective control shall not be based on the fulfilment of certain abstract criteria, but is rather to be inferred from the circumstances of the particular case.[101]

---

[97]Bemba Appeals Judgment (n 70), p. 172 ("[...] Mr. Bemba's power to investigate crimes committed in the CAR was limited [...]"), p. 173 ("[...] the limitations alluded to by Mr. Bemba did not completely curtail his ability to investigate crimes").

[98]ICC OTP, *amicus curiae* brief (n 69). The brief was initially filed confidentially but was leaked to the media and subsequently published online.

[99]Ibid section B. See also, ICC OTP, Report on Preliminary Activities (n 67), p. 145.

[100]ICC OTP, *amicus curiae* brief (n 69), p. 22; Bemba Trial Judgment (n 70), p. 188. Critical in this regard, Kai Ambos, 'La absolución de Jean Pierre Bemba y la responsabilidad del Superior', Semana, 15 June 2018. Retrieved January 27, 2021 https://www.semana.com/opinion/articulo/la-absolucion-de-jean-pierre-bemba-y-la-responsabilidad-del-superior-columna-de-kai-ambos/571182. See in this regard also James Steward, 'The Role of the ICC in the Transitional Justice Process in Colombia', 30 May 2018, p. 96 et seq. Retrieved January 27, 2021 https://www.icc-cpi.int/iccdocs/otp/201805SpeechDP.pdf.

[101]Bemba Appeals Judgment (n 70), p. 170 ("The trial chamber must specifically identify what a commander should have done *in concreto*. Abstract findings of what a commander might theoretically have done are unhelpful and problematic [. . .]"). See in this regard also Cote (n 63) 189-90; Rodrigo Uprimny, 'Responsabilidad del mando y JEP: un debate complejo y polarizado', La Silla Vacía, 27 February 2017. Retrieved January 27, 2021 https://lasillavacia.com/blogs/responsabilidad-del-mando-y-jep-un-debate-complejo-y-polarizado-59906.

3.2 Causation

Trans. Art. 24 does not include any reference to a nexus of causation between Security Forces commanders' omissions and their subordinates' crimes.[102] While the absence of such a nexus is consistent with the ad hoc tribunals' approach,[103] it is controversial in light of the wording of Art. 28 ICC Statute ("as a result of his or her failure") which seems to point to such a causality requirement. While some argue that a strict "but for" standard is required, others advocate for a less restrictive risk approach. The *Bemba* Appeals Judgment is silent on the matter. However, it has been dealt with by Judge Eboe-Osuji in his Concurring Separate Opinion, stating that the phrase 'as a result of' "is at the center of th[e] appeal."[104] He argues that "[w] hat is required is merely that the defendant's 'contribution must be more than negligible or not to be so minute that it will be ignored under the "*de minimis*" principle."[105] Arguing in favour of endangerment liability,[106] he notes that there is "no question of strict liability."[107]

The Trial Chamber affirmed the causation requirement as an essential element of command responsibility pursuant to Art. 28 ICC Statute[108] but did not discuss it in depth. It only stipulated a "nexus requirement,"[109] thereby apparently dismissing a but-for causation standard as too strict ("higher than that required by law"), but did not further define what sort of nexus is required.[110] Judges Steiner and Ozaki discussed the "as a result of" requirement in more detail in their Separate Opinions to the Trial Judgment.[111] Especially Judge Steiner raises two important questions:

---

[102]In this regard, Olasolo and Canosa Cantor (n 23) 83-85, 103.

[103]See, for example, ICTY, *Prosecutor v. Halilovic,* Trial Judgment, IT-01-48, 16 November 2005, p. 76 "[...] the very existence of the principle of superior responsibility [...] demonstrates the absence of a requirement of causality"; ICTY, *Prosecutor v. Hadzihasanovic,* Trial Judgment, IT-01-47, 15 March 2006, p. 188 stating that the Prosecution does not have to prove "a causal link to impose command responsibility".

[104]Bemba Concurring Separate Opinion of Judge Eboe-Osuji (n 83), p. 154.

[105]Ibid., p. 166.

[106]Ibid., p. 239.

[107]Ibid., p. 246.

[108]Bemba Trial Judgment (n 70), p. 211 ("The Chamber concurs with Pre-Trial Chamber that the portion of text emphasised above does not require [sic!] [...] the establishment of "but for" causation [...]").

[109]Bemba Trial Judgment (n 70), p. 211 ("it is a core principle of criminal law that a person should not be found individually criminally responsible for a crime in the absence of *some form of personal nexus* to it"). See also p. 213, stating that it would be too much to require that "the crimes would not have been committed, [...] had the commander exercised control properly [...]".

[110]Ibid., p. 213, leaving the question open ("in light of the factual findings below").

[111]ICC, *Prosecutor v. Jean Pierre Bemba Gombo,* Separate Opinion of Judge Sylvia Steiner to the Bemba Trial Judgment, ICC-01/05-01/08-3343-AnxI, 21 March 2016; ICC, *Prosecutor v. Jean Pierre Bemba Gombo,* Separate Opinion of Judge Kuniko Ozaki to the Bemba Trial Judgment, ICC-01/05-01/08-3343-AnxII, 21 March 2016, pp. 18–23.

First, what is the threshold of causation[112] and second, what is the degree of risk required?[113] The second question becomes only relevant if the answer to the first question follows a—here so-called—risk approach. Thus, the gist of the issue is, what is actually needed to conclude that the lack of countermeasures "caused" the crimes: is an increase of the risk of commission of the crimes sufficient (that is Judge Steiner's and, apparently, the TC's view)[114] or is certainty as a strict causality ("but for") standard required (as the Defense argues)?[115] In the confirmation decision, the Pre-Trial Chamber (PTC) also followed the lower standard, arguing that an increase of the risk of commission of the crimes suffices,[116] invoking essentially considerations of practicability.[117] The issue is not further discussed in the case law.

In the doctrinal writing, the causality requirement is mostly accepted.[118] In cases of actions, it is a minimum threshold of criminal responsibility.[119] If action and

---

[112]Bemba Separate Opinion of Judge Steiner (n 111) 16 et seq.

[113]Ibid., p. 24.

[114]Ibid., p. 24 ("I [. . .] agree with the Pre-Trial Chamber, that "it is only necessary to prove that the commander's omission increased the risk of the commission of the crimes charges [. . .]", "I believe "high probability" is the appropriate threshold"); Bemba Trial Judgment (n 70), p. 213 ("A nexus requirement would clearly be satisfied when it is established that the crimes would not have been committed [. . .] had the commander exercised control properly [. . .]"). Bemba Separate Opinion of Judge Kuniko Ozaki (n 111), p. 23 ("[...] I have concurred in the Chamber's findings that [. . .] the requirement of a causal link under Article 28 would be clearly satisfied when it is established that the crimes would not have been committed [...] had the commander exercised control properly [. . .]").

[115]ICC, *Prosecutor v. Jean Pierre Bemba Gombo,* Defence for Mr. Jean Pierre Bemba Gombo, Confidential, Appellant's Reply to "Prosecution's Response to Appellant's Document in Support of Appeal", ICC-01/05-01/08-3483-Conf 20-12-2016 1/30 EC A, 20 December 2016, pp. 52–56.

[116]Bemba Confirmation Decision (n 70), p. 425 ("[. . .] the Chamber considers that it is only necessary to prove that the commander's omission increased the risk of the commission of the crimes charged"), referring, *inter alia*, to *Ambos* (2002), in: Cassese/Gaeta/Jones (eds.), The Rome Statute of the International Criminal Court. A Commentary, Vol. 1, OUP, p. 860.

[117]Bemba Confirmation Decision (n 70), p. 425 "[. . .] the effect of an omission cannot be empirically determined with certainty [. . .]" and "it would not be practical to predict exactly what would have happened if a commander had fulfilled his obligation to prevent crimes".

[118]Triffterer (2002), pp. 197–202 ("causal connection"), 203–204; Nerlich (2007), p. 665, 673 ("(quasi-) causal link"), 677–678 (regarding the superior "after the fact"); Boas (2007), pp. 260–262 (explicitly p. 262 speaking of "Article 28's causation requirement"); Mettraux (2009), p. 33 (p. 82 generally arguing in favour of causality as part of customary law); Ambos (n 116) 850, 860-861; Weigend (2010), p. 76 ("hypothetical causation"); Robinson (2012), p. 1, 5 ("[. . .] Rome Statute expressly requires causal contribution [. . .]"), 12, 53 ("properly requiring causal contribution"); van Sliedregt (2012), p. 199 ("express recognition of a causal link"); Cryer and others (n 71) 376 ("form of causation"); Meloni (2010), pp. 173–178 (at least regarding preventive countermeasures).

[119]See the seminal treatment by Engisch (1931), p. 5; see also Jescheck and Weigend (1996), p. 277; Fletcher (1998), p. 61. For ICL literature see Kiss (2015), p. 608, 634; from an IHL perspective: Egorov (2009) p. 561, 572.

omission are treated as equivalent in terms of criminal liability,[120] the conditions upon which this criminal responsibility rests must be the same, too.[121] For the element of causation, this means that the standard must be in both cases—action and omission—the *conditio sine qua non* formula which only needs to be converted to a but for test in the case of omission.[122] To compensate for the lack of action in cases of omission something more is required and this 'more' consists of the respective defendant's duty to act, that is his/her position as a 'guarantor' (*garante, Garant*) with regard to the protected interests.[123] In cases of command responsibility, the commander is held responsible for his failure to intervene *with regard to the crimes of his subordinates* (by omission).[124]

It is for the latter reason—the direct imputation of the subordinates' crimes to the commander—that the requirements of command responsibility, including especially the causality element, must be interpreted strictly. To put it differently: A fair imputation of the subordinates' crimes to the commander requires more than mere risk increase (or any contribution in the sense of the above-quoted TC's findings), namely proof that the crimes would not have been committed if the commander had

[120]In ICTR, *Prosecutor v. Kambanda*, Judgment and Sentencing, No. ICTR-97-23-S, 4 September 1998, p. 40 the ICTR Trial Chamber pointed out that all acts of genocide could be committed by omission; in the same vein Schabas (2009), p. 177 ("The actus reus of an offence may be either an act of commission or an act of omission. This principle applies to all of the acts of genocide enumerated in article II, including killing."); an equation of actions with omissions with regard to the commission of the war crimes of murder, torture, wilfully causing great suffering, inhuman treatment and cruel treatment can also be found in ICTY, *Prosecutor v. Delalic et al.*, Judgment, No. ICTY-96-21-T, 16 November 1998, p. 424, 494, 511; ICTY, *Prosecutor v. Blaskic,* Judgment, No. ICTY-95-14-T, 3 March 2000, p. 154, 186; ICTY, *Prosecutor v. Kordic*, Judgment, No. ICTY-95-14/2-T, 26 February 2001, p. 236; Olasolo (2009), p. 82 et seq.

[121]For a basic statement: Wilson (2017), p. 84 ("The basic stance adopted in the criminal law is that criminal liability for omitting to act can be incurred if, as a matter of interpretation, the offence definition is consistent with such liability and if the defendant is placed under a duty to act"). Focusing on causality Sistare (1989), p. 55 ("We assume that omissions, though often difficult to define, are a kind of human conduct. It is on this basis that we believe omissions to be grounds of responsibility and causes of other events. For, although omissions usually are not causally efficacious in the sense of mechanical production, they are causal events through which agents are related to the world. Hence, the act doctrine does not bar liability for omissions as it would liability for non-events." (footnote omitted); see also Paul and Hall (2013), p. 177 et seq.; Mitsch (2016), p. 11; Murmann (2019) § 29, p. 3.

[122]Ambos, Treatise on ICL (n 71) 216 ("If omissions cannot display 'causal energy' and therefore recourse must be taken to a normative (instead of a naturalistic) concept of causation, this does not, a limine, exclude the application of a concept of causation in cases of omission. Indeed, it is, as explained above, perfectly possible to apply an inverted *conditio sine qua non* or 'but for test'; in fact, the Chamber formulated such a test but seemed to consider it inapplicable in these cases.", footnote omitted); Kiss (n 119) 608, 634-635. From a general criminal law perspective cf. *Fletcher*, Basic Concepts, *supra* at fn. 119, p. 67 ("If the implications of the "but for" test are followed through, there is no important difference between the causal role of acts and of omissions"); Fletcher (2000), pp. 371–372; Jefferson (2015), p. 73; Murmann (n 121) § 29 para. 3.

[123]Ambos, Treatise on ICL (n 71) 183-184 with the discussion of the relevant duties.

[124]Boas and others (n 118) 261 et seq., 277, 623, 636-637; Arnold and Jackson (n 71), mn. pp. 6–16, 52]; Levine (2007), p. 52, 81; Nerlich (n 118) 668, 670-671; Ambos (2007), pp. 177–178.

properly supervised his subordinates (but for causation). If, despite the above arguments, the risk approach is opted for, the *degree of risk* required has to be defined. Here again the structure of command responsibility and general considerations of fairness call for a strict approach: not any risk or any probability of a risk suffices but only a high probability that the failure to intervene resulted in the relevant crimes.[125]

3.3 Knowledge (Mens rea)

Trans. Art. 24(d) LA 1/17 calls for "actual or updatable knowledge", in light of the information at the commander's disposal prior, during or after the commission of subordinates' crimes.[126] In contrast, Art. 28 ICC Statute establishes that the commander's knowledge must either actually exist ("knew", Art. 28(a)(i)) or could have existed but does not because of negligence ("should have known", ibid.).[127]

While the ICC Statute's positive knowledge requirement corresponds to the "actual knowledge" standard of Trans. Art. 24(d), this is not the case for the second alternative. The ICC's "should have known" standard, amounting to negligence,[128] is clearly stricter than the "updatable knowledge" standard of Trans. Art. 24(d), which seems to refer to knowledge of already committed crimes and thus imply direct knowledge.[129] "Knowledge", however, means awareness, as follows from plain legal terminology,[130] and is 'a state of mind in which a person has *no*

[125]In the same vein, Bemba Separate Opinion of Judge Steiner (n 111), p. 24; Kiss (n 119) 608, 636; Bundesgerichtshof (German Supreme Court), Judgment, No. 3 StR 442/99, 19 April 2000, reprinted in Neue Juristische Wochenschrift 53 (2000), 2754, 2757; 2010, 1087, 1091; Bundesgerichtshof (German Supreme Court, Decision, No. 4 StR 157/00, 23 May 2000, Neue Zeitschrift für Strafrecht 20 (2000), 583; Frister (2020), Ch. 22, p. 25; against every risk increase as being sufficient also Meloni (n 118) 178.

[126]Cf. the fourth requirement (d) of Trans. Art. 24 LA 1/2017, cited at Sect. 2.2.1.

[127]The *ad hoc* tribunals use a comparative wording, establishing the "had reasons to know" standard, see Arts. 7 (3) of the ICTY Statute and 6 (3) of the ICTR Statute.

[128]Bemba Trial Judgment (n 70), p. 192; cf. also Bemba, ICC Prosecutor, Public Redacted Version of "Corrected Version of 'Prosecution's Response to Appellant's Document in Support of Appeal'", 19 January 2017 (filed originally on 21 November 2016), ICC-01/05-01/08-3472-Conf, ICC-01/05-01/08-3472-Corr-Red 1/199 RH A, 19 January 2017, pp. 178–194. See also Arnold and Jackson (n 71), mn. p. 49; Nerlich (n 118) 674; Triffterer (n 118) 199, 200 ("negligent lack of awareness"); Mettreaux, (n 118) 210; Cryer and others (n 71) 373; O'Keefe (n 71) 206; Schabas (n 71) 616-617; Werle and Jeßberger (n 71) 669; Cassese and others (n 71) 190.

[129]Pappier (n 21).

[130]Garner (2019), pp. 1042–1043 ('Knowing: having or showing awareness,' 'Knowledge: An awareness or understanding of a fact or circumstance'); Oxford Dictionaries, "Knowledge: Facts, information, and skills acquired through experience or education; the theoretical or practical understanding of a subject: [...] *Awareness* or familiarity gained by experience of a fact or situation" Retrieved January 27, 2021, from https://en.oxforddictionaries.com/definition/knowledge, emphasis added); Merriam Webster, 'Legal Definition of knowledge: awareness or understanding especially of an act, a fact, or the truth' (Merriam Webster, 4 October 2020) Retrieved January 27, 2021, from https://www.merriam-webster.com/dictionary/knowledge#legalDictionary.

substantial doubt about the existence of a fact.'[131] Thus, a person who knows/is aware of certain circumstances, i.e., that crimes have been committed by the subordinates, (s)he can be certain of these circumstances or, in other words, is "convinced" that these circumstances have occurred. In conclusion, this is a high threshold not to be confused with anything below actual knowledge or "virtual certainty."[132] Otherwise, the delimitation between knowledge and the lower "should have known" standard becomes blurred. This also explains why the negligence standard of Art. 28 ICC Statute only requires proof of constructive knowledge that is construed from information and indicia which would not suffice to affirm the superior's direct knowledge.[133] Trans. Art. 24(d), by using the term "updatable knowledge", blurs the line between these two standards.

On the other hand, "updatable knowledge" in Trans. Art. 24(d) may refer to the commander's active duty to take the necessary measures to secure knowledge of the conduct of his/her troops and to inquire, regardless of the availability of information at the time, on the commission of the crime.[134] This seems to be supported by the further wording of Trans. Art. 24(d) specifying that any—actual or updatable—knowledge must be "based on the information at his or her [the commander's] disposal before, during or after the commission of the respective conduct". This reminds of the standard ICTY language requiring that a commander has information "available" that would have put him/her on notice of the crimes.[135] However, in the *Blaškić* Appeals Judgment, the Chamber held that a standard beyond this, which would oblige the superior to remain constantly informed of his subordinates'

[131]Garner (n 130) 1003. See also Merriam Webster, 'Definition of certain: [. . .] known or proved to be true' (Merriam Webster). Retrieved January 27, 2021, from https://www.merriam-webster.com/dictionary/certain.

[132]ICC, *The Prosecutor v. Thomas Lubanga Dyilo*, ICC-01/04-01/06-3121-Red, AC, 1 December 2014, p. 447 ("virtual certainty" with regard to future events).

[133]Cf. Meloni (n 118) 181; Kiss (n 119) 641; Cryer and others (n 71) 373; also Ambos, Treatise on ICL (n 71) 221.

[134]Bemba Confirmation Decision (n 70), p. 433.

[135]ICTY, *Prosecutor v. Delalić et al. (Čelebići Camp)*, Trial Judgment, IT-96-21-T, 16 November 1998, p. 241 ("only if information was available to him which would have put him on notice of offences committed by subordinates"), p. 383 ("[. . .] a superior may possess the *mens rea* required to incur criminal liability where [. . .] he had in his possession information of a nature, which at the least, would put him on notice of the risk of such offences"). This 'has reason to know' standard was confirmed in the ICTY, *Prosecutor v. Blaškić*, Appeals Judgment, IT-95-14-A, 29 July 2004, p. 62, 67 (Blaškić Appeals Judgment). See also ICTY, *Prosecutor v. Delalić et al. (Čelebići Camp)*, Appeals Judgment, IT-96-21-A, 20 February 2001, p. 241 ("a superior will be criminally responsible [. . .] only if information was available to him which would have put him on notice of offences committed by subordinates"). In the same vein, Pappier (n 21).

actions,[136] is inconsistent with ICTY jurisprudence.[137] Thus, the Chamber affirmed that a superior is not liable for the "neglect of a duty to acquire [. . .] knowledge."[138] Given that the ICTY's 'had reason to know' standard (enshrined in Art. 7(3) ICTY Statute) is considered as either substantially the same as the ICC's 'should have known' standard (pursuant to Art. 28 ICC Statute)[139] or even less strict than the latter,[140] the requirement of "available" information does not serve as a sound basis for the additionally required "updatable" knowledge in Trans. Art. 24(d) LA 1/17.

In sum, and irrespective of this last interpretation, the Colombian standard is clearly narrower than the ICC's negligence standard and thus more generous for Security Forces' commanders. In this sense, the ICC Prosecutor is right if she describes this language as "ambiguous and possibly more restrictive" than the standard set out in the ICC Statute.[141] So far, the JEP has not developed any views on this issue. However, the Constitutional Court, in its important 2018 ruling on the JEP's Statutory Law, may have shown a way out of the predicament created by the Colombian legislation: While the Court made clear that the ICC Statute cannot be applied directly in the domestic legal system (including that of the JEP), it allowed a "complementary or subsidiary" application of ICL to avoid impunity.[142] Consequently, the JEP could apply Trans. Art. 24(d) LA 1/17 and at the same time use Art. 28(a)(i) ICC Statute as a corrective in order to comply with Colombia's obligations under international law and to avoid an intervention of the ICC.

---

[136]This standard had been previously established by the ICTY, *Prosecutor v. Blaškić,* Trial Judgment, IT-95-14-T, 3 March 2000, p. 329 ("keep constantly informed of the way in which his/her subordinates carry out the tasks entrusted them").

[137]Blaškić Appeals Judgment (n 135) p. 62 ("The Trial Judgment's interpretation of the standard is not consistent with the jurisprudence of the Appeals Chamber in this regard and must be corrected accordingly.").

[138]Ibid., p. 62.

[139]Ambos, Treatise on ICL (n 71) 221-227; Nerlich (n 118) 674 ("It has been argued persuasively that the 'had reason to know' standard developed by the ICTY is the same as the 'should have known' standard for military commanders under Art. 28(a)(i) ICC [Statute]"); Werle and Jeßberger (n 71) 623 ("weitgehende sachliche Übereinstimmung"). For a differentiated approach see Schabas (n 71) 616; Arnold and Jackson (n 71), mn., p. 53, ("seemingly lower standard of 'should have known'"), p. 60 "Textually, at least, the standard looks a little more relaxed than the 'had reason to know' standard in the statutes and case law of the ICTY and ICTR."), mn. pp. 63–64.

[140]Weigend (n 118) 78 (stating that Art. 28(a)(i) ICC uses a formulation that "is even stricter than [. . .] ICTY jurisprudence in not requiring that there was specific information available to the commander but neglected by him"); O'Keefe (n 71) 205-206; Cassese and others (n 71) 190 ("The ICC Statute employs a lower 'should have known' standard to establish constructive knowledge").

[141]ICC OTP, *amicus curiae* brief (n 69), p. 28.

[142]Constitutional Court of Colombia, (n 15), p. 407.

4 Concluding Remarks

The provisions on command responsibility contained in the Final Peace Agreement, LA 01/2017 and the JEP Statutory Law changed the legal landscape in Colombia: For the first time, Colombian Security Forces and FARC-EP superiors can be held criminally responsible for international crimes related to the armed conflict that were committed by their subordinates on the basis of command responsibility. Colombia has thus made a decisive step in addressing the previously existing gaps in domestic law regarding the criminal responsibility treatment of military commanders.

Notwithstanding, these positive developments come with caveats. The progressive development suffered several setbacks, particularly due to the political discourse and infights that evolved around the peace negotiations. Most notably, all references to international law have been eliminated from the provisions regarding command responsibility for Colombian Security Forces. Furthermore, the definition of command responsibility has been modified, establishing additional requirements and thus restricting the definition's scope of application for the Security Forces significantly. None of these changes affect the treatment of FARC-EP superiors which leads to a worrisome imbalance when it comes to command responsibility.

These modifications also lead to a more restrictive approach to command responsibility compared to international standards, especially Art. 28 ICC Statute. The ICC Prosecutor has repeatedly expressed concerns in this regard and it cannot be denied that the privileged treatment of the Security Forces by LA 01/2017 gives rise to serious concerns. This becomes particularly relevant in light of the ICC's complementarity principle as a consequence of which Colombia's deviation from the standard enshrined in Art. 28 ICC Statute may be interpreted as a sign of "unwillingness" to investigate or prosecute international crimes committed by Colombian Security Forces. The OTP's next steps thus depend on whether the JEP will, with regard to the Security Forces, apply the restrictive definition of command responsibility (as laid down in LA 01/2017) or interpret it in line with international standards and particularly Art. 28 ICC Statute. It is therefore fair to say that the JEP's treatment of command responsibility will be a—if not *the*—decisive factor influencing Colombia's efforts to try the most responsible perpetrators. Given the JEP's integration into a larger transitional justice project, the prospects that Colombia achieves a just peace relies to a great extent on accomplishing that goal.

References

Ambos, K. (2016). *Treatise on international criminal law* (Vol. III, p. 266). Oxford, UK: Oxford University Press.

Ambos, K. (2007). Joint criminal enterprise and command responsibility. *Journal of International Criminal Justice, 5*, 159.

Ambos, K. (2013). *Treatise on international criminal law* (Vol. I, pp. 210–211). Oxford, UK: Oxford University Press.

Arnold, R., & Jackson, M. (2021). Article 28. In K. Ambos (Ed.), *The Rome statute of the international criminal court. A commentary* (4th ed., pp. 25–28). Hart, Nomos: C.H. Beck.

Boas, G. (2007). *Forms of responsibility in international criminal law* (Vol. I, pp. 260–262). Cambridge, UK: Cambridge University Press.

Cassese, A. (Ed.). (2013). *Cassese's international criminal law* (3rd ed., p. 188). Oxford, UK: Oxford University Press.

Cryer, R., Robinson, D., & Vasiliev, S. (2019). *An introduction to international criminal law and procedure* (4th ed., p. 370). Cambridge, UK: Cambridge University Press.

Egorov, S. (2009). International legal protections for Persons *Hors de Combat*. In J. Doria, H.-P. Gasser, & M. C. Bassiouni (Eds.), *The legal regime of the international criminal court* (p. 561). Leiden, Netherlands: Martinus Nijhoff.

Engisch, K. (1931). *Die Kausalität als Merkmal der strafrechtlichen Tatbestände* (p. 5). Heidelberg, Germany: Mohr Siebeck.

Fletcher, G. (2000). *Rethinking criminal law* (pp. 371–372). Oxford, UK: OUP.

Fletcher, G. (1998). *Basic concepts of criminal law* (p. 61). Oxford, UK: Oxford University Press.

Frister, H. (2020). *Strafrecht allgemeiner teil* (9th ed.). Munich, Germany: C.H. Beck.

Garner, B. (2019). *Black's law dictionary* (11th ed., pp. 1042–1043). Eagan, MN: Thomson West.

Jefferson, M. (2015). *Criminal law* (12th ed., p. 73). London, UK: Pearson.

Jescheck, H.-H., & Weigend, T. (1996). *Strafrecht allgemeiner teil* (5th ed., p. 277). Berlin, Germany: Duncker & Humblot.

Kiss, A. (2015). Command responsibility under Article 28 of the Rome statute. In C. Stahn (Ed.), *The law and practice of the international criminal court* (p. 608). Oxford, UK: Oxford University Press.

Kremnitzer, M. (2004). Präventives Töten. In D. Fleck (Ed.), *Rechtsfragen der Terrorismusbekämpfung durch Streitkräfte* (pp. 201–222). Baden-Baden, Germany: Nomos.

Kremnitzer, M., & Cohen, M. A. (2005). Israel. In A. Eser (Ed.), *National prosecution of international crimes* (pp. 317–409). Berlin, Germany: Duncker & Humblot.

Levine, J. (2007). The doctrine of command responsibility and its application to superior civilian leadership: Does the international criminal court have the correct standard. *Military Law Review, 193*, 52.

Meloni, C. (2010). *Command responsibility in international criminal law* (pp. 173–178). The Hague, Netherlands: Asser Press.

Mettraux, G. (2009). *The law of command responsibility* (p. 33). Oxford, UK: Oxford University Press.

Mitsch, W. (2016). § 21 Das Unterlassungsdelikt. In J. Baumann (Ed.), *Strafrecht allgemeiner teil* (12th ed., p. 11). Cambridge, UK: Lehrbuch.

Murmann, U. (2019). *Grundkurs strafrecht* (5th ed., p. 3). Munich, Germany: C.H. Beck.

Nerlich, V. (2007). Superior responsibility under article 28 ICC statute. For what exactly is the superior held responsible? *Journal for International Criminal Justice, 5*, 665.

O'Keefe, R. (2015). *International criminal law* (pp. 5–105). Oxford, UK: Oxford University Press.

Olasolo, H. (2009). *The criminal responsibility of senior political and military leaders as principals to international crimes*. Oxford, UK: Hart.

Olasolo, H., & Cantor, J. C. (2019). The treatment of superior responsibility in Colombia: Interpreting the agreement between the Colombian Government and the FARC. *Criminal Law Forum, 30*(1), 106.

Paul, L., & Hall, N. (2013). *Causation* (p. 177). Oxford, UK: Oxford University Press.

Robinson, D. (2012). How command responsibility got so complicated: A culpability contradiction, its obfuscation, and a simple solution. *Melbourne Journal of International Law, 13*, 1–5.

Schabas, W. A. (2016). *The international criminal court. A commentary on the Rome statute* (2nd ed., pp. 613–614). Oxford, UK: Oxford University Press.

Schabas, W. (2009). *Genocide in international law* (2nd ed.). Cambridge: Cambridge University Press. p. 177.

Sistare, C. (1989). *Responsibility and criminal liability* (p. 55). Alphen aan den Rijn, Netherlands: Kluwer.
Triffterer, O. (2002). Causality, a separate element of the doctrine of superior responsibility as expressed in article 28 Rome statute. *Leiden Journal of International Law, 179*, 197–202.
van Sliedregt, E. (2012). *Individual criminal responsibility in international law* (p. 199). Oxford, UK: Oxford University Press.
Weigend, T. (2010). Superior responsibility: Complicity, omission or over-extension of the law? In C. Burchard (Ed.), *The review conference and the future of the international criminal court* (p. 76). Alphen aan den Rijn: Kluwer Law International.
Wilson, W. (2017). *Criminal law - doctrine and theory* (6th ed., p. 84). London, UK: Pearson.

Peace and Punishment: Reflections from the Perspective of International Criminal Law

Florian Jeßberger and Julia Geneuss

1 Introduction

The promise that international prosecutions would contribute to a more peaceful world marked the dawn of modern international criminal justice. In his opening speech at the post-World War II trial against the surviving major political and military leaders of Nazi Germany at Nuremberg US Chief Prosecutor *Robert Jackson* stated: "This Trial is part of the great effort to make peace more secure."[1] And: "Thus may the forces of the law be mobilized on the side of peace."[2] A few decades later, with the revival of international criminal justice in the mid-1990s, the UN Security Council determined that the conflict situations in the former Yugoslavia and in Rwanda constituted "a threat to international peace and security", and was convinced that "the establishment [. . .] of an international tribunal and the prosecution of persons responsible for serious violations of international humanitarian law [. . .] would contribute to the restoration and maintenance of peace."[3] In 2004, the

[1]Jackson (1947), p. 153.

[2]Jackson (1945), p. 53.

[3]Security Council resolution 827, S/RES/827 (25 May 1993), Preamble paras 4 and 5 (ICTY); Security Council resolution 955, S/RES/955 (8 November 1994), Preamble paras 5 and 7 (ICTR). The wording of ICTR UN SC resolution, Preamble para 7 is slightly different: "Convinced that in the particular circumstances of Rwanda, the prosecution of persons responsible for serious violations of international humanitarian law would enable this aim to be achieved and would contribute to the process of national reconciliation and to the restoration and maintenance of peace."

F. Jeßberger (✉)
Humboldt-Universität zu Berlin, Berlin, Germany
e-mail: florian.jessberger@uni-hamburg.de

J. Geneuss
Universität Hamburg, Hamburg, Germany
e-mail: julia.geneuss@uni-hamburg.de

K. Ghanayim, Y. Shany (eds.), *The Quest for Core Values in the Application of Legal Norms*, https://doi.org/10.1007/978-3-030-78953-4_16

Council "commended" the "important work of both Tribunals in contributing to lasting peace and security and national reconciliation and the progress made since their inception."[4] In its first report to the UN General Assembly and Security Council then President of the Yugoslavia Tribunal *Antonio Cassese* noted that the ICTY would work as a "tool for promoting reconciliation and restoring true peace."[5] Similarly, the UN General Assembly recognized "the role of the International Criminal Court in a multilateral system that aims to end impunity, establish the rule of law, promote and encourage respect for human rights and achieve sustainable peace."[6] Finally, in the Preamble of the 2010 Kampala Declaration state parties affirm that they are "[c]onvinced that there can be no lasting peace without justice and that peace and justice are thus complementary requirements", and emphasize "that justice is a fundamental building block of sustainable peace."[7]

Peace through punishment? While international criminal law and the establishment of international criminal courts and tribunals have always, at least rhetorically, been tied to the notion of peace, discussing (much less determining) the *impact* of international criminal justice on peace is not an easy task, as the concept of peace—as well as the concept of international criminal justice—remains ambiguous:[8] What peace? Whose peace? Positive peace or negative peace? Peace as a binary or peace as a relative concept? Peace as condition or peace as process? World peace or regional peace? Peace as objective or peace as aspiration? Imminent peace or long-lasting peace? However, despite this terminological and conceptual vagueness, international criminal justice and peace are seen in intimate liaison with one another. At the same time, the effects which the establishment, existence and practice of international criminal courts and tribunals can have on peace are put into question. As some commentators argue "some of the most serious doubts that have been expressed about international criminal law relate to the claim that it promotes peace and reconciliation."[9]

From an empirical point of view, these doubts seem valid. It is true that, as of now, research has not established that the threat and imposition of international punishment has a consistent and predictable effect—positive or negative—on the establishment, restoration and maintenance of peace, notwithstanding a certain "criminological turn" in international criminal law scholarship over the past few years. Case studies concerning the ICC's legal interventions in Libya and Uganda

[4]Security Council resolution 1534, S/RES/1534 (26 March 2004).

[5]General Assembly, Security Council, Report of the International Tribunal for the Prosecution of Persons Responsible for Serious Violations of International Humanitarian Law Committed in the Territory of the former Yugoslavia since 1991, A/49/342, S/1994/1007 (29 August 1994), para 16.

[6]General Assembly resolution 65/12, A/RES/65/12 (23 November 2010).

[7]Assembly of States Parties, ICC, *Kampala Declaration*, RC/Decl.1 (1 June 2010), Preamble paras 7 and 3.

[8]For the various understandings of the notion of peace in international law, see, e.g., Bailliet and Larsen (2015), p. 1.

[9]Cryer et al. (2019), p. 42.

show unclear results.[10] Studies on the work of the ICTY demonstrate that the perceptions within the affected communities of international efforts to prosecute and punish (as possible indicators for reconciliation and, ultimately, peace) differ significantly from the international narrative, according to which the Tribunal contributed to a stable and long-lasting peace in the region through its fair trials, its proportionate sanctions and its evenly distributed proceedings against civilian and military personnel at all levels of hierarchies and from each major ethnic or national party involved in the conflict. In 2004, 10 years after his more hopeful remarks as President of the ICTY, *Antonio Cassese* admitted that "[t]he much-hoped-for beneficial impact of ICTY trials on persons and groups living in the former Yugoslavia is meagre and tardy."[11] After all, it appears that on the available empirical basis neither a positive nor a negative impact of international punishment on the making, restoration or maintenance of peace can be established. Neither possible hypothesis is sustained by robust empirical data. In short: We just do not know. It is probably fair to assume that criminal justice can assist the peace processes *if*, and only if, powerful international institutions and states complement the "justice track" with diplomacy and political strategies, and, as some would argue, also military intervention. In this perspective, only as part of a holistic international commitment can international prosecutions be an effective tool. But even then, the presumed even indirect causality between the institutional and penal objectives to the effect that punishment automatically promotes peace is more of an "article of faith."[12]

Leaving empiricism aside, the very modest aim of this paper it to inquire into the various dimensions of the relationship between international criminal justice on the one hand and peace on the other, and to look more closely if, how, and where peace—and which type of peace—is integrated into the (normative) fabric of international criminal law in general and the ICC's law, mandate and role, more specifically. Two preliminary remarks are in order:

First, our topic, of course, intersects with the well-known and never-ending debate about how to "reconcile" or "sequence" peace and justice.[13] We are not intending to repeat the debate here, neither is our ambition to contribute to this debate. Positions extend from the idea of criminal justice as an "indispensable ingredient" of any process of national reconciliation and stable peace ("no peace without justice"), to a sharp dichotomy of peace and justice ("peace v justice"), to a conception of (criminal) justice as an instrument or tool to achieve peace ("peace through justice"). One of the most recent examples for a "peace v justice" approach and the strict separation between the "justice project" and the "peace project" relates to the (attempted) withdrawal of South Africa from the ICC Statute. In this context the South African Government declared: "Under these circumstances South Africa is of the view that to continue to be a State Party to the Rome Statute will compromise

---

[10]See Kersten (2016).

[11]Cassese (2004), p. 595.

[12]On "articles of faith" in international criminal jurisprudence: Vasiliev (2019), p. 45.

[13]For a summary, see, e.g. Kersten (2016); Rodman (2011).

its efforts to promote peace and security on the African Continent."[14] In South Africa's view you cannot be both: a state party to the ICC and a state that promotes peace on the African continent.

Secondly, it is important to note that in approaching the role peace plays in international criminal justice, the analysis also seems to depend on whether you look at it more from a criminal law perspective or more from an international law perspective. From an international law perspective, the peaceful relationship between states and the peaceful conflict resolution seems to be a central motive. From a criminal law perspective, on the other hand, at least at first glance, international peace seems to be more removed from the traditional concerns of criminal law: criminal law is the instrument to define crimes, to determine individual responsibility, to render judgment and impose sanctions. At closer inspection, however, it will be shown that the relationship between criminal justice and peace is not unique to international criminal law. Rather, the link between criminal justice and peace which is known in the domestic context can be used as a starting point for further inquiry into the relationship in the international context.

Our hope is that by addressing a topic at this very intersection our paper may be met with at least some interest by Mota Kremnitzer, to whom we dedicate these lines, a determined promoter of peace and a world leading scholar of (criminal) justice who has always been wandering so brilliantly across the worlds—the worlds of the international and the domestic, the worlds of criminal law and public international law, and, ultimately, the worlds of peace and justice.

2 Peace in Domestic Criminal Law

Taking the German criminal justice system, its doctrine and academic debate, as an example, there seem to be three different types, or better: dimensions, of peace when it comes to domestic criminal law. First, in German criminal law peace is regarded as a legal interest (*Rechtsgut*) protected through criminal law. The protection of peace refers to both internal and external peace. The former, internal public peace, is regarded as a collective legal interest (*kollektives Rechtsgut*), which concerns the protection of societal peace, i.e. peaceful co-existence within society.[15] Crimes that disturb internal societal peace are, for instance, the crime of incitement of masses (*Volksverhetzung*, § 130 of the German Penal Code), or the crime of threatening to commit certain grave offences (*Androhen von Straftaten*, § 126). External peace, on the other hand, refers to the criminalisation of aggressive war, i.e. inter-state

[14] Declaratory Statement by the Republic of South Africa on the Decision to Withdraw from the Rome Statute of the International Criminal Court (Depositary Notification), C.N.786.2016. TREATIES-XVIII.10 (19 October 2016).

[15] In German criminal law scholarship there is much debate on the term "public peace" and the concept of "kollektive Rechtsgüter", see only Hefendehl (2002).

violence. While the crime of preparing a war of aggression (§ 80 of the German Penal Code) had been incorporated into German criminal law already in the late 1960s,[16] since 2017 the crime of aggression can be found in the German Code of Crimes Against International Law (§ 13).[17]

Secondly, in the domestic criminal law discourse, peace is part of the theoretical justification of the criminal sanction, at least to the extent one is ready to follow a consequentialist approach. Under the deterrence paradigm, for instance, the threat of punishment deters from the commission of crimes and thus, a breach of societal peace. In addition, according to the theory of positive general prevention or affirmative prevention, criminal law and punishment have a "pacifying effect" (*Befriedungseffekt*).[18]

Thirdly, and most fundamentally, the ulterior objective of the criminal justice system as such, irrespective of the theoretical justification of the criminal punishment, is regarded to be the establishment, restoration and maintenance of a peaceful social order.[19] Societal peace is aimed to be achieved through the interplay of a broad range of different—political and legal—instruments and mechanisms of conflict resolution. Criminal justice is just one of those mechanisms, a mechanism of last resort (at least in theory). Only attacks against the more important legal interests, that is values whose violation is more likely to cause unrest and tensions and lead to impulses of revenge and vigilantism, are criminalized and punished. Lesser valuable interests are protected though other legal instruments and mechanisms. Therefore, criminal justice is selective and protects the status quo. By prosecuting and punishing the perpetrator, so the argument goes, the cycle of inter-individual violence is disrupted and peace is re-instated: crimes disturb societal peace which has to be restored through a collective organised and institutionalised reaction in order to prevent an uncontrolled and vengeful reaction of individuals or groups. As *Hans-Heinrich Jescheck* states, it is the aim of any criminal justice system to maintain public peace, as a precondition for any individual to exercise his or her fundamental rights.[20]

However, not each and every violation of a legal interest is prosecuted; here a procedural dimension of peace is unveiled. Domestic criminal law systems introduce exemptions from criminal law enforcement in cases where criminal prosecution would pose a threat to peace. In German criminal law, despite the dominance of the principle of mandatory prosecution (*Legalitätsprinzip*), a number of procedural norms allow for prosecutorial discretion for various reasons. One of those reasons to dismiss proceedings, at least for certain crimes, is that they "would pose a risk of serious detriment to the Federal Republic of Germany", § 153d of the German Code

[16]Article 26 of the German Basic Law (*Grundgesetz*) imposes a duty to criminalise aggressive war.

[17]For details see Jeßberger (2017), p. 180.

[18]See, e.g., Jescheck and Weigend (1996), p. 1 ff.

[19]See also van der Wilt (2017), p. 436 f., with a reference to Durkheim's works on the social function of criminal law.

[20]See Jescheck and Weigend (1996), p. 3; see also Jescheck (1975), p. 13 f.

of Criminal Procedure. That is, the prosecutor can—arguably must—abstain from proceedings if they would cause a threat to Germany's external or internal peace or security. The idea behind this provision is that certain situations should be taken out of the (criminal) "justice track"—even if just for a period of time—and dealt with in the political sphere only.[21] However, under German law, this discretionary norm does not apply when it comes to crimes under international law. Here, at least according to the books, justice always trumps peace.

3 Peace, International Criminal Justice and the Rome Statute

While, of course, it would be too simplistic to simply transfer the considerations from the domestic to the international level, the role peace plays in domestic criminal law can be a starting point for the reflections regarding peace, its location, role, types and dimensions, in the international criminal justice system.[22]

While few would attempt to argue against any relationship between international criminal justice and peace, the links between impunity, prosecution, and peace remain unclear. In the ICC Statute only one explicit reference to peace can be found. Paragraph 3 of the Preamble recognises "that such grave crimes threaten the peace, security and well-being of the world."[23] Further links between the ICC and peace are hidden in its institutional design, prosecutorial mandate and normative fabric.

3.1 Activating the ICC

The link between the ICC Statute and peace is most obvious when it comes to the role of the Security Council within the Rome Statute's system of international criminal justice. If the Council has determined "the existence of any threat to peace, breach of peace, or act of aggression" under Article 39 of the UN Charter,

---

[21] See Teßmer (2016, § 153d StPO para 11.

[22] See van der Wilt (2017), p. 438 ("[...] the ICC prosecutor has to operate in a conflict-ridden context that fundamentally differs from the run of the mill peaceful society.") Further Greenawalt (2007), p. 604 f. ("the political goals of domestic justice may be described, broadly speaking, as preservational: sustaining and improving an existing social order. The political goals of international criminal tribunals are, by contrast, transformational"); Schabas (2006), p. 68 ("This accounts for important distinctions between international criminal justice and national justice that, as a general rule, is addressed to individual offenders in peacetime and is targeted at social stability in a more mundane sense.").

[23] On the connections between peace and justice in the ICC Statute, see also Méndez and Kelley (2015), p. 479.

it may refer (Article 41 UN Charter) a situation to the Court (Article 13 ICC Statute) or defer an ongoing investigation or prosecution for a (renewable) period of 12 months (Article 16 ICC Statute). Thus, in case of a referral there is, one may argue, the implicit understanding that the ICC's legal intervention will contribute to peacebuilding. In case of a deferral, however, at least the UN Security Council is of the opinion that the ICC's activation and its enforcement of international criminal justice will pose a risk to the establishment or maintenance of peace. Thus, the institutional function of the ICC within the larger UN system reveals the link between the Court and peace.

The close relationship between the ICC and the UN Security Council begs the question of how the concept or notion of peace is understood within the UN system. In fact, the UN system includes aspects of the concept of positive peace.[24] Under this broader conception peace is defined as the absence of structural and indirect violence, i.e. the existence of a structure of oppressive, discriminative, unequal relationships.[25] This concept of peace includes, inter alia, respect for human rights protection, provision of social justice, and the elimination of structural violence causing poverty, inequality and exclusion. However, the notion of peace in Chapter VII of the UN Charter seems to refer to a narrower understanding of peace, i.e. the conception of negative peace.[26] Negative peace is understood as the absence of large-scale, direct forms of physical violence. Within the UN system, it is closely related to the prohibition of unlawful use of force. As will be discussed in a moment, the concept of peace traditionally referred to *inter*state relations, but the definition of violence developed over decades now also includes *intra*state armed conflict and violence.

The concept of negative peace is, arguably, also the concept on which international criminal justice is built. In international criminal law peace is understood as negative peace, that is the absence of personal or direct large-scale violence. This narrow conception of negative peace in international criminal justice and its repercussion on an equally narrow conception of justice, which both entail the status quo, have been criticised.[27] In this context, as a mere side note however, the ICC's role as "reparations court" can be mentioned. The Court, through the Trust Fund for Victims

[24]See Bailliet and Larsen (2015), p. 5, referring to the "holistic purposes" in Art. 1 of the UN Charter and that taken together with the Preamble it is noted that "peace is more than the absence of war" (citing Wolfrum (2012), p. 110. See also General Assembly resolution 71/189, A/RES/71/189 (19 December 2016) adopting the Declaration on the Right to Peace. E.g. Preamble para 16 ("[r] ecognizing that peace is not only the absence of conflict but also requires a positive, dynamic participatory process where dialogue is encouraged and conflicts are solved in a spirit of mutual understanding and cooperation, and socioeconomic development is ensured.").

[25]Galtung (1964), p. 1; Galtung (1969), p. 167; Galtung (1975).

[26]Ibid.

[27]See Drumbl (2007), p. 123 ff.; Nouwen and Werner (2014), p. 157 ff.; see also de Hoon (2017), p. 591 ff. ("oversimplification and unhelpful generalization of what justice means for different people and societies in different conflicts and circumstances and the related inability to 'deliver' justice in a one-size-fits-all and top-down manner.").

can award reparations to individual victims or victim groups to provide for relief of the affected individuals or the affected community. The reparations scheme of the ICC can be regarded as part of a positive peace conception.[28]

While the idea of criminal proceedings was already part of a peace treaty—the Versailles Peace Treaty—after World War I, international criminal justice had its breakthrough not before the end of the Second World War. At the Nuremberg trial before the International Military Tribunal against the major war criminals, the concept of international criminal law was closely linked to state sovereignty, aggression and peace. With Nuremberg, the international community chose criminal law as one legal tool to contribute to the establishment and maintenance of "perpetual" peace. The IMT trial and international criminal law were understood as part of a "peace project" ("peace through law").[29] Peace, however, was understood in the narrow sense, as the absence of war between states.[30] Crimes against peace were at the center of the IMT proceedings, the German war criminals were, first and foremost, prosecuted and punished for breach of the peace by initiating or contributing to the initiation of the aggressive war.

Since Nuremberg, however, there has been a development of "humanization" of international law.[31] The focus of both, international criminal law as well as the notion of peace within the UN system (and the international law system more generally) has shifted. From the establishment of the UN ad hoc Tribunals up until today, the focus in international criminal law is on *atrocity crimes*, namely crimes against humanity, genocide and war crimes. Unlike aggression, atrocity crimes, at least crimes against humanity and genocide, are not crimes against another state's sovereignty, but often crimes committed by the sovereign state against its own population, motivated by racism, political oppression, and hate more generally.[32] A shift from the protection of state sovereignty to an emphasis on human rights occurred. As a consequence, the connection to peace changed and is less immediate.

At the same time, the notion of peace expanded.[33] It no longer only includes the absence of inter-state violence, but also the absence of (inter- or intra-state) armed conflict as well as the absence of widespread and massive violence. Since crimes

[28]The ICTY also recognized that reparations for victims are important for peace: "The Tribunal cannot, through the rendering of its judgments alone, bring peace and reconciliation to the region: other remedies should complement the criminal trials if lasting peace is to be achieved, and one such remedy should be adequate reparations to the victims for their suffering." President of the ICTY (2011) Letter addressed to the President of the UN Security Council dated 12 May 2011, S/2011/316, para 90.

[29]Mégret (2018), p. 839 ("international criminal justice was largely seen as a project to civilize the relations of states between themselves.").

[30]See also Kelsen (1950), p. 19 ("In ordinary use of language, 'international peace' is a condition of absence of force in the relations among states. 'International' peace is to be distinguished from 'internal' peace, peace within one and the same state.").

[31]See, e.g., Meron (2006); Teitel (2011), p. 2.

[32]Mégret (2016), p. 1404.

[33]Similarly, Bailliet and Larsen (2015), p. 6 f.

against humanity and genocide can be committed in peacetime, a breach of peace, understood in the narrow, traditional sense of inter-state violence, is no longer a sufficient or even necessary condition of their commission. At the same time, however, genocide and crimes against humanity that take place within a state's territory are considered to be not only a breach of domestic and internal peace, but a threat or breach of international peace.[34]

Ultimately, it is argued that the original "peace project" developed into a "justice project":[35] international criminal law is meant to fight impunity for perpetrators of mass atrocities and to bring to justice perpetrators of international crimes. At the same time, its perspective is less state centred; instead the focus is on individualization of criminal responsibility, the move towards humanization put victims and human rights at the forefront.

In addition, while at Nuremberg the prosecution of perpetrators (of crimes against peace) was regarded as a unique task of the international community, today international criminal tribunals are seen only as stepping in for domestic criminal courts whenever the latter are unable or unwilling to punish perpetrators of atrocity crimes.[36] This development could be characterized as "crimification" of international criminal law (*Verstrafrechtlichung des Völkerstrafrechts*)—a shift in focus from the traditional international law perspective as the leading paradigm to a criminal law perspective. Through this development the ulterior objective of maintaining social or public peace of (domestic) criminal justice systems has been adopted by the international system. This leads to a transformation of the notion of peace: the focus shifted from the protection of international peace (in the narrow sense as absence of war) to the prosecution of atrocities, which in turn re-shaped and broadened the notion of peace also in the UN system.[37]

It is argued that this development leads to at least two consequences regarding peace:[38] First, states are less inclined to militarily intervene in ongoing conflicts, because they fear that their soldiers will be prosecuted for (war) crimes. Second, the commission of atrocity crimes serves as trigger for humanitarian intervention or responsibility to protect and thus makes international law more interventionist. Although somewhat contradictory, in both cases international criminal law would bring about less peace, either because it frustrates or because it triggers military intervention.

---

[34]After 1945 there has been a sharp decline in the number of inter-state armed conflicts, see, e.g., Szayna T S et al. (2017) What Are the Trends in Armed Conflicts, and What Do They Mean for U.S. Defense Policy?. www.rand.org/pubs/research_reports/RR1904.html.

[35]On the development and for a historicization of the relationship of international criminal justice to peace, see Mégret (2018), p. 835.

[36]This has led to a special status of the crime of aggression. This is reflected, e.g., in that in German criminal law in contrast to genocide, crimes against humanity and war crimes, the crime of aggression is not subjected to universal jurisdiction, see § 1 (first sentence) VStGB.

[37]See Mégret (2018), p. 835.

[38]On both points, Ibid., 835, p 848 ff.

3.2 Substantive Law

It is often said that the list of crimes under international law protects the most valuable interests of the international community, namely "peace, security and the well-being of the world" (Preamble ICC Statute). However, regarding peace as protected legal interest, it seems as if a distinction needs to be made between the crime of aggression on the one hand and the other crimes under international law, i.e. war crimes, genocide and crimes against humanity, as it is apparent that the crime of aggression—as "crime against peace"—is more directly linked than the other crimes to peace, at least in the traditional sense of the absence of inter-state violence. In the case of aggression, peace is what is directly protected by the norm and what is directly breached by the perpetrators. In its binary logic, if a crime of aggression is committed, a state of non-peace ensues. It was made explicit by the IMT that aggression is not only an attack against another state's sovereignty, but also affects world peace and is thus of interest to the international community as a whole. An aggressive act against another state forces the state to defend itself, so that an international armed conflict and possibly atrocity crimes can follow. In addition, other states might be involved in the conflict. As the IMT stated in relation to crimes against peace: "Its consequences are not confined to the belligerent States alone, but affect the whole world."[39]

When it comes to war crimes, genocide and crimes against humanity, things seem different. First of all, as already mentioned, these crimes are not connected to a narrow notion of peace, but rather to a broad notion that includes the absence of internal armed conflict and widespread and systematic violence. Second, peace here does not seem to follow the binary logic of peace found in the crime of aggression. Instead crimes against humanity and genocide seem to operate on a scale where peace is a relative concept; peace not as the absence of direct violence, but as diminished level of violence. The crimes only pose a threat to (international) peace once they have passed a certain threshold, and perpetrators do not as such breach peace, but with their crimes they add to the degree of "non-peacefulness" or "dispeace." As a consequence, in order for an international criminal court to have a positive effect on peace in ongoing conflicts, the work of the court must be associated with at least a decrease in inter-personal violence.[40]

As for war crimes the state of "non-peace" or "dispeace" in the sense of absence of armed conflict is a requirement of their application. So even if war crimes were not committed during the conflict, there would not be peace, just less "non-peacefulness". Instead, the criminalization of the conduct that constitutes war crimes is intended to "humanize" the conflict, to cause less harm than needed to both, the

[39] International Military Tribunal (1947), p. 426.

[40] Kersten (2016), p. 37 ("In this context, in order for the ICC to have a positive effect on peace, the work of the Court must be associated with a decrease in, or cessation of, direct, physical violence. Conversely, the effects of the ICC on peace are negative if the Court's intervention precipitates or is associated with continued conflict or intensified violence.").

affected civilians and the combatants, to control the level of violence and try to prevent the escalation of the conflict. Genocide and crimes against humanity on the other hand, can be committed in "peacetime" (although they can also be committed in the midst of an armed conflict), which refers to the absence of an (intra- or inter- or transnational) armed conflict. Yet, at the same time, they pose a threat to (international) peace, referring to situations of widespread or systematic collective violence.

3.3 Purposes of Punishment

Similar to the domestic context, peace is also often referred to when it comes to purposes of (international) punishment. In fact, for many the prime justification for international criminal justice, the deterrence rationale and its ability to prevent atrocities has been linked to peace. As has already been mentioned, pre-conflict deterrence can, in theory, prevent breaches of peace—at least when high-ranking political or military figures are deterred from unleashing violence.[41] During conflicts, deterrence of mid- or-lower-level figures could at least lead to less violence. As has been stated above, the empirical evidence of such a deterrent effect is unclear.

But peace is not only linked to deterrence and prevention as aims of punishment. In recent sentencing decisions, the ICC, building on ICTY case law, drew a line between retribution—or maybe expressivism—and peace. In *Al Mahdi*, for instance, the Trial Chamber explained that: "With regard to retribution, the Chamber clarifies that it is not to be understood as fulfilling a desire for revenge, but as an expression of the international community's condemnation of the crimes, which, by way of imposition of a proportionate sentence, also acknowledges the harm to the victims and promotes the restoration of peace and reconciliation."[42]

A claim that has also been made, the so-called rule-of-law rationale, is that the ICC, through its post-conflict intervention, can contribute to rebuilding the rule of law in the state affected by the conflict, either directly through its own proceedings or indirectly in its role as "watchdog court"[43]—i.e. monitoring domestic proceedings through positive complementarity—by activating the capacity of domestic tribunals to address crimes and thus fostering an environment that helps the maintenance of peace.[44] Either way, the trials are meant to increase the appeal of a peaceful conflict resolution and (criminal) law as the primary mechanism for dealing with perpetrators of atrocities.

Finally, two other purposes of criminal punishment specific to international criminal justice are often linked to the maintenance of long-lasting peace: The

[41]On deterrence and the (leadership) crime of aggression, Holtermann (2019), p. 137.

[42]ICC, Prosecutor v. Ahmad Al Faqi Al Mahdi (2016) Judgment and Sentence, ICC-01/12-01/15, Trial Chamber, 27 September 2016, para. 67.

[43]Jeßberger and Geneuss (2012), p. 1081.

[44]Vinjamuri (2015), p. 18.

purpose of establishing the truth about the commission of mass atrocities on the one hand, and the individualization of guilt on the other.[45] As regards the truth function, it is argued that international criminal trials can produce an accurate historical record of the facts that lead to the atrocities which creates a "shrinking space of denial."[46] Without such a historical record and societal confrontation of a violent past, the denial of the crimes is easier, which in turn would pose a barrier to reconciliation; this again would make a return of the conflict more likely. In a similar vein, the individualization of guilt is seen to contribute to reconciliation and to a more peaceful society by attributing criminal responsibility to specific individuals instead of to the whole group, thus diminishing collective stigmatization and rage and disincentivizing collective revenge.[47]

3.4 Prosecutorial Discretion

Turning to procedural law and peace, the controversial role of the ICC's Office of the Prosecutor is often highlighted. It is argued, that the exercise of prosecutorial discretion about which situations to investigate and whom to prosecute may have repercussions on the prospects of peace, the success of current peace-processes and, ultimately, the making of long-lasting peace. It is primarily with regard to the Court's possibility to intervene in ongoing conflicts, the question whether this intervention would promote peace or endanger peace and the debate about "peace v justice", "no peace without justice" or "peace first, justice second" ensues.

According to Article 53 of the ICC Statute the Office of the Prosecutor in deciding whether to take up an investigation or a case, shall consider, inter alia, whether there are "substantial reasons to believe that the investigation would not serve the interests of justice". Peace or "interests of peace" are not mentioned. It is therefore an open debate, whether the Office of the Prosecutor should take into account the effects of the Court's intervention on the peacemaking process. In other words: Is promoting peace in the interest of justice?

In a policy paper the ICC's Office of the Prosecutor provided an explanation of its understanding of the interests of justice and their relationship to peace processes. It stressed the difference between the concepts of "interests of justice" and "interests of peace" and explained that the latter falls within the mandate of other institutions: "the broader matter of international peace and security is not the responsibility of the Prosecutor; it falls within the mandate of other institutions."[48] At first glance, this

[45] See Werle and Jeßberger (2020), para 133 f.

[46] Phrase from Orentlicher (2008).

[47] Werle and Jeßberger (2020), para. 134.

[48] Office of the Prosecutor, ICC (2007) Policy Paper on the Interests of Justice. See also Bensouda F (2013) International Justice and Diplomacy. New York Times: "As the [ICC] is an independent and judicial institution, it cannot take into consideration the interests of peace, which is the mandate of

seems surprising given that the ICC Statute's Preamble states that the ICC crimes "threaten the peace, security and well-being of the world." So, one would imagine that the Prosecutor of such institution is somehow concerned with "the broader matter of international peace", or, as *William Schabas* has argued that, as a result of the inclusion of peace in the Preamble of the Rome Statute, the "interests of peace" become germane to the Court's activities, including the prosecutorial policy.[49] And indeed, the Office of the Prosecutor also stated that peace cannot be achieved without the prosecution of crimes under international law.

While this may seem contradictory, it seems as if two dimensions of peace, or moments in the peace process are at play: The peace that refers to the ending of ongoing inter-personal violence on the one hand, and the long-lasting peace that has to be secured after the conflict has ended. As regards the former, the Office of the Prosecutor argues that the pacification of ongoing conflicts is not their mandate and the substance of Article 16 of the Statute seems to agree with this. As regards the latter, it is argued that international criminal law and its enforcement through the ICC is one of the many mechanisms that helps to construct the diverse grounds for long term peace, one of the instruments that can help post-conflict reconciliation, addressing thereby one of the root causes for the cycle of violence and, thus, advancing long term peace.[50]

In this regard, a widely discussed problem is whether—due to financial, institutional and political constraints[51]—the inherent selectivity of international criminal justice and the discretionary prosecutorial decisions regarding the selection of cases hinder reconciliation and therefore undermine the efforts to achieve long-lasting peace.[52] While it is undisputed that selectivity in international criminal law is inevitable and not all serious crimes can be prosecuted, at least not by the ICC, there are claims that the factors that are taken into account by the OTPs regarding their selection of cases are detrimental to reconciliation and the furtherance of peace.[53]

There are at least two aspects to this argument. The first applies to the non-equal prosecution and punishment of representatives from all sides to a conflict. The problem of one-sided prosecutions, only targeting members of one side of the conflict whilst neglecting the other, has regularly been criticised in connection

other institutions, such as the United Nations Security Council. However, justice can have a positive impact on peace and security: this is what the U.N. Secretary General, Ban Ki-moon, calls the 'shadow of the Court' – its preventative role, and its capacity to diffuse potentially tense situations that could lead to violence by setting a clear line of accountability."

[49] Schabas (2016), p. 44.

[50] The "interests of justice" in Art. 53 to the ICC Statute arguably refer to possible tensions between criminal justice and other non-criminal justice elements of transitional justice, like truth and reconciliation commissions or certain forms of amnesties. On this, e.g., Robinson (2003), p. 481; Stahn (2005), p. 695.

[51] van der Wilt (2019), p. 305.

[52] In detail, van der Wilt (2017), p. 435.

[53] For details and references see the following two paragraphs.

with the prosecutorial policy of both ad hoc Tribunals, but also other international criminal tribunals including the ICC.[54] It has been argued that one-sided prosecutions deepen the rifts between the conflicting parties, between perpetrator and victim groups in particular when those groups are defined in terms of characteristics such as race, religion, and ethnicity, which undermines reconciliation and therefore the prospects for lasting peace.[55] However, studies on prosecutorial decision-making at the ICTY and the present policies applied by the ICC's Office of the Prosecutor indicate that this potential effect on peace-making is *not* taken into consideration. *Alexander Greenawalt*, for instance, has shown that the ICTY made its prosecutorial decisions strictly on the basis of the gravity of the crimes—and did not take account the membership of defendants in rival groups.[56] The ICC's Office of the Prosecutor, on the other hand, may—again according to its own policy—considers as one of several factors "the impact and the ability of the Office to pursue cases involving opposing parties to a conflict in parallel or on a sequential basis."[57]

The second aspect of selectivity creating a tension with the objective of reconciliation and long-lasting peace is concerned with the levels of hierarchy of the selected perpetrators, and, although arguably to a lesser extent, the categories of crimes that are investigated. For example, it has been argued that the prosecution and punishment of the senior leaders, that is, those most responsible not for singular crimes, but for the totality of crimes, for the breach of peace (in the broadest sense) leads to the removal of those leaders from the political scene, their delegitimization, or at least marginalization, through prosecution and punishment, works as a form of incapacitation—either during or post-conflict.[58] In practice, however, this often is possible only after those persons have been vanquished, for which more than legal intervention and diplomacy is often necessary.[59] On the other hand, it is argued that if the prosecutorial focus is on high-level perpetrators and victims see the low-level direct perpetrators remain untouched by international criminal law intervention, this can also create resentment in the affected communities and hinder reconciliation.[60] A similar argument can be made if only a certain category of crimes is investigated. This prosecutorial policy excludes certain groups of victims from the international criminal justice function. This again can hinder reconciliation and peace.

While the high degree of selectivity and the need to spell out factors for a coherent and comprehensible prosecution strategy for sure is one of the most complex issues of international criminal justice politics, it illustrates that whatever policy is followed, international criminal justice needs to be complemented by domestic prosecutions and non-criminal transitional justice mechanisms.

---

[54]Reydams (2005), p. 977.

[55]See deGuzman (2012), p. 294.

[56]Greenawalt (2007), p. 583.

[57]Office of the Prosecutor, ICC (2016) Policy Paper on Case Selection and Prioritisation. p. 15.

[58]See, e.g. Akhavan (2009), p. 634.

[59]van der Wilt (2017), p. 443.

[60]Ibid.

4 Conclusion

Not surprisingly, there is no easy, and, in particular, no uniform answer to the peace and punishment conundrum. What we have tried to show is that within the fabric of international criminal law, one has to distinguish different notions, dimensions, and aspects of peace which may be relevant at different levels, both theoretical and practical, of international criminal justice. To keep this in mind, we believe, is important when addressing – and assessing—the international justice system's capacity and efficiency to eventually make or keep peace.

References

Akhavan, P. (2009). Are international criminal tribunals a disincentive to peace?: Reconciling judicial romanticism with political realism. *Human Rights Quarterly, 31*, 624.

Bailliet, C., & Larsen, K. (2015). Introduction. In C. Bailliet & K. Larsen (Eds.), *Promoting peace through international law* (p. 1). Oxford: Oxford University Press.

Cassese, A. (2004). The ICTY: A living and vital reality. *Journal of International Criminal Justice, 2*, 585.

Cryer, R., Robinson, D., & Vasiliev, S. (2019). *An introduction to international criminal law and procedure* (4th ed., p. 42). Cambridge: Cambridge University Press.

de Hoon, M. (2017). The future of the international criminal court – On critique, legalism and strengthening the ICC's legitimacy. *International Criminal Law Review, 17*, 591.

deGuzman, M. M. (2012). Choosing to prosecute: Expressive selection at the international criminal court. *Michigan Journal of International Law, 33*, 265.

Drumbl, M. A. (2007). *Atrocity, punishment and international law* (p. 123 ff). Cambridge: Cambridge University Press.

Galtung, J. (1964). Summit meetings and international relations. *Journal of Peace Research, 1*, 1.

Galtung, J. (1969). Violence, peace and peace research. *Journal of Peace Research, 6*, 167.

Galtung, J. (1975). *Strukturelle Gewalt. Beiträge zur Friedens- und Konfliktforschung*. Reinbek: Rowohlt.

Greenawalt, A. (2007). Justice without politics? Prosecutorial discretion and the international criminal court. *NYU Journal of International Law and Politics, 39*, 583.

Hefendehl, R. (2002). *Kollektive Rechtsgüter im Strafrecht*. Köln: Heymanns.

Holtermann, J. V. H. (2019). "Can I Be Brought Before the ICC?" Deterrence of mass atrocities between Jus in Bello and Jus ad Bellum. In F. Jeßberger & J. Geneuss (Eds.), *Why punish perpetrators of mass atrocities? - Purposes of punishment in international criminal law* (p. 137). Cambridge: Cambridge University Press.

International Military Tribunal. (1947). Judgment, 30 September 1946. In *Trial of the Major War Criminals Before the International Military Tribunal* (vol 22, p. 426). Nuremberg.

Jackson, R. (1945). *Report of Robert H. Jackson: United States representative to the international conference on military trials* (p. 53). London: Department of State Publications.

Jackson, R. (1947). Opening Statement, 21 November 1945. In: *Trial of the Major War Criminals Before the International Military Tribunal: Proceedings Volumes (The Blue Set)* (Vol II, p. 153). Nuremberg.

Jescheck, H. (1975). Strafrechtsreform in Deutschland. *Schweizerische Zeitschrift für Strafrecht, 91*, 1.

Jescheck, H. H., & Weigend, T. (1996). *Lehrbuch des Strafrechts - Allgemeiner Teil* (5th ed., p. 1 ff). Berlin: Duncker & Humblot.

Jeßberger, F. (2017). Implementing Kampala: The new crime of aggression under the German code of crimes against international law. In M. Böse, M. Bohlander, A. Klip, & O. Lagodny (Eds.), *Justice without Borders: Essays in honour of Wolfgang Schombourg* (p. 180). Leiden: Brill.

Jeßberger, F., & Geneuss, J. (2012). The many faces of the international criminal court. *Journal of International Criminal Justice, 10*, 1081.

Kelsen, H. (1950). *Law of the United Nations: A critical analysis of its fundamental problems: With supplement* (p. 19). New York: Frederick A. Praeger.

Kersten, M. (2016). *Justice in conflict*. Oxford: Oxford University Press.

Mégret, F. (2016). What is the specific evil of aggression? In C. Kreß & S. Barriga (Eds.), *The crime of aggression - a commentary* (p. 1398). Cambridge: Cambridge University Press.

Mégret, F. (2018). International criminal justice as a peace project. *European Journal of International Law, 29*, 835.

Méndez, J. E., & Kelley, J. (2015). Peace making, justice and the ICC. In C. De Vos, S. Kendall, & C. Stahn (Eds.), *Contested justice - the politics and practice of international criminal court interventions* (p. 479). Cambridge: Cambridge University Press.

Meron, T. (2006). *The humanization of international law*. Leiden: Martinus Nijhoff.

Nouwen, S., & Werner, W. (2014). Monopolizing global justice: International criminal law as challenge to human diversity. *Journal of International Criminal Justice, 12*, 157 ff.

Orentlicher, D. (2008). *Shrinking the space for denial: The impact of the ICTY in Serbia*. New York: Open Society Institute.

Reydams, L. (2005). The ICTR ten years on - Back to the Nuremberg paradigm? *Journal of International Criminal Justice, 3*, 977.

Robinson, D. (2003). Serving the interests of justice: Amnesties, truth commissions and the international criminal court. *European Journal of International Law, 14*, 481.

Rodman, K. (2011). Peace v. Justice. In D. Chatterjee (Ed.), *Encyclopedia of global justice*. Dordrecht: Springer.

Schabas, W. A. (2006). *The UN international criminal tribunals: The former Yugoslavia, Rwanda and Sierra Leone* (p. 68). Cambridge: Cambridge University Press.

Schabas, W. A. (2016). Preamble. In *The international criminal court: A commentary on the Rome statute* (2nd ed., p. 31). Oxford: Oxford University Press.

Stahn, C. (2005). Complementarity, amnesties and alternative forms of justice: Some interpretative guidelines for the international criminal court. *Journal of International Criminal Justice, 3*, 695.

Teitel, R. G. (2011). *Humanity's law* (p. 2). Oxford: Oxford University Press.

Teßmer, D. (2016). In H. Schmeider (Ed.), *Münchener Kommentar zur Strafprozessordnung: Band 2*. München: C.H. Beck.

van der Wilt, H. (2017). "No peace without justice or no justice without peace?" some reflections on a complex relationship. *Diritti Umani e Diritto Internazionale, 11*, 435.

van der Wilt, H. (2019). Selectivity in international criminal law. In F. Jeßberger & J. Geneuss (Eds.), *Why punish perpetrators of mass atrocities? - Purposes of punishment in international criminal law* (p. 305). Cambridge: Cambridge University Press.

Vasiliev, S. (2019). Punishment rationales in international criminal jurisprudence - two readings of a non question. In F. Jeßberger & J. Geneuss (Eds.), *Why punish perpetrators of mass atrocities? - purposes of punishment in international criminal law* (p. 45). Cambridge: Cambridge University Press.

Vinjamuri, L. (2015). The ICC and the politics of peace and justice. In C. Stahn (Ed.), *The law and practice of the international criminal court* (p. 13). Oxford: Oxford University Press.

Werle, G., & Jeßberger, F. (2020). *Principles of international criminal law* (4th ed.). Oxford: Oxford University Press.

Wolfrum, R. (2012). Article 1. In B. Simma et al. (Eds.), *The charter of the United Nations: A commentary* (3rd ed., p. 110). Oxford: Oxford University Press.

Part IV
Core Values in Legal Research

Law as 'Argumentative Science': Functional Transfer of Basics of Scientific Theory

Otto Lagodny and Julius Lagodny

Legal research is in doubt: Is it really scientific research? Or is it something else? Is it only skilful argumentation? Such questions seem to be unacceptable and outrageous for lawyers and scholars of law. They are, however, very commonly raised by colleagues working in the natural sciences or other empirical sciences. First, these colleagues regularly wonder, how can one possibly pursue systematic research without a formulated research question. Second, how can one already think about "methods" without having fixed at least one research question ahead of starting the work. From the perspective of these other disciplines, this comes close to building a house without any plan or structure.

First, we give an overview of the relevant basics of empirical research (Sect. 1). We then elaborate on the function of a research question in those disciplines that use empirical methods. This is, in a most general way, 'finding the truth' (Sect. 2). As a next step, we transpose this function on legal research and ask: What is the functional equivalent in legal research to finding 'the truth' (Sect. 3). We will then argue that this equivalent ('validity') is not framed by content but by procedure: the search for convincing arguments for a legal problem. After having dealt with these decisive questions we discuss our findings from Sects. 2 and 3 (Sect. 4). Our general idea, however, is: If the concept of research guided by research questions in empirical disciplines is valid for all scientific research then it must be possible to transfer the general concept to legal research.

We would like to thank Shubha Kamala Prasad, Max Weber Postdoctoral Fellow at European University Institute, and Nazli Konya, Visiting Assistant Professor of Government at Colby College, for their insightful feedback during the writing of this article.

O. Lagodny
Paris London Universität, Salzburg, Austria

J. Lagodny (✉)
Cornell University, Ithaca, NY, USA
e-mail: jsl364@cornell.edu

K. Ghanayim, Y. Shany (eds.), *The Quest for Core Values in the Application of Legal Norms*, https://doi.org/10.1007/978-3-030-78953-4_17

The research question of this article, thus, can be summarized as follows: What is the functional equivalent in legal sciences to empirical disciplines' pursuit of finding 'the truth'?

Our approach and our research question for this article must be rather new for law researchers. We have found only two works dealing with research questions in law:[1] *Claes Martinson,*[2] Göteborg, explicitly does not deal with the existing law, which in his view is an 'overfiction'. He exemplifies this in the area of banking law. *Petri Mäntysaari,*[3] advocates the necessity of research questions in the legal area as a basis to establish a whole new discipline. We understand a research question, however, as a concept dealing with the existing 'lex lata' or/and the law to be created in the future ('lex ferenda'). In this chapter, we do not focus on the development of a new system. Instead, we want to develop our ideas based on the currently accepted systems, existing law and ways of general law research.

Just to avoid misunderstandings: We *do not* at all want to 'mix' empirical and legal thinking. Nor do we think one approach is superior to the other. In other words, we do not intend to merely replace arguments in legal sciences with empirical evidence. Often people arguing for one or the other try to bolster their side of the argument using empirical evidence. For example, one could say that allowing women to become priests in the Catholic church could help render the perspective of progressive women and men towards the Catholic church as more favourable. But even if empirically grounded, the discussion about something being normatively 'right' or 'wrong' is only marginally related to the empirical findings underlying a debate. In fact, 'empericalizations' of debates like the debate concerning the 'empirical, scientific beginning of life' in the US can lead to even harsher fights because both sides use 'scientific' evidence to prove their inherently normative point. Another example is the debate surrounding 'fake news' and 'alternative facts'.[4] In law, it is established for a long time—albeit often ignored—that one may not conclude from the facts, i.e. from "what is", to the normative consequences, i. e. "what should be".[5] The present situation of how to deal with the Covid-19-problems shows this: Even when the facts seem the same on a world-wide level, the legal solutions throughout the world, however, differ dramatically. In sum, we focus only

[1]Even recent works do not mention the problem, see Dreier (2018), pp. 1–65; Rottleuthner (2015), pp. 207–222.

[2]Martinson (2018). We are very much indebted to *Claes Martinson* for his help understanding his book (especially his research interest) in the Swedish language, and to our colleague from Salzburg, *Wolfgang Faber*, who enabled the contact with *Claes Martinson*.

[3]Mäntysaari (2017).

[4]From an empirical standpoint we would like to point out that some scientific facts tend to be closer to the truth than others. We are not trying to say that we should always listen to 'both sides'. In fact, often enough established empirical research shows that there are no 'other' sides. However, we would like to make the point that data and 'facts' that seem valid on the surface are used to bolster arguments by everyone in public debates since there is a need for the public to feel that something that is 'right' should also be 'true' and vice versa.

[5]See e.g. Kirste (2020), pp. 115–116 referring to Hume (1711–1776) and Moore (1873–1958).

on the comparison of legal research on the one side and on empirical research in political sciences as one example of empirical research on the other hand. As a follow-up question which cannot be covered by this article one may analyse other areas of research in political science or in other non-empirical sciences like e. g., theoretical philosophy, literature or theology.

1 Overview on Relevant Basics of Empirical Research

As a legal researcher it has—until the last 10 or 15 years—been absolutely unusual to be asked for the 'scientific objectives' or the 'intellectual merit' of a legal project. The same is true for the requirement to explain 'what methods' are used. Only if a legal researcher has applied for funds from an external society like the "Deutsche Forschungsgemeinschaft" (German Research Foundation) has he or she been confronted with questions like:

> Please give a concise description of your project's research programme and scientific objectives[6]

The US National Science Foundation insists in such cases on the following:

> The Project Description must contain, as a separate section within the narrative, a section labeled "Intellectual Merit." The Project Description should provide a clear statement of the work to be undertaken and must include the objectives for the period of the proposed work and expected significance [. . .][7]

Apart from such applications for budgets, law colleagues tend to react with irritation when you ask them about the objectives or the intellectual merit of their projects: „How dare you ask such a question?" is a remark which is sketched on their faces! By contrast, in research-projects which originate from empirical political science, such questions are considered normal and are taken for granted. It would even be confusing, *not* to ask the so-called 'so what?' question. We think, therefore, that time is more than ripe to deal with these issues in general with regard to research of legal questions.

1.1 The Three Steps in Empirical Research

In empirical sciences the different steps of research are well-established: We formulate at least one research question (step 1). Second, we formulate a testable and

[6]Deutsche Forschungsgemeinschaft (2018) DFG form 54.01 – 09/18, p. 4.

[7]The National Science Foundation (2019) Proposal & Award, Policies & Procedures Guide. NSF 19-1, II-12.

falsifiable hypothesis based on a theoretical argument.[8] In this step we also test this hypothesis by empirical means (step 2). Depending on the research question, the researcher chooses an empirical method to test the hypothesis. On the one hand, if the research question is 'why is the naturalization law of Austria so much more conservative than the German one?' an empirical researcher could, for example, engage in a comparison of the history of law in both countries or consider the political actor constellations in both countries over time on the policy.[9] On the other hand, if the research question is 'why do immigrants participate less in politics?' the set of methods and factors changes dramatically. For example, the research question is not country specific and suggests a general 'truth' about a subgroup of any country's population. Testing the results quantitatively using surveys or field experiments[10] would be a straightforward option. In a third step, the researcher discusses the results from the empirical analysis. Here they either confirm or falsify the hypothesis stated earlier (step 3).

This pattern has also been formulated similarly by *Popper* who pointed out that the decisive issue is not the verification but the exclusion of falsification.[11] Without discussing this differentiation of *Popper* here, we try to ask generally: What does the adaptation of this approach to law research mean?

1.2 Empirics in Political Science

Empirical political science is based on the use of data to test arguments.[12] One method often considered the 'golden standard' of empirical research, are experiments. Their advantage is that random distribution of respondents into treatment and control groups helps identifying an 'average treatment effect' of factor 'X'. Most

[8]Within empirical sciences there is of course a wide variation of ways to establish these steps. For example, in social sciences, a hypothesis is embedded in a 'theoretical argument' or 'theory' that establishes why the proposed explanation of a phenomenon should hold true in the first place. In natural science, the hypothesis is more straight forwardly derived from prior research and less derived from a 'theoretical argument'.

[9]Of course, there are factors to look at when answering this particular research question. These different factors furthermore establish which research method is best to be used.

[10]Field experiments are quite literally used in real fields and real acers in food science. However, here we are referring to experiments that social scientists use in a 'natural setting'. I.e., researchers use an experimental design and manipulate an explanatory factor, for example by giving money to one set of people and no money to the control group. Then they observe how having more money changes the behaviour of the treatment group compared to the control group.

[11]Popper (1999), pp. 3–22. There are many variations of this 3-step-approach.

[12]Arguments in the empirical sense are statements about a causal relationship between two concepts. The hypothesis needs to be falsifiable with data. There exists a multitude of other types of research in political science from interpretative approaches to political philosophy. However, here we would like to contrast law as a science with the empirical political science since the latter seeks to imitate positivist natural science at its core.

intuitive in natural sciences are trials of new drugs. The researchers hand out placebo pills to one randomly selected group of patients while handing out the new drug to another set of random patients. Then the researchers test how (and if) the associated vitals are improving in the treatment group compared to the control group with the placebos. The difference is the 'average treatment effect' or 'causal effect' of the new drug. Due to the randomization in an environment controlled by the researchers, they only manipulate one thing: the handing out of drugs and placebos. All other potential observed (or unobserved) impact factors cannot play a role due to the randomization. Hence, all differences in outcome have to be associated with the new drug. These concepts are used in the trials for the efficacy of new Covid vaccines as well.

Empirical social scientists also try to adapt this principle. For example, to understand how immigrants react emotionally and politically to political campaigns targeted against them compared to other types of political campaigns, empirical political scientists conducted survey experiments.[13] In this case, they divided a group of immigrant-origin respondents in a control group and a treatment group. The control group watched a campaign add in which a politician talked about the state of the economy. However, the treatment group watched a video targeting specific ethnic groups and immigrants in general and how they symbolize the downfall and corruption of society.[14] The idea here was to see how this act of campaigned discrimination against a particular group affects the emotional and political response of this particular subgroup. They would not expect great changes in the control group. The state of the economy should not necessarily affect our outcomes of interest. However, the effects of the negative, discriminatory campaign on the negative emotions and political participation should be significant—and it is.[15]

In many cases, the control group is literally a placebo. In medical research, the control group gets literally nothing except for a little bit of sugar. In social sciences this cleanest of control groups is often not possible. For example, in the case of negative campaigning the researchers were interested in the effects of negative, discriminatory campaigning on emotions and political participation. The control cannot be 'nothing' as in an 'empty' treatment because then we would compare the effects of some kind of campaigning compared to no campaigning. However, the research interests lies in the effects of different kinds of campaigning since, in reality, people are always exposed to some kind of campaigning. Hence, a test using an 'empty' control group would answer a *different* research question than

[13]Of course, a survey experiment is only one of many methods to track down 'causal effects' and 'causal mechanisms' but experiments are probably the most intuitive way of explaining what a 'scientific method' is.

[14]Besco et al. (2021), p. 6.

[15]Besco et al. (2021), pp. 7–10.

the one we are interested in (What affects do negative campaigns have compared to no campaigns?)

These types of experiments can show us how to use empirical, scientific methods to answer a wide array of research questions. In particular when one is interested in the 'causal effect' of variable of interest X—in other words, the effects of causes, not the causes of effects.

1.3 Argumentative Sciences

In this article, we are not able to deal with research questions for all non-empirical sciences. We only target law as a starting point. You can call law an "argumentative science". This is rather new as our colleague *Kurt Schmoller* from Salzburg law faculty spontaneously created the notion of "argumentative sciences" which includes law, theology, (political) philosophy etc. These sciences share the (total or at least decisive) lack of empirical methods. And they are based on discussion. With this in mind, we realized: the notion of "argumentation science" for law is gaining followers.[16]

1.4 Discussion on 'Methods' in Law: Without any Research Question

Empirical sciences discuss questions of methods in step 2 as mentioned supra. This means for example: Do we use quantitative or qualitative empirical methods? Do we rely on existing data or do we need to collect our own data? Legal research, however, is generally based on ways of interpretation which is one of the general methods of research. Thus: When we think of 'methods' in law, we regularly think of 'methods' (or better: ways) of interpretation of an existing or intended normative text: Has the meaning of the text as such been analysed? This is called the 'grammatical interpretation'. What meaning of the text has been intended by parliament at the time when the law was passed? ('historical interpretation'). How does a specific interpretation match with the meaning of the interpreted word in a different provision in that law? ('systematic interpretation') What does the purpose (the 'telos') of the norm require as result? ('teleological interpretation').[17] This is nothing more than rules of interpretation of a normative text.

[16]The leading German book on methods in law, Möllers (2019), stresses this in the Foreword and right in the beginning of the 570 pages (§ 1 note 1) citing Angelika Nußbaumer, the Vice-President of the European Court on Human Rights.

[17]See ibid., pp. 107–251.

This meaning of 'method' has nothing in common with 'methods' in the sense of scientific theory, e.g. quantitative or qualitative methods. There is only one field where a discussion of methods in this general sense takes place: In comparative law, it is necessary to think about the method of comparison when having fixed a comparative question (which is nothing else but a form of a research question!).

Example 1 A parliament wants to know what kind of legal solutions other legal orders have provided for a given problem: e.g. unlawfully parking in front of a private garage. Here the concepts used may range from private law (the owner of the garage has to do something) to public law (the state acts as such and the police takes away the parked car). Thus, it may suffice to show the different models and its implications. We call this method 'comparison of legal texts'. This method is appropriate for the research question because the research question only requires the literal comparison of different legal texts.

Example 2 Legal research in the existing patterns of the legal problem of abortion. Here the methods of comparative research used are much more differentiated. They will have to explore, amongst others, e.g. the practice of the courts, in other words, how a legal order is implemented in real life of a given society as well as other legal norms directly or indirectly influencing the regulations on abortion.[18]

Example 3 Research in the vast *de facto* and *de jure* differences of the cultural and historical origins between criminal law in Austria and in Germany. For example, how do socio-cultural particularities in daily interactions affect the procedures of criminal law in both countries? This requires in addition to these two examples to be involved in "everyday life", because one only becomes aware of deeply rooted differences when you live there in the role of a "participant observer" or have close contacts in another way with the relevant legal system.[19]

Similar to the examples given above (naturalization law in Germany and Austria versus political participation of migrants in general), the different 'research questions' in comparative law require different depths, foci, and actors depending on the project.

The question of 'the' proper method is vividly discussed in comparative research in law:[20] which of the many different methods of comparative research is the 'one and only', the "King's method" of comparative research in law.

Similarly, in social science there are different understandings of the 'gold standard' of methods. Often, experiments are called the 'gold standard' of social science research.[21] Some authors even say so-called randomized controlled experiments are

---

[18]See Eser and Koch (1999).

[19]As to this empirical method see e.g. Kawulich (2005), Art 43. As to a practical example, see Lagodny (2021), pp. 35–40. The author uses the method of participant observation discussing his own experiences of the reality of the Austrian legal order.

[20]See for further references: Eser (2016), pp. 929–1135.

[21]See Gerber and Green (2012).

the only way to conduct 'proper' research. However, this would significantly decrease the range of research questions social scientists could ask. For example, how does one randomize and control the environment for the following questions: Why are democracies richer than autocracies? How do insurgencies impact economic integration?[22] In these cases, randomization into treatment and control groups directly is impossible. Hence, researchers need to be creative and use observational data instead to answer these questions. This is to show that an almost ideological methodological war also appears within empirical social science. And if method comes before the research question, it substantially limits the questions we can ask.

2 The Research Question and Methods in Disciplines Working on an Empirical Basis

2.1 Overview

The considerations concerning the research method become even more evident when we realize the role of the research question in empirically motivated sciences. Here, we have empirical tests or experiments in order to falsify or verify a hypothesis. Empirical tests or experiments must have the properties to be replicable anywhere in the world by anyone and produce the same results.

The differentiation (true/false) makes sense as long as empirical tests make sense. This is the case as long as the research question concerns 'reality' as it is. Only then something may be considered as 'true' or 'false'.

The empirical sciences rely on a perception of the 'truth' as the decisive criterion for their work. It is, however, flexible what the 'truth' is. This can also change. e.g.: on earth, an iron ball falls down to earth quicker than a feather. In a vacuum they would fall at the same speed. This is 'true'.[23] However, other topics in particular in the societal context are not as straight forward. For example, homosexuality has been regarded as a physical or psychological illness for a long time. Similarly, Foucault shows another example: The way societies treated and described the 'insane' has significantly changed due to how society defines sanity and being sane.[24]

Instead of describing 'truth' we aim at deriving an argumentative equivalent for law research: '*validity*'. We will not go into details of the different empirical concepts of 'truth' in this sense. Neither will we look for a concept of 'truth' which works for both, the empirically and the non-empirically working sciences. Instead, we will look for a functional equivalent of 'truth' in legal research as our

[22] See Prasad S K (2020) State (In)security: The impact of insurgencies on economic integration. Working Paper. http://hdl.handle.net/10822/1060561.

[23] To say it in Poppers understanding: Newton's understanding of the 'free fall' law is still the best, so far unfalsified hypothesis of the relationship between speed, acceleration and time.

[24] See Foucault (1993).

(only) example of a non-empirical working science. This equivalent is 'validity'. We borrow this term from political philosophy or rather logic.[25] Validity and truth are not the same. However, in a world of argumentative sciences 'truth' as an absolute measure to which research has to uphold does not exist. Hence, we cannot test if an argument is 'true' or not. However, we can decide if an argument is valid or not. In other words, using logic, "a good argument is one whose conclusions follow from its premises; its conclusions are consequences of its premises."[26] In other words, theory of logic gives us tools to deduct if an argument is valid or not—rather than true or not.

Validity is the equivalent for truth in argumentative sciences. However, does this seemingly objective process to deduct the validity of arguments through reasoning govern research in law as well? Is 'validity' or a 'valid argument' always the same? If not, who is to decide what a valid argument is in law? How is validity established? In the following sections, we discuss the concept of 'truth' of facts and juxtapose it to 'validity' of an argument.

2.2 *The Function of 'Truth'*

In the natural sciences it is possible to falsify a hypothesis which relates to 'reality' (whatever reality means in the particular context). We are aware of the fact that 'reality' can be understood as a mere construction. What is decisive for us is that the way reality is construed does not exclude the necessity of empirical work. The borderline, thus, has to be drawn between empirically and not-empirically working sciences—as we have done already throughout the whole article.

What is the function of 'truth' in empirical tests and experiments? It is a criterion which provides—at least in the vast majority of cases[27]—a 'yes or no'- answer to the research question. In other words, does an asserted relationship 'truly' exist or not? It is the belief that something is causing something else if we can isolate it from all other potential causes by holding all other influences constant. More importantly, these methods should *not* require convincing another human. They either reject or

---

[25]E.g. see Kusch (2019). Many thanks to Nazli Konya, Cornell University, for the inspiration.

[26]Stanford Encyclopedia of Philosophy Archive (2014) Logical Consequence. https://plato.stanford.edu/archives/fall2014/entries/logical-consequence/.

[27]We understand our dichotomies of "true" and "false" as well as "right" and "wrong" as overlapping categories: In special and exceptional cases of empiric research one could use the couple of "right" and "wrong" instead of "true" and "false" and vice-versa: in special and exceptional cases one could possibly use the notions of "true" and "false" even in law. However, the discussion somehow turns to be somehow strange from the view of a non-lawyer if a norm clarifies what is evident: that animals are no "Sachen" ("material things") according to section 90a of the German Bürgerliche Gesetzbuch (Law on Private Relations). The legal logic thereof is, that the German law from the nineteenth century only knows two categories: "Persons" and "materials things". Animals as a third category did not fit into the dichotomy between "persons" and "material things".

confirm a hypothesis/argument.[28] If correctly done,[29] researchers will either find an effect or they will not. In theory, empirical tests of arguments do not need to convince another human being. They just *exist.* And this is decisive: An answer which does not require any additional human decision to be true or false. After an experiment we have a result which says: 'It is as it is'. Therefore, we have to formulate and reformulate a hypothesis as long as it can be—according to *Popper*—falsified in exactly this sense.[30]

Research questions in non-empirically working sciences do not require such a structure of the question. Questions can rather be answered very differently. There may be e.g. 'more-or-less'—answers which also exist in empirics; there may be answers like "normatively convincing" or simply "convincing" or other answers. And they need not at all refer to our concept of reality as a criterion. They rather refer to opinions.

We think one decisive difference between empirical science and argumentative science is that the answer to the research question in empirical science can often be narrowed to 'yes, something is *true*'/'no, something is *false*' while the analogy in argumentative science is 'yes, something is *right*'/'no, something is *wrong'*. Or—what could be discussed in follow-up contributions—as an equivalent of: something is "convincing" or "not convincing". This small shift implies a difference in magnitude: One is based on empirical differences and data, the other on normative perceptions and arguments. At the same time, we are not trying to discriminate between both types of research. We just want to point out that we as researchers have to be aware of how our way of doing research completely depends on what our research interest and our research question are.

But then, how do we answer legal research questions? Is it not all arbitrary if it is based on opinions? We argue that this depends on who has the power to answer (and decide) what is 'right' and what is 'wrong'. In a world of normative perception and arguments, how does one divide into what is 'right' and what is 'wrong'? Or rather, what is more convincing? Any decision made in a group, no matter the societal context or the set of rules implied, requires the exchange of arguments about the rightfulness or wrongfulness of a certain potential agreement or compromise. In

[28]Of course, an experiment can be in itself 'unconvincing' and a lot of debate in empirical research concerns exactly this: internal and external validity of experiments and other empirical research. However, this is a different debate. Here we are concerned with the idea that within an experiment (albeit be it valid or not) the data gives a yes or no answer to the research question.

[29]Just for the records: This is far from easy! And technically, in the Popperian tradition, a hypothesis can never be truly confirmed. They can only not yet be falsified—as in, represented the best-working hypothesis yet.

[30]We are aware that this depiction of empirical sciences is very idealistic and is rarely achieved. In reality, there are huge discussion concerning the 'correct' set ups for experiments, econometric modelling, and so forth. We try to make the case here, that the idealized idea of what 'truth' is in empirical science and argumentative science changes how researchers use different methods and/ or arguments to show that their 'truth' exists. Furthermore, an experiment is never the one answer. Research inspires other research and additional tests will be done to falsify or confirm similar hypothesis.

sum, arguments are always necessary—a first general rule for argumentative science.[31]

3 Functional Equivalent to a Hypothesis Including a 'Theory' (Step 2) and Discussion (Step 3): Making Arguments to Convince

The direct transfer of step 2 (theory and hypothesis) and step 3 (empirical tests) does not easily carry over to argumentative sciences. We argue that the equivalent of hypothesis and theory are foundations of arguments while the discussion and evaluation of the most 'convincing' argument is the argumentative equivalent to empirical testing (step 3).

There is a major obstacle to the direct transfer: the necessity of a theoretical foundation of a hypothesis. As *Mäntysaari* points out:

> Research questions are meaningful only in the context of prior theory. Findings are new only in relation to prior theory. Therefore, you need to study prior theory in order to choose meaningful research questions that may be able to new findings.[32]

We take this observation as a starting point. We are, however, fully aware that the 'theory'-problem might be approached differently, especially because there can be different views on law: Do we only focus on the existing law? On determining the existing law? Or do we also make suggestions on how the law should be in future? Or do we even think that existing law is an 'overfiction'?[33]

As we focus on the *lex lata* and the *lex ferenda* we already have to deal with 'theories'. This term is understood in law as a bundle of coherent reasons which have their basis in a general idea. E.g.: From a theory of 'international division of labour in transnational criminal prosecution' you may conclude several solutions to different single legal problems.[34]

If an empirically working scholar thinks about a 'theory' he or she wants to find the theoretical basis for the suggested hypothesis. This is a completely different meaning of the term 'theory'. And it is a meaning which makes little sense in law because there is no 'truth' to be verified or falsified.

---

[31]This might seem tautological as we called it 'argumentative sciences'. However, general rules in argumentative sciences are hard to come by, so we are sticking to it.

[32]Mäntysaari (2017), p. 51.

[33]This is what Martinson explicitly does *not* intend to do, see Martinson (2018), pp. 41–44. He points out that legal science has much more potential than just achieving at normative statements. We are very much indebted to *Claes Martinson* for helping us understand the Swedish language of his book.

[34]See Schomburg et al. (2012), pp. 1–50.

Research questions in law may be formulated without a 'theory' in the sense of empirical sciences.[35] The requirement of 'a theory', therefore, does not need to be transferred to legal thinking. We can, therefore, now go through all the three steps mentioned above.

The equivalent to step 3 (empirics) in argumentative is the discussion and evaluation of the most 'convincing' argument. Arguments and rationales are meant to convince those who have to be convinced, i.e. those who participate in making a decision, i.e. other members of a parliament, of a court, of any other decision-making institution or at least: the relevant scientific community or a part thereof. Convincing arguments, thus, are the functional equivalent for empirical tests. Arguments are either accepted or not. They cannot be 'true' or 'false'. And here we see the functional equivalent for empirics: convincing arguments and being convinced, establishing what is 'right' or 'wrong' from the view of the person or entity concerned. Who has to be convinced depends on the situation:

If the legal problem concerns a legal question which

- a court of last instance decides upon, it is exactly this court and no one else;
- is under debate between lawyers, it is exactly this group of lawyers;
- is under debate in a whole society, it is the society as such.

The concept of "being convinced", thus, is very relative. To clarify this approach from an extreme situation: Under a dictatorship, no court or parliament has to be convinced of the legality of a certain action. Not even the dictator has to be convinced by someone *else*. The dictator's will as such and his factual power are sufficient.

4 Discussion

4.1 The Three Steps

In legal thinking, we start with a legal 'problem' (or a legal 'question') as **step 1**. The array of legal 'problems' is wide: We can, e.g., discuss the question of how to interpret a given provision (interpretation problem). Example: Is it a crime to destroy something which has no economic value, e.g. a love letter written on one single page of paper? This question is discussed under Austrian law.[36] Such a question arises out of the view of, e.g., a judge having to decide on a single and concrete case.

[35] As mentioned above (supra Sect. 3) the perception of 'theory' and 'theoretical foundations' also varies across empirical sciences. For example, it is much more important in social sciences than in natural sciences.

[36] Birklbauer et al. (2018), Section (§) 125 annotation 6.

We can also discuss whether it is legitimate or legal to create a provision making it a crime to destroy such a love letter and comparable things. This is the view of a law-making institution, e.g. a parliament.

We can—as a third possibility—discuss e.g. how the legal order as a whole deals with love letters, etc. pp. This is a more general view of e.g. law philosophy.

Surely, there may be further examples for 'problems' in law. It has become apparent, however, that the term 'problem' means something very different in empirically working sciences and in law.

If we take the interpretation-problem as an example, the **step 2,** would be to give arguments for both legal interpretations ('theories'). These arguments can be divided into two main groups: The first group of opinions requires that the 'something' has to have at least 'some' economic value. We can call this the '*economic value*'-legal interpretation. The consequence is: destroying a love-letter is not a crime. The second group argues that an emotional value is already sufficient (and we call it: '*emotional value'* interpretation); consequence: it is a crime. These two groups of arguments may be labelled as 'theories'. Very often the foundation of a legal argument is not a complete 'theory'. Instead, only certain aspects of a theory (or even no coherent theory at all) are used in a legal argument.

Step 3 is done in natural sciences on the basis of empirically gained results. The equivalent in law has to be seen in the discussion and evaluation of the convincingness of arguments among those having to decide on a legal interpretation of the concrete problem, i.e. the judges of a court or a group of authors intending to write a legal book.

It is especially step 3 where the empirically working sciences and the non-empirically working sciences have to go on different paths. A normative question may not be answered by 'true' or 'false'. Instead, it will probably be answered normatively into 'right' or 'wrong'. Thus, we have to replace empirical evidence, or truth, with something else: the convincingness (or validity) of arguments.

Hence, 'validity' or how convincing an argument is in our view is the functional equivalent to empirics.

4.2 Does Content Determine Validity?

Validity is the measure of how convincing an argument is. The question is: what determines validity or convincingness? The most straight-forward answer would be: content! The content of an argument should decide over its validity. (i.e. human rights; the concept of "human dignity" as laid down in the Israeli Basic Law, the Philosophy of *Kant* or of *Dworkin*) and procedure: In normative questions there are no empirical methods to decide between 'true' and 'false'). In normative questions we have to decide ourselves between "convincing" and "not-convincing" or "right" and "wrong" outcomes. If content determines validity, we should be able to identify content-based 'truths' in law research that are universally applicable. In other words: If only content drives how valid an argument is, certain contents should be so 'valid' that they are considered universal 'rights'. Hence, we discuss the most universally agreed content in international law: human rights. As we will show below, not even in this content, we have no unanimity about what is convincing (what is right and, hence, most valid) and what is not (what is wrong, and invalid). The direct follow-up problem is: If no content is universally "convincing" or "not-convincing", what else does?

We think one should not focus on *what* but rather on *who.* Who makes this decision? Who is competent to decide (regardless of what this person or legal entity decides)? It is procedure that conditions validity.

To show how validity changes, we look into the development of one of the most internationally accepted principles of law: basic human rights. First, we compare how aspects of human rights differ across legal traditions (horizontal) and have changed historically within legal traditions (vertically). We show that what is 'valid' and universal differs across country and time. This shows that what is 'valid' in argumentative science is not so much contingent on content but rather on procedure (as in: who has to be convinced). We have to be aware that 'comparative' can be regarded upon from two directions: from the *vertical* view. Then we, second, compare between two legal orders in the same state in different times. We call this legal history. Or we compare two legal orders at the same time. This is *horizontal* comparison, what we normally call comparative law. However, for our purposes it does not matter whether we take our examples from horizontal or vertical comparison.

With regard to human rights we have to realize that the notion and the concept of "human rights" is not perceived identically across the globe. The discussion on the 'universality' of human rights'[37] shows this very clearly. We do not have to go into details of this discussion. It suffices to say that there is no unanimity on something so fundamental as abolishing the death sentence. In Europe, it took 14 additional protocols to the European Convention on Human Rights until the death penalty was completely abolished. In the US, we are far away from that. Similarly, Prasad and Nooruddin (2021) show that countries, in particular democracies, that sometimes violate human rights to fight back internal adversaries, tend to be less adamant in condemning human rights internationally.[38]

In addition: vertical comparison also shows that concepts and their validity vary dramatically over time. One example from the field of human rights always strikes us: Today, it goes without saying—first—that torture is prohibited world-wide by international law and this prohibition is—second—not observed, even by defenders of human rights' when it comes to traceless forms like 'water-boarding' or treatment by noise. When going back 500 years in Europe we see when looking at the persecution of witches that torture at that time was very well accepted and formal-

[37]See e.g. Di Fabio (2008), pp. 63–97.

[38]Prasad and Nooruddin (2021), p. 1.

ized. This enormous difference can only be explained by changes in the discourse today and 500 years ago. We do not want to go this far and say: 500 years ago, torture was a step 'forward'. Even so, historically, torture became part of due process because a paradigm shift implied that subjects could not be convicted unless they admitted the crime they were accused of. The confession first had to come from the subject's lips in court and not from 'God's Judgment' (like the proof in trial by ordeal: if the accused drowns she/he is considered to be innocent; if she/he does not drown, she/he has lied). As has been shown by *Zagolla*, the creation of a pivotal law, the 'Carolina' of 1532, has led to a restriction of torture to proceedings concerning only very severe crimes. Thereby, the gravity and the seriously harm caused by torture has been the reason that torture has since then not been used in minor cases and on a totally discretionary basis.[39]

This is, of course, an example from history. But we may use arguments from history in comparative law as history is comparative law on the *vertical* level whereas comparative law normally works on the *horizontal* level by comparing two legal orders at the same time.

We could extend this view also to the horizontal level and look on the contradiction between Western law concepts—focusing on the individual—and socialist concepts of law—focusing on collectives. The example of the former German Democratic Republic (GDR) shows that there was legal research.[40] Legal interpretation in the GDR, however, was based on a socialistic concept of law as a cogent starting point of any legal research.

The same is true for specific models of philosophy: Can the philosophy of e.g. *Kant* or *Plato* be decisive and 'convincing' anywhere? Especially in German legal literature there is a tendency to put *Kant* or *Hegel* or else in a an exceptionally bright spotlight and to conclude that any work which does not take them into account as the 'true' philosophers does not deserve even being discussed. Or: Is the whole concept of methodology of *Kelsen* valid for the whole rest of the world? Or just take the notion of 'Rechtsstaat' which is even very difficult to translate at all into English.[41]

In other words: We cannot talk about the contents of what law should be or what convincing arguments are, because there are too many basic differences: If we cannot take the contents of human rights as a common, general starting point because there are too many differences even on this level, then we wonder what other starting point we should take.

Given the different traditions in law, it seems inevitable that a world-wide common understanding of legal concepts is basically impossible. However, if we reduce the requirement of 'world-wide', we have to face the problem: Is there research following merely regional patterns, e.g. European, Jewish or Islamic

[39] See Zagolla (2006), pp. 53/54, 56–63.

[40] See Arnold (1995). The habilitation of Arnold has been one of the very few habilitations in law which has been accepted in former West-Germany.

[41] See Kirste (2014), pp. 29–43.

thinking? Such a regionalization would be a contradiction in itself as far as the discussion on research in *general* is concerned. Again: there is no national 'law of gravity'. There is only one 'law of gravity' in the whole world.

These considerations may be generalized. Any definition of whatever world-wide contents for a general research objective would collapse when confronted with the afore-mentioned comparative views. And this is applicable to philosophical views as well. To put it clearly: Is the human-dignity-concept of *Kant* transferable, for example, to a Buddhistic or an Islamic theory of law? We suppose: no—and it should not! Such questions can be formulated in many ways. The lesson of comparative law is that it is very unlikely to find such world-wide concepts of content.

We showed what is valid changes across time and space. Thus, we look at procedure as another potential indicator forming validity. In the following, we argue that validity is conditional on procedure. We call this concept: *Conditional Validity*.

4.3 Conditional Validity: The Procedure Frames **how** *Valid an Argument Is*

If the validity of an argument is not generalizable what then determines validity? How does an argument become *more* valid? What is valid and what is not valid in a legal argument? We argue that we have to think about the procedure: The answers differ from state to state or even from case to case as far as the creation of laws or their interpretation is concerned. The constitution and parliamentary law are decisive concerning the regulation of the process of law-making. As far as court-decisions are concerned, the rules laid down in the law of the procedure (e.g. the Code of Criminal Procedure) are decisive to inform a general framework of what is valid and what is not and who (or what) has more weight on what is a valid argument.[42]

For example, procedures decide if a judge's legal argument or opinion is decisive for a legal outcome. In other words, the rules of the game show if a judge's opinion is important for the outcome itself. In a case where the judge's opinion is crucial (in terms of procedure) for the outcome, the same argument from a different participant does not have the same weight or factual validity (as in the factual basis for the outcome of the case) as the argument of the judge. The validity of arguments is conditionally dependent on who is saying the argument and the relative power position he or she is in. We call this concept *Conditional Validity*.[43] The

[42]Many of our arguments might come close to many thoughts of *Kelsen* (Reine Rechtslehre) who at his time never has asked for a research question and therefore did not ask the follow-up questions raised here. He, however, intended to make legal research come close to natural science as fostered by the 'Vienna Circle'.

[43]There are, of course, several additional factors that determine the perceived validity of arguments. Other constructs like race, or gender play a major role in determining the validity of an argument regardless of the procedure. In the legal context, we argue that given a legal procedure in place, the

"condition" in this sense is that the person (or entity, e. g. like courts) has the (legal or factual) power to decide on the validity.

Another example are hierarchies implied by the procedure. The same argument from a supreme court justice weights much more than the exact same argument from a lower court judge. Similarly, in an academic legal discussion, citing a full professor is more 'valid' than citing the same argument but from a student. Hence, validity dependents also on hierarchy imposed by the procedure.

We have argued that it is impossible to find general 'truths' or even general beliefs that establish what is valid and what is not in argumentative sciences. However, we can show that it is generally true that (internal) procedures decide, first, how validity is conceptualized and, second, who has to be convinced of valid arguments. This changes what is valid and how 'convincing' arguments are made and addressed. We acknowledge, of course, that procedures (formal or informal) are established in a certain context. We would, hence, argue that validity is also *contextual*. For example, a young female lawyer of colour in a legal procedure in Germany or Austria will have to address the court differently from an old, white, male lawyer to make an argument 'convincing'. We merely want to point out that while procedures can tell us more about the general framework of how validity is established, procedures alone do not determine validity itself. This is symbolic for the argumentative sciences generally speaking: there is no general recipe!

Hence, we ask ourselves: What are the consequences for argumentative sciences if 'what is valid' is contingent on procedures, actors and many more conditions—in other words, highly conditionally and contextually dependent!

4.4 General Consequences of Conditional Validity for a More Conscious Understanding of Law

As we have already indicated, there are a lot of consequences in the whole area of research in law. We want to really "pick out" some features which in our view are striking. This does neither mean that these features are exhaustive nor that they are beyond any doubt. However, they are not more than a starting-point for a new discussion.

(a) The general objective of legal research as we worked it out now does not mean that any work of legal research is confined to it. Every project, every work will and must have its own objective(s) as defined by the individual researcher. However, it is not possible for this researcher to claim superiority of his or her

procedural position of a person making an argument gives a substantial framework for the changes of validity of an argument. In other words, a defendant arguing for his or her own innocence will not have the same validity weight as a judge or an attorney—based on their position in the legal procedure.

objectives. As we pointed out before, the objectives may not be in a general way defined by contents. Thus, there is no possibility to argue in this direction.

(b) A second consequence for legal research is that we acknowledge a basic equality of any legal argument. It does not matter whoever has used it: A court of the own legal order or of a foreign legal order, a law professor or a law student, and so on. The only aspect that should count is the argument itself—or at least we should consciously acknowledge that arguments are perceived as more valid conditional on the person who makes them in a certain context. This has, by the way, enormous consequences for the teaching of law. These observations have to be strictly separated from the practically decisive aspect of whom the legal order determines to decide on a legal problem.

(c) The creation of citation cartels ('Zitierkartelle') is contradicting the general objective. Such a cartel exists if researchers cite always the same other researchers or exclude certain other researchers from being cited. If the general objective is to create or search for the best argument, the use of citation cartels brings about the impression of greater validity: We position our opinion among other 'great' (often white, old) men. In legal research, citing one's colleagues often seems to be a matter of collegial decency. Following the discussion above, using citation cartels is not only a question of politeness but one of unscientificness. Citation cartels are contrary to the idea of engaging in research. The same may be argued about academic 'schools' which are often considered being an acceptable form of academic conduct which in reality is nothing but misconduct.

(d) We can generalize these considerations: Legal citations ought to be representative. Of course, representativeness is a lose concept in itself, but it clearly cannot be sufficient, just to grasp the journal or book which are 'on the researcher's desk' anyhow. One has to look for a representative citation to hear more voices. Citations are not a question of being 'nice' to colleagues.

(e) The Anglo-American style of citations in law issues has to be reconsidered. In the US, a citation of other legal researchers is not thought of as a reference to someone who has said exactly this and at exactly that place. This may be the case, but not necessarily. A citation is often meant to only give hints as to where the reader may find something comparable as well. This has nothing to do with the legal argumentation as such.

(f) We also have a solution to a general question: Why is it not necessary to cite 'student papers' on a large scale?[44] Most of these papers are written for learning purposes. They are not—per se—meant to participate in the academic concourse. The main reason, why law researchers do not cite student papers is not the general validity of their arguments but rather that the validity is conditional: adding them will not make an argument more convincing or more valid. This is a sad 'truth' and we might want to reconsider this.

[44]See Lagodny and Lagodny (2019), pp. 354–366, 361–363.

(g) With our approach it is quite obvious that legal research and politics may be separated as well as intentionally (or by chance) mixed. This depends on the project's definition of the research objectives. And it becomes clear that the separation of both, of law and politics, is not inherent in legal research as it is the basis of the 'Reine Rechtslehre' of *Kelsen*.

4.5 Special Consequences in the Field of Law

Lawyers are used to create divisions, sub-divisions, sub-sub-divisions etc. of a given legal problem. There are a lot of such sub-divisions which we are very familiar with legal problems like:

- How do we organize the legal order of a sovereign state as such, i. e. the "federal level" (e. g. Germany, Italy, India, the United States of America)?
- Subdivision of this question: How do we organize the subdivision of the federal level (the "Länder" of Germany, the Federal States of the U.S.)?
- How do we organize supranational entities like the European Union.

Within "the" law we are all familiar with subdivisions like:

- public law as opposed to private law
- criminal law and administrative law
- etc.

Our approach points out that such subdivisions are more or less artificial and intertwined with the units (states, legal orders etc) they refer to. They make sense in a given legal order but not necessarily in another one. This is pivotal for all work in legal comparison. Just to illustrate this:

(a) A lawyer who is familiar with the way of thinking in the field of human rights in the western hemisphere of the world is very well used that any check of the conformity of a state's act (e.g. the prohibition of a public authority vis-à-vis a private person with a certain human rights guarantee) starts with the 'purpose' of that state act.[45] We know from this way of thinking that the broader the purpose is formulated, the easier is the justification for that act of the state. While the "purpose" is self-defined, it is the one and only criterion for all follow-up questions. This is the pivotal point.
(b) When looking at the 'divisions' between the various 'branches' of law, e.g. public or private law; labour law, criminal law etc. one becomes aware of the fact that these lines are drawn very differently in every legal order. In a common law order like the US, the procedural law concerning private law (i.e. civil proceedings) and criminal procedure have the same basis: A jury trial and mechanisms to avoid such a trial (e.g. plea bargaining). In other

[45] See in detail: Lagodny (1999), pp. 575–591.

words: civil and criminal procedure are very similar in its starting point and its consequences. This is not at all true for the central European perspective: These criminal proceedings are called 'inquisitorial' because the judge himself is 'inquiring' the witnesses, not only the parties.

If we look at this question from a comparative view, we realize that this 'division' of law depends on the specific legal order. Minor traffic-offences for example are considered in Austria to be part of administrative law whereas in Germany they are part of criminal law and procedure: 'Ordnungswidrigkeit'.[46] Punitive damages are considered as being private law in the US whereas in Germany they "belong" to public law.

(c) Another question in this direction: Is the objective only to be seen in matters of law as opposed to other disciplines (ethics? moral issues? cybernetics? etc). If we confine the research question right in the beginning to law and exclude other ways of dealing with problems like relaying also to ethical solutions or—the other extreme—to decisions by algorithms, then we exclude important and sometimes decisive questions.

5 Conclusions for Our Work as Legal Researchers

Are legal scholars really 'a special breed of academic' as *Herbert Gintis* who fostered the 'game theory' formulated his scepticism?[47] We ask ourselves: Is every legal question, e.g. the question how to interpret a certain word in a specific legal provision, already a complete research question? In addition, there are a lot of comparable and other questions arising out of our approach.

With this article we generally intend to raise some questions for legal researchers. It is necessary to reflect more on what their research questions are and on what implications that has for their modes and methods of research.

We do not think, however, that this implies a direct, mechanical translation of scientific concepts into legal research. Exactly because general truths and general conceptions of validity are impossible to define beforehand and out of context. We do not think that legal research should aim at a 'scientification' or 'mechanisation' of substantive argumentative patterns.

We also introduced the concepts of 'Conditional Validity' to show how procedures define who has to be convinced, who has the power to convince, and how the validity of arguments changes over time, space, and procedure—in other words, validity is highly conditional.

When preparing this article, we were more than once struck by the experience that exactly the same notions are perceived very different in political sciences and in law (e.g. 'solutions', 'theory', 'methods'). It was also fascinating to see that political

[46] Administrative offense.

[47] Martinson (2018), p. 100. Citing Gintis (2008) Reputation is not enough, in footnote 196.

sciences range from strictly empirical branches to those being very close to legal thinking.

We dedicate these thoughts to Mordechai Kremnitzer who enabled us—as early as 1994—to breathe impressions of "never a dull moment" in Israel. We are very grateful for that.

References

Arnold, J. (Ed.). (1995). *Die Normalität des Strafrechts der DDR*. Freiburg: Max Plank Institute.

Besco, R., Garcia-Rios, S., Lagodny, J., Lajevardi, N., Oskooii, K. A. R., & Tolley, E. (2021). *Explicit racism and the political engagement of minorities*. Working Paper.

Birklbauer, A., Hilf, M. J., Konopatsch, C. J., Messner, F., Schwaighofer, K., Seiler, S., & Tipold A. (2018). StGB [criminal code]. *Journal für Strafrecht*.

Di Fabio, U. (2008). Menschenrechte in unterschiedlichen Kulturräumen. In G. Nooke, G. Lohmann, & G. Wahlers (Eds.), *Gelten Menschenrechte universal? Begründungen und Infragestellungen* (pp. 63–97). Freiburg: Herder GmbH.

Dreier, H. (2018). Rechtswissenschaft als Wissenschaft – Zehn Thesen. In H. Dreier (Ed.), *Rechtswissenschaft als Beruf* (pp. 1–65). Tübingen: Mohr Siebeck.

Eser, A. (2016). Strafrechtsvergleichung: Entwicklung – Ziele – Methode. In A. Eser & W. Perron (Eds.), *Strukturvergleich strafrechtlicher Verantwortlichkeit und Sanktionierung in Europa* (pp. 929–1135). Berlin: Duncker & Humblot.

Eser, A., & Koch, H. G. (1999). *Schwangerschaftsabbruch im internationalen Vergleich. Teil 3*. Baden Baden: Nomos.

Foucault, M. (1993). *Madness and civilization: A history of insanity in the age of reason*. London: Routledge.

Gerber, A. S., & Green, D. P. (2012). *Field experiments - design, analysis, and interpretation*. New York: W. W. Norton & Company.

Kawulich, B. B. (2005). Participant observation as a data collection method. *Forum Qualitative Social Research, 6*(2), Art 43. http://nbn-resolving.de/urn:nbn:de:0114-fqs0502430

Kirste, S. (2014). Philosophical foundation of the principle of the legal state (Rechtsstaat) and the rule of law. In J. R. Silkenat, J. E. Hickey Jr., & P. D. Barenboim (Eds.), *The legal doctrines of the rule of law and the legal state (Rechtsstaat)* (pp. 29–43). Cham: Springer.

Kirste, S. (2020). *Rechtsphilosophie. Einführung* (pp. 115–116). Baden-Baden: Nomos.

Kusch, M. (Ed.). (2019). *The Routledge handbook of philosophy of relativism*. London: Routledge.

Lagodny, J., & Lagodny, O. (2019). Fußnotenkulturen. Beobachtungen aus rechts- und aus politikwissenschaftlicher Sicht. *Zeitschrift für Internationale Strafrechtsdogmatik* (online) *6*, 354–366, 361–363.

Lagodny, O. (1999). Human dignity and its impact on German substantive criminal law and criminal procedure. *Israel Law Review, 33*, 575–591.

Lagodny, O. (2021). *Zwei Strafrechtswelten. Rechtsvergleichende Betrachtungen und Erfahrungen aus deutscher Sicht in Österreich*. Baden Baden: Nomos.

Mäntysaari, P. (2017). *User-friendly legal science: A new scientific discipline*. Cham: Springer.

Martinson, C. (2018). *Femton förmögenhetsrättsliga forskningsresultat*. Uppsala: Iustuts Förlag.

Möllers, T. M. J. (2019). *Juristische Methodenlehre* (2nd ed.). München: C.H. Beck.

Popper, K. (1999). The logic and evolution of scientific theory. In K. Popper (Ed.), *All life is problem solving* (pp. 3–22). London: Routledge.

Prasad, S. K., & Nooruddin, I. (2021). *States living in glasshouses...: The effect of domestic insurgency on how countries vote in the UN Human Rights Council*. Working paper, p. 1.

Rottleuthner, H. (2015). Methodologie und Organisation der Rechtswissenschaft. In E. Hilgendorf & H. Schulze-Fielitz (Eds.), *Selbstreflexion der Rechtswissenschaft* (pp. 207–222). Tübingen: Mohr Siebeck.

Schomburg, W., Lagodny, O., Gleß, S., & Hackner, T. (Eds.). (2012). *Einleitung. Internationale Rechtshilfe in Strafsachen* (5th ed., pp. 1–50). München: C.H. Beck.

Zagolla, R. (2006). *Im Namen der Wahrheit. Folter in Deutschland vom Mittelalter bis heute*. Berlin-Brandenburg: Be.bra verlag, pp. 53/54, 56–63.

CV of "Mordechai Kremnitzer"

Prof. (Emeritus) Mordechai (Mota) Kremnitzer, Faculty of Law Hebrew University of Jerusalem, and Senior Research Fellow at the Israel Democracy Institute, born on November 16, 1948 in Germany. Kremnitzer has studied law at the Hebrew University of Jerusalem, where he received his LL.B. 1970 with Cum Laude, and Ph.D. 1980. He served at the IDF (1970–1977) as prosecutor of the Navy, Deputy Chief Prosecutor and Military Judge. He received appointments at the Faculty of Law Hebrew University of Jerusalem as Lecturer in Criminal Law (1981), Senior Lecturer with Tenure (1985), Associate Professor (1990) and Full Professor (1999). Kremnitzer served as Dean of the Faculty of Law, 1990–1993, and held the Ivan C. Rand Professor of Criminal Law, 1992, the Bruce W. Wayne Professor of International Law, 2007. Lecturing and Research Subjects are Criminal Law, Constitutional Law, Military Law & Jurisprudence.

Functions/Tasks at the Hebrew University

- Member and co-organizer, research group on the Criminal Justice System, Institute for Advanced Studies, Hebrew University (1994–1995).
- Minerva Center for Human Rights, Academic Director (2002–2004), Chairperson of Academic Committee (2006).
- Chairperson, Tenure Committee, (2004–2005).
- President of the Disciplinary Tribunal for Faculty members (2004–2005).
- Member, Promotion Committee (2007).
- Member, International Monitoring Committee, Department of Communications (2008).
- Director of Prosecution, responsible for disciplinary action against faculty members of the Hebrew University of Jerusalem (2009–2011).

K. Ghanayim, Y. Shany (eds.), *The Quest for Core Values in the Application of Legal Norms*, https://doi.org/10.1007/978-3-030-78953-4

Service in Other Academic and Research Institutions

- Max-Planck-Institute for the Study of Crime, Security and Law, Freiburg, Germany
  - Researcher, 1983–1984 (Research subject: offences against the public interests)
  - Research Fellow, Alexander von Humboldt Fellowship, 1988–1989 (Research subject: specific offences)
- Open University, Israel
  - Member of Academic and Appointments Committee, 1995–2000.
  - Member of Executive Committee of the Open University, 2001–2008, 2013.
- University of Tulane, New Orleans, Louisiana
  - Visiting Professor, 1995.
- Wissenschaftskolleg zu Berlin, Germany
  - Fellow, 2005–2006.
- Central European University, Budapest, Hungary
  - Annual guest lecturer, 2005–2019.
    Teaching Subjects: Human Rights in Emergency Situations.
- McGill University, Montreal, Canada
  - Visiting Professor, 2008.
- University of Zűrich, Zürich, Switzerland
  - Visiting Professor, 2009.

Other Activities

- Legal Commentator of the daily Haaretz Newspaper,

  Board of the National Institute for Testing and Evaluation, Israel
- Chairperson, 1994–2000

  Knesset Channel, Israel
- Host of "Kremintzer Hosts" on the Knesset Channel, a television talk show interviewing leading jurists, academics, and politicians, 2012–2013.
- Intercontinental Academia: On Human Dignity

  Board of Editors and Advisory Boards
- Advisor, Constitutional Assembly of Thailand (1997).
- Member, Board of Editors Board, Journal of International Criminal Justice (2008, 2009).

Membership in Committees and organizations

- Member of Two-person Research Team (together with Prof. S. Z. Feller), appointed by the Ministry of Justice to draft a new Penal Code for the State of Israel (1982–1983).
  - A draft for a new general part was submitted to the Ministry and was adopted by the Knesset in 1994.
- International Association of Penal Law, (Board member, 1989–1993).
- Committee to examine the use of force by policemen, (Chairperson, 1993–1994).
  - A report was submitted to the Minister of Police in June 1994 and endorsed by the Minister and the Commissioner of Police.
- Committee nominated by the Minister of Justice on convictions based on confessions (Member, 1994–1995).
  - The report was submitted in 1995.
- Committee nominated by the Minister of Police to prepare a new police law (Member, 1994).
  - A report was submitted in 1998.
- Committee appointed by the Minister of Education on Education of Good Citizenship, (Chairperson, 1995–1996).
  - A report "On Being Citizens" was submitted and endorsed by the Minister in 1996
- Israel Democracy Institute (Senior Research Fellow, 1994–2000; Vice President for Research, 2000–2017).
- Committee appointed by the Minister of Finance and the Minster of Justice to examine the system of disciplinary measures for public employees (Chairperson, 1995).
  - A report was submitted in 1998 and endorsed by the Ministers
- Committee appointed by the Minister of Justice for recognition of extra-budgetary law schools, (Member, 1995–1996).
- Ministry of Education Committee to examine the Law College of Netanya (Member, 1996).
- Public Commission on the Reduction of Violence among Children and Youth, Vilnai Commission (Member, 2001).
- Pedagogical Council of the Ministry or Education, Israel (Member, 1999–2000).
- Israeli Press Council (President, 2002–2004)
- Assembly for preparing a draft constitution for the State of Israel (Member, 2001–2005).
  - The draft was presented to the Knesset in December 2005.

- Israel Association for Public Law, (Chairperson, 2002–2005).
- Committee appointed by the Minister of Justice to reform the Law regarding crimes against human life (Chairperson, 2007–2011).
  - A draft for a new law was submitted to the ministry, was endorsed by the ministry and the government and was adopted by the Knesset in 2019, with minor changes.
- Grants Committee, Israel Foundation for Legal Research (Chairperson, 2008).
- Committee appointed by the Council for Higher Education to examine the recognition of a law school in Sderot (southern Israel), (Member, 2008).
- International Committee appointed by the Council for Higher Education to monitor all departments of communication, Israel (Member, 2008).
- Committee appointed by the Council for Higher Education to examine the permanent recognition of a law school in Sderot (Southern Israel), (Chairperson, 2010).
- Committee appointed by the German Council of Science and Humanities to examine the legal studies research and education (Member, 2011–2012).
- Committee appointed by the government to propose a sentencing policy for Israel (Member, 2012–2014).
- International Anti-Corruption Academy (IACA), Member of the Board of Governors, 2013–2015).
- Council for Higher Education's Committee for Planning and Budgeting (Member of a sub-committee on extra-budgetary programs, 2013)

Prizes and Scholarships

- The Pinchas Rozen Award for Legal Research, 1989.
- The "Knight of Quality Government" of the Movement for Quality Government in Israel, 1999.
- The honor of lighting a torch at the ceremony opening Israeli Independence Day at Mount Herzl, 1999.
- The Zeltner Prize for Excellence in Research, 2003.
- The Humboldt Research Award, 2009.
- The "Ometz Award", given by Citizens for Good Governance and Social Justice, 2009.
- Honorary doctorate from the University of Lucerne, 2009.
- Honorary Fellow from The Open University, 2010.

Research Grants

- Co-Principal Researcher, German-Israel Foundation (GIF) research project on human dignity and the criminal law, (2005–2008).
- Principal Researcher, Proportionality in Public Policy: recipient of a five year grant from the European Research Council. (FP7), 2012.

List of Publications

Doctoral Dissertation

1. "Principles of the structure and organization of the specific offenses", Supervisor: S. Z. Feller, Ph.D. awarded on June 1980.

Books

1. "Israel: Toward a Constitutional Democracy" (co-written with Y. Ezrahi, M. Cohn & E. Alimi), 2001, 124 pp, Israel Democracy Institute, Jerusalem (in Hebrew).
2. "The Basic Laws as a Foundation for a Constitution" (co-written with D. Kretzmer, A. Benish), 2002, 202 pp, Israel Democracy Institute, Jerusalem (in Hebrew).
3. "Libel Law: De Lege Lata and De Lege Ferenda" (co-written with K. Ghanayim & B. Shnoor), 2005, 487 pp, Faculty of Law Hebrew University of Jerusalem & Israel Democracy Institute, Jerusalem (in Hebrew).
4. "Collateral Damage: The Harming of Innocents in the War against Terror" (co-written with D. Enoch, I. Porat & Re′em Segev), 2007, 215 pp, Israel Democracy Institute, Jerusalem (in Hebrew.
5. "Fraud and Breach of Trust: A Critical Examination and Recommendations for Improving Legislation" (co-written with D. Navot, N. Ben-Or, A. Fuchs and G. Wertheim), 2008, 384 pp, Israel Democracy Institute, Jerusalem (in Hebrew).
6. "Criminal Fraud", 2009, 251 pp, Nevo Publishing, Israel (in Hebrew).
7. "Anti-Democratic Legislation in the 18th Knesset (2009-2013)" (co-written with A. Fuchs, D. Blander), 2015, 213 pp, Israel Democracy Institute, Jerusalem (in Hebrew).
8. "A Handbook for Israeli Legislators" (co-written with N. Mordechay, Amir Fuchs), 2015, 237 pp, Israel Democracy Institute, Jerusalem (in Hebrew).
9. "How Confronting Terrorism Erodes Human Rights: The Israeli Experience" (co-written with A., Ben-Yehuda, N. Rosler, G. Rothschild Elyassi, and Y. Romm) (2017), 286 pp, Israel Democracy Institute, Jerusalem (in Hebrew).
10. "Libel Law: De Lege Lata and De Lege Ferenda" (co-written with K. Ghanayim & B. Shnoor, 2nd revised edition 2019), 565 pp, Faculty of Law Hebrew University of Jerusalem, Israel Democracy Institute, Jerusalem & Nevo Publishing (in Hebrew).
11. "The Reform of Homicide Offences (2019) in Light of Basic Principals and A Historical and Comparative Study" (co-written with K. Ghanayim). 2020, 575 pp, Faculty of Law Bar-Ilan University & Nevo Publishing (in Hebrew).

Books Edited

1. "Essays in honour of Justice Shimon Agranat" (co-edited with R. Gavison), 1986, 438 pp, Grep press, Jerusalem (in Hebrew).
2. "Current Trends in Criminal Procedure and Evidence - A Collection of Essays in Honor of Professor Eliahu Harnon" (co-edited with Anat Horovitz), 2009, 583 pp, Nevo Publishing, Israel (Hebrew).
3. "Conflict of Interests in the Public Sphere: Law, Culture, Ethics, Politics" (co-edited with D. Barak-Erez & D. Navot), 2009, 672 pp, Nevo Publishing, Israel (Hebrew).
4. "Proportionality: A Critical and Comparative Perspective", 2016, 393 pp, The Israel Democracy Institute, Israel (Hebrew).
5. "Human Dignity and Criminal Law: Würzburg Conference on Human Dignity" (co-edited with E. Hilgendorf, 2018, 223 pp, Duncker & Humblot, Leipzig.
6. "Basic concepts of criminal law" (co-edited with E. Hielkesser), 2018, 364 pp, Israel Bar Association, Tel-Aviv (Hebrew).
7. "Proportionality in Action: Comparative and Empirical Perspectives on the Judicial Practice" (co-edited with T. Steiner & A. Lang), 2020, Cambridge University Press.

Chapters in Collections (Not Including Chapters in Hebrew)

1. "Intention and Mens Rea", pp. 277–286, in R. Gavison (ed.) "Issues in Contemporary Legal Philosophy", 1987, Oxford University.
2. "Free Speech and Criminal Code Provisions for the Protection of State Security: The Israeli Case", pp. 86–92, in S. Shetreet (ed.) "Free Speech and National Security", 1991, Dordrecht.
3. "The World Community as an International Legislator in Competition with National Legislators", pp. 337–350, in A Eser and O. Lagodny (eds.) "Principles and Procedures for a New Transnational Criminal Law, 1991 Freiburg,
4. "The Israeli Proposal for a New General Part of a Penal Code – an Introduction," pp. 57–63, in R. Lahti and K. Nuotio (eds.) "Criminal Law Theory in Transition", 1992, Helsinki.
5. "National Security and the Rule of Law", pp. 153–172, in A. Yaniv (ed.) "National Security and Democracy in Israel", 1993, Lynne Rienner Publishers.
6. "Criminal Law", pp. 253–266, in A. Shapira (ed.) "Introduction to the Law of Israel", 1995, Kluwer.
7. "Criminal Law in Israel", pp.185–205, in R. Friedman (ed.) "Crime and the Criminal Justice System in Israel: Assessing the Knowledge Base Towards the 21st Century", 1998, Suny Press.
8. "The Use of Legislation to Change Social Perceptions", pp. 303–306, in S. Shetreet (ed.) "Women in Law", 1998 London: Kluwer.

9. "Strafbarkeit juristischen Personen aus angelsaechsicher und israelischer Sicht", pp. 215–242, in Hans-Joachim Hirsch (ed.), "Schriften zum Strafrecht, Krise des Strafrechts und der Kriminalwissenchaften", 2001, Berlin.
10. "Praventives Toeten in Rechtfragen der Terrorismusbekaempfung durch Streitkraefte", pp. 201–222, in D. Fleck (ed.) (Baden Baden, 2004, Nomos Verlag).
11. "Disqualification of Lists and Parties: The Israeli Case", pp. 157–170, in A Sajo (ed.), "Militant Democray", 2004, Utrecht, Eleven - International Publishing.
12. "Prosecution of International Crimes – Israel" together with M. Cohn, pp. 317–410, in A. Eser, U. Sieber, H. Kreicker, Duncker & Humblot (eds.), "National Prosecution of International Crimes, Vol. 5", 2005, Berlin.
13. "New Humanistic Trends in Israeli Criminal Law" together with K. Ghanayim, pp. 513–534, in Arnold and others (eds,), "Menschengerechtes Strafrecht - Festschrift fuer Albin Eser zum 70 Geburtstag", 2005, Verlag C. H. Beck Muenchen.
14. "Some Reflections on Comparative Criminal Law - Keynote Speech", pp. 2–14, in S. Beck, C. Burchard, B. Fateh-Moghadam (eds.),"Strafrechtsvergleichung als Problem und Lösung", 2011, Nomos Verlag Baden-Baden.
15. "The CIT in the Courtroom: Legal Aspects", pp. 276–290, together with G. Ben-Shakhar, in Verschuere, B., Ben-Shakhar, G., & Meijer, E. (eds.), "Memory detection: theory and application of the Concealed Information Test", 2011, Cambridge University Press.
16. "Coercive Interrogation in Israel – The process of shaping the norms", pp. 164–188, in M. Mahlmann (ed.), "Gesellschaft und Gerechtigkeit", 2011, Nomos Verlag Baden-Baden.
17. "Administrative Detention - An opportunity for Reevaluation", pp. 254–268, in E. Gil and others (eds.), "A Reexamination of Administrative Detention in a Jewish and Democratic State", 2011, Israel Democracy Institute (Jerusalem).
18. "Psychological and social consequences of terrorism on the targeted society", together with N. Rosler, pp. 41–52, in K-A. Schwartz (ed.), "10 Jahre 11. September – Die Rechtsordnung im Zeitalter des Ungewissen", 2012 Nomos Verlag Baden-Baden.
19. "Der Holocaust in Recht und Literatur", pp. 57–74, in M. Mahlmann and D. M. Nielaba (eds.), "Fechtschulen und phantastische Gärten": Recht und Literatur, Andreas Kilcher", 2013 Zuerich.
20. "Human Dignity - An Israeli Perspective", pp. 81–90, in A. Margalits, E. Hilgendorf (eds.), "Menschenwürde und Demütigung: Die Menschenwürdekonzeption", 2013, Nomos Verlag, Würzburg.
21. "Constitutional Proportionality- (Appropriate) Guidelines", pp. 223–238, in A. Barak, D. Barak-Erez, G. Sapir (eds.), "Israeli Constitutional Law at the Crossroads", 2013 Hart Publishing.
22. "Terrorism and Democracy - an Israeli Perspective", pp. 203–115, in T. Wuertenberger, C. Gusy, H-J. Lange (eds.), "Innere Sicherheit im Europaischen Vergleich", 2012, Berlin.

23. "Executive Measures Against the Liberties of Terrorism Suspects, together with L. Saba-Habesch", pp. 222–236, in Genevieve Lennon and Clive Walker (eds.), "Routledge Handbook of Law and Terrorism", 2015, Routledge Press.
24. "Commanders Responsibility", together with L. Saba-Habesch, pp. 121–141, in B. Burkhardt, W. Gropp, W. Perron and other (eds.), "Freundschaftsgabe fuer Albin Eser zum 80" Geburtstag, 2015, Berlin.
25. "Responsibility to Protect - a Right of Self Defense for All States Against Atrocities", in "The Responsibility to Protect at 10: The Challenge of Protecting the World's Most Vulnerable Population", 2015, Brandeis University Press NY.
26. "The Non-Separation of Religion and State in Israel: Does It Support the Racism and Nationalism Wave?" Together with Amir Fuchs, pp. 181–195, in E. Ben-Rafael, J. H. Schoeps, Y. Sternberg and O. Glocker (eds.), "Handbook of Israel: Major Debates" (vol. 1), 2016 De Gruyter Oldenbourg.
27. "Constitutional Proportionality: principles to its appropriate image", pp. 10–102, in M. Kremnizer (ed.) "Proportionality: A Critical and Comparative Perspective", 2016, The Israel Democracy Institute, Israel.
28. "Introduction: Analysing Proportionality Comparatively and Empirically", pp. 4–14. in M. Kremnizer, T. Steiner & A. Lang (eds.) "Proportionality in Action: Comparative and Empirical Perspectives on the Judicial Practice", 2020, Cambridge University Press.
29. "Comparative and Empirical Insights into Judicial Practice: Towards an Integrative Model of Proportionality", 452–606, in M. Kremnizer, T. Steiner & A. Lang (eds.) "Proportionality in Action: Comparative and Empirical Perspectives on the Judicial Practice", 2020, Cambridge University Press.
30. "Retrial in Israel – A need for a restart", with G. Harnik Blum, in B. Ariel, K. Campbell, I.Cotler, A.Horovitz (eds) "Wrongful Convictions in Israel and Canada", 2021, Routledge U.K.
31. "Cesare Beccaria's Integrative Deterrence Approach" in A. du Bois-Pedain & S. Eldar (eds) "Rereading Beccaria", 2021, Cambridge Press.

Articles (Not Including Articles in Hebrew)

1. "Grounds for Disqualifying a Judge", 18 Israel Law Review (1983), pp. 449–474.
2. "Proportionality and the Psychotic Aggressor - Another View", 18 Israel Law Review (1983), pp. 178–214.
3. "The Punishability of Impossible Attempts", 19 Israel Law Review (1984), pp. 340–387.
4. "Penal Responsibility for Offences of Omission", together with M. Gur-Arye, 55 Rev. Int. de Droit Penal (1983), pp. 691–703.
5. "Withdrawal from Attempt", together with S. Z. Feller, Report to the 12th Congress on Comparative Law, Israel Reports to the XII International Congress of Comparative Law: Jerusalem (1986), pp. 354–367.

6. "Interpretation in Criminal Law", 21 Isr. Law Review (1986), pp. 358–387.
7. "Capital Punishment – an Israeli Perspective", 8 Rev. Int. de Droit Penal (1987), pp. 475–483.
8. "General Security Service Pardon: A test for the High Court of Justice" reprinted from Vol. 8 Tel Aviv University Studies in Law (1988), pp. 157–184.
9. "Schwangerschaftsabbruch in Israel", together with A. Harel, A. Eser & H-G. Koch (Hrsg.), Schwangerschaftsabbruch im internationalen Vergleich, Nomos Verlag Baden-Baden (1989), pp. 465–536.
10. "The Landau Commission Report – Was the Security Service Subordinated to the Law, or the Law to the "Needs" of the Security?",23 Israel Law Review (1989, pp. 216–279.
11. "Is There a Rational Justification for Punishing an Accomplished Crime More Severely than an Attempted Crime?", 4 Brigham Young U.J. of Public Law (1990), pp. 81–95.
12. "Forty Years of Criminal Law – Further Comment", 24 Israel Law Review (1990), pp. 580–591.
13. "Sentencing as Art – a Response: Sentencing as a Just System", 25 Israel Law Review (1991), pp. 661–680.
14. "Constitutional Principles and Criminal Law", 27 Israel Law Review (1993), pp. 84–99.
15. "The Demjanjuk Case" 24 Israel Yearbook on Human Rights (1995), pp. 269–295.
16. "Proposal for a General Part of a New Penal Law – Introduction", together with S. Z. Feller, 30 Israel Law Review (1996), pp. 36–59.
17. "Israel's Direct Election", together with S. Goldman, 14 Justice (1997), pp. 3–9.
18. "On Premeditation", 1 Buffalo Criminal Law Review (1998), pp. 627–660.
19. "Constitutionalization of Substantive Criminal Law: A Realistic View", 33 Israel Law Review (1999), pp. 720–728.
20. "H-H Jescheck & T. Weigend: Lehrbuch des Strafrechts, Allgemeiner Teil, a Bookreview", together with K. Ghanayim, 34 Israel Law Review (2000), pp. 302–319.
21. "The Legality of Interrogational Torture: A question of proper authorization or a substantive moral issue?" together with R. Seger, 34 Israel Law Review (2000), pp. 509–559.
22. "The High Court of Justice and the Shaping of Public Policy - Equality and Gender" 7 Israel Affairs (2001), pp. 100–132.
23. "Die Strafbarkeit von Unternehmen", together with K. Ghanayim, 113 ZStW (2001), pp. 539–64.
24. "Trial by Polygraph – Reconsidering the Use of GKT in Court", together with G. Ben Shachar and M. Bar-Hilel, 26 Law and Human Behavior (2002), pp. 527–541.
25. "Proportionality and the Aggressor's Culpability in Self Defense" with K. Ghanayim, 39 Tulsa Law Review (2004), pp. 875–899.
26. "Judicial Activism: a Multidimensional Model", together with M. Cohn, 18 Canadian Journal of Law and Jurisprudence (2005), pp. 333–356.

27. "Targeted Killing Policy: Insufficiently Limited" 44 Justice (2007), pp. 38–43.
28. "The Use of Force by the Police" together with D. Menashe and K. Ghanayim, 53 The Criminal Law Quarterly (2007), pp. 67–97.
29. "Is the Subjective Mental Element Superfluous", 27 Criminal Justice Ethics, (2008) pp. 78–82.
30. "A Comment on Preventative Means in General and on Torture in Particular", together with L. Levanon, 42 Israel Law Review (2009), pp. 248–274.
31. "A Possible Case for Imposing Criminal Liability on Corporations in International Criminal Law" 8 Journal of International Criminal Justice (2010), pp. 909–918.
32. "Human Dignity and The Principle of Culpability" together with T. Hörnle, 44 Israel Law Review (2011), pp. 115–141.
33. "Human Dignity as a Protected Interest in Criminal Law", together with T. Hörnle, 44 Israel Law Review (2011), pp. 143–167.
34. "A suggested moral analysis of the Goldstone Report and its aftermath" 48 Justice (2011), pp. 21–22, 46.
35. "From Illiberal Legislation to Intolerant Democracy" with S. Krebs, 26 Israel Studies Review (2011), pp. 4–11.
36. "Israel as a Jewish state", 49 Justice (2011), pp.20–28.
37. Book review on "Hanah Lerner, Making Constitutions in Deeply Divided Societies (Cambridge: Cambridge University Press, 2011)", 26 Israel Studies Review (2014), pp. 144–148.
38. "Is Proportionality an Effective Protector of Human Rights? Proportionality and Constitutional Culture by M. Cohen-Eliya, I. Porat - a Critique" 10 Jerusalem Review of Legal Studies (2014), pp. 111–122.
39. "Mistaken Identity and Error in Performance: A Transferred Malice?" together with Khalid Ghanayim, 61 Criminal Law Quarterly (2014), pp. 329–360.
40. "House Demolitions", together with L. Saba-Habesch, 4 Laws Journal (2015), pp. 216–228.
41. "Offences Against the Democratic System of Government", together with K. Ghanayim, Oxford University Comparative Law Forum, 2016.
42. "Human Dignity and the Right to Due process" together with L. Saba-Habesch, in Human Dignity and Criminal law (Berlin, 2016), pp. 117–138.
43. "Facts, Preferences, and doctrine: An Empirical Analysis of Proportionality Judgment", with R-S. Kenan & S. Alon, 50 Law & Society Review (2016), pp. 348–382.
44. "A Comment to Simester's Aiding and Abetting", with H. Ben-Eliezer, Jerusalem Review of Legal Studies, 2021

Miscellaneous (in Hebrew)

1. "Menachem Begin on Democracy and Constitutional Values", with A. Fuchs, Israel Democracy Institute (2011).

2. "Ze'ev Jabotinsky on Democracy, Equality, and Individual Rights" with A. Fuchs, Israel Democracy Institute (2012)
3. "Democracy, Laws of War and Minority Rights: The Teachings of Nathan Alterman ", with Y. Avrech, Israel Democracy Institute (2013).
4. "Proposed Chapter on Democracy for Israeli Party Platforms", with A. Fuchs, Israel Democracy Institute (2015).
5. "A Plan to Combat Political Corruption in Israel", with D. Navot, Y. Feldman, L. Saba & T. Schwartz-Altshuler, Israel Democracy Institute (2015).
6. "Equality, Justice, and Judicial Review in the legacy of Edmond Levy", with A. Fuchs, Israel Democracy Institute (2018).
7. "Democracy and the Rule of Law in the legacy of Meir Shamgar", with A. Fuchs, Israel Democracy Institute (2019).
8. "Human Dignity: A Living Right in Medical Treatment", with D. Blander & K. Haber, Israel Democracy Institute (2019).

Policy Papers (in Hebrew)

1. "Freedom of Occupation: When Should the Government Regulate Entry into Professions?", with O. Ben-Shahar, S. Goldman, Policy Paper 11, Israel Democracy Institute (1998).
2. "Incitement, Not Sedition", with K. Ghanayim, Policy Paper No 7 in Hebrew, No 3 in English, Israel Democracy Institute (2002).
3. "Religious Feelings, Freedom of Expression, and Criminal Law", with S. Goldman & E. Tamir, Policy Paper 38, Israel Democracy Institute (2003).
4. "Religion and the High Court of Justice: Image and Reality – Part One: A Critical Examination of the Publication Manof", with M. Cohn, & E. Linder, Policy Paper 39, The Center for Jewish Information (2003).
5. "Religion and the High Court of Justice: Image and Reality – Part Two: A Three-Dimensional Model for Measuring Judicial Activism", with M. Cohn, Policy Paper 57, The Center for Jewish Information (2005).
6. "Disqualification of Lists", Policy Paper 59, Israel Democracy Institute (2005).
7. "Official Secrets: A Proposal for Amending the Penal Prohibition", with E. Rahaf, Policy Paper 56, Israel Democracy Institute (2005).
8. "Are All Actions Acceptable in the Face of Terror? Israel's Policy of Preventative, (Targeted) Killing in Judea, Samaria and Gaza", Policy Paper 60, Israel Democracy Institute (2006).
9. "Offenses against the State", with K. Ghanayim, Policy Paper 70, Israel Democracy Institute (2008).
10. "Human Dignity as A Supreme and Absolute Constitutional Value is German Law - In Israel Too?", with M. Kramer, Policy Paper 85, Israel Democracy Institute (2011).

11. "Regulation of Lobbying in Israel", with A. Shapira, H. Cidor, Motion for the Agenda, Israel Democracy Institute (2013).
12. "Distribution of Power, Not Separation of Branches: Preventing the Concentration of Political Power in Israel", with A. Fuchs, Policy Paper 133, Israel Democracy Institute (2019).
13. "The Crimes of Incitement to Racism and Violence", with A. Fuchs & I Weschler-Be'er, Policy Paper 132, Israel Democracy Institute (2019).

Motion for the Agenda

1. "Are your brothers to go to war while you stay here - A Proposal for Integrating the Ultra-Orthodox into the IDF", with A. Ben-Bassat & M. Dahan, Motion for Agenda, Israel Democracy Institute (2013).
2. "Merging the Israeli Police Prosecution with the State Attorney's Office", with G. Lurie, Motion for the Agenda, Israel Democracy Institute (2014).
3. "Legislative Impact Assessment on Right of Children", with N. Mordechay, & M. Ostrovsky, Motion for the Agenda, Israel Democracy Institute (2014).
4. "A Proposal to Amend the foundations of Law Act, with an Analysis and Critique", with B. Porat, Motion for the Agenda, Israel Democracy Institute (2016).
5. "Political Corruption: Mandatory Reporting by Officials", with Y. Ershied, Motion for the Agenda, Israel Democracy Institute (2019).
6. "A [Revised] Plan to Combat Political Corruption in Israel", with E. Harel-Fisher, Motion for the Agenda, Israel Democracy Institute (2019).
7. "Disqualification of Party Lists and Candidates – Does it Strengthen Democracy or Weakens it?" with A. Gal, Motion for the Agenda, Israel Democracy Institute (2020).
8. "Establishing a Unit for Structural and Systemic Treatment of Corruption", with Y. Wisel & E. Harel-Fisher, Motion for the Agenda 30, Israel Democracy Institute (2020).
9. "Public Officials and the Right to Silence", with Y. Wiesel, E. Harel Fisher, O. Has Rahav, Motion for the Agenda, Israel Democracy Institute (2021)

The manufacturer's authorised representative in the EU is Springer Nature Customer Service Centre GmbH, Europaplatz 3, 69115 Heidelberg, Germany. If you have any concerns regarding our products, please contact ProductSafety@springernature.com

Printed and bound by CPI Group (UK) Ltd, Croydon, CR0 4YY
30/09/2026
02225699-0011